Management of Marketing

Management of Marketing

Geoff Lancaster and Paul Reynolds

ELSEVIER
BUTTERWORTH
HEINEMANN

AMSTERDAM • BOSTON • HEIDELBERG • LONDON • NEW YORK • OXFORD
PARIS • SAN DIEGO • SAN FRANCISCO • SINGAPORE • SYDNEY • TOKYO

Elsevier Butterworth-Heinemann
Linacre House, Jordan Hill, Oxford OX2 8DP
30 Corporate Drive, Burlington, MA 01803

First published 2005

British Library Cataloguing in Publication Data

Library of Congress Cataloguing in Publication Data
A catalogue record for this book is available from the Library of Congress

ISBN 0 7506 6103 8

For information on all Elsevier Butterworth-Heinemann publications visit our website
at http://books.elsevier.com

Typeset by Newgen Imaging Systems (P) Ltd, Chennai, India
Printed and bound in Great Britain

Contents

Please find additional materials to accompany this text at: http://textbooks.elsevier.com

1
Marketing Philosophy

1.1 Introduction

The concept of marketing is neither complicated nor original. 'The customer is always right' is a view that has been cited ever since the Industrial Revolution. Marketing acknowledges consumer sovereignty and this has now developed into a management discipline. The subject of marketing as a management discipline originated in the USA in the 1950s, but its origins go back further. America was the birthplace of modern marketing, but in terms of its earliest practice, it was applied much earlier in Europe. The carpenter, tailor, saddler and stonemason knew their customers personally and were in a position to discuss individual needs of size, colour, shape and design at an individual level. Craftsmen appreciated they had to provide satisfactory service to customers. The Industrial Revolution gave rise to large scale manufacturing, so this personal contact ended. With mass production came mass markets and mass distribution. Manufacturers were no longer able to offer a personalised service, and techniques of marketing were developed to fill this gap.

There is no universally accepted definition of marketing. The way it is understood conditions people's perceptions of its value and the contribution it can make both to the success of an organisation and to the competitive health of the economy. As a student of marketing, it is important to appreciate that the term 'marketing' means different things to different people. We examine the subject from these different viewpoints later in this chapter.

Marketing is based on the premise that the customer is the most important person to the organisation. Most people think of the term customer in the context of a profit-making facility. Whilst it is true that the marketing concept has been more widely adopted and practised in the profit-making sectors of the economy, the fundamental principles of marketing are equally applicable in the not-for-profit sectors; a fact that is often overlooked.

Marketing as an organisational philosophy and activity is applicable to almost all types of organisation, whether profit-making or not-for-profit activities.

The term 'customer' is viewed in this text in this wider context, and not just as someone who interacts with a profit-centred business.

Examination candidates tend to be better at discussing marketing as a functional area of management than as an overall business philosophy. When properly understood, it will be appreciated that marketing is not necessarily narrowly confined to a particular office or department. Indeed, one of the most frequent problems that companies have is in the view of other departments (and sometimes in the marketing department itself) that somebody 'does' marketing in the process sense. In its widest sense, marketing is really an attitude of mind or an approach to business problems that should be adopted by the whole organisation. It is only when the discipline is understood in this wider context that students and practitioners can properly appreciate the role of marketing and its value to an organisation. At higher levels, examination questions tend to be more about marketing philosophy, whereas at less advanced levels the functional elements of marketing tend to attract more questions.

1.2 The importance of the consumer

In 1776, during the Industrial Revolution, Adam Smith (1776) widely regarded to be the founding father of modern economics, wrote in his classic work *The Wealth of Nations*:

> Consumption is the sole end and purpose of all production and the interests of the producer ought to be attended to only so far as it may be necessary for promoting that of the consumer.

In essence, it does not matter how good a firm may think its product to be, or how well organised it is in processing its orders, unless it has customers there is no business to conduct. In this statement, Adam Smith has given the essence of the central guiding theme of the subject of marketing. The key word is consumer, as it is the identification and satisfaction of consumer requirements that forms the basis of the modern concept of marketing.

Smith went on to say:

> The maxim is so perfectly self-evident that it would be absurd to attempt to prove it. But in the mercantile system, the interest of the consumer is almost constantly sacrificed to that of producers who seem to consider production, and not consumption, as the ultimate end and object of all industry and commerce.

What he was saying is that producers make what they deem the market needs. What he did through this classic statement was to point out the parameters of business orientation: the first part describes marketing orientation and the second part describes production orientation.

In order for a profit-making enterprise to prosper, its management must work hard to retain its existing markets against competition and must strive to counter technical obsolescence and changes in consumer tastes by attempting to secure new and profitable customers. Not-for-profit organisations must continually justify their existence in terms of their usefulness to society. They have to answer to interested parties who may well withdraw financial support if the goods or services they offer to the community do not match community requirements. The marketing concept, which puts the emphasis on customers and the identification and satisfaction of customer requirements, results in the consumer becoming the central focus of an organisation's activities.

Some people view the subject of marketing as a branch of applied economics. Other writers and practitioners have worked for a number of years in a specialised field of marketing such as advertising, brand management or marketing research. It is understandable that such people often regard their particular speciality as the most important facet of marketing. Some people take a myopic view of the subject and see marketing as a collection of well-developed management techniques, which when combined, constitute a functional area of the organisation's management operations. More enlightened people view the subject as an overriding business philosophy which guides the organisation in everything it does. Students approaching the subject for the first time might find the absence of a unified definition of the subject rather frustrating. It can rightly be regarded as somewhat ill-defined, with any definition coloured by the way the subject is approached. Marketing is often viewed as:

1 *A social process*: At a macro level, marketing is viewed as a social process by which individuals and groups obtain what they need and want by creating and exchanging items of value.
2 *A distributive system*: Marketing is viewed as a process whereby in a democratic society, operating within a free market or mixed economy, there evolves a system of distribution that facilitates transactions resulting in exchange and consumption.
3 *A functional area of management*: Marketing is seen as a functional area of management, usually based in a particular location within the organisation, which uses a collection of techniques, for example, advertising, public relations, sales promotion and packaging to achieve specific objectives.
4 *An overall business philosophy*: Many firms see marketing as the keystone of their business. Marketing is viewed not as a separate function, but rather as a profit-orientated approach to business that permeates not just the marketing department but the entire business. The central mission of the organisation is seen as the satisfaction of customer requirements at a profit (or, in not-for-profit sectors, at a maximum level of efficiency or minimum level of cost). This is achieved by focusing the attention of the entire organisation on the importance of the customer and the needs of the market-place.
5 *A targeting or allocation system*: Marketing is perceived as the way any organisation or individual matches its own capabilities to the needs and wants of its customers. From an organisational point of view, marketing is seen as the

primary management function that organises and targets the activities of the entire organisation in order to convert consumer purchasing power into effective demand. Its objective is to move the product or service to the final consumer or user in order to achieve company profit (or optimum cost efficiency).

 ## 1.3 Definitions of marketing

As a student of marketing, you are likely to have to sit examinations set by a university or a professional examining body. The generally accepted European definition of marketing is given by the Chartered Institute of Marketing (CIM). It might be wise to commit this particular definition to memory (whilst not forgetting that marketing is a very wide ranging subject which can be looked at from many different points-of-view):

> 'Marketing is the management process responsible for identifying, anticipating and satisfying customer requirements profitably.'

Some writers use the terms 'need' and 'wants' rather than customers 'requirements'. Kotler (1991) one of the world's leading academics in marketing, defines a 'need' as a basic requirement such as food, shelter, self-esteem etc. He defines a 'want' as a particular way of satisfying a 'need'. For example, a person may need food, but he or she may not necessarily want beans on toast!

A more technical definition is given for marketing by the American Marketing Association:

> 'Marketing is the process of planning and executing the conception, pricing, promotion and distribution of ideas, goods and services to create exchanges that satisfy individual and organisational objectives.'

Although this definition is not as succinct as that provided by the CIM, it is more correct, as the CIM definition highlights the 'profitability' criterion, whereas we have already discussed that marketing principles are also applicable in not-for-profit organisations.

 ## 1.4 Historical development

Marketing is primarily concerned with exchange or trade. Trade in its most basic form has existed ever since humankind became capable of producing a surplus. Typically, this surplus was agricultural produce which was traded for manufactured goods like textiles or earthenware. Exchange brought into existence places that facilitated trade such as village fairs and local markets. The emergence of trade allowed people to specialise in producing goods and services which could be exchanged in markets for other goods they needed.

1.4.1 The Industrial Revolution

The period 1760–1830 saw the UK economy transformed, losing its dependence on agriculture with a dramatic increase in industrial production. Before the Industrial Revolution, the production and distribution of goods tended to be on a small scale. Industrialisation resulted in dramatic gains in productivity, mainly due to the development of machines. Production became more geographically concentrated and was carried out in purpose-built mills or factories. Enterprises became larger, production runs longer and products more standardised. Firms produced in volume, not only for local markets, but for a national and international markets.

Although production expanded dramatically during this period, it brought with it many social problems. The simultaneous development of machines, communications, improved transport, agricultural improvements and advances in commercial practices transformed the UK economy, resulting in the growth of the 'factory system'. This caused the migration of the population from the countryside to the rapidly expanding industrial towns.

1.4.2 The dispersal of markets

Because of developments during the Industrial Revolution, firms could produce more in terms of volume than the local economy could absorb. Consumption, therefore, became dispersed over greater geographical distances and producers no longer had immediate contact with their markets. To overcome this problem of impersonality, entrepreneurs began plan their business operations in a 'marketing-orientated' manner, although this term was not formally used to describe the process until well into the twentieth century.

In order for producers to be able to manufacture goods and services that would appeal and sell in widely dispersed markets, it became necessary to carefully analyse and interpret the needs and wants of customers and to manufacture products that would 'fit in' with those needs and wants.

Prior to examining marketing as an entrepreneurial function it is appropriate to discuss the principal types of production:

- *Project* or *job production* is effectively 'one off' production where every aspect of construction (project) or manufacture (job) is done as a separate activity from the design to completion stage (e.g. the construction of a hospital [project] or construction of a ship [job]). Skilled personnel are needed during design and manufacturing. This means that the manufacturing process is a relatively skilled and expensive procedure.
- *Batch production* is where the numbers produced are more than one, but the skills required, and the means of production, are similar to job production and the reality is that batches produced are often in single figures.

The types of production just described applied in manufacturing activity until 1913. This is when Henry Ford set up the first ever continuous flow line production assembly plant in Detroit, USA to manufacture the Model 'T' car. The Model 'T' Ford was in fact developed in 1908 and was initially constructed using batch production principles. It was not until 1913 that Henry Ford brought in the first ever moving production line that was based upon the principles of the division of labour. Workers no longer assembled much of the car, but performed single tasks repeatedly so the task was completed faster and better. Another principle he established was that all components should be strictly interchangeable and precisely identical to the next. The result was that he was able to produce and sell his Model 'T' cars at US$550 each, or 35% less than when they were initially introduced in 1908. Moreover, the car remained in production, largely unchanged, for 19 years and by 1925 production line refinements meant that the price was down to US$260.

- *Flow (or flow-line) production* as just described is where all aspects of the manufacturing process are broken down into their simplest components of assembly. Less skilled, relatively inexpensive, labour can be used. The whole process is a quicker and more cost effective method of production. End prices are lower, and the implication is that all products are basically the same so there is a need for a mass market.

1.4.3 UK marketing implications resulting from developments in production line technology

Flow line production technology did not receive widespread application in the UK following the introduction of Ford's revolutionary process in the USA in 1913. This was largely owing to the fact that UK society was then divided into a small number of 'haves' who owned most of the wealth and a huge number of 'have nots' who could only afford the bare necessities of life, plus a relatively small number of middle class. This was unlike the USA which was a more equal society distributed typically along a bell shaped curve, so the circumstances were right in the USA to expand car production in the knowledge that there was a huge middle class ready to purchase these cheaper mass produced automobiles.

In the UK, the upper classes did not want anything that was mass produced and the middle classes were a relatively small market, whereas the large working class would not have been able to afford to run a car even if it was free. However, Ford did eventually produce a number of Model 'T' cars at Trafford Park, Manchester, but these were not principally for UK consumption.

The Second World War in 1939 was the trigger for the widespread adoption of flow production in the UK. Men were conscripted for war service and it meant that women were drafted into factories, which had switched over to the manufacture of war products. As women were basically unskilled and war products were needed desperately, flow line production technology was the ideal solution and American advisers helped to establish such facilities in the UK.

The war ended in 1945, but rationing did not end until 1954, so flow production was seen as the most effective way to fulfil demand.

A radical post-war Labour Government under Clement Atlee set about a programme designed to remove the inequality between rich and poor and redistribute wealth. Government Nationalised much of the country's infrastructure and increased death duties and personal taxes so that the base rate was 33% which moved up in 5% bands to 83%. Investment income commanded an extra slice of 15% on top of the top slice of tax, so effectively some people paid tax at 98%. It was not until 1979 when Margaret Thatcher was elected and headed a Conservative Government that this top band of 83% was reduced to 60% and later reduced to 40% in 1988.

The effect was a redistribution of wealth from the upper classes to the intermediate and lower classes. Its effect on marketing was profound. The consequence was that goods hitherto classed as luxury products that were not necessary became utility products that were necessary to live a modern lifestyle. An example is the telephone which in the 1950s was a luxury item, is now a virtual necessity and even mobile phones have now become a utility item. People nowadays need a greater 'raft' of goods to lead a modern lifestyle and indeed the number of individual products needed is also greater. For instance, in the 1950s in working class households, it was unusual to possess more than two pairs of shoes. This is very unlike today where multiple pairs of shoes are commonplace. Not only do customers now need a greater range of products to live a modern lifestyle, but they also need more of individual products as well.

The implications just outlined often form questions on marketing papers along the lines of:

- Marketing is the delivery of a higher standard of living. Discuss.
- Marketing is the creation of unnecessary wants and desires. Discuss.
- Marketing is the creation of unnecessary goods and services. Discuss.

1.4.4 Marketing as an entrepreneurial function

The process of matching resources of a firm to the needs and wants of the market place is termed entrepreneurship. People like Josiah Wedgwood (1730–95) came to epitomise the traditional entrepreneur with their ability to 'sense' what the market wanted in terms of design, quality and price, and then organise production and distribution to satisfy effective demand at a profit. These early entrepreneurs were practising an early rule of thumb form of marketing activity although it was not then called marketing.

It was not until 1908 that a Frenchman, Heri Fayol, investigated manufacturing practice and suggested a division of labour that the first theoretical foundations were laid for the discipline of business. Theory in business is unlike say chemistry, where theory is first hypothesised in a laboratory situation and then applied in practice. In business, practice takes place prior to the establishment of theoretical business guidelines. Many mistakes are made without guidelines for pointers to best practice, and it is only by observing practice that theories can then be established.

1.4.5 The effect of job specialisation

A craftsman, like a blacksmith or potter, develops skills in a particular activity. These craft industries were in fact based on an early form of division of labour which resulted in specialisation and greater productivity. Industrialisation took the processes of specialisation and division of labour a stage further. Specialisation resulted in greater productivity which, in turn, reduced costs and hence the selling price of products. However, the rise in job specialisation that was principally brought about by the development of flow production techniques, also increased the need for exchange. Larger-scale production meant that marketing channels had to be created to facilitate the distribution of goods to enable the effective demand from the much larger market to be met. This development laid the foundations of the modern industrial economy, which is still based on the fundamental concept of trade or exchange. Sellers establish customers requirements and develop products to satisfy their needs. The medium of this exchange is money.

During the first half of the nineteenth century Britain was the dominant force in the world economy. The main factor underlying industrial growth was the development in international trade. Britain was first and foremost a trading nation that had secured supplies of raw materials and held a virtual monopoly in the supply of manufactured goods to, and the receipt of produce from, the relatively underdeveloped countries which collectively made up the British Empire.

The first half of the twentieth century saw the emergence of Germany and the USA as competing world industrial powers. Although Britain faced strong competition from economically emerging nations in the areas of textiles, coal and steel, the British economy continued along a path of industrial expansion in the period to the First World War. The incomes generated in other countries resulted in a worldwide increase in total demand for goods and services. The total value of Britain's trade increased even though its share of international trade started to decline.

Today, we have a situation where a large number of producers compete for a share of a finite world market. Modern industry is based on mass production which necessitates mass consumption. In order for many sophisticated products (e.g. home computers, motor cars and consumer durables like washing machines) to be commercially successful they must be produced in a volume sufficient to bring unit costs down to a competitive level. It is no longer enough to produce a good product, as it was in time of shortages or rationing when producers enjoyed a 'sellers' market'. Today, for producers to achieve a sufficient level of effective demand, they must produce goods and services that the market perceives as 'valuable' and, more importantly, that the customers will actually buy in sufficient volume. The final customer's needs and wants not only have to be taken into account, but the identification and satisfaction of these needs and wants has become the most important factor in the long-term survival of a business.

1.5 The marketing-orientated organisation

Transition to marketing maturity tends to be a gradual developmental process. Many firms who have reached full marketing orientation have done so by evolving through secondary stages of development.

There are three basic types of business/customer orientation: production, sales and marketing orientations. These are hierarchical, and usually sequential, stages of development. Many production-orientated firms witness a downturn in sales that have always been taken up by the market, and develop greater sales awareness and begin to place greater importance on moving products to the consumer through the use of sales push programmes and techniques. Eventually, enlightened firms begin to appreciate that selling itself plays but a single part in the overall operation of moving goods from the factory to the consumer. The customer becomes much more than someone who is there merely to sell to. The satisfaction of consumers' needs and wants becomes the rationale for everything the company does. Such companies have progressed to marketing orientation. Of all the stakeholders in a business enterprise, the customer is by far the most important. It is through concentration upon satisfaction of customer needs, and the profits that result from so doing, that all other stakeholder needs are satisfied.

1.6 Different types of business orientation

An understanding of the preceding levels of business orientation is necessary for a full appreciation of how a marketing-orientated organisation is superior to other forms of business thinking. Each type of orientation is now examined:

1.6.1 Production orientation

In the nineteenth and most of the twentieth centuries, the primary purpose of business and industrial activity was felt to be production. The production manager was key to an organisation, and it was normally through production that managers reached the most senior positions in management.

Manufacturers were in a 'supplier's market' and were faced with a virtually insatiable demand for all that could be produced. Firms concentrated on improving production efficiency in an attempt to bring down costs. Generally, firms produced whatever they could produce well, expecting demand for company goods and services to present itself automatically. An understanding of customers' requirements was of secondary importance. A famous production-orientated statement reflected this thinking:

'Build a better mousetrap and the world will beat a path to your door.'

Ford also made a classic production-orientated statement that is often repeated today in relation to his Model 'T' Ford that was introduced in 1913:

'You can have any colour you want; as long as it is black!'

This production-orientated philosophy was feasible as long as a sellers' market pertained. The economic recession particularly that hit the USA but the UK as well in the 1920s and 1930s concentrated the minds of business people. To simply produce was no longer good enough, as warehouses were full of unsold goods and thousands of bankrupt businesses testified to the folly of this philosophy. The lesson to be learned from this experience was that firms that focused their attention on existing products and existing markets without paying attention to the changing needs of the market place ran the risk of being overtaken by events and becoming outdated.

Some companies still have this outdated philosophy. If they produce good products and customers do not purchase, there can be only two reasons: either the consumer does not appreciate the quality of the product, or the sales force is inept. It is true that many firms produce excellent products, but not necessarily items of the type of or design that potential customers want to purchase. The British motor cycle industry produced many fine machines in the 1950s and early 1960s, but lost their market to the Japanese on points of styling, design and choice.

Under a production-orientated philosophy, the salesperson's role is a relatively minor one. The salesperson is there to sell what the firm has produced. Such a firm is likely to be organised in the manner outlined in Figure 1.1.

1.6.2 Sales orientation

Business people began to appreciate that in a highly competitive environment, it was simply not enough to produce goods as efficiently as possible. They also had to be sold. The sales concept affirms that demand has to be created through

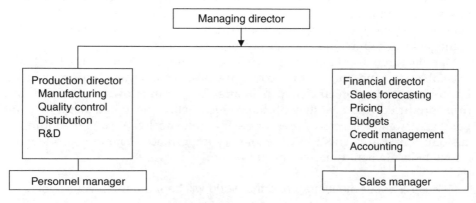

Figure 1.1 Typical organisation of a production-orientated firm

the art of persuasion using sales techniques. The sales department was perceived to hold the key to company prosperity and survival. Scant attention was paid to genuine needs and requirements of the final consumer, but it was at least understood that goods and services did not necessarily sell themselves without some kind of endeavour.

Many firms simply still think of marketing as a contemporary term for selling and change the name of their sales office to 'Marketing Department' to be 'modern'. In fact selling, although important, is but one of several functions for which the marketing department is responsible.

Drucker (1954) explained the relationship between selling and marketing eloquently:

> 'There will always, one can assume, be a need for some selling. But the aim of marketing is to make selling superfluous. The aim of marketing is to know and understand the customer so well that the product or service fits him and sells itself. Ideally, marketing should result in a customer who is ready to buy!'

In a sales-orientated firm, sales volume is the success criterion. Planning horizons tend to be relatively short term, with the actual customer and how they perceive the value of the goods being sold, being of secondary importance. The implicit premises of a sales orientation are that:

1 the firm's main task is to establish a good sales team;
2 consumers naturally resist purchasing and it is the salesperson's role to overcome this resistance;
3 sales techniques are needed to induce consumers to buy more.

In the UK, sales orientation was a well-established philosophy during the 1960s. Rationing ended in 1953, but it was not until the late 1950s and early 1960s that the Second World War shortages began to be filled. The first reaction on the part of management to a slowing down in sales was to import 'hard sell' techniques from the USA. There was little consumer protection legislation, so many consumers fell prey to such techniques with no redress to the law. Sales techniques like 'putting the customer in a position where they cannot say "no" ' flourished (i.e. putting questions such that they will receive assenting answers, so after having said 'yes' so many times it is difficult to say 'no' when asked for the order). However, the kind of activity just described was relatively minor in terms of dishonest practice. Many sales and advertising techniques that were then openly practised, now come under the criminal code (e.g. pyramid and inertia selling). It was during the 1970s that the UK Government reacted to assist consumers and a great deal of legislation was introduced to protect consumers in this era of what was called 'consumerism'. It is often argued that this era of sales orientation that lasted in the UK and Europe around the decade of the 1960s is what gave marketing a bad image in the collective mind of the public, and this negative image still

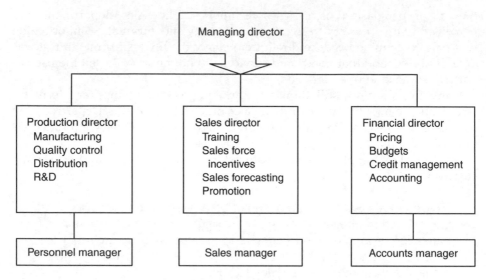

Figure 1.2 Typical organisation of a sales-orientated firm

persists to the present day. There was seen to be nothing inherently immoral in production orientation, for it gave customers the opportunity to say 'no', whereas sales orientation forced goods upon unwilling customers. As we discuss next, marketing orientation is the natural development that follows sales orientation.

In a sales-orientated firm, selling is a major management function, and is often given equal status to that of production and finance. This type of organisation is illustrated in Figure 1.2.

1.6.3 Marketing orientation

The market concept assumes that to survive in the long term, an organisation must ascertain the needs and wants of specifically defined target markets. It must then produce goods and/or services that satisfy customer requirements profitably. Under the marketing concept the customer who becomes the centre of business attention. The organisation no longer sees production or sales as the key to prosperity, growth and survival, and these are simply tools of the business. Marketing orientation acknowledges that what is required is the identification and satisfaction of customers' needs and wants. The marketing concept is shown schematically in Figure 1.3.

The main difference between production and marketing orientation is that company management in a production-orientated firm focuses its attention on existing products, paying minor attention to the changing needs and wants of the market place. The marketing-orientated firm produces goods and services it has ascertained that prospective customers want to purchase.

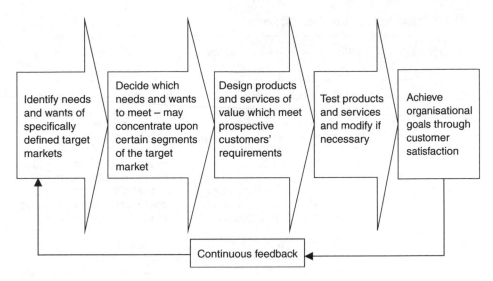

Figure 1.3 The marketing concept

The main difference between sales and marketing orientation is summed up by Levitt (1960):

> 'Selling focuses on the needs of the seller; marketing on the needs of the buyer. Selling is preoccupied with the seller's need to convert his product into cash; marketing with the idea of satisfying the needs of the customer by means of the product and the whole cluster of things associated with creating, delivering and finally consuming it.'

Sales-orientated firms tend to use shorter-run production methods and are preoccupied with achieving current sales targets. This philosophy extends down to individual members of the field sales force because of the way that their commission and earnings are structured through the sales quota and target system. In such a company, customer considerations and dealings with individual customers are often restricted to the sales department. In a marketing orientated organisation, the entire firm appreciates the central importance of the customer, and realises that there will be no business without satisfied customers. To be able to progress from a 'sales' to a 'marketing' orientation, senior management in the organisation must work to cultivate a company-wide approach to the satisfaction of customer requirements.

The main problem facing a sales-orientated firm in progressing to marketing orientation is managing organisational change. The marketing department is likely to require proportionally more influence and authority over other departments in order to bring about an integrated and cohesive organisation in which all departments pull in the same direction for the benefit of customers. Unless the philosophy of marketing permeates the entire organisation from top to bottom, it will never achieve its full potential.

Table 1.1 Departmental philosophical differences

Other department	Other department's priorities	Marketing department's priorities
Finance and accountancy	'Cost plus' pricing; rigid budgetary control; standard commercial transactions	Marketing-orientated pricing; flexible budgeting; special terms and discounts
Purchasing	Standard purchasing procedures; bulk orders; narrow product line; standard parts	Flexible purchasing procedures; smaller orders of necessary; wide product line; non-standard products
Production	Long production lead time; long runs; limited range of models; supplier-specified products	Short production lead time; short runs; extensive range of models; customised orders
Sales	Time horizon – short term; success criterion – sales; 'one-department' orientated; short-term sales	Time horizon – long term; success criterion – customer satisfaction; whole organisation-orientated; long-term profits

It is natural for departments like sales and production to experience a sense of anxiety that can be brought about by major organisational change, and they may even resent having to adjust their activities in line with marketing requirements. The human implications of such a change need to be taken into consideration. The reallocation of power within a company can be an uncomfortable experience for those with a vested interest in keeping the status quo. The main departmental differences and possible organisational conflicts between marketing and other areas of the firm are summarised in Table 1.1.

In a marketing-orientated company it is probable that the Managing Director will come from a marketing background. This marketing philosophy is not confined to the Marketing Director or to the marketing department, but it permeates the whole company.

The adoption of a proper organisational structure is a necessary condition for marketing orientation, but is not the sole condition. A change of management titles is purely cosmetic. Such changes will not bring about the necessary shift in company attitudes. A marketing-orientated firm is typically organised as outlined in Figure 1.4.

Marketing organisational issues arise quite frequently in examinations. The important thing is not to become too enthusiastic about the finer points of an organisation chart. Putting personalities and departments in the right boxes is necessary, but this is not enough on its own. When addressing such questions, always emphasise that it is the adoption of the marketing concept as a business philosophy, rather than the adoption of a particular organisational structure, that is really important. It is the company's whole approach to the business situation that is the key issue. This means an adoption of a business philosophy that puts customer satisfaction at the centre of management thinking throughout

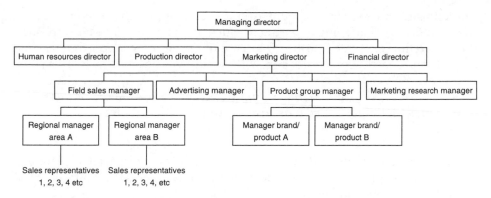

Figure 1.4 Typical organisation of a marketing-orientated firm

the organisation, and this is what distinguishes a marketing-orientated firm from a production or sales orientated organisation.

1.7 Marketing as a business philosophy

Marketing is sometimes seen as a rather confusing phenomenon, drawing its theories from a disparate number of sources. The main source of confusion is the combination of marketing as a philosophy of business and marketing practice. These are two separate, yet interrelated, areas:

1 a basic way of thinking about business that focuses on customers' needs and wants;
2 a functional area of management that uses a set of techniques.

Peter Doyle (1994) explains:

> 'The Marketing Concept is not a theory of marketing but a philosophy of business. It affirms that the key to meeting the objectives of stakeholders is to satisfy customers. In competitive markets this means that success goes to those firms that are best at meeting the needs of customers.'

To look at marketing as an business philosophy is to take a holistic view of the discipline. This approach is explained by Peter Drucker (1954):

> 'Marketing is not only much broader than selling; indeed, it is not a specialised activity at all. It encompasses the entire business. It is the whole business seen from the point of view of its final result, that is, from the customer's point of view. Concern and responsibility for marketing must, therefore, permeate all areas of the enterprise.'

Marketing cannot exist in a vacuum. An integrated approach is needed, not just the creation of a marketing department. Such an approach to business propels the marketing-orientated firm towards embracing new opportunities and away from a narrow preoccupation with selling existing products to existing customers.

Because of the difficulty of incorporating all the various facets of marketing into a single definition let us look instead at the distinguishing features of the subject:

1 Marketing is dynamic and operational, requiring action as well as planning.
2 Marketing requires an improved form of business organisation, although this on its own is not enough.
3 Marketing is an important functional area of management, often based in a single physical location. More importantly, it is an overall business philosophy that should be adopted by everybody in the entire organisation.
4 The marketing concept states that the identification, satisfaction and retention of customers is the key to long-term survival and prosperity.
5 Marketing involves planning and control.
6 The principle of marketing states that all business decisions should be made with primary consideration of customer requirements.
7 Marketing focuses attention from production towards the needs and wants of the market place.
8 Marketing is concerned with obtaining value from the market by offering items of value to the market. It does this by producing goods and services that satisfy the genuine needs and wants of specifically defined target markets.
9 The distinguishing feature of a marketing orientated organisation is the way in which it strives to provide customer satisfaction as a way of achieving its own business objectives.

1.8 Summary

In a modern organisation, the entrepreneurial function is rarely carried out by one individual as was often the case 50 years and more ago. The entrepreneurial function that has developed into a managerial function and business philosophy that views customers as the starting point of business planning activity is termed marketing. It is only since the end of the Second World War that marketing has developed as a formalised business concept with a codified philosophy and set of techniques.

Marketing is seen as both a functional area of management which utilises a set of management techniques, and an overall business philosophy. The sub-functions of marketing are examined as a whole in Chapter 3, then in more detail in specialised chapters throughout the book.

A marketing-orientated company achieves its business objectives by identifying and anticipating the changing needs and wants of specifically defined target markets. The subject of targeting is addressed in Chapter 5. The range of techniques used for identifying customer requirements is termed marketing research, and this is discussed in Chapter 13.

The fundamental principles of marketing are equally applicable to not-for-profit organisations, where efficiency or minimum cost criteria can be substituted for profit objects. These issues, along with a number of specific examples, are discussed in Chapter 16.

References

Doyle, P. (1994), *Marketing Management and Strategy*, Hemel Hempstead: Prentice-Hall, p. 37.

Drucker, P. (1954), *The Practice of Management*, New York: Harper and Row, p. 65.

Kotler, P. (1991), *Marketing Management: Analysis, Planning, Implementation and Control*, 7th edition, Englewood Cliffs, NJ: Prentice-Hall, pp. 4–5.

Levitt, T. (1960), 'Marketing myopia', *Harvard Business Review*, July–August, 38(4), 45–46.

Smith, A. (1776), *An Enquiry into the Nature and Causes of the Wealth of Nations*, London: Methuen and Co. Ltd.

Further reading

Brennan, R., Baines, P. and Garneau, P. (2003), *Contempory Strategic Marketing*, London: Palgrave Macmillan, Chapter 1.

Cravens, D.W., Lamb, C.W. Jr. and Crittenden, V.L. (2002), *Strategic Marketing Management Cases*, 7th edition, New York: McGraw-Hill, Chapter 1.

Hartley, R.F. (2004), *Marketing Mistakes and Success*, 9th edition, New York: John Wiley & Sons, Chapter 1.

Jobber, D. (2004), *Principles and Practices of Marketing*, 4th edition, New York: McGraw Hill, Chapter 1.

Kotler, P., Armstrong, G., Saunders, J. and Wong, V. (2001), *Principles of Marketing*, 3rd European edition, Pearson Education, Ltd., Chapter 1.

Lancaster, G. and Massingham, L. (2002), *Essentials of Marketing: Text and Cases*, 4th edition, Maidenhead: McGraw-Hill, Chapter 1.

Questions

Question 1.1

Distinguish between a 'need' and a 'want'. Give specific examples.

Question 1.2

In what way is the marketing concept relevant to non-profit making organisations? Use examples.

Question 1.3

Why should the customer be the most important person that any organisation has to deal with?

Question 1.4

What is meant when it is said that marketing should be viewed as an 'overall business philosophy' rather than merely another functional area of management?

Question 1.5

Outline and discuss those factors you believe have given rise to the need for modern companies to be marketing-orientated.

Question 1.6

Discuss the contention that successful marketing stems more from the adoption of a sound organisational philosophy rather than the application of functional skills.

Question 1.7

Many companies confuse marketing and selling. How do you explain the differences between the two?

Question 1.8

'The marketing concept has failed to live up to the high expectations of its early protagonists'. Using examples of companies and products with which you are familiar, critically evaluate this statement.

Question 1.9

What characteristics distinguish a truly marketing-orientated organisation from a production- or sales-orientated organisation?

Question 1.10

List your three most effective marketing-orientated organisations and give the reasons for judging them to be the best. Now list the three worst and do likewise.

2

Marketing Environment

2.1 Introduction

Companies operate within a complex and dynamic external environment. It is the task of marketing-orientated companies to link the resources of the organisation to the requirements of customers. This is done within the framework of opportunities and threats present in the external environment. Change is an unequivocal fact of life, and organisations have to adapt. Usually, change occurs very slowly, almost imperceptibly. At other times it occurs quickly, and although it is obvious to everybody at the time, it can be so rapid that organisations might find it difficult to react in time (e.g. the 'dot.com' boom).

Charles Darwin, author of *Origin of the Species (1859)*, put forward the theory that living organisms have been able to survive in a constantly changing and potentially hostile world, because of their ability to adapt to changing environmental conditions (see also Darwin, 1887). Companies operate in an ever-changing business environment. They too, in order to survive, need to take account of, and adapt to, changing economic and technological conditions. Change is inevitable and in a free enterprise system firms have to be free to use their judgement in order to adapt to the ever changing commercial environment which is the mark of a free society (see Friedman, 1962).

In Chapter 1, we discussed the importance of the customer at the core of the business philosophy we call 'marketing'. Although a clear understanding of customer requirements is of supreme importance in putting such a business philosophy into practice, this alone is not enough. Firms must monitor not only the changing needs and wants of target markets, but also changes in the wider, external or 'macro' environment. This is necessary if the organisation is to be able to prepare to adapt to changing conditions.

2.2 Monitoring the external environment

2.2.1 Capitalising on environmental change

With environmental change, organisations should attempt to capitalise on it rather than reacting to it in a defensive manner. Firms can rarely control their macro-environment, but they can understand, and even anticipate it.

The ability of companies to understand and react to environmental forces is of vital importance to marketing success. In fact an individual organisation's new technology may be the external environmental force of technology that might be affecting other organisations! In a seminal article Zeithaml and Zeithaml (1984) give examples of environmental management strategies that firms can use to influence the largely uncontrollable environment, the principles of which are still used till date by many firms.

The general marketing environment is made up of factors and forces that affect or influence the marketing function. These include inter-departmental relationships (referred to as the intra-firm environment) and all other external factors (the macro-environment).

The macro-environment can, in turn, be broken down into two broad categories:

1 The marketing company's immediate environment is the marketing function itself consisting of the 'four Ps' plus an extra people 'P'. This element ensures the smooth operation of the marketing function. This leads to the 'intra-firm' environment consisting of other departments in the company like: finance, production, human resource management and research, design and development. The next layer is called the 'micro-environment', that consists of suppliers, customers, competitors, distributors and marketing intermediaries like advertising agencies and marketing research companies.
2 The wider external environment is termed the 'macro-environment' and this includes political, economic, socio-cultural and technological factors (remembered through the acronym 'PEST'). Lately, 'legal' factors have been isolated from 'political' factors, making the acronym 'SLEPT'. More recently still, the acronym became 'PESTLE' with the extra 'E' standing for 'environmental'. Its latest incarnation is 'STEEPLE' with another 'E' standing for 'ecological'. As a student of marketing it is important that you know these various acronyms because they are often referred to in these shorthand terms in marketing strategy examination papers.

In order for organisations to be able to adapt successfully to changing conditions, management needs to understand the many factors and forces influencing such changes. Firms like to be in a position to adapt to changes as they occur, or better still, be able to adapt in advance of change by anticipating events. By identifying environmental trends early, management can better determine how they might affect the future of the business. If they cannot identify and react to changes quickly, they run the risk of being dictated to by circumstances beyond their control and be forced into being 'market followers', rather than playing a part in such change, influencing the course of events and being 'market leaders'. In recent times there has been a move towards greater 'globalisation' of markets. This in turn has driven many developments in international marketing strategy especially in the field of market segmentation and branding. Today many brand have global recognition and are truly 'global brands' whereas in the past firms involved in international markets were more likely to have different brands in different regions or even countries. For an interesting treatment of the development and importance of global branding see Moore *et al.* (2000) and also the work of Ehrenberg and Goodhardt (2000) world renowned experts in the field of branding. The future direction of branding is covered in a book by Clifton and Maughan (1999).

2.2.2 Speed of response

In terms of speed of response and an ability to react to changing conditions, there are three acknowledged types of organisation:

1 *Companies that make things happen*! Such organisations identify and under-stand the forces and conditions that bring about change. They continually strive to adapt, and stay 'ahead of the game'. These companies may them-selves play some part in influencing the rate and direction of change.
2 *Companies that watch things happen*! These organisations fail to adapt to changes early enough to become part of that change. Such firms have little opportunity to influence events, but are usually forced to make changes to survive. Such changes are 'reactive' rather than planned and are often instigated as part of a defensive 'crisis management' programme.
3 *Companies that wonder what happened*! Companies in this category are those that are blind and impervious to change. Such firms sometimes even fail to realise that circumstances have altered. Even when such change is acknow-ledged, management often refuses to adapt to an ever-changing environment. Such firms are unlikely to survive in the long term.

2.2.3 The need to constantly monitor environmental factors

In mixed economies like those in Europe and North America, companies have a great deal of autonomy in the management of their business affairs. Company management has control over how they choose to organise and integrate func-tions and responsibilities within the organisation. Generally, management is free to decide what to produce, methods of manufacture and to make decisions concerning distribution, pricing, packaging and communications. Providing management operates within the law of the country, it is relatively free to conduct its business affairs as it chooses.

The business variables that are the responsibility of the marketing function, such as price, advertising, new product development, packaging and the customers to whom the products are marketed, are collectively referred to as the marketing mix. The functions of marketing and the concept of the marketing mix are discussed in greater detail in Chapter 3.

Although marketing-orientated firms have direct control over their mix elements, they do not formulate plans and strategies in a vacuum. As we have discussed, organisations are influenced by a plethora of environmental factors largely outside their control. Environmental change poses both opportunities and threats to the marketing firm. The success of the firm in meeting the challenge posed by change will depend on the ability of management and individual managerial skills in carrying out the following tasks:

1 monitoring the external environment and anticipating significant changes;
2 evaluating the likely effect of change or potential change on the business activities of the firm;
3 drawing up short-, medium- and long-term plans to deal with the new environmental scenario (this will include the formulation of contingency plans);
4 using controllable variables under management's command (the marketing mix elements) to successfully adapt to changes in the external environment;
5 monitoring the ability of plans and strategies to successfully cope with, and ideally capitalise on, changed conditions and to undertake corrective action where necessary.

2.3 The general marketing environment

The general marketing environment is made up of a number of separate, but interrelated elements. From a conceptual point of view, it is easier to think of these individual elements as 'sub-environments'. Marketing management is primarily concerned with anticipating and reacting to perceived changes occurring outside the organisation itself. This external environment, as already noted, is referred to as the 'macro-environment'.

The term 'general marketing environment' refers to all factors and forces that impinge upon marketing management's ability to conduct its affairs successfully. This also includes inter-departmental factors and influences. In Chapter 1, it was explained that the marketing concept is a customer-orientated philosophy that should permeate the entire organisation. A distinction was also made between marketing as an overall concept or philosophy and the more narrowly held view of marketing as a specific functional area of management. As a functional area of management, marketing invariably has to both compete and co-operate with other departments within the firm. Again, as stated earlier, we term this 'micro' area of the general marketing environment the 'intra-firm environment' and this is all part of the company's 'micro-environment'. These terms are reiterated as they often appear as a part of questions in marketing examination.

2.4 The intra-firm environment

Companies have a finite amount of money and other resources. The marketing function often has to compete with other management functions to secure that share of the firm's overall budget it needs to accomplish its tasks effectively. Marketing needs a revenue budget to spend on advertising, exhibitions, direct mail, sales personnel, marketing research and other activities that form part of the process of winning orders. It also needs a capital budget in order to purchase equipment like computers.

Other management departments such as production, finance and human resource management feel that they too provide important services and hence deserve an equal share of the company's budget.

The marketing department not only has to 'compete' with other departments for financial resources, but it has to work in co-operation with these other functions. For example, marketing research may identify a 'gap' in an existing market that the firm can commercially exploit. In order to produce products or services that might fill this gap, the marketing department will have to call upon the services of other departments such as finance, research, design and development, production and the legal department. Hence, marketing tasks cannot be achieved in isolation, but need the full co-operation of other departments.

When considering the overall environment in which marketing operates, it is important to appreciate that although the marketing function is the process through which the organisation adapts to changes in external conditions, it also has to consider internal factors. Marketing managers make decisions that directly affect other functional areas of the firm. Likewise, decisions made elsewhere within the organisation affect marketing's ability to carry out its job effectively. When addressing environmental problems facing the marketing department, students sometimes fail to appreciate the importance of understanding the degree of conflict and co-operation inherent in the interaction between marketing and other functional areas of the firm.

2.5 The macro-environment

Although departmental rivalries and conflicts that present themselves within the company's intra-firm environment can be a problem, they are to a certain extent within the control of the organisation's management. It is generally uncontrollable forces in the external macro-environment that pose the most important sources of opportunities as well as threats to the company.

The term 'macro-environment' denotes all forces and agencies external to the marketing firm itself. Some of these forces and agencies will be closer to the operation of the firm than others, for example, a company's suppliers, agents, distributors and other distributive intermediaries and competing firms. These 'closer' external factors are collectively referred to as the firm's 'proximate macro-environment' to distinguish them from the wider external forces found, for example, in the legal, cultural, economic and technological sub-environments.

2.6 The proximate macro-environment

The proximate macro-environment consists of people, organisations and forces within the firm's immediate external environment. Of particular importance to marketing firms are the sub-environments of suppliers, competitors and distributors (intermediaries). These sub-environments can each have a significant effect upon the marketing firm.

2.6.1 The supplier environment

Suppliers are generally other business firms, although they can be individuals (e.g. a marketing consultant). Suppliers provide the firm with raw materials, components, services, or in the case of retailers, the finished goods themselves. Companies often depend on numerous suppliers, but it is not a case of one-way dependence; supplying firms also depend on the future prosperity of the buying firm for future orders. The buyer/supplier relationship is one of mutual economic interdependence, both parties relying on the other for their commercial wellbeing. Changes in the terms of the relationship can have a significant effect on both parties. Any such changes are usually the result of careful negotiation rather than unilateral action. Both parties seek a degree of security and stability from their commercial relationship that is increasingly viewed as being long term. This is borne out by the development of 'just-in-time' manufacturing techniques, that was pioneered by the Japanese Toyota Company, but has now seen widespread adoption by companies worldwide. This philosophy of management demands absolute reliability from suppliers to deliver goods that are never sub-standard ('zero defects' is the term used) so inspection at the customer's works is eliminated before they are committed to the production line. This philosophy also demands that goods and components are delivered exactly when they are required (so the ordering company does not effectively have to hold any stocks).

Although both parties to a commercial contract are seeking stability and security, it would be wrong to believe that factors in the supplier environment are not subject to change. Suppliers may be affected by industrial disputes that might affect delivery of materials to the buying company. Other changes (e.g. a sudden increase in raw material prices) may force suppliers to raise their prices. Whatever is being purchased, unexpected developments in the supplier environment can have an immediate and serious effect on the firm's commercial operations. Because of this, marketing management, by means of its market intelligence system (dealt with in detail in Chapter 13), should continually monitor possible changes in the supplier environment and have contingency plans ready to deal with potentially adverse developments.

2.6.2 The competitive environment

Factors in the competitive environment can affect the commercial prosperity of a company. Management must be alert to the potential threat of other companies marketing product substitutes. Many UK manufacturers in industries like steel and textiles have experienced intense competition from imported foreign products. For example, the UK carpet industry has traditionally had a reputation for producing excellent quality Axminster and Wilton woven carpets. Much of this production is still carried out in the textile town of Kidderminster in the Midlands, which has been traditionally acknowledged as the 'carpet centre of the world'. Over recent years, the market has changed with cheaper 'tufted' carpets (not woven, but with the yarn punched into a backing material) becoming more popular. Since people have become increasingly mobile and inclined to move home more often, many are reluctant to invest in a top-quality woven carpet, which may well last 20 years or more, especially as it is widely recognised that it is impractical to take up a fitted carpet when moving home. A further reason for the increase in popularity of tufted carpets is that not only are they significantly cheaper than traditional woven carpets, but the quality and visual appearance of synthetic fibres has dramatically improved. To a certain extent, the UK carpet industry failed to react fast enough to changes in consumer tastes and to the changes in technology required to produce tufted synthetic carpet. Nowadays, much of this type of carpet is imported into the UK from Belgium and the USA. The UK carpet industry is much smaller today than it was 20 years ago and many manufacturers of traditional woven carpets have been forced into liquidation.

In some industries, as in the carpet industry, there may be numerous manufacturers worldwide posing a potential competitive threat. In other industries, such as aerospace or motor vehicle manufacture, there may only be a few. Whatever the type, size and composition of the industry, it is essential that marketing management has a full understanding of competitive forces. Because of the 'globalisation' of the market place for many products, some firms have formed strategic alliances, for example, Louis Kraar (1989) discusses the case of Ford and Volkswagen setting up a joint company in Brazil. Companies need to establish exactly who their competitors are and the benefits they are offering to the marketplace. Such knowledge means that the company will have a better opportunity to compete effectively. Greater internationalisation of markets and even the globalisation of many markets have meant that few firms are immune from the competitive pressures globalisation has brought with it. For an interesting discussion on the globalisation effects and implications of many European markets see Stone (1989).

2.6.3 The distributive environment

Many firms rely on marketing intermediaries to ensure that their products reach the final consumer. Some firms supply directly to a retailer, whilst others use a more complex 'chain' including intermediaries such as wholesalers, factors, agents and distributors. The use of intermediaries is more common in the distribution of consumer goods that are usually targeted at a mass market. Firms manufacturing industrial products, particularly where these are custom made, or buyer specified, rather than supplier specified, are more inclined to deliver their products direct to the final customer. However, this is a generalisation, as a number of industrial marketing firms make use of factors, distributors and other intermediaries.

It may seem that the conventional method of distribution in any particular industry is relatively static. To a certain extent this is true, although distribution channels are subject to evolutionary change, just like any other business function. The rate of change in the distributive environment can be likened to the hour hand of a watch. The hand of the watch is always moving, although each individual movement is so small as to be imperceptible. Taken over time, the cumulative movement can be very significant. Because changes in the distributive environment occur relatively slowly, there is a danger of marketing firms failing to appreciate the commercial significance of cumulative change. Existing channels may decline in popularity over time, whereas new channels may be developing unnoticed by the marketing firm and an obvious recent has been advances that have been made in this direction by e-commerce companies.

The subject of distribution, and in particular factors and forces influencing change, is discussed in greater detail in Chapter 8. At this stage, it is sufficient to appreciate that the distributive environment, like any other environmental factor, is likely to be subject to change.

2.7 The wider macro-environment

We have examined a number of factors present in the 'proximate macro-environment' that are the macro-environmental forces closest to the marketing firm (i.e. suppliers, competitors and marketing intermediaries). Changes in the wider macro-environment may not be as immediate to the marketing firm's day-to-day operations, but they are just as important. Factors making up these wider macro-environmental forces fall into four groups:

1 political (and legal) factors,
2 economic factors,
3 social (and cultural) factors,
4 technological factors.

As mentioned in Chapter 1, these are remembered through the acronym 'PEST'. It was also stated that this definition has expanded to include additional factors that go to make up the acronym 'STEEPLE'. However, the view is taken that excessive sub-divisions make for a detail of complexity. Such finite divisions are only appropriate in circumstances when, say, the final ecological 'E' in

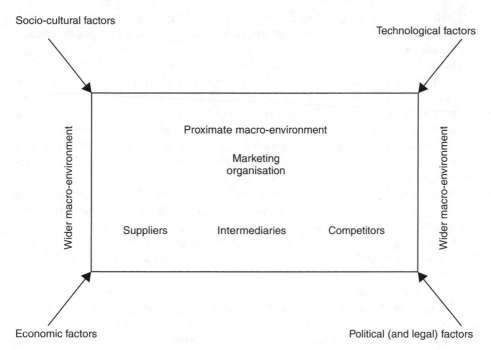

Figure 2.1 Macro-environmental factors influencing the marketing organisation

'STEEPLE' has a great bearing on the company's operations as it might be operating in an environment where ecological issues might be particularly sensitive (e.g. drilling for oil). For our purposes, the sub-divisions under the acronym 'PEST' is appropriate for the discussion that follows.

Changes in these sub-environments affect not only the marketing firm, but also those organisations and individuals that make up the proximate macro-environment. The two parts of the overall macro-environment (the proximate and wider macro-environments) are therefore closely related. A change in the supplier or competitive environment may, for example, have its basic cause in wider changes taking place in the technological or political arenas.

In Figure 2.1 we show the organisation's inner proximate marketing environment surrounded by its wider macro-environmental influences.

We now examine each of these wider macro-environmental influences in more detail:

2.7.1 The technological environment

Technology is a macro-environmental variable that affects business, as well as all elements in the company's proximate macro-environment including its customers. The rate of technological change is accelerating. Marketing firms themselves play a part in technological progress through their own research departments or through co-operative ventures. Organisations must make use of current technology that can play a part in generating new developments and applications.

Technology has influenced the development of many of the products that we now take for granted, for example, television, calculators, aerosol sprays, compact disc players, video recorders and home computers. In advanced industrial nations, mature 'smoke stack' industries such as steel making are in relative decline. New 'sunrise' industries such as biotechnology, electronics and information technology have developed, and it is these new industries to which advanced industrial nations should look for manufacturing and trading opportunities.

Of the 'sunrise' industries, the development of IT has had particularly wide reaching effects on marketing organisations. The development and large scale production of the microprocessor has enabled the development of new products (e.g. calculators and digital watches). It has also revolutionised the collection, processing and dissemination of information, which has in turn affected the whole spectrum of marketing activity. The area of marketing research provides a good illustration of change in practice resulting from the adoption of the new technology. Questionnaires can now be designed and coded by computer, and data collected from respondents can go directly back to the computer via optical readers. 'Computed-aided telephone interviewing' (CATI) provides sophisticated screen presentations and enormous capacity in terms of the complexity, scope and sample size of the respondents to be interviewed. Response speed and fast data-processing turnaround time are the principal advantages of this system.

Sales forecasting is another example of an important marketing activity revolutionised by advances in IT. Before the advent of computers, sales forecasts were usually subjective 'educated guesses'. Computers, and the software packages that go with them, have given organisations access to powerful, sophisticated, quantitative forecasting techniques. Large amounts of data can now be stored and numerous, complex equations inherent in sophisticated quantitative methods can be solved and updated automatically by the computer. Routine sales forecasting can now largely be left to a computer, leaving the manager free to tackle non-routine activities.

The impact of technological change on marketing activities can be seen at retail levels where electronic point of sale (EPOS) data capture is now applied by most retailers. The laser checkout reads a bar code on the product being purchased and stores this information. It is then used to analyse sales and re-order stock, as well as to give customers a printed readout of what they have purchased as well as the price charged. Such a system has obviated the tedious task of marking every item with the retail price and the need for the checkout person to key the price of each item into the till. Manufacturers of fast-moving consumer goods (FMCGs) particularly packaged grocery products have responded to these technological innovations by incorporating bar codes on their packaging.

Business in general and certainly marketing in particular has become more and more affected by, and dependent upon, technology. Furthermore, technological progress itself is altering and accelerating. Technology seems to be developing at an exponential rate that is at an ever-increasing rate. The rate of development increases because scientists and technologists can learn from what has happened in the past, in a sense they are 'standing on the shoulders of giants'. For example, the digital computer was developed in a laboratory in Manchester University, England and since then other people have developed the basic technology to what we can see today. We shall examine some of the more salient of these changes and advances in technology as they affect the marketer in more detail in this chapter. Suffice it to say at this stage, that advances in technology are now beginning to basically change the nature of marketing and other business and commercial activities. So much so that many consider that in as little as ten years the process of marketing will be changed beyond recognition compared to what it is today. Some experts go so far as to say that the traditional marketing model or 'paradigm' is no longer applicable in the world of the Internet and that a new model is called for. Certainly, at the very least, the modern-day marketer needs to be familiar with the key advances in technology, which are at this time impacting the marketing process. See Reed Hoke (2000) for an interesting discussion of how developments in technology, especially the Internet have impacted and driven developments in global marketing. Developments in business related technology often contributes to the growth of the international company and a move towards the global market and consumer. Smaller firms in particular benefit from Internet based business technologies as it reduces their size disadvantage. Electronic commerce has no geographic boundaries; it is just as easy to interact with consumers in New Zealand from the UK as it is to interact with consumers in the next town. Many firms, in order to both differentiate their products and reduce their costs are increasingly using computer-based technology. Just-in-time ordering and stock holding systems saves firms millions in inventory and logistics costs compared with the more traditional way of doing things in the past. Computers have facilitated the use of these new systems and processes. Some of the developments in business related computer technology allow the marketer to be much more customer focused and marketing oriented with, for example, much faster and flexible responses to customer needs. The use of database marketing and data mining has improved the accuracy and efficiency of many marketing operations particularly marketing communications such as direct mail. See Tapp (2001) for an interesting discussion on the strategic importance of direct marketing and the use of information technology in marketing.

As far back as 1989 *Business Week* reported that developments in communications have been particularly striking especially in mobile telephone, satellite and Internet technologies. These developments have continued particularly in Internet and mobile telephone technology and their integration (see Hardaker and Graham, 2001). In the same year Dreyfuss (1989) commented on the significant developments in fibre optics and high definition television (HDTV). Over the past decade scientists and technologists have continued to make remarkable advances in these areas. The examples that have been provided illustrate how changes in the technological environment can affect products and services that firms produce and the way they carry out their business operations. Technological change, like all other factors in the macro-environment, pose threats and opportunities to the marketing firm.

2.7.2 The economic environment

Economic factors are of concern as they are likely to influence, among other things, demand, costs, prices and profits. The business press is particularly concerned with levels of industrial output, levels of retail buying, inflation, unemployment, balance of payments and exchange rates. These economic factors are largely outside the control of the individual firm, but their effects on individual enterprises can be profound. One of the weaknesses of economics as a social science is the poor predictability of economic variables. Not even 'experts', such as Nasar (1988) in the USA, could produce anything like accurate long-range economic forecasts for economic conditions throughout the 1990s. The problem with such forecasts in the minds of people who apply them in business settings is that they tend to assume a spurious accuracy, as many such forecasts are mathematically based and produce a forecast down to the last single unit of measurement. How accurate such forecasts turn out to be, is a matter that only the passage of time can tell. When the forecast does not closely match reality, people lose confidence in such techniques.

Political and economic forces are often strongly related. For example, the Middle East War in Autumn, 1973, which was a political and military conflict between Israel and its Arab neighbours, produced economic shock waves throughout the Western world, that probably had greater economic implications for the world than the Second World War. Indirectly, the conflict resulted in the Arab nations dramatically increasing crude oil prices, a commodity upon which the economies of advanced Western nations were principally dependent. This contributed significantly to a world economic recession, which lasted for more than a decade. Increased oil prices meant increased energy costs (hence, increased transportation, power and heating and lighting costs) as well as increases in the cost of many oil-based raw materials such as plastics and synthetic fibres.

This 'oil crisis', demonstrated to the world that any state or confederation, possessing prime resources has far more economic, and therefore political, power than had been hitherto realised. It demonstrated how dramatic economic change can upset the traditional structures and balances in the world business environment.

Another economic development that has had a significant effect on individual UK enterprises was in joining what was then called the European Economic Community (EEC) on 1 January 1973 (now called the European Union or EU). The EU, or 'Common Market', was initially set up as a customs union. This implies that all tariffs between member states on all goods and services should be abolished and that a uniform tariff be adopted for all goods and services imported into the customs union area from non-member countries. However, as we have seen, the EU has expanded beyond its original customs union remit and is now a political union and this was particularly evidenced when the words 'Economic' and 'Community' were dropped from the original EEC nomenclature to become 'Union'. The issue of the EU is dealt with in more detail later in Chapter 16 when international marketing is examined.

As has been already demonstrated, changes in world economic forces are potentially highly significant to marketing firms, particularly those engaged in international marketing. However, an understanding of economic changes and forces in the domestic economy is also of vital importance, as these forces have the most immediate impact.

A factor that has persistently troubled the UK economy over the past 20 years has been, only until relatively recently, the high level of unemployment. This level of domestic unemployment has consistently decreased demand for many luxury consumer goods, which, in turn, has adversely affected the demand for the industrial machinery required to produce such goods. In some regions of the UK, particularly in those that have switched from 'old' industries like coal production to newer 'high-tech' industries, the local economy and in particular retail and service sectors that served them, have suffered because of persistent, long-term unemployment.

Other domestic economic variables are the rate of inflation as well as the level of domestic interest rates (i.e. the variable that determines the cost of borrowing). These can of course be significantly influenced by world economic factors. High levels of inflation, and high levels of interest rates used to combat inflation, affect the potential return from new investments and can inhibit the adoption and diffusion of new technologies. Governments have attempted to encourage economic growth through various policy measures. Tax concessions, Government grants, employment subsidies and capital depreciation allowances are some of the measures that have been used to stimulate growth.

Examples used here demonstrate, the importance to marketing firms of continually monitoring the economic environment at both domestic and world levels. The complex interaction of economic forces and the political responses made by individual governments in an attempt to influence and manage their national economies, can have dramatic effects on individual firms' business operations. Economic changes pose a set of opportunities and threats to the marketing organisation. By understanding and carefully monitoring the economic environment, firms should be in a position to guard against potential threats and capitalise on the opportunities.

2.7.3 The political and legal environment

For clarity, we have examined factors in the firm's macro-environment in isolation. In reality, these factors are very much interrelated. This is particularly true when considering political factors. The political environment cannot be examined in isolation, as this would be an academic exercise with little practical substance. It is only of practical use when it is translated from theory to practice or from rhetoric into action.

The outcomes of political decisions are manifest in government legislation. Changes in the legal environment are preceded by political debate and decisions. This is why political and legal forces are grouped together, but in the context of 'PEST' the 'legal' part of 'P' is often subsumed under 'political' when it appears in question papers.

Many of the legal, economic and social developments in society are the direct result of political decisions in practice. The UK Government has followed a basically 'free market' philosophy, particularly since the late 1970s. This started with the privatisation of many previously nationalised state industries in 1979. There is now a belief amongst the major UK political parties that business enterprise should be in the hands of private shareholders rather than being controlled by the state.

The guiding objective of government economic strategy is the control of inflation. To this end, great significance is attached to controlling the monetary supply, reducing and attempting to eliminate the Public Sector Borrowing Requirements (PSBR) and keeping public expenditure to a level commensurate with a balanced budget. Entrepreneurship, private ownership, self-help, reasonable profit levels and low levels of taxation are viewed as being vital to the country's prosperity. This illustrates the fact that many aspects of the economy are directly influenced by the political climate of the day.

To many companies, domestic political considerations are likely to be of prime concern. However, firms involved in international operations are faced with the additional dimension of international political developments. Many firms export and may have joint ventures or subsidiary companies abroad. In many developing countries, the domestic political and economic situation is less stable than in the UK. Change is often brought about by force, rather than through the democratic process. Marketing firms operating in such volatile conditions have to monitor the local political situation very carefully.

2.7.4 The socio-cultural environment

Of all the elements making up the marketing macro-environment, perhaps socio-cultural factors are the most difficult to evaluate, and pose the greatest challenge to the marketing firm. Social and cultural change is found in changing tastes, purchasing behaviour and changing priorities. The type of goods and services demanded by consumers is a function of their social conditioning and their resultant attitudes and beliefs.

In essence, a society's culture is a distinctive way of life of a people that is not biologically transmitted, but a learned behaviour that evolves and changes over time. Cultural influences give each society its particular attributes. Although the norms and values within a society are the result of many years of cultural conditioning, they are not static. It is the cause and effects of cultural change and the resulting revised norms and values within a society that are of specific interest to marketing firms.

UK culture was greatly influenced during the late nineteenth Century by the Victorian Protestant work ethic that prescribed hard work, self-help and the accumulation of material wealth. Other industrial societies are also materialistically orientated. Cultural values do change over time, and such change is particularly marked amongst the young, for example, many young people question the desirability of a culture with core values based upon materialism.

Core cultural values are those firmly established within a society and difficult to change. Such beliefs and values are perpetuated through the family, religion, education, the government and other institutions within society. As a result, core cultural values act as relatively fixed parameters within which marketing firms operate.

Secondary cultural values tend to be less strong and are more likely to undergo change. Social and cultural influences are so interrelated that it is difficult to evaluate the effects of each in isolation. Generally, social change is preceded by changes over time in a society's secondary cultural values. The following are examples of changes in the secondary cultural values of UK society that have caused dramatic social changes in the UK and the West in general.

Changes in social attitudes towards credit

As recently as the 1960s, credit was generally frowned upon. It was acceptable to finance major purchases such as cars and houses on credit, although even these financial arrangements were rarely discussed openly as they are nowadays. There tended to be a stigma attached to buying goods on credit. Credit was referred to in derisory terms such as 'on tick' or the 'never-never'.

Today, offering instant credit has become an integral part of marketing activity. Many people have credit accounts at garages and stores and most people use credit cards and charge cards like Visa and Access. Credit transactions are conducted openly in stores and elsewhere without any hint of social stigma. Credit transactions are so prevalent nowadays that the person who never finances purchases on credit is unusual.

For many people today it is often the availability and terms of credit offered that are the major factors in deciding to purchase a particular product. Credit has lost its stigma and is an accepted part of everyday life. Indeed, it is demanded by many customers, for without it the purchase would probably never take place. Marketing companies' response to this change in attitudes can be seen in the large number of credit schemes on offer today.

Changes in attitude towards health

People are more concerned about personal health than they were a few decades ago. They question the desirability of including artificial preservatives, colourings and other chemicals in the food they eat. Even as recently as the early 1980s, people who ate special 'health' foods and who took regular exercise like jogging were considered to be rather odd. Today, eating wholesome foods and taking sensible, regular exercise is an important part of many people's lives. Marketing firms have responded to this increase in general health awareness amongst the population. Today, many food products are advertised as being 'natural' or 'additive-free' and food producers have to specify the ingredients on the package. Sports equipment and sportswear marketing is now aimed at all sectors society, irrespective of age, sex or social class. The interests of people who were then viewed as 'eccentrics', has since grown into a multi-million pound industry. This has resulted in increased business opportunities for firms who provide goods and services that satisfy the requirements of a more health conscious population.

Smoking, once thought to be the height of sophistication, is now acknowledged as being detrimental to health, and is generally regarded as being anti-social. Many people today never start smoking, and many who do, attempt to stop. It is now the norm to look for smoking sections in public places rather than for non-smoking sections. This is an example of how changes in social attitudes have posed a significant threat, in this case, to the tobacco industry. Manufacturers are diversifying out of these products into new areas of growth in an attempt to counteract the general decline in their traditional markets.

Changes in attitudes towards working women

The cliché that 'a woman's place is in the home' reflects the chauvinistic attitude held by many people (including women) a few decades ago. In the UK today, social attitudes are more enlightened and a high proportion of economically active people are women. Approximately 60% of working women are married, combining running a home with the demands of a job or career.

Marketing firms have reacted to these changes. The fact that many women now have less time for traditional 'housekeeping' has doubtless contributed to the proliferation and acceptance of convenience foods as a normal part of everyday life. To a certain extent, the development of convenience foods raises conflict between this development and health awareness; a conflict that is being resolved by food manufacturers producing ranges of 'healthy', additive-free convenience foods.

The high proportion of working women has contributed to the development of 'one-stop shopping'. When both partners are working, leisure time is at a premium. Hypermarkets allow people to do most of their shopping under one roof. Today it is common for couples to make one major shopping expedition to a hypermarket, travelling by car and purchasing a week's or even a month's major supplies. Freezers and timesaving devices such as food processors and microwave ovens have all increased in popularity. Meals can be pre-cooked, stored in the freezer and rapidly defrosted and cooked when required.

Changes in moral attitudes

The 1960s is described as being the era of the 'social revolution'. This period witnessed the birth of the so-called 'permissive society'. Throughout the 1960s society's values went through a period of dramatic change. Attitudes towards marriage, divorce, sexual relationships, drugs, religion, family, economic and social institutions and towards authority in general, underwent considerable change. Many members of the 'older generation' were shocked to see how values and beliefs they had held for generations were cast aside or totally ignored by younger people. Younger people became more responsive to change. This was a period of 'individualism', where behaviour considered socially unacceptable a few years earlier became tolerated and even accepted as being typical.

Since the 1990s, society has experienced something of a reversal in moral attitudes among the young. Young people have witnessed periods of economic recession, high unemployment, a dramatic increase in the divorce rate and single parent families and have seen the consequences of drug abuse and sexual permissiveness and the advent of AIDS. Today, there is a tendency amongst younger people to place a greater emphasis on health, economic security and more stable relationships.

2.8 Summary

The macro-environmental factors discussed so far are not an exhaustive list, but these demonstrate the main areas of environmental change. Other sub-environments may be important to marketing management. For example, in a number of countries the religious environment may pose an important source of opportunities and threats.

Demographic changes are important to many companies. The UK population has been stable at under 60 million for a number of years, but the birth rate is falling, whilst people are living longer. Companies that produce goods and services suitable for babies and small children (e.g. Mothercare) have seen their traditional markets remain static. Such companies have diversified, offering products targeted at older age groups. A larger older sector of the population offers opportunities for companies to produce goods and services to satisfy their particular needs. Special products and services like holidays and pension related financial services are being marketed to meet the needs and wants of this relatively affluent sector, the over 55 year age group, which has more dis-posable income available than most other age groups. This group consists of many people who have retired early on generous occupational incomes. SAGA specifically set itself up to target this age group with a range of products including holidays and insurance provision.

Some of the environmental variables discussed in this chapter are covered later in greater depth in Chapter 15 that covers marketing intermediaries, par-ticularly the forces influencing change in the structure of retail distribution.

Technological advances in the field of marketing practice itself are discussed further in Chapter 13 in the context of marketing research, and in Chapter 17 in the context of planning and control, as well as Chapter 14, which deals with sales forecasting.

Culture and cultural change is discussed further in relation to the arena of international marketing in Chapter 16 which also examines marketing intermediaries with particular reference to overseas agents and distributors.

References

Business Week (1989), 'Super television: the high promise – and high risks – of high definition TV', 30th January p. 56.

Clifton, R. and Maughan, E. (1999), *The Future of Brands*, London: Macmillan.

Darwin, C. (1859), *On the Origin of Species by Means of Natural Selection, or the Preservation of Favoured Races in the Struggle for Life*, London: John Murray [Facsimile of 1st ed.]: Cambridge, Mass., Harvard University Press, 1964.

Darwin, C. (1887), *The Life and Letters of Charles Darwin*, New York: D. Appleton and Co.

Dreyfuss, J. (1989), 'The coming battle over your TV set' *Fortune* 13th February, pp. 64, 104.

Ehrenberg, A. and Goodhardt, G. (2000), 'New brands, near instant loyalty', *Journal of Marketing Management* 16(6), 607–618.

Friedman, M. (1962), *Capitalism and Freedom*, Chicago: University of Chicago Press.

Hardaker, G. and Graham, G. (2001), *Wired Marketing: Energising Business for e-Commerce*, New York: John Wiley and Sons, pp 1–20.

Kraar, L. (1989), 'Your rivals can be your allies', *Fortune* 27th March p. 66.

Moore, C., Fernie, J. and Burt, S. (2000), 'Brands without boundaries: The internationalisation of the designer retailer's brand', *European Journal of Marketing* 34 (8), 919–937.

Nasar, S. (1988), 'Preparing for a new economy' *Fortune* 26th September p. 86.

Reed Hoke, H. (2000), 'Loyalty, Internet and global marketing hot issues', *Direct Marketing* 62(9), 52–55.

Stone, N. (1989), 'The Globalization of Europe: An Interview with Wisse Decker', *Harvard Business Review*, May–June, 90–95.

Tapp, A. (2001), 'The strategic value of direct marketing: What are we good at?' *Journal of Database Marketing* 9(1), 9–15.

Zeithaml, C.P. and Zeithaml, V.A. (1984), 'Environmental management: revisiting a marketing perspective', *Journal of Marketing*, 48, 46–53.

Further reading

Brassington, F. and Pettitt, S. (2005), *Essentials of Marketing*, Englewood Cliffs, NJ: Prentice-Hall, Chapter 2.

Dibb, S., Simkin, L., Pride, W.M. and Ferrell, O.C. (2001), *Marketing Concepts and Strategies*, 4th European edition, Houghton Mifflin Company, Chapter 2.

Hill, L. and O'Sullivan, T. (2004), *Foundation Marketing*, 3rd edition, Englewood Cliffs, NJ: Prentice-Hall, Chapter 3.

Kotler, P. (2000), *Marketing Management – The Millenium Edition*, Englewood Cliffs, NJ: Prentice-Hall, Chapter 5.

Kotler, P. and Armstrong, G. (2004), *Principles of Marketing*, 10th edition, Englewood Cliffs, NJ: Prentice-Hall, Chapter 4.

Masterson, R. and Pickton, D. (2004), *Marketing an Introduction*, McGraw-Hill. Chapter 3.

Oldroyd, M. (2004), *CIM Coursebook 04/05: Marketing Environment*, London: Butterworth Heinemann.

Palmer, A. and Hartley, B.L. (2002), *The Business and Marketing Environment*, 4th edition, Maidenhead: McGraw-Hill.

Questions

Question 2.1

What do you understand by the term 'macro-environment'? Use examples to illustrate the importance of this macro-environment to the marketing management of an organisation with which you are familiar.

Question 2.2

The Chartered Institute of Marketing's definition of marketing includes the following: 'Marketing ... is responsible for identifying, anticipating and satisfying customer requirements profitably'.

To what extent can the monitoring of the technological, economic and social environments contribute to 'anticipating customer requirements?' Illustrate your answer with examples drawn from your own knowledge and experience.

Question 2.3

'Whatever the product or service being purchased by the marketing firm, developments in the supplier environment can have an immediate and possibly serious effect on the company's commercial operations'.
Critically evaluate this statement using examples to illustrate the points made.

Question 2.4

Under what circumstances is it possible for a firm to exert influence over its distributors and intermediaries? If so, what kind of influence, and how can this be achieved?

Question 2.5

Give examples of how the changing roles of people in society have affected marketing practice over the past 25 years. How do you envisage developments over the next 25 years, and how do you feel this might affect the practice of marketing?

Question 2.6

List and discuss the main elements in:

 (i) the micro-environment or proximate environment,
(ii) the wider general macro marketing environment.

Question 2.7

Discuss the most important international 'macro-environmental' factors that are affecting marketing firms operating in today's international business environment.

Question 2.8

Explain, making use of specific examples, why the modern marketing manager needs to be aware of developments in the technological environment which impact on the way firms may carry out their marketing function.

Question 2.9

List the major changes in the retail environment over the last 20 years. What factors have driven these changes?

Question 2.10

Outline a procedure you might recommend for a firm to undertake on-going environmental scanning.

3
Constituents of Marketing

3.1 Introduction

In Chapter 1, marketing was described as a concept-based business philosophy that has as its primary objective the realisation of profit through customer satisfaction. This philosophy is implemented through the various functions that make up marketing. Marketing should not be regarded as a limited set of activities like advertising, sales promotion and marketing research. A marketing-orientated company should ensure that the marketing concept is uppermost in the thoughts and actions of all personnel.

Marketing specialists are of course the people most directly concerned with implementing the marketing concept and are most closely associated with customers. Individual areas of marketing expertise are known as marketing's functions. The role of functional specialists is to identify the needs of the market, to interpret these, to bring products and services to the market place in a manner that is appealing and to ensure lasting customer satisfaction.

3.2 Marketing in practice: the mix

Marketing strategy can be likened to a recipe. The ingredients of the recipe are the various functions of marketing. Just as recipes vary according to the dish being prepared, so different marketing strategies require differing levels and combinations of functional ingredients. Even if a relatively minor ingredient is incorrect, the recipe will not be successful. The same is true of marketing strategy where all functional ingredients depend on each other for success.

The idea of the 'four Ps': product, price, promotion and place (distribution) was suggested by McCarthy (1960). These are the key elements of the marketing function. Each of these mix elements possesses a number of variables (see Figure 3.1) whose emphases can be varied according to a chosen strategy. Inherent in any marketing strategy is a series of inter-mix variables as well as several intra-functional variables. These functional aspects of the marketing mix which include the 'four Ps' in addition to customer segmentation, targeting and positioning are referred to as the marketing mix – a term put forward by Borden (1965). Marketing mix variables are under the direct control of marketing, and the manipulation of the four Ps is how the company reaches its target segments.

Figure 3.2 is a representation of how the marketing mix can be utilised. A marketing strategy takes the tools of the marketing mix and assigns to them variable degrees of importance that marketing considers appropriate to a given set of circumstances. This placing of emphasis is described as marketing effort. Marketing effort has human resource allocation as one of its components. Considered in financial terms, the use of the marketing mix concept allows

Price Level Discrimination Discount	Promotion Advertising Sales promotion Personal selling
Product Design Packaging Display Brand	Place Warehousing Transportation Service Stockholding

Figure 3.1 The marketing mix – available marketing tools to target customers

Price Level [Discrimination] Discount	Promotion [Advertising] Sales promotion Personal selling
Product Design Packaging Display [Brand]	Place Warehousing Transportation [Service] Stockholding

Figure 3.2 A hypothetical marketing strategy

management to arrive at a total budget for marketing strategy, and then allows for this budget to be allocated at different levels across the mix and within each element of the mix.

As the marketing mix is composed of closely interrelated elements, it is necessary to examine each of these in turn to be clear about its respective role. Each of these functions has at least a chapter devoted to it later in the text, so the purpose here is to examine these functions at an introductory level and to put them in relative perspective to each other.

Markets are dynamic in nature and can be affected by a wide range of environmental, uncontrollable variables. The task of marketing is to devise strategies that take account of these variables using available marketing tools. These tools of the marketing mix are controllable variables to be applied to a given situation with creativity and imagination. The major constraint on creativity is the level of financial support that the company can give to its marketing effort. Each of the functions of marketing is now considered.

In the present economy, services is now the fastest growing segment of the economy and intelligent companies are paying attention to the unique opportunities and challenges of marketing and managing services. The 7-Ps or extended marketing mix of Booms and Bitner (1981) is a marketing strategy tool that expands the number of controllable variables from the four in the original marketing mix model (i.e. the 4 P's) to seven. The traditional marketing mix model was primarily directed and useful for tangible products. The 7-Ps model is more useful for services industries and arguably also for knowledge-intensive environments.

The western nation economies are now considered 'post-industrial' with around 60% of gross domestic product (GDP) attributed to services. Other experts in this area such as Parasuraman, *et al.* (1985, 1998, 2000) recommend the use of an extended '7P' marketing mix framework more suitable specifically for services. These 'extra' three mix elements or 'P's' are:

- *People*: Services are delivered by people and so obviously people are absolutely crucial to the success of services delivery.
- *Processes*: The process used to deliver the service is again absolutely crucial to service delivery. The UK airline British Airways experienced problems in processing customers at Heathrow Airport, London in August 2004. This failure of process resulted in many customers vowing never to fly with 'BA' again.
- *Physical evidence*: The ability and environment in which the service is delivered, both tangible goods that help to communicate and perform the service and intangible experience of existing customers and the ability of the business to relay that customer satisfaction to potential customers.

3.3 Product (or service)

The marketing mix is a combination of many factors, but consumers tend to view marketing effort in more tangible terms of the product (or service).

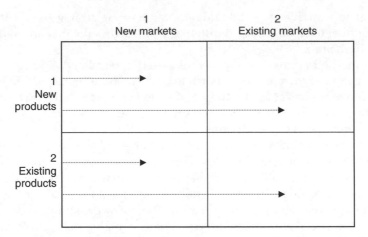

Figure 3.3 Strategic options (Ansoff's matrix). (Originally proposed by Igor Ansoff 'Strategies for Diversification' Harvard Business Review, September 1957)

Marketers should recognise that much of the 'want-satisfying' nature of the product is derived from consumer perceptions. The true nature of the product is what the consumer perceives it to be, and not what the company thinks it is, or would like it to be. Marketing management is responsible for finding out what perceptions will contribute to consumer satisfaction, and then manage the marketing mix to ensure that the product embodies these perceptions.

The product (or service) is the cornerstone of the marketing mix that should be considered as the starting point for marketing strategy, because without it there is nothing to promote, or to price, or to distribute.

Marketing strategies have a variety of options available in their design. These vary in their levels of sophistication and long-term impact. Figure 3.3 illustrates the potential strategies that can be derived from a simple matrix.

Companies making 2/2 decisions (concentrating on existing products in existing markets) lack imagination and run the risk of becoming outmoded. 2/1 decision makers (existing products into new markets) represent attempts to extend the 'product life cycle' (see Chapter 6). 1/1 and 1/2 decisions are more adventurous and risky. In the long-term new product (or service) development is the principal means of survival for a company.

The key aspects of the product as a marketing function can be summarised as follows:

1 *Product planning*:
   (a) Product/market decisions – to whom, where and in what quantity?
   (b) New product decisions, research and development programmes, marketing research studies.
2 *Product management*:
   (a) Organisational decisions relating to human accountability for the success of the product.

(b) Marketing decisions relating to the numbers and types of product on offer. These are product line and product mix elements.
3 *The physical product*:
   (a) design decisions,
   (b) quality/image decisions,
   (c) packaging decisions.

It should be recognised that the terms 'service' and 'product' are interchangeable. Marketers in banking and insurance often refer to individual services as 'products'. This point is dealt with more fully in Chapter 6.

3.4 Price

Price is important because of its direct impact on customers, the company and the economy. To consumers, price is an indication of quality and an important factor in decision-making. For the company, selling price represents the means of recouping costs and making a profit.

The price customers are prepared to pay determines the level of demand for a product. This affects overall company prosperity and may have a bearing on the company's competitive position in the market place. Price levels in general have implications for the national economy. They influence wages, interest rates and Government policy.

Some claim that price is all-important. In some commodity markets, companies have achieved similar levels of service, product quality and promotional support so price has become the major method of product differentiation. However, we should not overlook the major marketing efforts these companies have made to reach such a state of similarity. In addition, if a company can differentiate its products on a non-price basis, or conversely, fails to maintain the standards of its competitors, then price should decrease in importance as the major determinant of product choice. Certainly, price is important, but not all-important.

Marketing management faces problems when arriving at a specific price level, as price is difficult to define. Whilst it is possible to think of the price of a product as the monetary value given in exchange, this definition is simplistic when we consider price in relation to other elements of the marketing mix.

The buyer and seller have different views of the price of an item. Whatever a buyer's motive for purchase, economic consideration of price as an opportunity cost cannot be ignored. The decision to spend a certain amount of money on one product leaves the purchaser with less to spend on other products or services. Whilst price is often thought of as an indicator of quality and prestige in the minds of consumers, it also has negative aspects. If the quality of two products is perceived to be equal, buyers will naturally choose the cheaper one. Whilst there is scope for product differentiation by the seller, price remains an important yardstick that buyers use in reaching a purchase decision.

Price is the principal mechanism for making profit. There is normally a close relationship between the selling price of a product and the cost of production. The marketer does not view price as being something that is 'attached' to the product after all the other components (tangible and intangible) have been assembled. Rather, the marketing orientated seller anticipates that price will be considered as a product feature, viewed by the buyer in conjunction with a variety of other product attributes. In this way, the marketer never loses from sight the reality that price is one, albeit important, element of overall marketing effort.

Pricing decisions are complicated by the fact that they can create conflict in the firm, within marketing channels and within the competitive environment. Marketing management may arrive at a price that fits perfectly with total marketing effort at a price they believe will be considered to be optimal by the customer. The application of price can be frustrated by other management interests (e.g. accounting might consider it inappropriate in terms of immediate rate of return or distributive intermediaries may consider it to be unfair). An effective pricing strategy can be disrupted by competitive action and this is discussed further in Chapter 7, along with options available to companies facing competitive pricing pressures.

If an element of the marketing mix is mismanaged, consequences for a company can be severe. Where pricing is concerned, the effects of bad judgment are more immediately apparent in terms of their influence on the financial well being of the organisation. Companies cannot survive unless the value of sales exceeds costs. An overly high price might damage the effectiveness of a well-conceived marketing mix strategy. If a price is set too low and the volume of sales cannot offset this disparity, it is unlikely that a subsequent increase in price will be readily acceptable to the marketplace. The financial or survival implications associated with pricing strategy make this functional area one of key importance to a company.

3.5 Promotion

Promotion is an element of the marketing mix that is subject to much variation according to the type of product or service on offer. For some products, promotion may only play a minimal role in marketing effort; for others, marketing strategy may be almost solely based on this mix element.

A product cannot be sold if the target market is unaware of its existence. Promotion cannot sell a product that is unacceptable to the market place and this is a major defensive argument against critics who claim that advertising is over persuasive and over pervasive. In consumer markets, promotion often has the highest budget allocation of all mix elements, especially after the product has been launched. For this reason promotion receives much attention as a marketing function. The effects of promotional expenditure are difficult to measure, and although recognised procedures exist for measuring its effectiveness, the task is complex. Lord Leverhulme of washing detergent fame has said: 'Half the money I spend on advertising is wasted, but I don't know which half!'

Promotion is difficult to evaluate, as it does not create immediately tangible success. It is an investment, but problems often arise when fixing a company's promotional budget. Unlike the purchase of machinery, recruitment of extra staff or improved warehousing facilities, the promotional budget provides nothing that can be easily perceived as 'value for money'. This is a recurrent source of company dispute and confusion that can be overcome by ensuring that promotional strategy is preceded by setting clear objectives. By so doing, one can then better make judgments about the effectiveness of a strategy.

The term 'promotion' traditionally covers four basic activities: advertising, personal selling, public relations and sales promotion techniques. An element of overlap occurs, but there are definitions that clarify the respective roles of each area:

1 Advertising is concerned with communicating messages to selected segments of the public to inform and influence them in a manner which leads them to favourably perceive those items featured in the advertisement. Advertising is clearly identifiable in terms of the product being promoted. It is also a commercial transaction between the advertiser and the management of the chosen media.
2 Whilst advertising tends to be aimed at a group, personal selling (as the description implies) tends to be tailored towards individuals. The seller may convey the same basic messages that are included in advertising, but the presentation can be modified where necessary to suit specific situations and potential customers.
3 Public relations (PR) is a set of communicational activities through which an organisation creates or maintains a favourable image with its various 'publics'. These publics range from customers, company employees, shareholders and even Government. PR has its major role as a marketing activity, but it also extends to other aspects of an organisation.
4 Sales promotion involves matters like temporary price reductions, displays, coupons, in-store demonstrations and free samples.

There are other aspects to promotion whose aim is to create and stimulate demand. How they are 'blended' together is referred to as the promotional mix or, more correctly, the communications mix. Just as individual marketing functions go to make up the marketing mix, communications functions can be employed to form an intra-functional mix. Integration is the key: sales are made easier when consumers are informed and made interested by prior advertising. The effectiveness of advertising is in turn increased when it is co-ordinated with specific sales promotional techniques.

Other elements of the marketing mix – price, product and place – are all indispensable. In contrast, advertising, public relations and sales promotion, but not personal selling, is a more abstract activity that can sometimes be omitted from a marketing programme without immediate detrimental effects. Harm would occur over of time, sooner or later, depending on the nature of the product being marketed (e.g. branded foodstuffs would be more quickly affected than quality furniture because of its shorter purchasing cycle). Non-marketing-orientated management has a tendency to treat advertising, PR and sales promotion as the least significant marketing mix elements. In times of entrenchment these areas are more readily cut back.

Assessment of advertising effectiveness can be difficult, but a good product, an efficient distributive system and an appropriate price are often insufficient to provide overall success without the aid of promotion. A marketing mix without advertising and sales promotion might appear dull when compared to efforts of competitors, and such a strategy would be vulnerable to competition.

The importance of promotion clearer when we consider that its task is to stimulate demand by communication which, if effective, should convince buyers that the featured products are 'right' for their particular needs. Chapter 4 identifies stages in the purchasing process and communication at every stage is vital. Even when the buying decision has been made, promotional communication is necessary to convince the buyer that the correct decision has been made so positive attitudes are reinforced and repeat purchases are made.

Promotion is a communication process whose basic objectives are to modify behaviour, to inform, to persuade and to remind. Chapter 10 deals more thoroughly with the overall and specific aims of promotion.

3.6 Place

Place is concerned with activities needed to move the product or service from the seller to the buyer and its origin is in the word 'placement'. To understand 'place' (more correctly termed 'distribution') as a separate function and an element of the marketing mix we divide the function into two categories:

1 A structure or network through which transactions are made so the product is made available and accessible to the final user. This structure is termed a 'distribution channel'.
2 When a channel of distribution has been established, the company must address the task of moving its products through the distributive system. This is termed 'physical distribution management'.

3.6.1 Distribution channels

Changes in retail trends during the past 30 years have increased the number of goods that flow directly from manufacturers to retailers who sell to consumers through super- and hyper-markets. Intermediaries are significant for the movement of many goods. Manufacturers feature, as they are also recipients of goods in the form of raw materials and components.

The use of intermediaries in a channel system has advantages:

1 The number of transactions made is dramatically reduced when sales are affected through intermediaries or middlemen. Instead of a manufacturer selling to many retail outlets or other manufacturers, distributors or wholesalers can assume this task, reducing manufacturers' transactions to more easily manageable proportions.
2 Middlemen relieve some of the financial burden that manufacturers need to bear when marketing directly to the end user.
3 Manufacturers' costs of transport, storage and stockholding are reduced, as these are 'broken up' (a wholesaling function known as 'breaking bulk') and shared throughout the channel network.
4 Channel members possess knowledge of local markets that would be impractical for the producer to possess.
5 Middlemen market a variety of related (sometimes competing) products and have established contacts and means of entry into local markets that the producer might find difficult to approach if acting independently. They can promote products and employ a sales force with an intimate knowledge of the local market.

Advantages of the channel system are summarised by describing the utilities channels create:

1 *Time utility*: Distribution is coordinated so products reach users when they are demanded.
2 *Place utility*: Describes the physical movement of goods from one place to another.
3 *Possession utility*: Intermediaries ensure that possession is facilitated. Financial risks are reduced with the change of title (ownership) that occurs as goods move through the channel towards the ultimate consumer.
4 *Form utility*: Goods are progressively changed into a more usable form as they proceed along the chain of distribution.

The benefits of channel systems come with costs. When responsibilities are shared or passed on, the cost to a company is less control. Ideally, a channel structure should operate to the mutual satisfaction of all members. In reality, there is a tendency for behavioural dimensions of the channel to cause power struggles and conflict. Channel members may disrupt the status quo if they perceive that actions of others are working to the detriment of their own interests. To protect themselves from such action, channel members might attempt to establish positions of power to regain control over their products that was lost when responsibility was delegated.

The main sources of power are financial strength and strong brand leadership. For example, Kellogg Company has successfully retained power over supermarket chains by refusing to supply 'own label' products. Kellogg's brands are strong enough for the company to control its distribution and production, as indicated by a consistent advertising theme: 'We do not make cereals for anyone else'. Channel power is further developed in Chapter 8.

3.6.2 Physical distribution management

Physical distribution management (PDM) is also referred to as 'logistics' and is concerned with transporting finished goods to customers, stock control, warehouse management and order processing. A key task of this element of the 'place' function is to ascertain the level of service that the customer requires, then to ensure that this is adhered to and that the product arrives in good condition to the customer. Physical distribution, like promotion, represents a financial cost. The art of PDM is to achieve a preordained level of service at a cost that is acceptable to the profit objectives of the company. This is a critical area of marketing because failure to deliver on time not only negates market-ing effort, but it can irrevocably lose customers. PDM is important in two other ways:

1 Depending on the product, physical distribution costs can represent as much as 30% of the cost of sales (mostly the cost of transportation). Clearly, if dis-tribution savings can be achieved, the company can have a competitive advantage in terms of pricing.
2 If a company is able to offer a particularly efficient service to customers, this can reduce customer sensitivity to price.

Distribution is, therefore, a valuable weapon for companies whose strategy is one of non-price competition.

The usual measure of a company's distribution efficiency is in the order cycle or lead-time, that is, the length of time that elapses between receipt of an order and delivery of goods. Although always a critical factor, this lead-time has increased in importance over the past 25 years as economic pressures have forced companies to reduce stock levels to save working capital, which helps to finance stockholding. In most industries, the responsibility for stockholding is placed on the supplier. Automotive manufacturers have now taken this prac-tice to such an extreme that in some cases they only take receipt of goods hours before they are required. Such manufacturers operate a production technique known as JIT manufacturing, or, more correctly, 'lean manufacturing'. The objective is for components to be discharged from transport and directly marshalled to the production line. Sophisticated statistical techniques are employed to arrive at optimum order quantities and to ensure logistical coor-dination between raw material supply, production and distribution.

Management is faced with two problems when dealing with physical distribution:

1 It must ensure that the efforts of all elements are optimised. This means that efficiency is judged on the end result and not upon individual results of separate departments.

2 The other consideration is termed the 'total cost approach' to distribution. If a lead-time of 5 days is the distributive objective, this might involve maintaining high stock levels or using an expensive transport mode. Other managers in the company may strive to reduce costs in their own areas of activity, but it must be ensured that these efforts are not detrimental to achieving the overall distribution objectives that end customers have been promised.

It is sufficient here to suggest the following guidelines for PDM:

1 Managers must decide the level of service the company wishes to achieve, using the overall distribution mix strategy.
2 When the service level has been decided, the company can examine the most economic method of achieving this.
3 The costs involved must be realistic, but service objectives should not be sacrificed in the interest of cost saving.

We conclude by saying that it is not possible to both maximise service and minimise costs.

3.7 Personal selling

Personal selling has been explained in its context as a function of the promotional or communications mix. Selling is so important that it is considered as a function of marketing in its own right, even though it is not included separately as one of the 'four Ps' of the marketing mix. In its promotional role, selling contributes to the effectiveness of marketing effort, but it has a more fundamental role to play, as the act of selling is the end result of all marketing activity.

Sales personnel perform marketing tasks in addition to those of selling. These may include gathering marketing information or carrying out public relations activity. These are valuable duties, but they should not detract from the primary role of the salesperson: that of selling the company's products or services.

Selling is a process of communication. Companies promote a particular image. This may be one of a small family firm whose strong point is personal service. Others may wish to emphasise their size and ability to provide expert service. A company's philosophy of business and its particular merits combine to form a company message. It is the task of the salesperson to communicate this message to customers. Buyers usually require more than the physical product when they consider potential suppliers. As well as selling skills, it is important when recruiting sales personnel that companies take into account how well the applicant fits into the desired company image and how well this image will be transmitted to customers.

The salesperson relies upon the company for support in meeting delivery times and providing satisfactory levels of quality. The company's marketing effort may only go part of the way in reaching customers. The efficient projection of the company message provides a 'backdrop' in front of which the salesperson carries out his or her role. Between the company and customer a 'communication gap' might exist. This can be partially filled by advertising, but it is not an easy form of two-way communication. Personal selling fills the gap and completes the company's marketing effort, reinforcing company message by providing an interpretation that is personally and specifically tailored to the customer.

In addition to the communication process, the salesperson's role requires physical sales to be made. The salesperson must utilise communication as a means to 'persuade' customers that the company's products can offer something that is superior to competitive offerings. Buyers arrange their needs and requirements according to a scale of preference that is linked (consciously or subconsciously) to a budget. Where this scale already includes the products a salesperson is offering (as is usually the case) the selling task requires that a competitive preference scale that is not merely one of financial negotiation should be considered. The word 'persuasion' should be interpreted with caution. It does not imply that to sell is to encourage buyers to purchase items that they do not want or offer no advantage. Rather, persuasion implies that the buyer should be convinced of the advantages that the proposed product can provide.

Sales personnel are employed to further the communications process, but the level of direct persuasion required varies according to the sales task. During the process leading up to a sale (which can vary from minutes to months) the salesperson is likely to be required to adopt different approaches according to the stage in the buying process that has been reached or to the type of customer being canvassed.

The typical caricature of the 'salesman' usually refers to the 'cold canvass' or 'lead' seller. The prominence of such salespersons has declined because of changing retail structures, but has re-emerged with the advent of products and services such as double glazing, cavity-wall insulation, alarm systems, prefabricated home extensions and 'one off' life insurance policies. The seller, in many such circumstances, has little prior knowledge of customers and relies heavily upon persuasion. This mode of selling is unsuitable in industrial situations. Lead selling is similar, but in this case the seller is supplied with lists of customers who have expressed at least a potential interest in the product. Such lists might be compiled from replies to advertisements or names that have been gathered as a result of a 'survey' purporting to be a market research survey. The real intention of many such 'surveys' is to gain names and addresses as 'leads' for potential canvassing (this practice is termed 'sugging' which is short for 'selling under the guise of market research').

'Canned selling' is where the salesperson is allowed little deviation from an 'approved presentation' which has been based on careful research of customer reactions, needs and objections and is a method of presentation that has been proved to be effective in certain situations. Whenever a customer objection is voiced, the 'canned sales' approach attempts to overcome this by a rote-learned presentation of an answer to the objection. Salespersons are trained to ask question that will produce assenting answers, so it will then be more difficult for customers to say 'no' at the end. This method is often used when selling goods direct to the public in retail or home environments. The level of creativity required of the salesperson is low, although his or her personality is important in ensuring success.

The types of selling discussed represent the negative image of selling which has done much to diminish the importance and standing of selling as a profession and as an essential element of marketing. The vast majority of salespersons are employed selling on a business-to-business or development sales basis. They are involved in competitive selling. A high degree of product knowledge is required as well as skill in the techniques of selling. The salesperson attempts to achieve a sale in the face of direct competition from other producers. Emphasis is placed on building up cooperation and trust. The persuasion element is concerned with convincing the buyer that the correct company has been chosen with which to make the business development. The missionary salesperson performs a similar function to that described except that where development sales are usually concerned with established products; missionary selling is more concerned with communicating the company and product message in new markets than in securing sales. Here, the salesperson visits customers to inform and influence rather than to sell; such selling will then be the task of a competitive seller. Many large companies employ different personnel to perform development, missionary and competitive selling tasks, and it is easy to see that each task requires a different personality type. In fact missionary salespeople have sometimes been dubbed 'commando salesmen'. In industrial markets it is common for the sales force to carry out all of these tasks and a variety of skills and extensive product knowledge is required (see Lancaster and Jobber, 2003).

3.8 Marketing information

Gathering marketing information is the least visible of marketing functions from a consumer perspective. However, it is fundamental to marketing activity. It must be considered that satisfactory products reflect needs and wants of customers that can only be ascertained by gathering information. Information provides the means for a company to fulfil the marketing concept.

Figure 3.4 illustrates how the information process works. To be of value, it should be a constant process. Market requirements are established and then translated into products and action. The reaction of the market is then assessed. This provides feedback and guidance as to whether customer needs have been correctly interpreted and suggests any remedial action that may be required.

The primary need of any company is to assess the requirements of the market and then act accordingly. In order to function efficiently a company must augment its information requirements beyond this basic need.

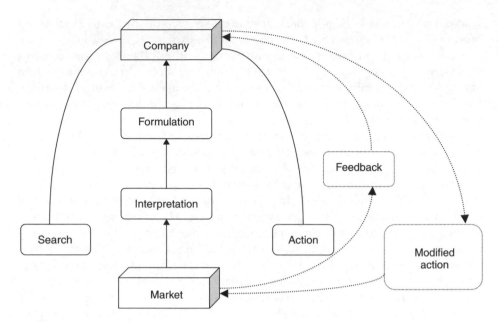

Figure 3.4 The information process

Figure 3.4 indicates that we should interpret 'market' in a wider sense than simply consumer or customer needs. An examination of the market should also encompass the macro-environment, competitive and public environments. The company should also address itself to information that is available from its internal management system. The sum of all such information and activity is grouped together to constitute a formal system designed to collect, process and report. This is known as a marketing information system (MkIS). The components of the MkIS are shown in Figure 3.5. This shows that the information sources are fed into an analytical process that guides decision-making and provides feedback that can then suggest modifications to the original course of action.

Marketing research is the well-known function of the information process. It is concerned with discovering needs of customers and subsequent testing to ensure that these needs have been correctly interpreted. There are techniques pre- and post-testing elements of the marketing mix such as advertising research and sales research. Pre-testing products and predicting their penetration into the market come under these headings. These activities come under the heading of consumer research. Market research focuses on the marketplace and includes market size and market share analysis. These are just some elements that come under the broader description of marketing research. Marketers view the research process as a continuous activity that involves fact-finding, monitoring and problem solving.

Market intelligence is concerned with broader issues that affect a company as well as market monitoring. Monitoring of environmental factors discussed

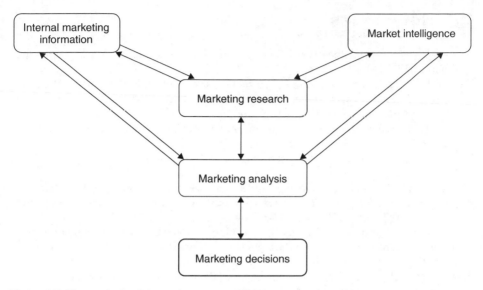

Figure 3.5 The marketing information system (MkIS)

in Chapter 2 is the responsibility of market intelligence. Its role is to provide information that precedes action and also to forewarn management of any developments that might significantly alter the market.

A lot of marketing information exists within the organisation itself. Utilising such information depends on liaison between various company departments so that information is presented in a useful form for purposes of marketing analysis. Financial and sales data form the basis for customer and profit analysis. Analysis of performance of individual products builds up a picture of company performance and provides an indication of market trends. Such information can also provide the basis for desk research, dealt with in detail in Chapter 13.

Various information functions have been described separately, but marketing management relies on them in the decision making process. Information does not make decisions; it provides the basis for making them.

 ## 3.9 Summary

Marketing functions combine to form a single strategy. Functional specialists provide a convenient and practical method for operating the marketing mix, but this does not detract from the integral nature of marketing mix management. It is a function of senior management to ensure that this integration takes place.

Many people develop a specific interest in a particular marketing function. The aim of this chapter has been to demonstrate that specialisms are approached in the context of the total marketing mix.

References

Ansoff, I. (1957), 'Strategies for diversification', *Harvard Business Review*, September, Boston, 35(5), 113–124.

Booms, B.H. and Bitner, M.-J. (1981), 'Marketing strategies and organisation structures for service firms', in Donnelly J.H. and George, W.R. (eds), *Marketing of Services*, Chicago: American Marketing Association.

Borden, N.H. (1965) 'The concept of the marketing mix', in Schwatz, G. (ed.), *Science in Marketing*, New York: John Wiley.

Lancaster, G.A. and Jobber, D. (2003), *Selling and Sales Management*, 6th edition, London: Prentice-Hall, pp. 57–71.

McCarthy, E.J. (1960), *Basic Marketing: A Managerial Approach*, Homewood, IL. Irwin.

Parasuraman, A. (1998), 'Customer service in business-to-business markets: an agenda for research', *Journal of Business and Industrial Marketing* 13(4/5), 309–321.

Parasuraman, A. and Grewal, D. (2000), 'Serving customers and consumers effectively in the 21st century: a conceptual framework and overview', *Journal of the Academy of Marketing Science* 28(1), 9–16.

Parasuraman, A., Berry, L.P. and Zeithaml, V. (1985), 'Quality counts in services too', *Business Horizons*, May–June, 44–52.

Voss G.B., Parasuraman, A. and Grewal, D. (1998), 'The roles of price, performance, and expectations in determining satisfaction in service exchanges', *Journal of Marketing*, October, 46–61.

Further reading

Brassigton, F. and Pettitt, S. (2005), *Essentials of Marketing*, London: Prentice-Hall, Chapter 1.

Jobber, D. (2004), *Principles and Practices of Marketing*, 4th edition, New York: McGraw-Hill, Chapter 1.

Kotler, P. and Armstrong, G. (2004), *Principles of Marketing*, 10th edition, Pearson Prentice-Hall, Chapter 2.

Kotler, P. Armstrong, G. Saunders, J. and Wong, V. (2001), *Principles of Marketing*, 3rd European edition, Pearson Education, Ltd., Chapter 15.

Masterson, R. and Pickton, D. (2004), *Marketing an Introduction*, New York: McGraw-Hill, Chapter 2.

Questions

Question 3.1

Marketing concept:

(a) 'Marketing is satisfying customer needs at a profit'.
(b) 'Marketing is the process of creating unnecessary needs and wants'.

Discuss the issues to which the above two statements give rise.

Question 3.2

Marketing mix: Consider which of the marketing mix variables is most important in:

(a) consumer goods marketing,
(b) industrial goods marketing.

What are the extended marketing mix '7P' classification?

Question 3.3

Product: Product is generally regarded as being the most important of the 'Four Ps'. Why is this?

Question 3.4

Promotion: Does the fact that selling is included as part of the promotional mix weaken its role as a sub-element of marketing?

Question 3.5

Place: Do you feel that channels of distribution and physical distribution management are sufficiently linked to warrant a combined grouping under 'place'?

Evaluate the importance of a fully integrated physical distribution system (business logistics system) to the successful application of the marketing concept within the firm.

Explain the concepts of time and place utility in the context of both channels and physical distribution.

How does the 'level of service' experienced by the customer relate to the distribution element of marketing? Use examples to illustrate the points made.

Question 3.6

Marketing information: Describe the concept of a modern, integrated 'Marketing Information System' and examine its usefulness in marketing decision making. Why are companies increasingly seeking to establish marketing information systems, when in the past marketing research has been sufficient for a company's information needs?

To what extent do you agree that information is the very life-blood' of successful marketing? Give full reasons for your point of view.

4

Buying Behaviour

4.1 Introduction

As consumers, we are continually exposed to different experiences and influences. Some of us are more susceptible to change and influences than others, but nobody goes through life remaining the same as they were at birth. Some of our responses to the environment are because of our psychological makeup. As our situations change, opportunities emerge as we become subject to a wider range of influences to which we might respond in a positive or negative manner. Changes in circumstances may arouse innate needs or promote new needs and wants in our consumption patterns.

The job of marketing is to identify needs and wants accurately and develop products and services that will satisfy them. The role of marketing should not be to 'create' wants, but to fulfil them. Chapter 1, which discussed the marketing concept, provided some explanation of what this means in terms of business practice.

It is not sufficient to simply discover what customers require. It is more valuable to find out why it is required. Only by gaining a comprehensive understanding of buyer behaviour can marketing's goals be realised. This understanding works to the advantage of both the consumer and marketer, because marketing becomes better equipped to satisfy customer needs efficiently. This should enable a company to establish a loyal group of customers with positive attitudes towards its products.

4.2 Definitions

Consumer behaviour can be defined as:

> The acts of individuals directly involved in obtaining and using economic goods and services, including the decision processes that precede and determine these acts.

The underlying concepts we now discuss form a system in which individual consumers are the core surrounded by an immediate and wider environment that influences their goals. Such goals are satisfied by consumers passing through a number of problem-solving stages that lead to purchasing decisions.

Marketing draws on many sources that contribute theory, information, inspiration and advice. Pricing, for example, uses economics to provide a framework for price determination and an associated pricing strategy. The main input to the theory of consumer behaviour comes from psychology. Its interdisciplinary nature also means that sociology, anthropology, economics and mathematics contribute.

4.3 Cultural and social influences

If a company does not understand the culture of the market in which it operates, it cannot develop products and market them successfully. Marketers should recognise how culture shapes and influences behaviour. Culture can be defined as a group of complex symbols and artefacts created by humans and handed down through generations as determinants and regulators of human behaviour in a given society. These symbols and artefacts include attitudes, beliefs, values, language and religion. They also include art and music, food, housing and product preferences. Culture is 'learned' behaviour that has been passed down over time. It is reinforced in our daily lives through the family unit and educational religious institutions. Cultural influences are powerful and cannot be easily classified as they concern unwritten laws about what is socially acceptable or appropriate in a particular society. A comparison of Far Eastern culture with that of Western Europe provides an example of two contrasting cultures. Even within Western Europe, distinct cultures exist, e.g. differences in social etiquette and sense of humour. Such generally accepted norms of behaviour are called 'social mores'. The importance of culture is more appropriate to international marketing is this is discussed further in Chapter 16.

Much of our life is directed by 'customs'. Similar to social mores in the way they have developed, customs can be deeply rooted in society. Customs associated with birth celebrations, marriages and funerals have changed little over centuries. Many customs are so deeply rooted in society that they have not changed or 'evolved' to reflect the existing cultural climate.

Laws relating to Sunday trading and the licensing of alcohol consumption in the UK are examples of laws that have been changed to catch up with the liberalising demands of changing attitudes within UK society. Marriage remains an important custom, but this has been challenged in the UK over recent years. When couples began to co-habit and raise families outside marriage, society adopted an attitude of condemnation. Today, society has adopted a more relaxed attitude to those who ignore the convention.

Changes in attitudes usually reflect changes in culture. Culture, although powerful, is not fixed forever. Changes in culture are slow and often not fully assimilated until generations have passed.

The twentieth century witnessed significant cultural change, for example, changing attitudes towards work and pleasure. The idea that it work is 'good for the soul' has faded since the Victorian era. It is no longer accepted that work should be difficult or injurious to mind or body. Many employers now make great efforts to ensure that the workplace is a pleasant environment realising that this might increase productivity. Employees more frequently regard work as a means to an end, rather than a raison d'être. When people worked to earn money, it is now more socially acceptable to reward themselves by spending this on goods or services that give pleasure. Many products and services whose function is to provide enjoyment now rank alongside those, in terms of purchasing necessity, as those that provide the necessities of life. Increased leisure time follows from this changed attitude to work as the working week is shorter and holiday time has increased. At home, labour saving devices release more time to be spent on enjoyment. The quantity of leisure time available influences consumer purchases.

A major cultural change last century that accelerated since the early 1960s was the changing role of women in society. Working women have helped alter traditional stereotypes that society had applied to women. Increased independence and economic power not only changed the lives of women, but also influenced society's perception of their socio-economic role.

Society has witnessed profound changes in family structure. We have moved away from the extended family towards the 'nuclear family'. Increased mobility of labour has produced a migrant mentality with family units tending to move away from their native regions and close relations. Increased affluence and better transport communications have increased mobility within regions, creating large suburbs and less-populated inner urban areas, although there has recently been a trend back towards 'trendy' inner city apartment dwelling amongst the young. Average family size is becoming smaller and couples are waiting longer before having children.

In many societies when considering culture we must also consider subcultures. Immigrant communities have become large enough in many countries to form a significant proportion of the population of that country. Just as society itself cannot ignore subcultures; marketers must consider them because of their interactive influence on society. In some cases, they constitute sufficiently large individual market segments for certain products. Subcultures are often identified on a racial basis, but this is a limited view. Subcultures can exist within the same racial groups sharing common nationality and such bases may be geographical, religious or linguistic.

4.4 Specific social influences

4.4.1 Social class

Social class is the most familiar social influence. Chapter 13 explains that marketing research uses social class as the principal criterion when identifying market segments as this classification reveals a great deal about likely behaviour. An important determinant of social class has traditionally been income. Although this might be an indication of the social class to which an individual might belong, salary structures have altered a lot during the past 30 years, such that the 'professions' do not necessarily earn more than the 'skilled trades'.

Classification of consumers on the basis of 'lifestyle' is perhaps more meaningful. If a group of consumers with approximately the same income are considered, their behavioural patterns and lifestyles are likely to vary markedly because these will reflect the social class to which each belongs. Social class is an indicator of lifestyle and its existence exerts a strong influence on consumers and their behaviour. Whatever income level a consumer reaches during a lifetime, evidence suggests that basic attitudes and preferences do not change radically. It would, however, be reasonable to expect the 'level of consumption' to rise in line with income. As consumers, we usually identify with a particular class or group. Often it is not the specific social class that is revealing, but that to which the consumer aspires. People who 'cross' social class barriers usually begin to do this when they are young. Income and education allows younger people to adopt lifestyles that are different to those of their parents. Young consumers tend to absorb the influences of the group to which they aspire, and gradually reject the lifestyles of their parents and their parents' friends and relations. For this reason, 'occupation' is a useful pointer to social class.

'Eating out' and drinking wine were once pleasures only enjoyed regularly by upper class members of society. Today, wine marketers address a broad range of consumers, with a different marketing mix strategy being designed for each group.

A study of social class should be approached without preconceptions. It is important that marketers do not associate social class or social stratification with any derogatory interpretation of the term. Marketing does not make value judgements in its distinctions of social class; a 'lower' or 'higher' social grouping does not imply inferiority or superiority. Such a classification is merely an aid to the identification of market segments and how they should be approached. The marketer should make decisions on the basis of information revealed by objectively designed research, as this how changes in behaviour can be identified.

4.4.2 Reference groups

A reference group has a more intimate role to play in influencing consumers. This refers to a group of people whose standards of behaviour influence a person's attitudes, opinions and values. In general, people tend to imitate and seek advice from those closest to them. Reference groups can be quite small, like the family group. They can also be large. For instance, a persons involved in a certain occupation are likely to behave in the manner expected and accepted by their immediate colleagues and the wider occupational group. Reference groups can be found in a person's social life, perhaps through membership of a club or organisation concerned with a particular hobby or interest. In order to foster a sense of 'belonging', such individuals are unlikely to deviate too far from the formal or informal behavioural norms laid down by the group.

One only needs to consider school children to see how reference groups influence individuals. Although children are strongly influenced by their family group, they are also keen to 'fit in' with their peers, and it is never long before a new hairstyle or fashion or other fad has spread through classrooms.

Not all individuals imitate those in their reference group. Reference group theory does not suggest that individualism does not exist, but it does suggest that even individualists will be aware of what is considered 'normal' within their group.

The smaller and more intimate a reference group, the stronger its influence is likely to be. Within a small social circle, or within the family, the advice and opinions of those who are respected as knowledgeable and experienced will be influential. Such persons are termed opinion leaders. There can also be influences from outside the group. 'Snob appeal' is often due to the existence of opinion leaders outside the immediate reference group who are emulated by opinion followers. Some companies make a direct appeal to this 'snob' instinct. A marketing strategy can be based on the assumption that if a company can make its products acceptable to social leaders and high-income groups, then other sectors of the population will follow them. Another variation is to deliberately segment markets by appealing to snobbery. Credit and charge cards are frequently marketed in this manner. The strategy is to create an aura of exclusivity around the target group, whilst effectively intimidating and isolating those not targeted. For a number of charge cards, this strategy is reinforced by income requirements set down for applicants. American Express is an example of such a marketing strategy, and this company also makes appeals within reference groups (i.e. cardholders) encouraging them to enlist new members.

While snobbery 'between' reference groups is a basis for approaching consumers, this is not viable for all products. Snobbery within a reference group, for example, the syndrome of 'keeping up with the Jones's's' can also be used. Snobbery apart, influence and information flow on a 'horizontal' basis within the reference group is of greatest value to the marketer.

4.4.3 Family

Of all the different types of reference group, the family merits specific attention, as it is the most intimate group. The nature of the family can be identified by considering the 'family life cycle'. Eight stages can be identified, although many texts quote different divisions.

Unmarried: This carries the 'young, free and single' label. Financial and other responsibilities are low, whilst relative disposable income is high. Young, unmarried consumers tend to be leisure orientated and are opinion leaders in fashion. As such, they constitute a very important market segment.

Newly-married couples – no children: This group does not have responsibilities of children. They concentrate expenditure on items considered necessary for setting up a home and have been dubbed 'DINKY' meaning 'double income, no kids yet'.

Young married couples with youngest child under 6 (Full nest I): Expenditure is children-orientated. Although spending is high there is little 'spare' money for luxury items. Much recreational activity takes place in the home. Such consumers are eager for information and receptive to new product ideas, but they are economy-minded.

Married couples with youngest child 6 or over (Full nest II): Children are still dependent, but expenditure has switched to more durable items for children like bicycles and computers. Fashion clothes purchases for children become important and a lot of recreational activity tends to take place away from the home.

Older married couples still with children at home (Full nest III): The amount of disposable income may have increased. Often both parents are working and children are relatively independent, possibly working part- or full-time. Parents are likely to be more independent, with more time for their own leisure activities. Consumer durables might be replaced at this stage. Furniture purchases may have an aesthetic, rather than functional, orientation.

Older married couples with no children living with them (Empty nest I): At this stage the family unit has been transformed. Income is likely to be at a peak. Such consumers are likely to be conservative in their purchasing patterns. Whilst spending power is high, marketers may experience difficulty in changing existing attitudes and preferences. They have been dubbed 'WOOPIES' meaning 'well off older persons'.

Older retired couples (Empty nest II): The family unit has made most major purchases in terms of consumer durables. The thrust of fast moving consumer goods (FMCG) marketing is not directly aimed at this group as their consumption is relatively low and buying patterns are firmly established. In demographic terms, the number of older and retired consumers is increasing rapidly and marketers are paying increasing attention to this group. Although income has probably reduced significantly, many retire with an occupational pension, which allows them to lead full and active lives. The tourist industry is increasingly addressing itself to these consumers.

Solitary survivor: The solitary survivor has been traditionally typified by a pensioner whose spouse had died. Increasingly this category includes divorced people. This latter category is a group to whom marketing appeals can be made on the basis of their particular circumstances. Many, having come to terms with their new 'single' status, seek a more fulfilling life through the pursuit of educational, social and leisure activities and they often like to entertain at home and be entertained.

Within the family unit the marketer should be conscious of the need to identify the principal decision-maker and ascertain the level of influence exerted by other family members. Traditional thinking holds that the male takes responsibility for car, garden and DIY purchases, and the female makes decisions on furnishing and kitchen-related purchases. Social changes over recent years have affected these traditional precepts. Marketers should not approach a market with preconceptions; their strategies should be based on careful enquiry and research into purchasing motivations.

4.5 The consumer as an individual

We have considered consumers as occupants of a wider environment whose behaviour is influenced by cultural and social structures. Specific influences such as reference groups and the family unit affect consumer behaviour. We now consider the individual principally from an 'inner' or psychological point of view. This will help us to understand how consumers respond to external influences.

As the consumer is a physical being, it is not difficult to define characteristics that may provide explanations for some of those actions described collectively as 'behaviour'. Consumers can be male or female; some live in towns, some in the country; they are tall, small, young or old. The psychological state of the consumer, on the other hand, is more difficult to determine. The consumer as an individual absorbs information and develops attitudes and perceptions. Personality also develops. This will affect the needs a person has as well as methods chosen to satisfy them. Any need-satisfying action is preceded by a motive. Although each human being is physically and psychologically unique, marketing attempts to identify patterns of behaviour that are predictable under given conditions. This increases a marketer's ability to satisfy human needs, which is the essential aim of marketing.

The psychology of human behaviour is complex. We focus on five psychological concepts which are generally recognised as being most important in understanding buyer behaviour: personality and the self concept; motivation; perception; attitudes and learned behaviour.

4.5.1 Self concept and personality

'Self concept' or 'self image' is an important determinant of individual behaviour as it is concerned with how we see ourselves and how we think other people see us. Individuals are inclined to create a personal image that is acceptable to their reference groups. This 'inner picture' of the self is communicated to the outside world by behaviour.

Behaviour that interests marketers relates to the consumption of goods e.g. choice of clothes, type of house, choice of furniture and decoration and type of car. The sum of this behaviour is a 'statement' about 'self' and the person's lifestyle. Consumption is a non-verbal form of communication about the self. The individual will also reinforce personal image through verbal statements that express attitudes, feelings and opinions. Individuals express their self image in a way that relates to their inner 'ideal' and this promotes acceptance within a group. This self-statement can also be an expression of rejection. For example, the music, fashion and values adopted by the so-called 'punk' movement of the early 1980s showed a reference group process in action. The 'punk' movement also rejected much within society that was considered to be 'normal' amongst other reference groups.

Marketing can make direct appeals to 'self image' through advertising. Many car advertisements appeal to the 'executive' whose 'self-image' is one of confidence, success and sophistication. The advertising theme for the Guinness beer drink is esoteric. Advertising propositions are changed regularly, but the implication for Guinness drinkers is that they are set apart from the 'masses' and are unorthodox in a mysterious way. Guinness had to do this, because the success of their earlier advertising, with the theme of 'Guinness is good for you' and the implication that 'Guinness gives you strength' meant that its consumers were typically middle aged to older men. What Guinness wanted was to attract younger consumers yet not alienate traditional consumers. Hence, they have introduced 'extra-cool Guinness', which is the traditional product only served at a colder temperature. They introduced advertising themes that were difficult to interpret in the early 1990s, with a 'mysterious man' who was dressed in black and meant to personify a glass of Guinness. For a very interesting and innovative discussion of the consumer behaviour aspects of advertising see Reynolds and Gutmann (1988).

'Self-image' is influenced by social interaction and people make purchases that are consistent with their 'self-concept' in order to protect and enhance it. We are subjected to a changing environment and changing personal situations, so individuals are involved in a constant process of evaluating and modifying their 'self-concept'. Personality has a strong influence on buyer behaviour and it is a component of self concept. Attempts to further define personality are less clear-cut. It is overly simplistic to define personality merely as 'an expression of the self concept', but we know that certain purchase decisions are likely to reflect personality. We would expect the owner of an ostentatious sports car to have a confident outgoing personality, but there is nothing conclusive to provide us with such a specific rule and this assumption could be misplaced. Marketing must consider personality, because of its close connection with 'self'.

Marketers can learn from psychoanalytical theories of personality, pioneered by Sigmund Freud. These suggest we are born with instinctive desires that cannot be gratified in a socially acceptable manner and are thus repressed. Indirect methods of satisfying these desires are sought by individuals in an attempt to find an outlet for repressed urges through socially acceptable channels. The implication for marketing is that a consumer's real motive for taking certain actions or buying certain products may be hidden in the subconscious. The stated motive may be an acceptable translation or substitution for the inner desire. The task of marketing is to appeal to inner needs, whilst providing products that enable these needs to be satisfied in a socially satisfactory manner.

4.5.2 Motivation

Motivation can be defined as goal-related behaviour. Marketers are interested in motives when goals are related to purchasing activity. They are also interested in why consumers make certain purchases. We know that in order for a motive to exist there must be a corresponding need. Motives and needs can be generated and classified in a variety of ways. Some motives like hunger, thirst, warmth and shelter are physiological; others, such as approval, success and prestige are psychological.

Having made this distinction, we can distinguish between instinctive motives such as survival and learned motives that include cleanliness, tidiness and efficiency. Still further, we can distinguish between rational economic motives and emotional ones. However, this last distinction is imprecise as many purchase decisions are compromises due to economic restrictions.

Motivation is a complex psychological issue. Marketers acknowledge a classification of motives, based on a hierarchy of needs. This classification has since been refined, but the most convenient reference model is that developed by Maslow in 1943 (Figure 4.1). He suggests that an individual's basic (or lower-order) needs must be relatively well satisfied before higher needs can begin to influence behaviour. As lower-order needs are satisfied to an increasing degree, so the individual will have time and interest to devote to higher needs. Once the basic physiological needs (e.g. hunger, thirst) are satisfied the individual will concentrate on acquiring products and services that increase social acceptability (e.g. love, sense of belonging) and status (e.g. esteem,

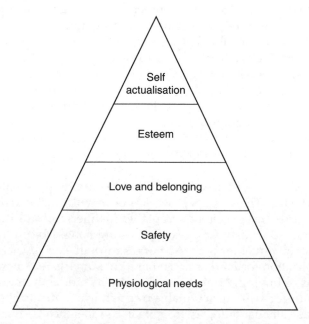

Figure 4.1 Maslow's hierarchy of needs (*Source*: Maslow, A.H. (1943), 'A theory of human motivation', *Psychological Review* 50, 370–396)

recognition). Maslow describes the ultimate need as one of self actualisation. When somebody has reached a stage in life when basic needs, love and status have been achieved, then the overriding motivation is one of acquiring products and carrying out activities that permit self-expression. This may take the form of hobbies or a series of purchases that have been desired for a long period, but have been relegated until those needs which are lower in the hierarchy have been satisfied.

Within this hierarchy, marketers should appreciate that enormous differences exist between individuals. Goals differ widely so in the short term an element of hierarchy stage 'hopping' is likely. Moreover, a product which represents self-actualisation for one person may only satisfy a lesser need for another. So complex is the question of motivation that it is impractical to devise marketing strategies based on the hierarchy theory alone. Motivation research has developed considerably over the years, although this is more directly related to specific consumer and product problems. The hierarchy of needs has general value in that it suggests that marketers of consumer products should understand and direct their effort at the higher needs of their customers. The theory also provides a useful starting point when attempting to explain the basic nature of consumer behaviour.

4.5.3 Perception

Whilst motivation is an indication of willingness to act or respond to a stimulus, perception concerns the meaning that the individual assigns to that particular stimulus. Marketers are concerned with influencing a buyer's perception of their products in relation to factors like price, quality and risk. The product image is only as good as the consumer's perception of it. The product only exists (in commercial terms) if the consumer perceives that it is capable of satisfying a need.

Any stimulus is received through the five senses (sight, hearing, smell, taste and touch). The perception of the stimulus is, therefore, affected by its physical nature, by the environment of the individual and by his or her psychological condition. Before any form of perception can take place, it is necessary that the stimulus (in this case the product) receives consideration.

An individual is exposed to a multitude of stimuli most of which receive little or no attention. Advertisers face a challenge in attempting to ensure that their particular stimuli receive individual consumer attention. Having gained that attention, the marketer must attempt to ensure that it is retained. At this point, the task becomes more difficult as perception is constantly selective. Consumers are exposed to a limited proportion of all marketing stimuli that are available: we do not read all newspapers and magazines, nor do we visit every part of a store. Even when a medium of communication has our attention (e.g. a magazine or television) we do not read or watch every advertisement. Individuals have many sources of stimuli competing for their attention. Thus, an advertisement may only be partially read and easily forgotten; consumers can only act on information that is retained in the mind. Marketers cannot provide 'blanket' exposure for their products, so they attempt to place their stimuli where they think they are most likely to be well received. This is the basis of media selection whose practical aspects are covered in Chapter 10.

A well-known cliché says that 'beauty is in the eye of the beholder'. Although marketers may succeed in gaining maximum attention, perhaps because the consumer has identified a problem and is actively involved in the search process, there is no guarantee that a consumer's perception of a particular product will be the interpretation that the marketer desires. Previous experience of a similar product may influence perception, either favourably or unfavourably. Experience, environment, the immediate circumstances, aspirations and many other psychological factors combine together to shape, alter and reshape consumer perceptions.

4.5.4 Attitudes

Attitudes can be defined as a set of perceptions an individual has of an 'object'. This can be a person, product, brand or a company. For example, our attitude towards imported goods might be influenced by our feelings about the country of origin. Similarly, our attitudes towards a certain store or company are likely to be favourable if the staff are particularly helpful, or if we know that some profits are donated to a worthwhile cause. As discussed earlier, the influence of reference groups on the individual tends to be strongly emphasised. Social interaction plays a major part in attitude formation. Attitudes may be learned from others. In particular, many of our attitudes are due to the influence of the family group and many attitudes developed in our formative years remain with us throughout our lives.

Attitudes can be positive, negative or neutral. In general, attitudes can be firmly held by individuals who tend to resist attacks made on such attitudes. This is not to say that attitudes never change or cannot be changed. A bad experience can rapidly alter an attitude from positive to negative, while a small product modification may generate a favourable attitude when the previous attitude to the product was neutral or negative. Marketers must be aware of the importance of generating a favourable attitude towards their companies and products. Once established in the mind of consumers, attitudes are difficult to alter. Even slight dissatisfaction can cause a radical change in attitude. In a competitive environment, such a process can work both for and against a producer or retailer. An attractive promotion or advertisement may appeal to the consumer's emotions and temporarily change patterns of action, but this will not necessarily result in a change of the basic attitude.

4.5.5 Learned behaviour

Learning results from 'experience'. This is an important element in the study of behaviour because it has the power to change attitudes and perceptions. Learning not only provokes change; it is able to reinforce a change in behaviour. A consumer may 'learn' that certain products are more acceptable than others to their family or reference group. In an attempt to promote this acceptability, the purchaser might reinforce the acceptable purchase with similar repeat purchases. Marketers realise that a prime objective is to influence consumers sufficiently to make a first purchase. The ultimate success of marketing effort depends on a succession of repeat purchases.

Such learning by 'trial and error' principles is referred to as 'conditioned learning'. Each time a satisfactory purchase is made the consumer becomes less and less likely to deviate from this behaviour. This type of learning results in 'brand loyalty', which, once established, tends to be unchanging.

Learning also occurs as a result of information received. The information source may be a reference group or a direct approach to the consumer through advertising, publicity or promotion. From the marketer's viewpoint, learning for the sake of stored or accumulated information is of little value. For learning to have an effect on motives or attitudes, the marketing effort of a particular company should attempt to direct these changes towards products or services that are offered for sale.

It has been shown that the consumer is subject to the combined and continuous influences of the socio-economic and socio-cultural environment as well as to social interactions and psychological influences. Having discussed some of the issues that make up consumer behaviour, it is worthwhile to reflect on the consumer's fundamental goal. When consumers buy products, their aim is to achieve satisfaction. This might seem obvious, but it has two important implications:

1 Companies that provide most satisfaction will enjoy the greatest success. (The basis of the marketing concept.)
2 Because consumers are constantly engaged in a search for satisfaction, competition will always have potential appeal.

It is not, therefore, sufficient to provide satisfaction. Companies must strive to maintain and improve the level of satisfaction they provide. Complacency is the worst enemy of the marketer.

For the majority of consumers, it is unlikely that total satisfaction in relation to 'all needs and wants' can ever be achieved. Marketing might have the theoretical wherewithal to supply total satisfaction, but we must be realistic enough to admit that satisfaction also depends on the financial status of the consumer. Consumers are subject to a variety of competing demands that are made on limited financial resources. The family life cycle is a good example of changing circumstances. Of necessity, satisfaction may only be partial, and is a compromise. We should be careful not to judge satisfaction purely as a function of 'spending power' as this is simply a materialistic interpretation. It is, however, realistic to suggest that freedom from financial worries helps us to achieve material satisfaction, which in turn, contributes to complete satisfaction. Marketers should also consider that consumer goals have an aesthetic component that concerns quality of life rather than simply the quantity of products that money can buy.

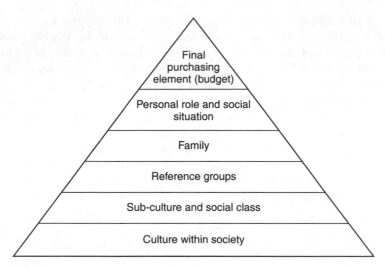

Figure 4.2 Purchasing influences on individual consumers

4.5.6 Pyramid of influences

To sum up the various elements that affect consumer choice, a hierarchy is suggested in Figure 4.2 that suggests how purchasing behaviour is affected from a general cultural level to an individual purchasing level. It is suggested that each subsequent stage in the hierarchy might have a closer effect on the purchase decision than the preceding stage.

4.6 Models of consumer buying behaviour

We have examined the consumer as an individual in terms of psychological influences and have considered wider forces that influence consumer behaviour. Should we consider them as a whole or as a group of influences that exert themselves simultaneously and continually on the consumer? Models of consumer behaviour attempt to do this. They relate to the total buyer/decision process and to the issue of new product adoption. Consumer behaviour is complicated and behavioural models attempt to reduce this complexity. There is much written on the subject of consumer behaviour and the aim now is to bring together a series of simple models that attempt to explain buying or decision processes in relation to relevant variables.

4.6.1 Buyer-decision process

In Chapter 6, we examine how products are classified according to the degree of complexity their purchase demands, but an example explains the process. We acknowledge that the purchase of shower gel (a 'fast moving consumer

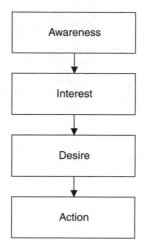

Figure 4.3 Mental states of buying

good') is less complex than purchasing a new car. Whatever the buying task and associated degree of complexity confronting the consumer, it is important to consider the steps leading to a purchase as a problem-solving process.

Figure 4.3 is a model of the mental states the buyer passes through during the buyer/decision process.

'Awareness' is considered in details under 'new product adoption' in Section 4.6.2. The consumer is aware of many products, but does not necessarily experience a desire to purchase. This state of awareness becomes important when a product is perceived as being capable of solving a problem. For this reason, Figure 4.4, first put forward by Robinson *et al.* (1967) is a more useful model of the buyer/decision process, as it describes the activities involved.

Our lives are made up of processes of problem recognition and need satisfaction. We need to buy food to satisfy hunger. Our problem is deciding what kind of food and which brand to purchase from which store. We are invited to a special function and want to buy a new outfit. We go through the stages of the buyer-decision process. By identifying or feeling a need or want, we then recognise a problem.

If a person moves from an apartment to a house with a garden, then there will be a recognised need to mow the lawn. The person will be aware that lawnmowers exist, but this basic knowledge may constitute the full extent of awareness at that point in time.

The next move towards purchase involves information search. A lawnmower might be relatively expensive and the potential consumer knows little about the product, so in this case the search process will be extensive (in contrast to the routine search activity carried out for everyday shopping items). Information sources may include the family, neighbours, colleagues and the marketing actions of lawnmower manufacturers. The degree of influence each source has on the consumer will depend on the nature of the product and on

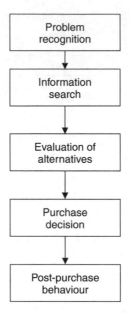

Figure 4.4 Steps in the buyer/decision process (*Source*: Robinson, P.J., Jarvis, C.W. and Wind, Y. (1967) 'Industrial Buying and Creative Marketing', Boston, MA: Allyn and Bacon, p. 14.)

the individual making the purchase. We know that reference groups, in particular family, exert a powerful influence. In the lawnmower example, the consumer is likely to turn to parents and relatives and friends for information and advice. Marketing provides information through advertising. Magazines and newspapers may feature articles and advertisements for selected products. By the time the search period nears completion, the consumer will have rejected certain lawnmowers as being unsuitable in some way, perhaps being too expensive or too heavy. A preference for a country of origin might have ruled out some machines. A mental short-list of possible alternatives will remain.

This 'short-list' allows the consumer to move to the next buying stage, that of evaluation of alternatives. The relative merits of each option are assessed so the chosen product maximises or optimises satisfaction. Often an ideal choice is arrived at easily, but financial limitations might oblige another alternative to be the product finally chosen.

During information search the short-list is usually easy to establish and basic product features bring about attraction or rejection in the consumer's mind. When the range of choices has been narrowed down, evaluating alternatives is more difficult. This is especially true when the potential purchase has necessitated an extensive search. Here, differences in product features or attributes are likely to be more subtle and difficult for the consumer to evaluate. For FMCGs, brand and brand image are major influences.

Looking at the buyer decision process from the marketer's viewpoint, segmentation strategy is considered to be most influential during the information search stage. Thus a dual process takes place, and the consumer quickly eliminates some products from those on offer, as they are clearly unsuitable. By segmenting the market, a company is eliminating some consumers from the total population of potential purchasers, and concentrates its efforts on segments more likely to 'short-list' its products. As well as segmenting the market, the marketer's task is to ensure that because of certain attributes, products receive high rankings in the consumer's mind during the evaluation stage. The creation of product attributes is thus the 'fine tuning' of a segmentation strategy. This can only be achieved after detailed marketing research.

Finally, the purchase decision must be made. When making a choice, the consumer is not only seeking satisfaction, but is also aiming to reduce risk. This is especially true when a product is costly and the purchase decision is accompanied by some anxiety. This relates to making the right choice from the chosen product group, and also concerns the wisdom of having made the purchase in the first place. In the lawnmower example, there will be a wide range of demands on the consumer's limited resources; perhaps it would have been more sensible to pay a gardener to do this work and purchase something else instead.

Immediately prior to purchase, the consumer is still susceptible to 'influence'. A decision not to purchase may be the result of influence from any of the motivations mentioned. Conflicting influences only serve to confuse and make the purchaser's task more difficult. The salesperson can be highly influential at this stage. 'Forcing' a sale at this delicate stage might help the salesperson's commission, but from a marketing standpoint it does not give the kind of satisfaction that might lead to repeat purchases. Often a 'hard sell' will only reinforce anxiety, termed 'cognitive dissonance'. Marketing strategies should concentrate on reducing anxiety and perceived risk.

It might be assumed that post-purchase behaviour is beyond marketing's control. Control can be exercised if the product is marketed skilfully and thoughtfully before the purchase is made. Marketers must be aware of post-purchase behaviour, because this directly affects repeat sales. Simply stated, consumers can be satisfied or dissatisfied with a purchase. If the consumer is satisfied then all is well. Advertising must take care not to build consumer expectations too high as this might lead to dissatisfaction. Post-purchase dissonance, or cognitive dissonance, is a feeling of dissatisfaction or unease that consumers sometimes feel following a major purchase. The product may be perfectly acceptable, yet the consumer may feel that the purchase was not as good as it could have been. Despite these feelings of unease, consumers frequently rationalise and reinforce their purchase decision. They will not voice dissatisfaction and appear to be poor decision-makers in the eyes of their reference group. They prefer to feel positive in their own minds about their actions and actively seek information that justifies their purchase, and tend to ignore any doubts they might still have.

If consumers publicise dissatisfaction, marketers face a problem because of the power and influence attached to word of mouth communication. If a product is faulty, or does not perform as claimed, the marketer is in error, but marketers should be aware of the negative effects of dissonance when nothing is wrong. Whilst actions to reduce potential dissonance can be taken before the purchase is made, marketers can do much to instil confidence and security after the sale. Companies should attach as much importance to after-sales service as they do in making the sale in the first place. This reduces dissonance in the case of genuine complaints. In addition, companies can follow up sales by some form of communication with customers. This builds customer confidence in having made the 'right' decision and some advertising campaigns are expressly designed with this purpose in mind. The term that relates to after sale follow-up is 'customer care'.

The importance of each stage of the buyer/decision process varies according to the type of product under consideration. For some product groups the whole process is routine, whilst for others each stage involves careful consideration by the consumer. Understanding how the buyer/decision process works is vital to the success of marketing strategy. Where purchases are routine, the task of marketing is to break that routine in favour of the company's products. The more complicated the buying process, the more important it is that companies assist consumers in the problem-solving process and reassure them that their choice has been a wise one.

4.6.2 Adoption process

Marketers are interested in consumer behaviour as it relates to new products. Figure 4.4 showed a sequential model of the buyer/decision process. It referred to situations for existing products or services and focused initially on problem solving and search. Figure 4.5 shows the adoption process for an innovatory new product. The key difference between the two models is that the adoption model begins with awareness. It is the task of marketing to create awareness and then guide the consumer through subsequent stages of the process. Without awareness of a new product, consumers cannot consider it as a solution to need related problems. To be worthwhile, innovative products should be problem solving in nature so far as the consumer is concerned.

Awareness can come about by 'word-of-mouth' communication or the marketing effort of firms. The individual is exposed to the innovation and becomes aware of its existence. If the product has initial appeal, further information is sought. At the evaluation stage, the consumer 'weighs' the relative advantages of the new product against those of existing products (and perhaps against directly competing products if these have been launched).

The consumer might make a 'temporary' adoption by obtaining a sample to trial. A lot of new FMCG products are produced in a 'trial size' and companies distribute free samples. It may be possible to borrow a product from somebody for trial purposes. If a trial cannot be made, the likelihood of adoption decreases.

At the adoption stage the decision is made whether or not to 'adopt' (buy or begin to use) the product, either singly or on a full-scale basis. Post-adoption confirmation is when the product has been adopted and the consumer might be seeking assurance and reassurance that the correct decision has been made. New information has been accepted and prior information rejected. Often, after

Figure 4.5 Stages in the adoption process

an important purchase, cognitive dissonance is present. As stated earlier, it is important that such dissonance is countered by providing some kind of follow-up using appropriate marketing means.

Figure 4.6 expands the adoption process model. At the beginning of the process, it is useful to regard the circles shown as a series of 'inputs' that flow into the 'melting pot' creating knowledge. It is important to remember that the 'self' input includes the psychological concepts of attitudes, perception, learning and motivation. Like the other inputs, they set the scene for knowledge to be translated into a favourable condition of awareness. Figure 4.6 also shows that persuasion, and hence the rate of adoption, is affected by the product's:

- relative advantage (over other products on the market),
- compatibility (with the needs of the consumer),
- complexity,
- trial-ability or trial opportunity,
- observability (e.g. a new car purchase is easily observed, whereas an insurance policy is more difficult to comprehend in this context).

The model allows for reviewed action after the decision stage. At this point, consumers are highly sensitive to the influence of information sources including reference groups.

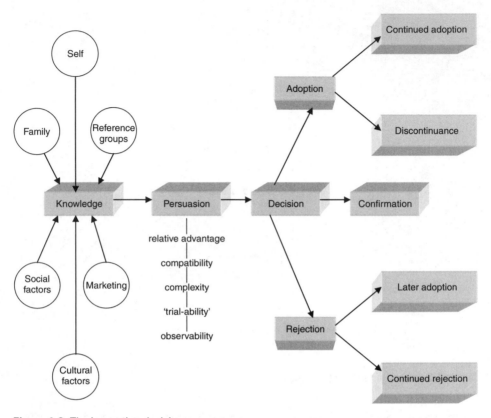

Figure 4.6 The innovation decision process

The rate of adoption for an innovation also depends on the type of consumer to whom the product is marketed. Chapter 6 deals with product policy issues and in particular with the product adoption process as explained in Figure 6.8. It shows how consumers can be divided into groups, or adopter categories, and the rate at which these adoptions are taken up. Some adopters are receptive and readily adopt innovations, whilst others are slow to adopt new products. This 'diffusion of innovation' process suggests that certain groups of consumers are highly influential and that this influence will 'diffuse' through to subsequent consumer groups. In the context of consumer buying behaviour we see how each of these groups possess distinct characteristics:

1 'Innovators' are likely to be younger, better educated, and relatively affluent with a higher social status. In terms of personal characteristics, they are likely to be broader minded, receptive people with a wide range of social relationships. Their product knowledge relies more on their own efforts to gather objective information than on company literature or salespeople.
2 'Early adopters', whilst possessing many of the characteristics of innovators, tend to belong to more 'local' systems. Although their social relationships are

less broadly based, they tend to be opinion leaders and are highly influential within their particular group. As such, they are a major target for marketers whose aim is to get their product accepted as quickly as possible.

3 The 'early majority' is a group that is slightly above average in socio-economic terms. They rely heavily on marketing effort for information and are influenced by opinion leaders of the early-adopter category.

4 'Late majority' adopters are more likely to adopt innovations that have already been accepted by previous groups. Social pressure or economic considerations are, therefore, more influential in this group than innate personal characteristics.

5 'Laggards' make up the cautious group. They tend to be older, with relatively lower socio-economic status. The innovator group may already be considering another, newer, product before laggards have adopted the original innovation.

The theory of the diffusion of innovations is useful in relation to the study of consumer behaviour. We should, however, be aware that consumers who exhibit particular adopter characteristics for one category of product might behave differently in the adoption of another product type. It should also be appreciated that the model refers to innovatory products and not to repeat purchases.

4.7 Organisational buying behaviour

It is common for industrial buying to be thought of as being devoid of the psychological and emotional connotations attached to consumer behaviour. After all, industrial purchasers cannot afford the luxury of 'impulse' buying. They are employed to make purchases for a specific reason. They have budgets and usually have a great deal of knowledge about what they purchase. Although there are differences, many parallels can be drawn between industrial and consumer buying.

First, though, note that the heading of this sections is 'organisational' buying behaviour, whereas, we are now referring to 'industrial' buying behaviour. 'Organisational buying' is a wider term used to cover industrial, buying for resale and public authority/utility (termed 'institutional') purchasing. However, the principles of organisational buying are, for our purposes, the same as those for industrial buying. In some marketing texts the terms 'organisational buying' and 'industrial buying' are interchanged, although the latter really refers to a narrower context.

The most apparent similarity between organisational and consumer buying is that both activities represent a need-satisfying process. Although these needs might differ, they should be fully recognised before any selling approach is made. Figure 4.7 is a model of the industrial buyer/decision process and it closely resembles the model that was used for consumers (Figure 4.4). The approach and reaction to new products is also similar. Diffusion theory can,

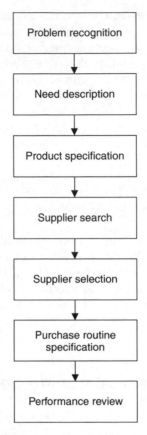

Figure 4.7 The industrial buyer/decision process

for example, be applied with equal validity to both types of buying situation. In fact Rogers' 'diffusion of innovations' model (dealt with in Chapter 6) was not originally developed for consumer markets. Finally, organisational buyers are also subjected to influences that affect their decisions: marketing effort influences industrial behaviour; reference groups exist within industrial situations; as individuals, buyers are influenced by their own psychological make-up.

A more detailed model was originally suggested by Wind in 1978 when he proposed 12 stages as shown in Figure 4.8.

An important question that organisational marketers must ask is: 'Who are the powerful buyers?'

This does not necessarily correlate with rank within the purchasing organisation. Those with little formal power may be able to stop a purchase or hinder its completion.

Five major power bases are highlighted:

1 *Reward*: Ability to provide monetary, social, political, or psychological rewards to others for compliance.

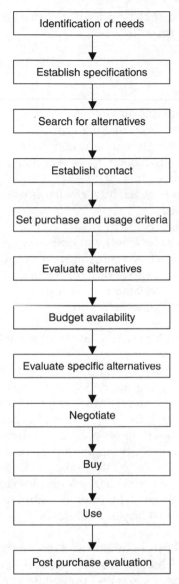

Figure 4.8 Wind's 12 stage model (*Source*: Wind, Y. (1978), 'The boundaries of buying decision centres', *Journal of Purchasing and Materials Management*, 14(2), Summer, 27.)

2 *Coercive*: Ability to provide monetary or other punishments for non-compliance.
3 *Attraction*: Ability to elicit compliance from others because they like you.
4 *Expert*: Ability to elicit compliance because of technical expertise, either actual or reputed.
5 *Status*: Compliance through the capacity of a legitimate position of power in a company.

In general, it can be said that organisational markets differ from consumer markets in the following respects:

1 rationality of buying motives,
2 derived demand,
3 smaller numbers of buyers,
4 larger number of influences on buyer,
5 often a multi-person decision making unit,
6 customers are sometimes in economic competition,
7 industrial customers may have more power than sellers,
8 many products are 'buyer specified',
9 economic relationship between buyer/seller is often long term,
10 high value of purchases,
11 distribution is more direct,
12 sales are often preceded by lengthy negotiation,
13 company policies may act as a constraint on the buyer,
14 possible 'reciprocal' buying (we buy from you and you buy from us),
15 unequal purchasing power amongst customers,
16 often there is geographic concentration.

Such characteristics should be taken into account when the marketing firm develops its communications strategy.

Having made these general observations we now focus on specific factors that pertain to organisational buying situations. Most apparent is the fact that it is an 'organised' process. Whilst consumer markets attract much of marketing's attention, we should not overlook the magnitude of organisational sales and purchases. Every time a consumer makes a purchase from a retail outlet, a derived demand is created for a series of component parts and materials in earlier parts of the supply chain that make up the finished product. We can add to this complex chain those companies who buy and sell machinery, packaging materials and maintenance equipment. In order to control this constant flow of goods and services, companies must organise their buying activity so that they have:

- a constant supply (in terms of quality and delivery);
- a system of control which monitors performance specifications;
- a review policy towards existing and potential suppliers.

The larger the organisation, the more structured tends to be the methods of buying. A formal process should be established for each of the activities that make up organisational purchasing procedure as outlined in Figure 4.7.

For the most purchases made by consumers the negative aspects of an ill-advised purchase are shorter term and can be more easily rectified. In contrast, for a large company, whose machinery might be in use 24 hours a day, even a small quality or delivery problem from suppliers could cause considerable loss in terms of 'down-time' on the production line. Organisational purchasing must, therefore, adopt a formal structure because of the responsibility that it bears.

Just as consumer behaviour varies according to product types, industrial purchases demand more or less attention according to their nature. This is not to say that the approach for routine purchases should be any less formal than that for more critical items. A formal classification of industrial products is given in Chapter 6. The purchasing approach for each type of product bought varies according to the buying situation.

4.7.1 Buying situations

Three major types of organisational buying situation can be identified:

1 *'New task'*: This is a challenging task for purchasing. The product item might be a new machine or new material for a new product. Although buyers have professional expertise, they might be unfamiliar with the product and need to engage in extensive need description, product specification and supplier search.
2 *'Straight rebuy'*: This involves little effort and it is routine within the current purchasing structure. It is important to appreciate that this 'routine' is only possible because careful buying in the past has established a reliable supply pattern.
3 *'Modified rebuy'*: For a variety of reasons, the product specification or supplier has to be changed. In many ways modified rebuy can be as challenging as the new task situation. Although the basic product may be well known, any change involves risk. Often industrial buyers keep alternative suppliers as minor suppliers, buying a little from them from time to time to test their reliability in preparation for greater participation should the need arise. With the same risk reducing goal in mind, product modifications are usually introduced gradually so that problems can be resolved before a greater commitment has been made.

The main difference between consumer and organisational buying is that the latter usually involves group decision making. Here, individuals have different roles in the purchasing process. An idea was put forward by Frederick E Webster (Jr.) and Yoram Wind (1972) termed the 'buying centre' concept. The categories described are also referred to as the 'decision making unit' (DMU). He said that in any organisational purchasing situation, various influences can be identified:

- 'Users' work with, or use, the product and are sometimes involved in product specification.
- 'Buyers' have authority to sign orders and make the purchase. They might help shape the specification, but their principal role is in supplier negotiation and selection.
- 'Deciders' make the final buying decision (frequently the decider and the buyer is the same person).
- 'Influencers' can affect the buying decision in different ways (e.g. technical people may have helped in a major or minor way to develop the product specification).

- 'Gatekeepers' control the flow of information to and from people who buy (e.g. the chief buyer's secretary or even the receptionist who might handle initial enquiries).

Organisational buyers' roles vary widely. In technical sales situations, the salesperson may hardly meet the buyer, as it is a technical manager who conducts negotiations. The buyer finally takes over to handle commercial aspects of the sale. Many companies employ buyers who are skilled in purchasing procedures, but only have limited technical knowledge of products being purchased. Other companies employ buyers for specific product areas. Whatever buying structure operates, the industrial salesperson should appreciate that the buyer is not necessarily the final decision-maker. Clearly, the real decision-maker should be the principal target for sales effort (see Johnston and Lewin (1996) for an integrated approach to modelling the organisational buying process).

Purchasing should not only be considered in terms of transactions between buyers and sellers because the purchase has repercussions on other aspects of the company. Sales and marketing managers are, for example, concerned with product quality and delivery. Technical and production managers are concerned with performance. Marketers should be aware of factors that influence organisational buyers (see the discussion by Möller (1985) for the use of research in organisational buying).

It is important to ensure that problems faced by purchasers are fully understood and marketing and sales strategies designed accordingly. Whilst price is important, it is not the only influence in organisational purchasing decision making.

Figure 4.9 highlights the main tools available to industrial markets for targeting DMUs.

With a move towards companies holding less stock of raw materials and components in the interests of saving working capital, reliable delivery and quality is vital. As mentioned in Chapter 2, in certain flow-production manufacturing situations using JIT/lean manufacturing principles, stockholding is virtually non-existent. Buyers require a constant stream of goods with zero defects. Should defects occur, the company's entire production can be stopped, so reliability of supply is of paramount importance. In these situations, relationships tend to be long term and it is just a common for buyers to visit sellers as it is for sellers to visit buyers (the traditional pattern). This notion is termed 'reverse marketing' where buyers take the commercial initiative and actively source suppliers who match up to criteria of reliability of quality and supply. There is now a notion of 'open accounting' where price does not enter the negotiation equation, as buyers are fully aware of the exact price make-up of components they have sourced. In turn, suppliers also know profit margins of their customers, and buyers and sellers agree a common mark-up. If the supplier then devises ways to make components more cheaply without compromising quality, then savings from the new process are divided between the supplier and the customer. Needless to say, such agreements imply long-term relationships from which has been coined the phrase 'relationship marketing'.

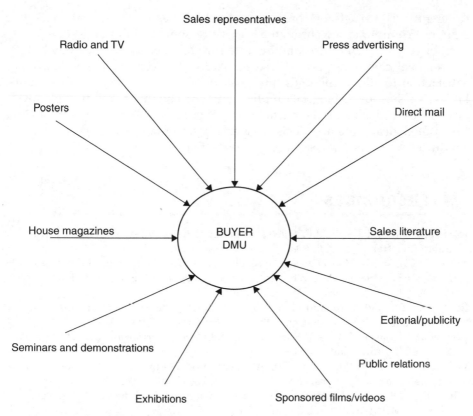

Figure 4.9 Targeting the DMU

Buyers are of course individuals as well as being purchasing professionals. In many industrial markets, levels of service and price are such that there is little to distinguish suppliers. The personal impression that the individual buyer or the DMU has of a supplier's image, as well as the personal rapport that the salesperson can achieve, can influence buying decisions. Just as purchasers of consumer goods are responsive to the actions of sellers, organisational buyers have personalities that sellers must take into account. Some buyers may be aggressive, devious or indecisive. The salesperson should not adopt a 'blanket' approach to customers. Human factor also extend to the buyer's relationships with contemporaries within the organisation. Companies themselves have 'personalities' in more abstract terms of attitudes and policies that can make them more or less susceptible to particular sales and marketing approaches.

4.8 Summary

Although we can identify factors common to both consumer and organisational buying behaviour, it is clear that the two markets should be approached differently. The needs of consumers should be ascertained and marketing response communicated through a variety of sources. In organisational markets, buyers and sellers do communicate through media, but they rely heavily on personal communication. These professional buyers endeavour to obtain satisfaction for the company's 'physical' needs, whereas much of consumer behaviour has psychological implications. Although organisational buyers have a clear rationale for their actions, this is not to say that they are insensitive to psychological influences. This is especially important in a market where the products on the offer are essentially comparable.

References

Johnston, W.J. and Lewin, J.E. (1996), 'Organizational buying behaviour: Toward an integrative framework', *Journal of Business Research* 35, 1–15.

Maslow, A.H. (1954), *Motivation and Personality*, New York: Harper and Row, pp. 80–106.

Muller, K.E.K. (1985), 'Research strategies in analyzing the organisational buying process', *Journal of Business Research* 13, 3–17.

Reynolds, T.J. and Gutmann, J. (1988), 'Laddering theory, method, analysis, and interpretation', *Journal of Advertising Research*, February–March 11–31.

Robinson, P.J., Jarvis, C.W. and Wind, Y. (1967), *Industrial Buying and Creative Marketing*, Boston, MA: Allyn and Bacon, p. 14.

Webster, F.E. (Jr.) and Wind, Y. (1972), 'A general model of understanding organisational buying behaviour', *Journal of Marketing* 36, April, 12–19.

Wind, Y. (1978), 'The boundaries of buying decision centres', *Journal of Purchasing and Materials Management* 14(2), Summer, 23–29.

Further reading

Blackwell, R.D., Miniard, P.W. and Engel, J.F. (2001), *Consumer Behaviour*, Harcourt Brace Jovanovich, Chapters 1–7.

Brennan, R., Baines, P. and Garneau, P. (2003), *Contempory Strategic Marketing*, London: Palgrave Macmillan, Chapter 4.

Cravens, D.W., Lamb, C.W. (Jr.) and Crittenden, V. L. (2002), *Strategic Marketing Management Cases*, 7th edition, International edition, McGraw Hill pp. 434–448.

Schiffman, L.G. and Kanuk, L.L. (2000), *Consumer Behaviour*, London: Prentice-Hall, Chapter 7–10.

Solomon, M., Bamossy, G. and Askegaard, S. (1999), *Consumer Behaviour: A European Perspective*, London: Prentice-Hall, Chapters 1–3.

Questions

Question 4.1

Advertising and consumer behaviour: How far do you agree with the statement that advertising is the biggest single influence on consumer behaviour?

Question 4.2

Industrial buying: It is common to think of the purchasing decision processes of industrial buyers as being devoid of emotion. How far would you agree with this?

Question 4.3

Customer care: Why is the idea of 'customer care' such a relatively recent one?

Question 4.4

Buyer behaviour: How far do models of buying behaviour go towards providing marketers with better tools for targeting customers?

Question 4.5

Organisational buying: How does organisational buying relate to industrial buying?

Question 4.6

DMU: Do you define the DMU as a committee of people or something more informal?

Explain how buyers in business to business or 'organisational buying' situations differ from consumer buyers in their purchasing decision making processes.

Discuss the idea of an organisational decision making unit (DMU) and examine the role within the DMU of the people involved in a business purchasing decision.

Examine the role of direct marketing within an overall marketing communications campaign targeted at customers in:

(i) consumer markets,
(ii) business-to-business markets.

If possible use examples to illustrate the points made.

Discuss how Abraham Maslow's theory of motivation may help marketing management in understanding the dynamics of individual consumer behaviour.

What are the different types of organisational markets? Define each one and suggest examples of products and organisations that fit each description.

Explain the nature and characteristics of each type of organisational buying situations.

5

Segmentation, Targeting and Positioning

5.1 Introduction

Market segmentation and targeting can be defined as:

> The process of breaking down the total market for a product or service into distinct sub-groups or segments, where each segment may conceivably represent a distinct target market to be targeted with a distinctive marketing mix.

To improve opportunities for success in a competitive market environment, marketers must focus their effort on clearly defined market targets. The intention is to select those groups of customers that the company is best able to serve in such a way that it does this in a superior manner to competitors. The sequential steps in this process are segmentation, targeting and positioning. We now examine each of these steps.

There are increasingly more segmentation bases available, which means that targeting and positioning strategies are becoming more meaningful.

5.2 The need for segmentation

The essence of the marketing concept is to place customer needs at the centre of the organisation's decision making. In addition, the need to adopt this approach is a result of increased competition, more informed and educated consumers and changing patterns of demand. It is this latter point that has given rise to the need to segment markets.

People do not purchase exactly the same kinds of products as each other. They may have different tastes in clothes or in the type of holidays they take. Perhaps they purchase different brands of toothpaste or breakfast cereals. This obvious example shows that market segmentation and the subsequent strategies of targeting and positioning start by recognising that increasingly, within the total demand/market for a product, specific tastes, needs and amounts demanded may differ.

We refer to a market that is characterised by differing individual preferences as being 'heterogeneous'. Market segmentation breaks down a total differently behaving market for a product or service into distinct sub-sets or segments, with customers who share similar demand preferences being grouped together with each segment. This is illustrated in Figure 5.1.

Effective segmentation is achieved when customers sharing similar patterns of demand are grouped together and where each segment differs in the pattern of demand from other segments in the market (i.e. where clustering gives rise to 'homogeneous' demand within each segment and 'heterogeneous' demand amongst different segments). Most markets for consumer and industrial products can be segmented on some kind of basis.

5.3 Targeted marketing efforts

As most markets are made up of heterogeneous demand segments, this means that companies have to decide which segments to serve. Most companies recognise that they cannot effectively serve all segments in a market so they must instead target their marketing efforts.

Varied patterns of demand require that marketers develop specific marketing mixes aimed or targeted at specific market segments. Targeting versus mass marketing approach has been likened to using a 'rifle approach' as opposed to using a 'shotgun approach'.

This idea of how companies target their marketing efforts was put forward by Abell (1980) when he suggested targeting strategies based upon customer group concentrations or customer need concentrations, or a combination of each. Figure 5.1 illustrates how this idea works in practice.

Figure 5.1(a) shows a marketing strategy of complete coverage. This is termed 'undifferentiated' marketing and an appropriate example here might be a popular brand of washing powder/liquid.

Figure 5.1(b) shows a strategy that concentrates on a specialist want or wants that cover different customer groups. This is a 'differentiated' marketing strategy. An example here is an adhesives manufacturer who supplies the engineering, textiles, schools, office supplies and 'do-it-yourself' markets.

Figure 5.1(c) shows a strategy that concentrates on supplying a variety of wants to a specific customer group, for example, a mining machinery

Customer wants	Customer groups		
	Group 1	Group 2	Group 3
Want 1			
Want 2			
Want 3			

Figure 5.1 Customer wants/groups

	G1	G2	G3
W1	X	X	X
W2	X	X	X
W3	X	X	X

Figure 5.1(a) Complete coverage

	G1	G2	G3
W1			
W2	X	X	X
W3			

Figure 5.1(b) Want satisfaction specialisation

	G1	G2	G3
W1			X
W2			X
W3			X

Figure 5.1(c) Customer group specialisation

manufacturer supplying all machinery requirements for the coal industry. This is also a 'differentiated' marketing strategy.

Figure 5.1(d) shows a strategy of specialist supply where the company serves customer groups 2 and 3 with wants 1 and 3, respectively. An example is a spinner of carpet yarns who supplies carpet manufacturers, but who also

	G1	G2	G3
W1		X	
W2			
W3			X

Figure 5.1(d) Selective specialisation

manufactures and sells needle punch carpets to the motor trade. This is known as a 'concentrated' market strategy.

A number of factors affect the choice of targeting strategy. For example, smaller companies with fewer resources often have to specialise in certain segments of the market to be competitive, so they must pursue a concentrated strategy. Competition will also affect the choice of strategy. In the final analysis, choosing a targeting strategy is a matter of striking the optimum balance between the costs and benefits of each approach in the particular situation.

Specifically, the advantages of target marketing are:

1 marketing opportunities and 'gaps' in a market may be more accurately identified and appraised;
2 product and market appeals (through the marketing mix) can be more finely tuned to the needs of the potential customer;
3 marketing effort can be focused on the market segment(s) that offer the greatest potential for the company to achieve its objectives.

5.4 Effective segmentation

The base(s) used for segmentation should lead to segments that are:

1 *Measurable/identifiable*: Base(s) chosen should lead to ease of identification (who is in each segment?) and measurement (how many potential customers are in each segment?).
2 *Accessible*: Base(s) used should lead to the marketer being able to reach selected market targets through marketing efforts.
3 *Substantial*: Base(s) used should lead to segments that are large enough to be worthwhile serving as distinct market targets.
4 *Meaningful*: Base(s) used should lead to segments that have different preferences and needs, and should show clear variations in market behaviour or response to specialised marketing efforts. For example, in the consumer durables market, for example, motor cars, brand loyalty can be used as an effective segmentation variable (see Hooley *et al.*, 2003).

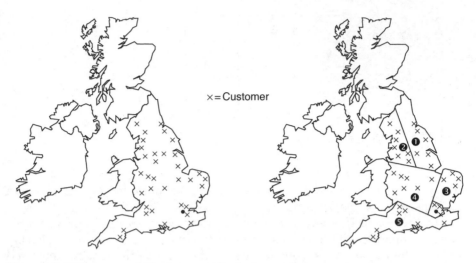

Figure 5.2 Market segmentation for a machine tools manufacturer

This latter criterion, that segments are meaningful, is very important as this is an essential prerequisite in identifying and selecting market targets.

Before we examine the steps of segmentation, targeting and positioning in detail we need to understand further what market segmentation means, and how this relates to our criteria for effective segmentation. A simple illustration is shown in Figure 5.2. Here, the country (England) is broken down into five distinct selling regions, each served by a regional sales representative.

In segmentation, targeting and positioning, the goal is to identify distinct subsets of customers in the total market for a product where any subset might eventually be selected as a market target, and for which a distinctive marketing mix will be developed.

For instance, taking the geographical segmentation example in Figure 5.2 when we examine the North–West region we might find that it breaks up into an 'assisted region' and a 'non-assisted region' as shown in Figure 5.3.

An 'assisted region' attracts various grants and benefits from the Government and the European Union. An industrial goods supplier selling certain types of capital equipment (machine tools in this illustration) will target firms to whom it sells in an Assisted Region with a different message (perhaps emphasising grants that are available) than to those firms it sells to in a non-assisted region.

In this illustration we are assuming that buyers in assisted regions will be more prone to the cost savings motive (through grants), whereas those in non-assisted regions will react more to general commercial criteria like reliability, price and service. The important element to note is that the bases selected for segmentation (geography and assistance status) are meaningful ones. It only makes sense to continue to subdivide markets in this way as long as the resulting

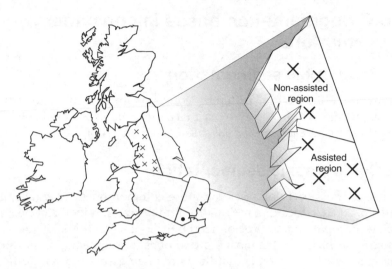

Figure 5.3 Further segmentation on the basis of assistance status

segments are worthwhile serving as distinct market targets with distinct marketing mixes. There are some markets where complete segmentation (i.e. tailoring the marketing mix to individual customers) is not only desirable, but essential. In shipbuilding each customer may be treated as a separate market, but for most consumer product markets such customising of marketing effort would be impractical.

The following represents the sequential steps when conducting a segmentation, targeting and positioning exercise:

1 select bases(s) for segmentation and identify segments,
2 evaluate and appraise the market segments resulting from step 1,
3 select an overall targeting strategy,
4 select specific target segments in line with step 3,
5 develop 'product positioning' strategies (see Section 5.9 for more detail) for each target segment,
6 develop appropriate marketing mixes for each target segment in order to support positioning strategies.

The remainder of this chapter discusses each of these steps individually.

The machine tools example used the bases of geography and benefits to segment the market. There is no prescribed way to segment a market and different combinations of bases should be sought. There are, however, a number of relatively common bases frequently used by marketers that are now discussed.

5.5 Segmentation bases in consumer markets

5.5.1 Geographic segmentation

In international marketing, different countries might constitute different market segments. Within a country a market can be segmented into regions that might represent each individual salesperson's territory.

5.5.2 Demographic segmentation

This consists of a variety of bases the more common ones being: age, gender (see Oreclin, 2002), education, nationality, family size, family life cycle, income, social class/occupation and type of neighbourhood (ACORN).

Demographic bases are the most popular ones for segmentation in consumer product markets. The reason is that they are often associated with differences in consumer demand (i.e. they are meaningful).

Family life cycle segmentation is based on the idea that consumers pass through a series of distinct phases in their lives. Each phase gives rise to, or is associated with, different purchasing patterns and needs. For example, the unmarried person living at home will probably have different purchasing patterns to someone of the same age who has left home and recently married. Similarly, it is recognised that purchasing patterns of adults often change as they approach and then move into retirement (see Wells and Gubar, 1966). The subject was also discussed in Chapter 4, but the stages are defined as:

1 young person;
2 young and single, no children;
3 couple, youngest child under 6 (full nest I);
4 couple, youngest child 6+ (full nest II);
5 older couple with children 18+ at home (full nest III);
6 older couple, family head in work, no children at home (empty nest I);
7 older couple, family head retired, no children at home (empty nest II);
8 older alone (in work);
9 older alone (retired).

A further development in the application of family life cycle has been developed by Research Services termed 'SAGACITY'. This combines life cycle with income and occupation in order to delineate different consumer groups. Consumers are divided into one of four life cycle groups:

1 *Dependent*: Adults 15–34 who are not heads of household or housewives unless they are childless students in full-time education.
2 *Pre-Family*: Adults 15–34 who are heads of household but childless.
3 *Family*: Adults under 65 who are heads of household or housewives in households with one or more children under 21 years of age.

4 *Late*: All other adults whose children have already left home or who are 35 or over and childless.

These four major life cycle groups are then broken down further by a combination of occupation and/or income to produce 12 major SAGACITY groupings:

		Approx. % of UK population
(DW)	Dependent white collar	6
(DB)	Dependent blue collar	9
(PFW)	Pre-family white collar	4
(PFB)	Pre-family blue collar	4
(FW+)	Family, better-off white collar	6
(FB+)	Family, better-off blue collar	9
(FW−)	Family, worse-off white collar	8
(FB−)	Family, worse-off blue collar	14
(LW+)	Late, better-off white collar	5
(LB+)	Late, better-off blue collar	7
(LW−)	Late, worse-off white collar	9
(LW−)	Late, worse-off blue collar	19

Occupation and *social class* are linked because in developed economies socio-economic group (social class) categorisations are based on occupation. Of all demographic bases, social class is still the most widely used basis for segmenting consumer product markets.

Social class scores highly against other segmentation criteria of being identifiable and accessible. It is easy to classify individuals on the basis of occupation, and to reach different social classes according to different media and shopping habits. The social class grading system used in the UK, together with a broad indication of the type of occupation associated with each is:

Social class grading	*Type of occupation*	*Approx. UK %*
A	Higher managerial	4
B	Intermediate management	11
C1	Supervisory, clerical, administrative	26
C2	Skilled manual	30
D	Semi-skilled/unskilled	25
E	Pensioner (no supplementary income) Casual and lowest grade workers	4

Some doubt has recently been expressed about social class being such a meaningful basis for segmenting markets. For instance, the skilled manual group (C2) can earn higher incomes than their counterparts in supervisory or even intermediate management (C1 or B). They are often able to purchase products and services that were traditionally the prerogative of the upper social grades.

Education

Education is related to social class because the better educated tend to get the higher paid jobs. Education is usually expressed as terminal education age (TEA). This classification is open to criticism because of an increase in the provision of part-time and distance learning education, which means that although a person's TEA might be low, education might have been enhanced through later part-time higher qualifications.

Type of neighbourhood/dwelling – ACORN

Partly because of the diminishing meaningfulness of social class/occupation as a basis of segmentation, new forms of social classification have begun to emerge that take into account a wider range of factors than the single index of occupation on which more conventional social grading systems are based. An example is the ACORN system (a classification of residential neighbourhoods). This system takes dwellings, rather than individuals, as a basis for segmentation. It is based upon the 10 yearly return made by the householder in the census enumeration district within which the house is situated. This census of population takes place in every year that ends in one (i.e. the last one was 2001) and householders must complete their return by law. There is also a 10% sample taken in every year that ends in six. In the United Kingdom, there are around 125,000 such census districts. The ACORN system has classified each of these into one of 11 major groups. Each of these major groups is further subdivided to yield a total of 36 specific neighbourhood types. The 11 major groups, and an example of how Group A is further subdivided into neighbourhood types, are given below:

A		Agricultural areas
	A1	Agricultural villages
	A2	Areas of forms and small holdings
B		Modern family housing, higher incomes
C		Older housing of intermediate status
D		Poor quality, older terraced housing
E		Better off council estates
F		Less well off council estates
G		Poorest council estates
H		Multi-racial areas
I		High-status non-family areas
J		Affluent suburban housing
K		Better of retirement areas
U		Unclassified

Essentially, the ACORN system is based on the idea that the type of area and housing in which an individual lives is a good indicator of his or her possible patterns of purchasing, including types of products and brands that might be purchased. There is evidence to suggest that this is the case and the ACORN system goes some way to fulfilling the 'meaningfulness' criterion for a segmentation basis.

ACORN was developed by Richard Webber, who has gone on to develop marketing applications for Consolidated Analysis Centres Inc. (CACI). 'Sample Plan', for instance, is a service that can be used for marketing research using a computer program to select ACORN areas. Individual addresses can then be chosen that provide a truly representative sampling frame for survey work.

The effectiveness of census data in providing segmentation bases, has been further refined. Pinpoint (PIN) analysis is based on census data and it claims 104 census variables to delineate 60 neighbourhood types that are clustered into 12 main types.

'MOSAIC' is another approach based on census data. It has added data on the financial circumstances of potential target customers living within each district by relating it to Royal Mail postcodes. Each postcode represents on average between 8 and 12 individual homes of a similar type and each is ascribed an individual 'mosaic' categorisation. For example, M1 is 'high status retirement areas with many single pensioners', M17 is 'older terraces, young families in very crowded conditions', M34 is 'better council estates but with financial problems' and M55 is 'pretty rural villages with wealthy long distance commuters'. The reason why it is called 'MOSAIC' is because if each of the 58 different MOSAIC categorisations ascribed to postal codes was represented as a different colour and then superimposed onto a map of the UK it would resemble a mosaic pattern.

This classification provides a powerful database for direct mail, because individual householders can be personally tageted according to the type of MOSAIC categorisation of their home, and in the specific geographical area in which their home is situated. For instance it is possible to specify that a personal letter goes out to all residents in South-East Huddersfield (HD8) who fall in the M46 'post-1981 housing in areas of highest income and status' MOSAIC category.

5.5.3 Lifestyle segmentation

This is termed 'psychographic segmentation'. It is based on the idea that individuals have characteristic modes and patterns of living that may be reflected in the products and brands they purchase. Some individuals prefer a 'homely' lifestyle, whereas others may have a 'sophisticated' lifestyle.

Young and Rubicam, the advertising agency, put forward a formal lifestyle classification called '4Cs' where 'C' stands for 'Customer Type'.

Consumers are put into one of the following categories:

- mainstreamers (the largest group containing in excess of 40% of the population),
- aspirers,
- succeeders,
- reformers.

The basic ideas of customer types are applicable the world over although the actual types may vary. For a good discussion on applying lifestyle segmentation in Chinese markets see Jobber (2004), Lord (2002) and Oliver (2002).

5.5.4 Direct or behavioural segmentation

The approaches to consumer segmentation described so far have been examples of associative segmentation. That is, they are used where it is felt that differences in customer needs and purchasing behaviour may be associated with them. For example, if we use age to segment a market, we are assuming that purchasing behaviour in respect of a certain product is a function of age. Most of the problems that arise from using associative bases are concerned with the extent to which the bases are truly associated with a reflection of purchasing behaviour.

Because of the problems of associative segmentation, an alternative is to use direct bases for segmenting markets. Such bases take consumer behaviour as the starting point for identifying different segments, and these are referred to as behavioural segmentation bases. They divide into three categories:

1 *Occasions for purchase*: Segments are identified on the basis of differences in the occasions for purchasing the product.
    In the market for men's ties, 'occasion for purchase' might include gift-giving, subscription to clubs or societies or purchasing a new shirt or suit.
2 *User/usage status*: A distinction may be made between 'heavy', 'light' and 'non-user' segments for a product.
3 *Benefits sought*: This is one of the most meaningful ways to segment a market. The total market for a product or service is broken down into segments that are distinguished by the principal benefit(s) sought by that segment.

The household liquid detergent market might include benefit segments like economy, mildness to hands, cleansing power and germ protection.

5.5.5 Loyalty status

A direct approach to segmenting markets is the extent to which different customers are loyal to certain brands (brand loyalty) or retail outlets (store loyalty). Identifying segments with different degrees of loyalty can enable a company to determine which customers are prone to brand loyalty (see Kendra, 2000). Such a segment is attractive for concentrating future marketing effort. Once convinced of the relative merits of a brand or supplier, such customers are less likely to switch brands. Understandably, where existing brand loyalty is strong in a market, would-be new entrants are faced with a difficult marketing problem (see Hooley *et al.*, 2003).

Consumers fall into one of four categories as far as loyalty status is concerned:

1 'Hard core loyals' who have total loyalty to a single brand (e.g. brands AAAAAA).

2 'Soft core loyals' who divide their loyalty between two, or more brands (e.g. brands AABABBA).
3 'Shifting loyals' who 'brand-switch' spending some time on one brand and then moving to another (e.g. brands AAABBB).
4 'Switchers' show no brand loyalty, often purchasing products that are lowest in price or have a special offer (e.g. brands BCBAACD).

5.6 Segmentation bases in organisational markets

The concept of segmentation, targeting and positioning is the same between consumer and organisational markets. Business to business marketers are continually finding new ways to segment their markets and customise their product and service offerings (for a good example of this see Kotler, 1999; Wind and Rangaswamy, 2001). Segmenting organisational markets suggests a number of additional bases and precludes others used for consumer markets, the most frequently used bases being:

1 Geographic e.g. north-west and south-east, Germany and Denmark.
2 Type of application/end use e.g. nylon for clothing or that used for ropes.
3 Product/technology e.g. plastic containers and glass containers.
4 Type of customer e.g. manufacturing industry, retail business, public authority.
5 Customer size e.g. by average value of order placed with the company.
6 Loyalty of customer.
7 Usage rate, for example, heavy or light.
8 Purchasing procedures, for example, centralised or decentralised, the extent of specification buying, tender versus non-tender procedures.
9 Benefits sought – based on the 'needs' that customers require from their purchase e.g. a car required for a company representatives, or for hiring out or as the managing director's personal car.

Shapiro and Bonoma (1984) have suggested a 'nested' approach to industrial market segmentation. They identified five general segmentation bases arranged in a nested hierarchy as shown in Figure 5.4.

● Demographic variables give a broad description of the segments and relate to general customer needs and usage patterns.
● Operating variables enable a more precise identification of existing and potential customers within demographic categories.
● Purchasing approaches look at customer purchasing practices (e.g. centralised or decentralised purchasing). It also includes purchasing policies/criteria and the nature of buyer/seller relationships.
● Situational factors consider the tactical role of the purchasing situation, and how much detailed knowledge might be required about the individual buyer.
● Personal characteristics relate to people who make purchasing decisions.

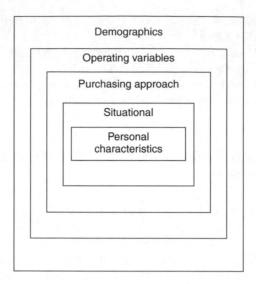

Figure 5.4 'Nested' approach to industrial segmentation

As with consumer markets, industrial market segmentation may be on an indirect (associative) or a direct (behavioural) basis. A variety of bases may be used together in order to obtain successively smaller sub-segments of the market. The criteria given for bases of consumer market segmentation – being identifiable, accessible, substantial and, most important, meaningful – are equally applicable to organizational market segmentation.

 ## 5.7 Evaluating and appraising market segments

Having decided a basis for segmentation and identified market segments, the marketer must evaluate the various market segments that have been identified. Overall, segments should be appraised with respect to sales and profit potential, or in the case of a not-for-profit organisation, the potential to contribute to overall organisational objectives. This, in turn, requires that each segment be appraised with respect to factors like overall size, projected growth, extent of existing and potential competition, nature of competitive strategies and customer requirements.

 ## 5.8 Selecting specific target markets

This step concerns organisations that decide to pursue a concentrated or differentiated targeting strategy. The company must decide which of the segments in the market it is best able and willing to serve. This decision should be based on some of the factors outlined, including company resources, competition, segment potential and company objectives. Four characteristics will make a market segment particularly attractive:

1 The segment has sufficient current sales and profit potential to meet company objectives.
2 The segment has the potential for future growth.
3 The segment is not over competitive.
4 The segment has some relatively unsatisfied needs that the company can serve particularly well.

5.9 Developing product positioning strategies

For each segment in which a company chooses to operate, it must determine a product positioning strategy. Product positioning relates to the task of ensuring that a company's products or services that it offers to the market occupies a pre-determined place in selected target markets, relative to competition in that market. This process is also called 'perceptual mapping' or 'brand mapping'.

The idea of product/brand positioning is applicable to both industrial and consumer markets. The key aspects of this approach are based on certain assumptions. All products and brands have both objective and subjective attributes that they possess to a greater or lesser extent.

Examples of objective attributes include:

Size	Large $\Longleftrightarrow$	Small
Weight	Heavy $\Longleftrightarrow$	Light
Strength	Strong $\Longleftrightarrow$	Weak

Examples of subjective attributes include:

Value for money	Good value $\Longleftrightarrow$	Poor value
Fashion	Very fashionable $\Longleftrightarrow$	Old fashioned
Reliability	Very reliable $\Longleftrightarrow$	Very unreliable

Customers consider one or more of these attributes in choosing between products and/or brands in a given segment. Customers also have their own ideas about how the various competitive offerings of products or brands rate for each of these attributes, that is, positioning takes place in the mind of the customer.

Using these criteria it is then possible to establish:

- important attributes in choosing between competitive offerings;
- customer perceptions of the position of competitive market offerings with respect to these attributes;

High price per gram

Brand (A)

Brand (B)

Brand (C)

Very sweet ———————————————————————— Not at all sweet

Brand (E)

Brand (D)

Possible positioning
strategies for the new brand

Low price per gram

Figure 5.5 Hypothetical product positioning map for the 'instant' breakfast food market

- the most advantageous position for the company within this segment of the market.

An example illustrates this process. Imagine a company is proposing to enter the market for 'instant' breakfast foods in which there are already five competitors, A, B, C, D and E. The company should first establish what customers believe to be the salient attributes in choosing between brands in this market. In addition, the perceived position of existing competitors with respect to these attributes should also be investigated. If the important attributes have been found to be 'price' and 'taste' a possible positioning map might be drawn as shown in Figure 5.5.

Using this information, the company must now decide where to position its product within the market. One possibility is to position the new brand in the medium-price, medium-taste part of the market; another, to position it at the low-price, less sweet taste area. (These possibilities are plotted on the position map, Figure 5.5). Both of these strategies would give the new brand distinctiveness, as opposed to positioning the brand next to one of the established brands, which would mean intense competition for market share.

5.10 Developing appropriate marketing mixes

This is the final step in the appraisal of segmentation, targeting and positioning. It involves the design of marketing programmes that will support the chosen positional strategy in the selected target markets. The company must now determine how to apply the '4Ps' of its marketing mix, that is what price, product, distribution (place) and promotional strategies will be necessary to achieve the desired position in the market.

5.11 Summary

Used well, the techniques and concepts described here can contribute significantly to overall company marketing success. Market segmentation, targeting and positioning decisions are strategic rather than tactical. Later we consider these areas in relation to strategic aspects of marketing planning.

References

Abell, D.F. (1980), *Defining the Business: The Starting Point of Strategic Planning*, Englewood Cliffs, NJ: Prentice-Hall, Chapter 3.

Day, G.S. and Shocker, A.D. (1976), *Identifying Competitive Product Market Boundaries – Strategic and Analytical Issues*, Cambridge, MA: Marketing Science Institute.

Hooley, G.J., Sanders, J. and Piercy, N. (2003), Marketing strategy and competitive positioning: The key to market success, Hamel Hampstead: Prentice-Hall, p. 148.

Jobber, D. (2004), *Principles and Practices of Marketing*, 4th edition, New York: McGraw Hill, p. 219.

Kendra, P. (2000), 'How do you like your beef?', *American Demographics*, January, 35–37.

Kotler, P. (1999), *Kotler on Marketing*, New York: Free Press, pp. 149–150.

Lord, R. (2002), 'Chinas WTO entry is not a passport to profit', *Campaign*, 16 August, 24–5.

Oliver, R. (2002), Exploding the myth, *Campaign*, 16 August, 30.

Oreclin, M. (2002),'What Woman watch', *Time*, 13 May, 65–66.

Shapiro, B.P. and Bonoma, T.V. (1984), 'How to segment industrial markets', *Harvard Business Review*, May–June, pp. 104–110.

Wells, W.D. and Gubar. G. (1966), 'Life cycle concepts in marketing research', *Journal of Marketing Research*, 3(4) November, 355–363.

Wind, J. and Rangaswamy, A. (2001), 'Customerization; the next revolution in mass communication', *Journal of Interactive Marketing*, 15(1), Winter, 13–32.

Further reading

Clow, K.E. and Baack, D. (2004), *Integrated Advertising, Promotion, and Marketing Communications*, New Jersey: Person Prentice-Hall, pp. 138–151.

Sterne, J. and Priore, T. (2000), *Email Marketing Using Email to Reach Your Target Audience and Build Customer Relationships*, New York: J. Wiley & Sons, Inc.

Weinstein, A. (April 2004), *Handbook of Market Segmentation: Strategic Targeting for Business and Technology Firms*, Haworth Pr Inc.

Questions

Question 5.1

Segmentation, targeting and positioning: How do you explain the importance now attached to effective market segmentation, targeting and positioning?

Question 5.2

Segmentation bases: Using two consumer goods examples and two industrial goods examples suggest segmentation bases for each of these.

Question 5.3

Targeting: Explain each of the following types of targeting strategy:

undifferentiated marketing,
differentiated marketing,
concentrated marketing.

Discuss the considerations that should be made when selecting specific target markets.

Question 5.4

Positioning: What do you understand by the term 'product positioning'?

Making use of specific examples, outline the principles of market segmentation, market targeting and positioning.

Discuss the main range of segmentation bases that are used by marketing firms in both consumer and industrial markets.

Outline the process of market segmentation, targeting and positioning and explain the issues management will have to address at each stage of the overall process. Use examples where possible to illustrate the points made.

Explain how management's choice of targeting and positioning strategy might influence the way in which they plan and manage the firms marketing mix.

Outline the main evaluative criteria that can be used by management to assess the effectiveness of marketing segmentation variables.

Using a 'perceptual map' or 'brand map' show how marketing firms can formulate a product positioning strategy within an individual market segment.

6

Product Strategy

6.1 Introduction

A marketing plan relies on how the 'four Ps' are used in its support. Different products and markets call for different mixes, but these elements must be applied to a marketing situation whatever the emphasis given to each of them. A product strategy is especially important and it presupposes the existence of something to 'take to the market'. It is the principal focus of the marketing mix because this is what is ultimately delivered to the consumer. The product or service ('product' and 'service' being interchangeable words in this discussion) is that which gives satisfaction to the consumer, fulfilling the overall aim of marketing.

Product policy or strategy is concerned with how the product is presented to the consumer and how it will be perceived.

6.2 Defining the product

Although consumers or customers (again, interchangeable terms) pay for something specific and identifiable, they are really paying for something that incorporates promotion, availability and perceived value. This is termed a 'bundle of satisfactions' that can be tangible and intangible (see Figure 6.1). Marketers must understand and utilise this broad view of the product or any strategy is likely to be disjointed, poorly targeted and unsuccessful. The marketer's task is to organise the marketing mix in such a way as to present consumers with an assortment of 'satisfactions' identified as being appropriate to their needs. The marketing mix creates the 'product' in this wider sense, and all its efforts are devoted to delivering something that most exactly matches defined consumer wants or needs.

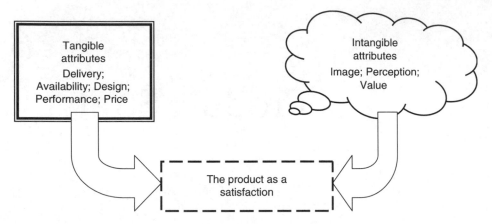

Figure 6.1 Product/service dimensions – the wider viewpoint

'Product' has been defined at its broadest level. Sometimes known as the 'extended product', this definition considers the product as the total sum of marketing effort. It is important not to restrict the view of a product to one of a physical object. It is necessary to include 'service' in any definition of the product. In fact today in most Western economies services make up most of the gross domestic product (GDP). According to Samiee (1999, p. 319), 25% of global trade is in services, this trend is growing and is expected to continue to grow. All products have some service element if only after sales service. Likewise most services have some tangible or 'product' component. Today when customers make a purchase it is often a mixture of product and service components (see Baker and Hart, 1999, Chapter 1).

A holiday is a product in the leisure market and an insurance policy is a product in the securities and investment market. To the consumer the product is a satisfaction. Although a washing machine is a physical object, the real product features in terms of customer satisfaction are labour- and time-saving. A frozen ready-prepared meal comprises physical ingredients; but the satisfaction is convenience. To an industrial buyer, the main feature of a product may be speed of delivery or technical support. The product can, therefore, be a physical object, a service or a benefit that can be either perceived or real. For the marketer, the product is a want-satisfying item; to the consumer, it is a satisfaction. Sometimes a 'product' may be a person. For example, political candidates, film stars, 'pop' stars and international sports personalities are marketed in a similar way to product marketing. Professors Philip Kotler, Gary Armstrong and others give a very informative treatment of the 'productisation' of the sporting personality 'Tiger' Woods and the fact that companies such as Nike, Buick, Disney and American Express pay more than $50 million a year to associate their products and services with Mr Woods. In fact Tiger Woods may earn as much from marketing activities as he does from golf prize money (see Cassidy, 2001; Fitzgerald, 2002; Hyman, 2000; Kotler and Armstrong, 2004).

Having clarified the concept of a product, we now describe products in terms of classification systems.

6.3 Product classification (consumer goods)

We have explained that a product has intangible as well as tangible attributes. With this perspective in mind, it is appropriate to consider products in identifiable groups. This is done through a classification that assists market planning. We also ascribe to each group a customer view of products to ascertain why and how they are purchased.

The first distinction made is between consumer and industrial goods. Industrial goods are those bought by manufacturers who use them to make a product that is in turn sold to make other products. Consumer goods are finished products that are sold to the ultimate user and these are sub-categorised as shown in Figure 6.2.

6.3.1 Convenience goods

These are relatively inexpensive items whose purchase requires little effort on the part of the consumer. The regular shopping list consists mainly of convenience goods. The decision process is clouded by the existence of brands that require the consumer to make comparisons and choices. A major task of competitive advertising is to attempt to predetermine the purchase decision for convenience goods, so the consumer buys, or subconsciously notes, a certain brand rather than first thinking of the generic product and then making a brand-choice decision.

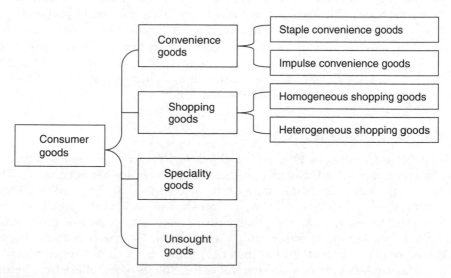

Figure 6.2 Formal classification for consumer goods

Convenience goods can be further divided into staple and impulse items. Staple convenience goods are those consumed almost every day (e.g. milk, bread and potatoes). Product differentiation for staple items tends to be negligible. If a sudden need arises for a product that might have been overlooked during a major shopping trip, then even less thought is put into the purchase decision. Small grocery stores owe much of their trade to the purchase of such overlooked items. As the name implies, there is no pre-planning with the purchase of impulse convenience goods. The decision to make an impulse purchase is made 'on the spot'. Supermarket displays and the provision of 'dump bins' are often designed to promote impulse sales.

6.3.2 Shopping goods

This classification includes major durable or semi-durable items. Because shopping goods are generally more expensive than convenience goods and purchase is less frequent, purchase is characterised by pre-planning, information search and price comparisons. The infrequency of such purchases usually means the consumer is not aware of product availability prior to purchase planning. The purchase of a furniture item, for example, will involve extensive consideration of the relative merits of the products on offer. In addition to product features the consumer will consider price, place of purchase, purchase (credit) terms, delivery arrangements, after-sales service and guarantees.

The quality of sales staff is a significant factor to success when marketing shopping goods. Promotional strategies aim to simplify the decision process for consumers by ensuring that they have a high level of brand awareness before purchase planning begins.

Shopping goods can be further classified into homogeneous or heterogeneous items. White goods, furniture, 'do-it-yourself' equipment and lawnmowers are homogeneous in nature because although they are important to the consumer, they are not really exclusive. They are goods that are basic necessities and are not too differentiated from each other in terms of price, prestige or image. Heterogeneous shopping goods are stylised and non-standard. Here, price is of less importance to the consumer than image. Behavioural factors play an important role in the purchase decision process.

6.3.3 Speciality goods

The purchase of speciality goods is characterised by extensive search and reluctance to accept substitutes once the purchase choice has been made. The market for such goods is small, but prices and profits can be high. Consumers of speciality goods pay for prestige as well as the product itself. Companies marketing these goods must create and preserve the correct image. If marketing is successful, the customer's search period can be reduced or even eliminated. For instance, some consumers will decide on a particular model of car or a designer label for clothes or jewellery long before the purchase is considered.

6.3.4 Unsought goods

Promoting and selling 'unsought' goods makes up an area of marketing that is sometimes the subject of criticism. By definition, the customer has not considered their purchase before being made aware of them, and could often do without them. Unsought goods often satisfy a genuine need that the consumer had not actively considered, for example, a life-insurance policy, or the need for a funeral arrangement. The consumer is often at a disadvantage when confronted with unsought goods because there might have been no opportunity for evaluation and comparison, so such goods should be marketed sensitively. The consumer may be suspicious of any 'special offer', which is often the hallmark of less scrupulous companies whose methods of marketing include direct mail, telephone canvassing, door-to-door calling and the practice of 'sugging' (or 'selling under the guise of market research' described in more detail in Chapter 13).

The marketing implication of the system of classification that has been described is that it accurately reflects buying behaviour for large groups of consumers. A company is likely to segment its market within a given product class, but the classification system allows for a basic understanding of buyer behaviour as a function of the product. A segmentation strategy that is consumer-orientated, as described in Chapter 5, can then be formulated using this classification basis.

6.4 Product classification (industrial goods)

A classification of industrial goods gives an insight into the uses to which goods are put and reasons for their purchase, which provides a better understanding of the market. Only certain goods classed as 'industrial' are directly essential to the manufacturing process. Machinery and raw materials are prime necessities. However, the company could not function without a whole range of other items, although not being integral to the manufacturing process, are still essential to the overall running of the company. For example, a company needs office furniture and equipment, stationery and cleaning materials, which are ancillary to the manufacturing process.

Goods and services required by industry are shown in Figure 6.3 and classified into a number of formal groups:

6.4.1 Installations

These are expensive and critical purchases like major items of plant and machinery required for the production of a manufacturer's products. If a company makes a mistake in its choice of office equipment or building maintenance services this can be costly, but it is unlikely to be a threat to the company's future. However, if a range of machinery is purchased that is subsequently found to be unsuitable, this could affect the entire production base. The purchase of installations should be the result of an extensive search process. Although price is important, it is seldom the single deciding factor. Much

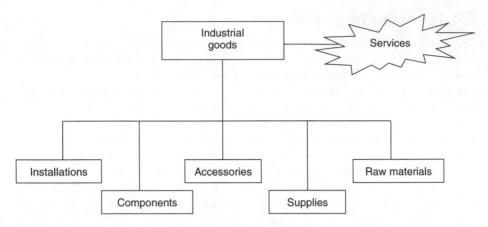

Figure 6.3 Classification of industrial goods

emphasis is placed on the quality of sales support and advice and subsequent technical support and after-sales service.

6.4.2 Accessories

Like installations, these are capital items, but they are usually less expensive and depreciated over fewer years. Their purchase is important, but not as critical as for installation purchase. Accessories include ancillary plant and machinery, office equipment and office furniture. In a haulage company, fork-lift trucks, warehousing equipment and smaller vehicles would be classified as accessories.

6.4.3 Raw materials

Buying raw materials can account for much of the time and work of the purchasing department. There is a direct relationship between raw material quality and the quality of company's own finished product, so quality, consistency of supply, service and price are important. Price is important because as such materials are purchased continuously and have a direct and continuous effect on costs.

Even in commodity markets, there are often distinctions in quality of service that can affect the speed of processing or the number of machinery break-downs. Raw material suppliers can do much in terms of differentiation to emphasise the fact that they provide a good service.

6.4.4 Component parts and materials

Supply criteria are similar to those for raw materials, and include replacement and maintenance items for manufacturing machinery. In this sense they are different to 'accessories'. This category is an important element of purchasing, particularly in assembly plants where purchases range from computer chips to casings to fascia panels to components like car bodies. It also includes products that facilitate the manufacturing process, but which do not form part of the finished product, for example, oils, chemicals, adhesives and packaging materials.

6.4.5 Supplies

These are the 'convenience goods' of industrial supply and include such items as office stationery, cleaning materials and goods required for general maintenance and repairs. Purchasing is more routine and undertaken by less senior employees. Most supplies are homogeneous in nature and price is likely to be a major factor in the purchasing decision.

6.4.6 Industrial services

The use of outside suppliers of industrial services, especially in the public sector, has risen over recent years. Many organisations find it is less expensive to employ outside agencies (with the expertise they can offer) to carry out certain tasks, than employing their own personnel. Cleaning, catering, maintenance, transport and even management consultancy are examples, and so long as suppliers meet standards required by the organisation, it makes economic sense to use outside providers whilst the company concentrates on its own areas of expertise in producing and marketing their products.

The industrial product classification system that has been described can be linked to organisational buying behaviour. Organisational purchasing has a more rigid routine than consumer purchasing. Organisational buyers deal with someone else's money, and the amounts spent are large in comparison to individual consumer purchases. This means that the consequences of error are greater. Industrial decision-making is thus more carefully planned than for consumer purchases. Industrial buyers are, however, only human, and base their decisions on a variety of less scientific criteria than those of price, quality and delivery.

6.5 Service marketing issues

Service marketing has a number of characteristics that make them more difficult to appreciate than physical goods. These are summarised as:

- Intangibility – in that they often cannot be seen, felt, tasted, smelt or heard prior to purchase (e.g. a visit to the hairdresser);
- Inseparability – relates to the fact that they are normally produced and consumed at the same time and cannot be separated from their providers (e.g. a concert performance);
- Variability – in that quality might vary depending upon who performed the service (e.g. the provision of a restaurant meal);

- Perishability – in that services generally cannot be stored, so if they are not sold at a specific point in time then the opportunity for a sale is missed for ever (e.g. a stay for a night in a room in a hotel).

In Chapter 1, we introduced the notion of the fifth 'P' as being an addition to the traditional 'four Ps', and mentioned that this stood for 'people' to ensure the smooth operation of the marketing function. In service marketing this is especially important because of its intangible nature. Booms and Bitner (1981) introduced the notion of the 7Ps of service marketing. These included the traditional 4Ps as well as people, process and physical evidence.

6.5.1 People

Services in particular are dependent on people who deliver and perform them. Personal interaction is often a key element in providing customer satisfaction and repeat business. Training is important to ensure that standards are maintained.

6.5.2 Process

Service usually demands a well-integrated means of delivery. The management of the process ensures availability and uniform quality often accompanied by immediate consumption (e.g. a visit to a hairdresser).

6.5.3 Physical evidence

This involves the appearance of the premises and factors like attention to ambience and image. The objective here is to make the service more tangible to customers.

6.6 New product development

New product development forms part of product strategy as well as being an element of overall marketing strategy. New products should be a prime concern of all levels within an organisation from top management to the shop floor.

New products are key to a company's continued survival, but their development is risky. Large sums of money might be lost, but product failure can also damage a company's image and allow other companies to gain competitive advantage. Naturally, the objective of new product strategy is to launch a successful product, but it is essential that any such strategy be designed to reduce risk throughout individual stages of development.

In consumer markets new products appear regularly. Confectionery firms, for instance, launch new products, many of which disappear shortly after the initial product promotion. Consumers are generally unaware of the work and investment that goes into product development. The development of a new car, for example, can be a multi-million pound investment, although success or failure is of little consequence to the consumer. For many companies, new products represent 'make or break' decisions.

As marketers, it is useful to consider definitions of various types of new products:

1 *Innovative products* are by definition 'new' to the market. They provide completely different alternatives to existing products in a market. Successful new drugs are 'innovative', as were laser beams and micro-processors, and in their day, the internal combustion engine and the television.

2 *Replacement products* are new to consumers, but 'replace' existing products rather than providing a total innovation. Photographic equipment has been 'replaced' constantly since cameras were invented. The compact disc player and microwave oven are replacement products ('replacing' other methods of sound reproduction and cooking). The technology and some of the component parts of such products are innovative in the marketing sense of new product definitions, but the products themselves are replacements.

3 *Imitative products* are the category into which most new products fall. Once a firm has successfully launched an innovative or replacement product, other firms usually follow. These are described as 'me too' products. Not all companies have the resources to develop new product ideas, but if a firm has resources, it is often preferable to be a market leader rather than a follower. Some companies, however, have a deliberate 'me too' approach, preferring to let another company complete costly market development before launching their imitative product. Often a powerful imitator can quickly gain market share from an innovative initiator.

4 *Relaunched products* form the final category. In more abstract terms, the nature of a product is to be found in the consumer's perception. If a product is successfully relaunched using a different marketing strategy (perhaps by changing the emphasis of product benefits) then it can be called a new product, even if its physical characteristics have not substantially altered.

The product is central to marketing strategy, because without a product, other marketing activity would be possible. Not only does the sale of the product or service provide revenue, it is the medium through which a company fulfils the marketing concept. Given the importance of new products, and the risks involved in their development, it is essential that any development programme be carried out in a predetermined and scientific manner through a new product development programme (see Danaher *et al.*, 2001, for a discussion on how the marketing mix might change for each new successive generation of new product innovations).

The notion for individual phases in new product development was developed by the American consultants Booz, Allen and Hamilton (1982), and is explained in Figure 6.4 (see also Boullier, 1989).

This study was done in 1968 and it was found that it took 58 new product or service ideas to generate one successful product. The study was repeated in

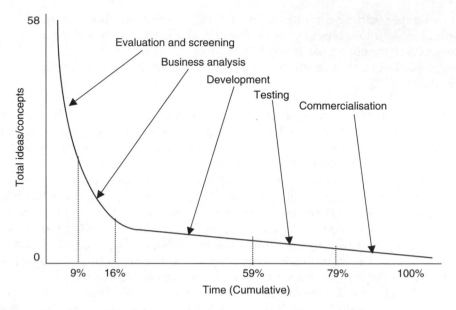

Figure 6.4 Decay curve of new product ideas

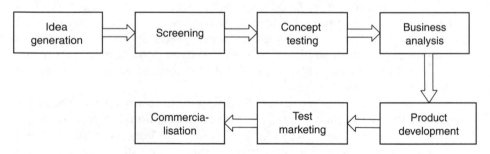

Figure 6.5 Stages in the new product development process

1981, but it was then found that it took only 7 new ideas to come up with one successful product. However, it is the 1968 study that is the most popularly cited one and it is our belief that it generally takes much more than 7 new concepts to produce a successful product.

Refinement has taken place since this experiment in relation to the stages of new product development and the process described in Figure 6.5 represents what is currently viewed as being each of the stages in this process.

Idea generation

Of prime importance here is the attitude of management and the atmosphere in which new ideas are encouraged and created. Ideas can spring from many sources including research and development or production, who are in a good position to see ways of modifying and improving the product. The sales team is well placed to report on competitive products and provide customer feedback.

Senior management, as well as creating an idea-orientated atmosphere, should hold regular meetings and brainstorming sessions concentrating on issues of new product development. Venture teams and planning committees can include a mixture of personnel from management to shop floor. Market information can provide ideas based on what other companies are doing or on changes that are taking place in the marketplace.

Screening

The aim of screening is to reduce the pool of ideas to a manageable number by identifying the most potentially viable ideas. Answers should be provided to a number of questions:

- Is there a real consumer need?
- Does the company have the resources and technical competence to market and manufacture the new product?
- Is the potential market large enough to generate profits that correspond to the company's needs?

If the answer to any of these questions is negative, then no further work should be undertaken. Many new products fail because these basic questions have not been asked.

To develop an effective screening technique, the firm should isolate factors that research has shown to be desirable in the market place. Factors desirable to the firm should be included because the firm should attempt to develop products that make best use of production and marketing strengths. An internal appraisal of the company's strengths and weaknesses, together with input from marketing research, should establish what these criteria should be. Statistical weighting techniques can be used to make the selections. Products that best satisfy these criteria should be selected for further development.

Concept testing

During this phase a small number of key decision makers from within the company, and possibly potential buyers as well, are presented with the product idea in a simple format, perhaps accompanied by drawings and a written description. This is in order to ascertain their feelings about the product's likely success in the market place. Concept testing uses few resources and it allows an organisation to test out initial reactions prior to any commitment to more costly research, design and development.

Business analysis

Business analysis is concerned with the more detailed financial, rather than practical viability concerns of the previous phase. The company should estimate demand, costs and profitability. Cost analysis needs to take into account marketing costs as well as the physical costs of raw materials and production.

Product development

Considerable time and energy would have already been expended, as well as some financial expenditure, especially if research surveys have been commissioned, but compared with the costs of physical product development, the energy and expense so far devoted to the product is likely to be small. By means of thorough pre-analysis, the company has attempted to minimise risk and isolate and validate a new product idea by this phase. During the product development stage, the company usually develops a prototype product in to confirm its validity in physical terms. Once a prototype has been developed satisfactorily, the company turns to the market place to obtain feedback on the product's suitability in terms of performance and customer attitude. The prototype should correspond as closely as possible to the envisaged production model so as to obtain accurate customer reactions. At this stage it is possible to modify or 'fine tune' the product.

It is possible to abandon the idea at this stage if market reaction is perceived to be negative. It is important that the company is ruthless in rejecting products at any stage of development. The fact that a flaw might be found in the feasibility of the product at this late stage should not influence the decision to abandon the idea, even though it might appear to be wasteful, as subsequent failure will be more costly.

If the product development stage is successful, the firm should have confidence to go ahead with a product launch. This decision is critical and requires competence and courage. If the product is rejected at this stage, a valuable opportunity might be lost. On the other hand, the decision to go ahead commits the company to the relatively large costs of production and marketing costs associated with a new product launch.

Test marketing

This is the final check on whether or not the new product is being marketed properly. It is wrong to consider a test market as a final 'screen' for a new product, because when a company enters a test market, the decision to launch the product has already been taken. The purpose of a test market is to test the appropriateness of the proposed marketing strategy and associated tactics, to refine them if necessary and to predict the effect of such strategy in terms of potential market penetration.

For consumer markets, test marketing is made simpler by the existence of Independent Television areas. These divide the UK into well-defined areas that can be used as test market areas. They are particularly appropriate when television advertising is a component of marketing strategy. It is important that the test market area should be as closely representative of the final total market as possible. If this is not the case, the objective of 'testing' is lost. Sometimes, companies will run two test markets at the same time in different geographical locations. This offers opportunities for experimentation. Variations of the marketing mix can be tested simultaneously to try to find the best balance possible within an optimum budget.

Market research agencies now provide sophisticated services to companies when they test market. In fmcg markets, it is important to establish the rate of 'penetration' for a given brand. Modelling techniques, aided by computer technology, has improved the accuracy of predictive analysis. Statistical analyses can also reduce the need for large scale testing.

Test markets are sometimes 'sabotaged' by competitors who can create artificial conditions of increased marketing activity in the test area for a short period with the intention of causing disruption and creating market conditions that are not representative. For this reason, test markets should be as unobtrusive as possible and many companies confine such test marketing activities to a small geographical location – smaller than a television area.

A number of 'test towns' exist in the UK, which are said to represent as closely as possible a microcosm of the UK. Examples are: Darlington, Croydon, Bristol and Southampton.

In industrial markets, where the number of customers may be small, testing can be achieved by initially marketing to a few co-operating customers who provide feedback before a full-scale launch takes place. There are more correctly termed 'product placement tests'. This testing technique is also used for consumer items like washing machines.

Commercialisation

Various ideas have been filtered out by now, so a viable proposition has been selected. Production, financial and commercial criteria have been examined and a suitable product, acceptable to the marketplace, has been prepared. Test marketing has permitted the company to make any final adjustments to the chosen marketing strategy. The product can now be 'commercialised' on a full-scale basis.

New products have a high failure rate and this can only be lessened through a scientific analysis of the market along the lines described. Figure 6.6 illustrates the relationship between cost and the various stages of product development.

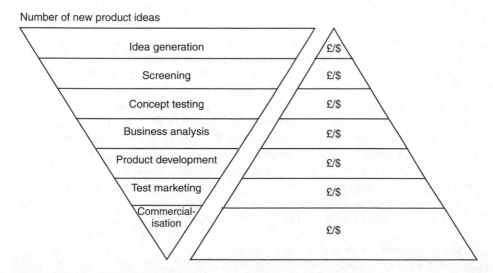

Figure 6.6 The relationship between cost and product development

Development costs increase as commercialisation comes closer. The importance of screening is re-emphasised. It is essential to reject unsuitable product ideas as early as possible to minimise development costs.

6.7 The product life cycle

The product life cycle (PLC) is central to product and marketing strategy. It is based on the premise that a new product enters a 'lifecycle' once it is launched on the market. The product has a 'birth' and a 'death' described as 'introduction' and 'decline' respectively. The intervening period is characterised by 'growth' and 'maturity'. By mapping a product's course through the market, it is possible to design marketing strategies appropriate to the relevant stage in the product's life. In addition to the stages outlined, an additional stage is that of 'saturation', which is a levelling off in sales once maturity is reached and prior to decline.

There is much enthusiasm for the PLC concept, but it must be used with caution. Not every product fits conveniently into the theoretical curve it proposes. It is also true that where a product's demise seems inevitable, there is often a great deal that creative management can do to extend the course of the curve (see Hollensen, 2003, p. 462, for a good discussion on the limitations of the PLC concept).

Figure 6.7 shows the course for the hypothetical life cycle of a product. The marketing environment is dynamic, so even basically similar products are likely to react differently during their life span. The PLC is influenced by:

1 the intrinsic nature of the product itself;
2 changes in the macro environment;
3 changes in consumer preferences, that are affected by the macro- and micro-environment;
4 competitive actions.

The 'market influence' on the shape of the curve can also influence the time span of the lifecycle that can range from weeks to decades.

A daily newspaper is cited as a product with a very short life cycle, because it is of little use the day after publication. However, this is a poor example because in considering a newspaper, the real product is the newspaper as a 'name', rather than an individual edition. Newspaper titles whilst not being perfect PLC examples (distribution strategy, for example, varies little over time) do, however, provide good examples of introduction and decline and in particular, life cycle extension. Changes in format, use of colour and changed editorial content are designed to revive flagging interest in a newspaper suffering from falling circulation figures.

In strategic terms, the task of marketing management is to:

1 estimate the likely shape of the total curve;
2 design an appropriate strategy for each stage;
3 identify the product's movement from one stage to another.

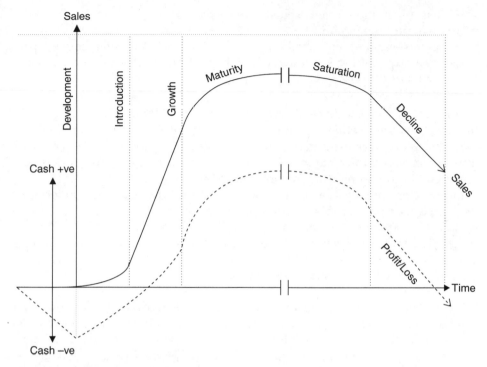

Figure 6.7 Product life cycle (PLC)

The value of the concept is that once the stage has been identified, markets are seen to display certain characteristics that suggest specific strategic reactions. We now examine the lifecycle stages that have been highlighted in Figure 6.7 along with their associated strategies.

6.7.1 Development

During this phase of course no sales are made, and as time proceeds, so development costs accrue as can be seen on the lower negative cash flow curve (see Topfer, 1995, p. 68, for a discussion on development costs).

6.7.2 Introduction

This is the period relating to new product launch and its duration depends on the product's rate of market penetration. The period ends when awareness of the product is high enough to attract wider user groups so sales then increase at a steeper rate.

Typical conditions associated with the introduction stage are:

- high product failure rate,
- relatively few competitors,

- limited distribution (often exclusive or selective),
- frequent product modifications,
- company losses because development costs have not yet been recouped, promotional expenditure is relatively high in relation to sales and economies of scale are not yet possible.

The goal at this stage is to create awareness. This usually involves a disproportionate level of marketing expenditure relative to sales revenue. This should be regarded as an investment in the product's future. Promotion is the marketing mix element used to create this product awareness. The sales function is also important in communicating the product's benefits to users.

Introductory pricing strategy will depend on the type of product in terms of its degree of distinctiveness. The company may wish to achieve high sales levels in a short space of time or slowly establish a profitable niche in the market place. Price is also affected by competitive activity as this determines how long any product distinctiveness is likely to last.

The company has two strategic options:

1 A skimming pricing strategy involves the application of a high price to a small target group of consumers (typically innovators and early adopters as discussed in the previous chapter). Whilst the product remains distinctive, growth can be encouraged by a planned series of progressive price reductions.
2 A penetration pricing strategy to attract the largest possible number of new buyers early in the product's life. This involves pricing the product at a low level and is appropriate where demand is elastic and high levels of competitive activity.

Skimming and penetration strategies are discussed in detail in Chapter 7. In both cases, the role of pricing is to establish the product in such a way as to permit further strategy to be implemented in the subsequent stages. A skimming approach should 'set the scene' for product distinctiveness to be retained as long as possible. Whilst profits are not necessarily forthcoming during introduction, the introductory pricing strategy should prepare for profitability in the future as discussed in Chapter 7.

Distribution decisions are determined by expected penetration or skimming and it is important that the product is available to the intended market. Out-of-stock situations provide competitors with opportunities to take market share that can be costly to win back.

6.7.3 Growth

During growth the product is still vulnerable to failure (although most failures occur early during this stage). Competitive products, launched by more powerful companies, can enter the market at this stage and pose a sufficient threat to cause some companies to withdraw.

The characteristics of growth are:

1 more competitors and less product distinctiveness;
2 more profitable returns;
3 steeply rising sales;
4 company or product acquisition by larger competitors.

Promotional expenditure still features strongly because this is the best time to acquire market share. It should, however, be at a level that does not drain profits, although it is not unusual for high levels of expenditure to continue throughout growth to achieve profitable market dominance during the maturity stage. The emphasis of promotional effort changes from creating product awareness to specific brand or trade name promotion.

Distribution retains its importance during growth. In FMCG markets in particular, success often depends on finding shelf space in retail outlets, although these now tend to be dominated by a small number of operators as discussed in Chapter 8. Once a 'hierarchy' of brand leaders has been established, powerful buyers in retail multiples may attempt to rationalise their list of suppliers. Distribution is a key factor in such decisions, because retailers will wish to keep their stock levels to realistic levels. In other markets, distribution is equally important, because during growth, suppliers are in competition with each other to establish dealership and distributive outlet agreements.

A company should attempt to optimise the product's price during growth, especially if a skimming policy is in operation, and towards the end of this period, profits are usually at their highest. The end of growth is often characterised by reduced prices at the end of skimming (even though profits may be still high as a result of higher volumes). As the growth period moves towards maturity, market shares tend to stabilise and a hierarchy of brand or market leaders will probably have emerged.

6.7.4 Maturity

The majority of a company's product portfolio is normally in the maturity stage of the product life cycle. Much marketing activity is devoted to this stage.

The major characteristics of the maturity stage are:

1 sales continuing to grow, but at a much decreased rate,
2 attempts to differentiate and re-differentiate products,
3 prices falling in battles to retain market share. Profits falling correspondingly,
4 increasing brand and inventory rationalisation amongst retailers and distributors,
5 marginal manufacturers retiring from the market when faced with severe competition and reduced margins.

A key task of marketing strategy during maturity is to retain market share. Promotion's role should be to reinforce brand loyalty.

It should be emphasised that exponential market growth has ceased by this stage. Any growth is achieved at the expense of competitors. There is, therefore, a need for sustained promotional activity, even if only to retain existing customers. Deciding levels of promotional expenditure can be a problem in view of contracting profit margins.

In line with the aims of promotion, distribution strategy should be designed to retain outlets. A retail outlet or distributorship that is lost during maturity is unlikely to be easily regained at a later stage. To this end, the major thrust of promotional effort may move from consumers towards distributors.

6.7.5 Saturation

This stage is the latter part of the maturity phase, but it does have characteristics that make it different. It is where the peak of 'maturity' has been passed and just before final decline. Saturation is the period when 'price wars' are common and lower priced producers have entered the marketplace, as they have been able to replicate the technology to be able to manufacture, often in low labour cost countries. Price wars should be avoided, although a problem is that the market might be so saturated that this is the inevitable result. The result is an overall reduction in revenue for all participants, although it is good for consumers. The aim of price-cutting should be to increase purchases sufficiently to offset any revenue loss, but the reality is that it is often a signal for more established players to exit from the marketplace before decline.

6.7.6 Decline

The shape of the PLC curve is theoretical and should not be regarded as inevitable, but persistently falling sales signify the decline stage of the product. Market intelligence should be able to identify and predict this phenomenon. Consumer preferences may have changed or innovative products may have displaced existing products.

Characteristics of decline are:

1 sales falling continually for the total period;
2 a further intensification of price cutting;
3 producers deciding to abandon the market.

The decision to abandon a market poses problems for the firm and is often made too late. However, some companies consider it worthwhile extending the product's life well into decline whilst the number of competitors is falling, in the belief that in a declined market there will be few competitors, but there is still residual demand. In such circumstances it is often the case that price reductions can be halted, or prices can even be increased, as there are few or no competitors to make a challenge. For those who remain until this phase, attention is likely to move from active marketing to cost control. Cost control and cost reduction is always an important element of management activity, but during decline this may be the only way to maintain profitability.

6.8 The PLC as a management tool

There are a number of detractors to the notion of the PLC, and like any theory it can pose a problem if it is taken too literally (e.g. a product might be prematurely discarded if there is a downturn in sales in the belief that it has started to decline, but what management might be witnessing is a temporary downturn at the end of the introduction stage). The key to successful use of the concept is an ability to accurately identify the transition from one stage to another that requires the company to use marketing research and intelligence. Management will then have the framework for using the PLC as a long-term strategic-planning tool. In particular, use of the PLC provides two valuable benefits:

1 a predictable course of product development for which appropriate strategies can be planned and budgeted;
2 the scope to plan beyond the life of the existing product.

In some cases there might be an overlap in the lives of two products. The launch of the second product should ideally be funded from the profits of the first product's growth period. The timing of a new product launch should be synchronised within the life cycles of existing products, enabling the company to perpetuate its presence in the market.

The PLC provides a 'framework' for planning, but management should be master of the theory. In difficult trading conditions it may be judicious to bring the product's life to a premature end to afford the company a better allocation of resources. Alternatively, the product need not necessarily fall into decline at all; its life can be extended by finding new end uses or markets.

Normally, an extension of the life cycle does not involve too many product modifications. If the basic product is altered radically, it can be argued that this is a new product, albeit not an innovative one.

In understanding the PLC concept, one should distinguish between the specific and the generic product. Following the launch of a truly innovative product (e.g. the video recorder) many imitative products emerged. Some of these followed the typical PLC pattern and others did not. This depended on the skill of company management and strategic decisions as to their future course in the marketplace. As a generic product, the video recorder followed a typical life cycle course, with a stretched maturity point, representing replacement buyers, until an innovative alternative was launched in the form of DVD recorders (see also Burgelman, 2000, for a discussion of innovation of other types of communication technologies and the work of De Bens, 2002, which covers a related area).

The identification of the transition period from one stage to another is difficult. Where innovative products are concerned, there will be no empirical data on previous products, so the product represents a unique situation. If the concept is adhered to too rigidly, management planners may 'think' themselves into successive stages and thus into decline which may not be the case. Critics contend that the PLC becomes a self-fulfilling prophecy and that management is liable to miss opportunities because of a too-dogmatic approach to the theory. Marketing is a creative process and the PLC concept is only meant to provide a guide to strategy.

6.9 The product adoption process

The product adoption process has been introduced in Chapter 4 in the context of buyer behaviour. The PLC concept has considered the product in relation to the market place. From the product adoption process, described in Figure 6.8, we can learn something about users or consumers who are the targets of marketing strategy. The relationship is simple, yet positive enough to enable us to draw conclusions about the characteristics of consumers in each adopter category. The theory is applicable to both industrial and consumer markets. It is important to remember that consumers will not necessarily fall into the same

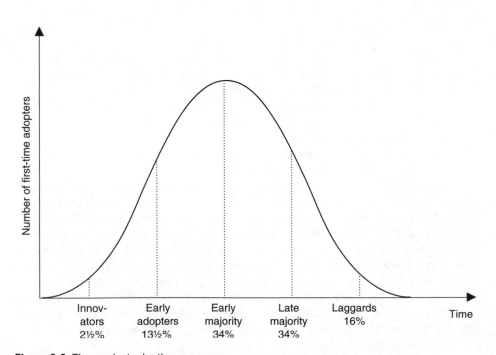

Figure 6.8 The product adoption process

category for all products. An early adopter of a photographic innovation could be a laggard in the garden-tool market.

The rate at which the product moves through these adopter categories is termed the 'diffusion of innovations', that is, the extent to which each adopter category successively influences the next towards adoption. This theory is widely acknowledged in marketing. Chapter 4 has already dealt with the diffusion process in terms of discussion of the various adopter categories, and this short discussion has examined it in the context of the product.

6.10 Product (and market) management

Product management is the function responsible for the 'fortunes' of the product, and covers tactical and strategic marketing issues as the product follows its course along the lifecycle curve. The Managing Director is of course responsible for managing the whole company, and managing the marketing of products is delegated to the Marketing Director or Manager. The Marketing Manager then delegates responsibility further throughout the marketing function. Just as many companies employ an advertising manager or a marketing research manager or a sales manager, there is often justification for employing somebody whose role is specifically concerned with products or brands. In FMCG companies, the term 'brand management' is usually substituted for product management.

How marketing is organised depends on the type of company, the nature of its products and the markets in which it operates. A simple marketing structure is outlined in Figure 6.9.

As the number of products to be marketed increases problems might develop, as responsibility for individual products may become blurred. Some products may become neglected and marketing mix elements might be misallocated.

A product-management structure offers a solution to this problem in that a manager is made directly responsible for each product's success and for the allocation of marketing resources. It is the product manager who decides the

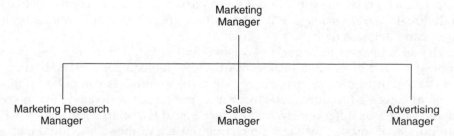

Figure 6.9 A functional marketing organisation

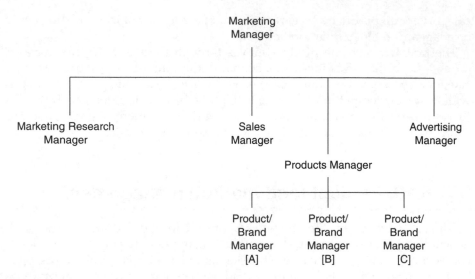

Figure 6.10 A product/brand management structure

level and type of support required from the marketing functions. Figure 6.10 shows the product manager's position in relation to other functional marketing specialists.

A products manager will oversee the overall management of the company's products or brands and is responsible to the marketing manager. In a large company, a group product manager might take control of a range of similar products (e.g. frozen foods, agri-chemicals or cosmetics). Product (or brand) managers serve under that person with responsibility for individual brands. In this way, control and management of the product is focused. The product manager is responsible for all aspects of the product's welfare, through liaison with other functional managers within the marketing function.

A product management system is appropriate when companies have a large number of products, or where products differ widely in nature. A criticism of this system is that product managers are not functional experts and must rely on liaison with the other functional managers to execute their ideas. This can lead to conflicts of interest between these parties and also to conflict between individual product managers. It is important, therefore, that individual roles are clearly delineated.

The term 'market manager' is occasionally used in a similar philosophical context to that of product management. Here, the company markets similar products, but to diverse customer groups. An example is computer applications to banks, educational establishments, public sector, retailing and so on. Here, user needs differ widely, so the overall head is a 'markets manager' with an individual 'market manager' in charge of each of these individual market groupings.

6.11 Product line and product mix

The product mix is the total assortment of products that a company markets. So that this assortment can be more easily managed, products can be grouped into product lines or groups of products that are similar in terms of their functions or because they are sold to similar groups of customers.

A food manufacturer might market a range of beverages as well as other products like convenience foods. Beverages can be arranged as a product line. It may even be appropriate to arrange different beverages into their own individual product lines. Thus, the coffee product line might include different varieties of instant coffee, coffee beans, ground coffee and coffee sachets. The length of a product line will then denote the number of individual products in the line; the width of the product mix denotes how many lines go to make up the mix.

This system allows management to look objectively at its product mix and decide whether or not certain lines should be 'lengthened', 'shortened' or even 'deleted'. As well as allowing the development of line strategies, this organised method of looking at the products of a company shows where profits are being made. These profits can then be directly related to marketing expenditure.

 ## 6.12 Summary

A study of the product is inevitably bound up with other areas of marketing, in particular with consumer and organisational buying behaviour, and this is a topic that has been covered in Chapter 4. In particular, the chapter highlighted how new products are accepted by purchasers, and to how information relating to these new products is disseminated throughout the marketing system. This chapter has now related this knowledge to its applicability to the notion of the product life cycle concept.

Another area that is linked up with the product is that of market segmentation and product positioning and this was the focus of Chapter 5.

The whole area of portfolio analysis is one of strategy that is tied in closely to product. A full discussion of this aspect takes place in Chapter 17.

 ## References

Baker, M. and Hart, S. (1999), *Product Strategy and Management*, Harlow: Prentice-Hall.

Booms, B.H. and Bitner, M.J. (1981), 'Marketing strategies and organisational structures for service firms', in: Donnelly, J. and George, W.R. (Eds), *Marketing of Services*, American Marketing Association (AMA).

Booz, Allen and Hamilton (1982), *New Products Development in the 1980's*, Booz, Allen and Hamilton Inc., New York.

Boullier, D. (1989), 'Du bon usage d'une critique du modèle diffusioniste'. Discussion prétexte et concepts de Everett M. Rogers'. *Reseanx: Communication, technologie, société*, 36, 31–51.

Burgelman, J.-C. (2000), 'Innovation of communication technologies: some general lessons for the future from the past', in: Cammaerts, B. and Burgelman, J.-C. (eds), *Beyond Competition: Broadening the Scope of Telecommunications Policy*, Brussel: VUB University Press, pp. 229–238.

Cassidy, H. (2001), 'Target, Tiger Swing TV Deal with TCG', *Brandweek*, December, p. 11.

Danaher, P.J., Hardie, B.G.S. and Putsis, W.P. (2001), 'Marketing-mix variables and the diffusion of successive generations of a technological innovation', *Journal of Marketing Research*, 28, 501–514.

De Bens, E. (2002), 'Het digitale communicatietijdperk maatschappelijke implicaties', in: Verleye, G. and Doolaege, B. (eds), *Nieuwe communicatietechnologie in Vlaanderen*, Een doorlichting: Academia Press, Gent, pp. 1–24.

Fitzgerald, K. (2002), 'Buick Rides the Tiger', *Advertising Age*, April 15, p. 41.

Hollensen, S. (2003), Marketing Management: A Relationship Approach, Financial Times, pp. 462–463.

Hyman, M. (2000), 'The yin and yang of the Tiger effect', *Business Week*, October 16, p. 110.

Kotler, P. and Armstrong, G. (2004), *Principles of Marketing*, 10th International edition, Person Prentice-Hall, p. 282.

Levitt, T. (1983), *Differentiation of Anything: The Marketing Imagination*, London: Collier Macmillan, pp. 72–93.

Rogers, E. (1962), *Diffusion of Innovations*, New York: The Free Press, p. 162.

Samiee, S. (1999), 'The internationalisation of services: trends, obstacles and issues', *Journal of Services Marketing*, 13(4/5), 319–328.

Topfer, A. (1995), 'New products – cutting time to market', *Long Range Planning*, 28(2), 61–78.

▌ Further reading

Blythe, J. (2001), *Essentials of Marketing*, Chapter 6, Products, Branding and Packages, Pearson Educational Ltd.

Crawford, M.C. and Di Benedetto, C.A. (2000), *New Products Management*, 6th edition, Boston: Irwin McGraw-Hill.

Hollensen, S. (2003), *Marketing Management – A Relationship Approach*, Chapter 11, Product and service decisions, Prentice-Hall.

Keegan, W.J. and Green, M.S. (2000), *Global Marketing*, 2nd edition, Chapter 11, Product and Branding Decisions, Prentice-Hall.

Kotler, P., Armstrong, G., Saunders, J. and Wong, V. (2001), *Principles of Marketing*, 3rd edition, Chapter 14, New Product Development and Product Life Cycle Strategies and Chapter 15, Marketing Services, Prentice-Hall.

McGrath Michael, E. (2001), *Product Strategy for High Technology Companies*, Boston: McGraw-Hill.

Nobil, M. (2002), *Business Superbrands: An Insight into the World's Strongest B2B Brands*, Brand Council: London.

Plamer, A. (2000), *Principles of Marketing*, Chapter 9, The Product and Chapter 10, Innovation and New Product Development, Oxford: Oxford University Press.

Wright, R. (2001), *Marketing: Origins, Concepts, Environment*, London: Thomson, Chapters 5–6.

Wright, R. (2004), Business to Business marketing – A Step by Step Guide, Prentice-Hall, Financial Times, Chapter 5, pp. 204–251.

Questions

Question 6.1

New products: Your company has traditionally been conservative with regard to new product development and has tended to wait until others develop and market products before venturing into that area themselves. However, your research and development department has come up with a new product idea that is revolutionary in terms of solving a relatively simple problem and they feel that the time is right to exploit this new product now. They are now seeking your advice as to what to do next. What suggestions can you make?

Question 6.2

Product classification: Prepare an outline for a presentation you have been requested to give upon the subject of the marketing implications of new product development. You have been specifically requested to concentrate your discussion on the advantages and disadvantages of:

- Innovative products
- Replacement products
- Imitative products

Question 6.3

Product life cycle: A key element of the role of a product manager is to accurately identify the transition of products from one stage of the product life cycle to another. Prepare a report outlining different strategies to be adopted at different product life cycle stages for the following types of product:

- a new breakfast cereal,
- an innovative light weight construction material,
- a bank's recently introduced long term investment account that carries a high rate of interest without risk of losing any of the capital.

Question 6.4

Product definition: The 'extended product' is a definition that considers the product as the total sum of marketing effort. Why is it important not to restrict the view of a product to one of a physical object? Why is it also necessary to include 'service' in any definition of the product?

Using a product of your choice explain the process of new product development from the inception of the original product idea to its eventual commercialisation and launch.

Describe an appropriate process of new product development (NPD) that marketing management should follow to avoid the possibility of product failure at the commercialisation stage of the NPD programme.

Explain the concept of the product life cycle (PLC) and comment on its practical usefulness as a strategic marketing tool.

Demonstrate how the components of the marketing mix and their relative importance alters within each stage of the PLC.

7

Pricing

7.1 Introduction

The end price of a company's products or services determines of the amount of money the company can make. Company objectives are guided and influenced by market conditions and price must be a function of such conditions, so the achievement of company objectives often necessitates compromise over the amount of profit that can be realised. The importance of price as a function of the marketing mix varies from market to market, but it is not always the most important factor in the buyer's decision-making process. For the seller, as price determines the amount of profit or loss, it is crucial that pricing is approached in a disciplined and orderly manner. Price provides revenue, whilst other elements of the marketing mix represent costs (see Jobber, 2004, p. 375).

Cost-orientated approaches to pricing are sometimes criticised. This is justified in that costs do not necessarily reflect market conditions or company goals at least in the longer term. Marketing strategies can be designed that put costs into the perspective of a long-range strategic approach. For example, the acquisition of a high market-share may drive down costs in the long term. An image-building strategy might invoke high costs initially, but it allows the company to charge higher prices in the long term. A purely cost-orientated approach to pricing might be too narrow as a basis for pricing. Cost is, however, the logical starting point, and prices charged must ultimately exceed costs if the company is to remain in business. Tellis explains:

> 'A *strategy* is a broad plan of action by which an organisation intends to reach its goal. A *policy* is more of a routine managerial guide to be implemented when a given situation arises. Giving certain price discounts when a certain amount of product is ordered in an example of a *policy*.'

Equipped with this awareness of costs, companies should consider price in terms of marketing objectives that are also designed to achieve financial goals.

The key to pricing is 'realism'. Pricing objectives should be well defined, attainable and measurable. Having laid down objectives, the company can use a variety of pricing strategies to achieve them.

7.2 The nature of price

Whether we are end consumers or involved directly in the commercial process, price affects living standards and work and ultimately the functioning of the economy. As marketers we are interested in the role of price in the buyer–seller relationship. The buyer views price as a cost that is paid in return for a series of satisfactions. Whatever these satisfactions, price itself is usually perceived as a negative factor. The seller sees price as a means of cost recovery and profit. Both buyer and seller need to understand how price works for pricing structures to be implemented and managed efficiently. Economics provides a starting point from which such an understanding can be gained.

From economic theory we learn about the related concepts of 'utility', 'value' and 'price'. Utility is an aspect of an item that makes it capable of satisfying a want or a need. Value is the expression used to quantify utility, whilst price describes the number of monetary units the value represents.

A further assumption of economic theory is that of the downward sloping demand curve, or the assumption that customers will buy more of a product as price falls as shown in Figure 7.1.

Conversely, the supply curve is the opposite way around, the assumption being that suppliers will be willing to supply greater amounts at a higher price and this is illustrated in Figure 7.2.

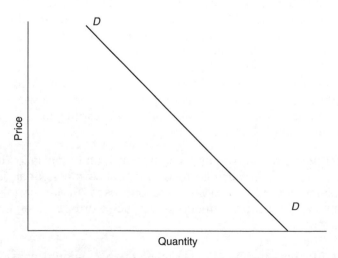

Figure 7.1 Downward sloping demand curve

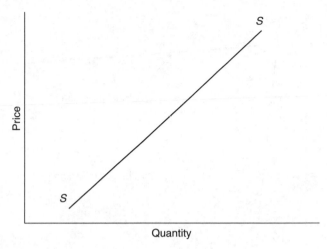

Figure 7.2 Upward sloping supply curve

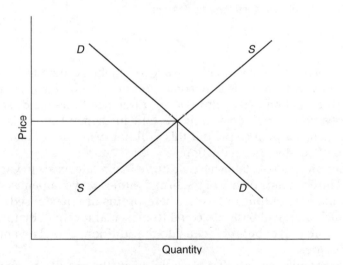

Figure 7.3 Demand and supply curves showing market price

Where demand and supply intersect is the market price, and this is shown in Figure 7.3. It can be seen that at price 'P', quantity 'Q' will be the amount demanded.

When a demand schedule is plotted companies must consider elasticity of demand. Elasticity describes the sensitivity of consumers to changes in price. A product can be said to have elastic demand when price changes greatly affect levels of demand. Inelastic demand is relatively insensitive to price changes. These two notions are explained in Figure 7.4.

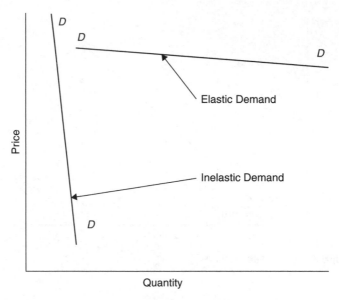

Figure 7.4 Examples of elastic and inelastic demand

Very few products have totally elastic or inelastic demand. Even when demand is elastic, there is usually some point on the demand curve where a further price reduction makes little or no difference to demand. Determining the exact position of this point is important in demand analysis, because it makes little sense to reduce price if this will not result in an increase in sales sufficient to offset the price reduction.

Companies must also establish a cost curve that relates costs to varying levels of output. The economic theory of the firm assumes that companies will always attempt to increase output to levels where profits are maximised. This is the point at which marginal costs are equal to marginal revenue, that is, when the cost of one more unit of output is equal to the addition to total revenue that this last unit provides.

A final economic concept that is explored in the marketing context is the notion of 'oligopoly', as many companies, especially in the FMCG field, operate in near oligopolistic situations. In such circumstances, there are relatively few sellers who produce similar goods and produce below their maximum capacity. Price as an instrument of competition is less effective, so rather than engaging in 'price wars', manufacturers place more emphasis on 'non-price competition'. This is typified by attempts to brand products and engage in advertising or 'above-the-line' promotion. Generally, advertising tends to be defensive as the market is saturated and demand is relatively inelastic as it reflects regular demand and not new or increased levels of demand. Pricing fixing and collusive pricing agreements by oligopolistic companies is illegal under EU and USA competition laws (see Sherwood, 2003).

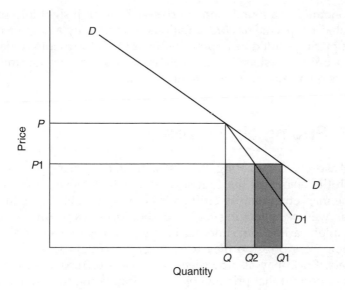

Figure 7.5 The concept of oligopoly

Examples of such products are washing detergents, breakfast cereals, canned and packaged soups, soft drinks, car tyres, aluminium producers and petrol companies. Figure 7.5 illustrates the concept of 'oligopoly'. It can be seen from demand curve 'D' that at price 'P', quantity 'Q' is be the amount that would be demanded under normal demand considerations. When price is reduced to 'P1', the expectation would be that 'Q-Q1' would be the additional amount demanded. However, under oligopoly, the demand curve kinks to 'D1' and effectively becomes more inelastic, which means that 'Q-Q2' is the additional amount demanded, so in such circumstances, price competition is less effective in producing more sales.

If a company lowers its prices it must expect competitors to lower their prices. Given inelastic industry demand, the company's own demand curve is relatively more inelastic at lower prices. Oligopolistic situations not only apply to product groups and industries, but to local markets as well. A community might be served by, for example, many petrol stations or hairdressing establishments competing for local custom, and in such cases their behaviour equates to oligopoly.

Only the simplest assumptions that economic theory makes about behaviour in the marketplace have been described here. Students of economics will appreciate that many variations in this behaviour can be described, and marketers will be aware that economics only describes markets to a limited extent. Economics largely ignores the effects of sociological and psychological influences on the consumer. However, when considering price, knowledge of economics is essential as a starting point for understanding the market. The fact that most marketing textbooks include a section on economics in relation to price illustrates this importance.

With economics as a foundation, marketers have an insight into pricing that can be related to specific pricing situations. As with any aspect of marketing, the task of pricing should be approached in a formal, structured manner. This helps to ensure professionalism as well as affording an opportunity to 'look back' if revision or modifications are necessary.

▮ 7.3 Pricing objectives

As with all aspects of marketing, the first stage in the pricing process should be to establish the objectives the company wishes to achieve. Price is an instrument of the marketing mix that differs from other mix elements in that it is a financial as well as marketing tool. We should be aware that some pricing objectives might arise from 'non-marketing' sources. For example, in public limited companies pressure may exist to pay a certain level of dividend to shareholders. Price may also be seen as a means of recouping recent investment. It is important that pricing objectives originating from outside the marketing department are established in conjunction with marketing strategy. There is little point in planning the role of price in the marketing mix if finance decrees that price should achieve a certain level of profit regardless of the marketing implications that such a price may have. Pricing objectives should, therefore, be set in cooperation with other departments so conflict with corporate objectives does not arise.

Most pricing objectives are set with the marketplace in mind as the market is a reality of business life, but these objectives should also reflect the financial objectives of the firm. Today many markets are globalised with not only global customers but also global suppliers. A global customer such as Microsoft may wish to initiate a global purchasing contract form its suppliers or demand it is charged the same price for component parts no matter where the part ids sourced from in the world. A good discussion of the effects of increased globalisation on pricing policies is provided by Narayandas *et al.* (2000).

7.3.1 Return-on-investment

A fundamental pricing objective in efficiently managed organisations is to achieve a target return-on-investment from net sales. When costs have been established, the company decides on the percentage profit it wants to achieve. Whilst this percentage may remain constant, fluctuations in demand will affect the total value of the profits made. To achieve this objective successfully and consistently, the company is likely to be a market leader, and is less vulnerable to changes in the market place than its competitors. Achievement of this objective is relatively easy to measure, but in reality it is not always practical to achieve for an individual product. Most companies have a clear idea of the annual revenue they need to realise, and can estimate the profit margins needed to achieve this. This overall profit margin is usually the result of several pricing strategies applied to a variety of products in response to changes in the market place. There is sometimes confusion between a 'target return' pricing objective and 'cost plan' that is a pricing technique.

7.3.2 Improvement in market share

Improvement or maintenance of market share is a market-based pricing objective. A firm might feel it is earning a reasonable return on investment, but if the market is expanding, existing prices may not encourage a corresponding improvement in market share. A price modification (i.e. a reduction) could increase sales in an expanding market to a level where the return-on-investment increases in monetary terms although percentage return may have fallen. The acquisition of market share for its own sake is a contentious issue. It appears though that high market share companies enjoy advantages over smaller competitors, and market share is regarded as the key to profitability. Certainly, market share is an accepted indicator of a firm's general health and a decline in share is a significant danger signal.

Maintenance of market share is at least a key to survival, and price carries much of the burden of responsibility in a marketing mix designed to maintain or improve market share. In terms of measuring success, it is not difficult to establish the size of the market, and estimate respective market shares.

7.3.3 Maintaining price stability

A pricing policy with the objective of maintaining price stability and margins might seem to detract from marketing creativity and free choice. Although it is true that some products can be promoted and priced as prestige items, most firms have little influence over the general level of prices in a market. They must organise their businesses so that costs are at a level that will permit them to fall in line with the prices charged by market leaders. Prices tend, therefore, to be 'market led' with little scope for deviation from established price structures.

Provided a company's returns are considered adequate, there is considerable justification for maintaining the status quo by meeting competitive prices established by the market leaders. The market or price leaders do not stand to gain very much by distancing their prices too much (either upwards or downwards) from smaller competitors. Price adjustments are usually only made in response to changing market conditions.

Certain conditions may require an aggressive approach to pricing. During the introduction and growth stages of the product life cycle, price usually plays a less significant role. During maturity and growth (where most products are situated) the major 'price wars' are usually fought. Whilst changes in market share can be achieved by price-cutting, as a general rule, this is to be avoided as it works to the detriment of everyone.

The idea of a 'price leader' does not imply a monopolistic situation, or that one company is exploiting the market because of its position of power. The position of leadership is not absolute; it can be threatened and will certainly be attacked by competitors if the power is abused. Finally, it should be noted that price leadership does not equate to absolute authority. Many price leaders are not the principal market shareholders, although they will be major participants. Price leadership does not render a firm impervious to competitors who engage in non-price competition. Companies can improve their market share by shrewd use of the marketing mix, whilst at the same time pursuing a price stability objective. The party with the ultimate influence in price setting is usually customers, although they have less influence in some markets than others. For example, the market for petrol is one where the consumer has no real choice of substitutes and consequently little influence on price.

7.3.4 Controlling cash flow

In Chapter 6 we discussed how pricing objectives vary according to the product's position in the product life cycle. Financial managers will be particularly anxious to recoup the often very high costs of development as early as possible in the product's life cycle. Controlling cash flow is, therefore, a common pricing objective. The financial manager may be willing to bear development and marketing costs of launching a new product, but will also highlight a variety of other demands on the company's limited resources.

7.3.5 Growth in sales

The advantages of price stability objectives notwithstanding, at certain times, and under certain conditions, a legitimate pricing objective is simply to achieve growth in sales. Providing the firm appreciates the competitive conditions under which it operates, price (in particular a low price) is probably the most effective competitive weapon at its disposal.

If rapid growth in sales is called for, price can be used as the major component of the marketing mix. Such a move should be made with caution. Sudden price reductions may affect the effectiveness of other marketing mix variables. In addition, it is easier to implement a growth-in-sales objective by price reductions, than it is to regain previous higher pricing levels.

7.3.6 Profit maximisation

Most companies have an overall pricing objective of profit maximisation. This runs parallel with any other pricing objectives that a company might employ. Market conditions usually make it impossible to maximise profits on all products, in all markets, simultaneously. For this reason, some companies employ pricing techniques that may promote sales, but reduce profits on certain products in the short term, with the overall objective being to maximise profit on total sales of the company. Here, the company's product mix should be considered as a unit rather than a series of products whose profits should be maximised individually.

The term 'profit maximisation' is often unjustly connected with exploitation. A company needs to make profits to survive. Attempts to overcharge are usually counterbalanced by competitors as well as buyers. The moral issues to which this gives rise are discussed in Chapter 15 under ethical issues.

7.4 Essential steps in price determination

To ensure profitability, prices must ultimately exceed costs. It is logical, there-fore, to consider cost as the first stage in price planning. In fact, the problem should be approached from the opposite direction. In line with marketing ori-entation in general, pricing strategy should begin with the consumer and work 'backwards' to the company. Costs cannot be ignored, but pricing must be consumer or customer orientated, the customer being the person who decides whether or not the product is purchased. The following steps should be followed.

7.4.1 Identify the potential consumer or market

This step may appear to be too obvious to be worthy of mention, but its purpose is to focus the planner's mind on the market from the outset. It also prevents price from being viewed as separate to other marketing mix elements.

7.4.2 Demand estimation

Likely volume of sales will directly affect a manufacturer's costs and the price necessary for profit maximisation. Demand analysis is a skilled process that is dealt with in detail in Chapter 14 that covers sales forecasting. Ideally, demand analysis should provide the company with a schedule of predicted demand lev-els at differing prices. This establishes the position and slope of the demand curve. The price a company is able to charge for a certain product will vary from market to market and also within markets and between different market segments. This variation calls for comprehensive market research before a decision is taken to enter a particular market. Both qualitative and quantitative primary research techniques can be used and these are discussed in detail in Chapter 13.

Demand analysis should provide the following basic information, from which it should be possible to construct a demand schedule showing levels of demand at varying price levels:

1 *General marketing information* – demographic and psychographic data that helps planners to understand consumer needs and preferences.
2 *Income* – in general, demand for a product rises in line with increases in disposable income. The effect of prosperity varies according to the nature of

the product and the company should try to establish the income sensitivity of demand for their products.

3 *Substitute products* – knowledge of the availability of substitutes will help the company form an opinion of price elasticity of demand.

The results of demand analysis must be used with caution; statistical methods are based on hypotheses that can only estimate real life behaviour. Those responsible for setting prices should be aware that potential customers may say that they would pay a certain price for a product, but in reality their behaviour might be totally different. A further consideration is that of the expected price. This is the value that consumers, consciously or subconsciously, place on a given product.

Regardless of their inherent or built-in value (from the producer's point-of-view) certain products fall into a group where the consumer 'expects' them to be at a certain price level. The manufacturer may price products too high or too low relative to the expected price. Irrespective of production and marketing costs, consumers would not, for example, expect to pay a very low price for a luxury item; a low price might even detract from the quality image of such a product.

7.4.3 Anticipating competitor prices and reactions

Consumers (both final consumers and other manufacturers) can easily compare selling prices, but this does not give any proper insight into competitive manufacturing pricing structures, as it relates to various members of the marketing channel. Buyers can compound this difficulty by 'inventing' 'special prices' and 'non-existent discounts', not really offered by competitors, but stated as being real during the negotiation process to help when bargaining for a lower price.

When products are easily initiated and markets are relatively easy to enter, the price of existing or potential competitive products assumes major importance.

Even when products have substantial distinctiveness, it is not usually too long before other companies will enter the market.

Competition stems from three major sources:

1 'Head-on' competition from directly similar products.
2 Competition from substitute products.
3 Competition from products that are not directly related, but which compete for the same disposable income. For instance, watch manufacturers are often in competition with fountain pen manufacturers because their products are often bought as gifts. Hand knitting is mainly a leisure activity, so yarn producers face competition from other 'hand-craft' hobbies to seek the potential customer's free time. This aspect of competition is often overlooked when setting prices.

7.4.4 Market share analysis

If the company is seeking a significant market share, the price for the product will need to be competitive. Management should ensure that production capacity is sufficient to meet demand that this anticipated market share might create. If production capacity is limited, there is little point in setting low prices that might attract orders that cannot be fulfilled.

The steps discussed so far in price determination have been concerned with the market place, rather than the internal workings of the firm. Market considerations should be the major determinant of price, so it would be illogical to develop a product whose price did not fall approximately in line with competitive prices. The level of potential demand at given price levels is, therefore, an important consideration. Marketers sometimes charge low prices to make profit else where. Many supermarkets have a few products that are very cheap which act as so called 'loss leaders' and draw customers into the store. It is the total profit on the shopping 'trolley' of goods that management is really interested in. By using loss leaders and changing higher prices on other goods that consumers are less aware of or familiar with the supermarket can increase its total profit per customer (see Eastham, 2002).

7.4.5 Cost analysis

The company should have established whether or not a potential market is attractive from a basic assessment of costs. If the market seems promising, a more detailed cost analysis should be the next step. The likely level of demand should by now have been estimated for varying levels of output. For example, if demand analysis has predicted that a price level of £1.80 per unit will generate a demand level of 100,000 units per annum, the company needs to know the effect that this level of production will have on costs. (In this example, the price of £1.80 per unit would be a figure derived from an overall market demand schedule, whilst 100,000 units could represent the share of the total market the company wishes to obtain.) In order to ascertain the viability of such a price and level of output, a break-even point must be calculated from an analysis of the relationship between costs and output.

There are fixed costs that the company must pay regardless of the level of output (e.g. depreciation and maintenance costs of machinery and the costs of a minimum labour force). Variable costs are a function of the level of output (e.g. energy and raw material costs and perhaps those of additional labour as production levels rise). Total costs are the sum of fixed and variable costs. Break-even occurs when the number of units sold at a given price generates revenue to exactly equal total costs.

In Figure 7.6 demand analysis indicates that a price of £1.80 per unit would be attractive to the market, and the desired market share would require a production level of 100,000 units per annum. Fixed costs for production of the product are £100,000. Variable costs rise as production increases; at a production level of 100,000 units, total costs are £150,000. The company knows, therefore, that it must charge at least £1.50 per unit in order to break even at this

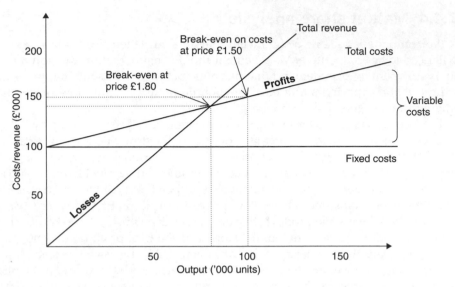

Figure 7.6 Application of break-even analysis

volume. However, this is a break-even figure based solely on cost. The break-even point can be modified by changing price; at a higher price fewer units are required to break even.

In this example, the company has already estimated that £1.80 is a desirable price in market terms. If this price is used with information from Figure 7.6, the following equation can be used to calculate the number of units required to break even at this price.

Fixed costs   = £100,000
Variable costs = £0.50 per unit
Selling price   = £1.80

Number of units required to break even at a given selling price = n
Total costs will be equal total revenue when: $100,000 + 0.5n = 1.8n$
Therefore, $n = 77,000$ (approx) and total costs = £138,500 (approx)

The company had planned to produce and sell 100,000 units. When the price is set at £1.80 per unit, break-even will be approximately 77,000 units. This price provides for profitable production at all points above 77,000 units.

This is a demand-orientated approach to pricing. The manufacturer determines the likely market price and then looks back at the cost structure to establish the feasibility of such a price.

7.4.6 Profit calculation

When pricing objectives were discussed, it was said that they differed according to the nature of the market. The cost and demand analysis just described does not reduce flexibility in setting price objectives. Rather, it provides management with information it requires to make further decisions. Taking the example in Figure 7.6, the company could use £1.80 at 100,000 units as its basis for setting a price if the objective was other than to break even. Once equipped with cost and demand data, various price levels that might be appropriate to a chosen marketing strategy can be considered. Several break-even points can then be plotted along the line of total cost. As long as the output level is to the right of any given break-even point, the company will generate profits. Thus the break-even point is a function of price that is, in turn, a function of the chosen marketing strategy.

Determination of price and profit is a practical and not an academic exercise. Marketers acknowledge that profit is the only means of survival for a company and price is the major tool through which profits can be realised. Once a price has been selected, management should review costs regularly in case savings can be made without affecting the product's quality. Provided production capacity and delivery permit, the sales force might attempt to increase the sale of units and so increase profits (seen in Figure 7.6 as moving output along the line of total costs away from the break-even point).

7.5 Price selection techniques

The chosen price will depend on marketing strategy. Examples are given of demand- and market-orientated treatments of price determination. Some pricing techniques pay less attention to demand, and concentrate on cost, whilst others put emphasis on the other elements of the marketing mix as well as aspects of consumer behaviour that affect the way price is perceived.

7.5.1 Break-even analysis related to market demand

The principal value of this technique is that as demand estimation is accurate, management is dealing with reality. We begin with the premise that at too high a price there will be no demand, whilst at too low a price the company will make losses. The company must, therefore, choose a price that is acceptable both to itself and to the market place. For simplicity, only one price is considered in Figure 7.6 and there is thus only one function for total revenue (i.e. total revenue = demand × unit price). If demand is estimated at various price levels it is possible to produce a series of total revenue lines. The various total revenue lines can be plotted to form a demand curve for the product in question. Usually, a company will choose a price and a corresponding level of demand that will maximise profit. In practice, this may not be possible because of limitations on the firm's production capacity, or because of a need to utilise production capacity as fully as possible.

Whilst demand-orientated pricing is preferable to cost-based pricing, we should be aware of practical limitations when it is related to break-even analysis. Firstly, it assumes that costs are static, whereas costs can vary considerably in a practical setting. Revenue too, is over-simplified, as market conditions can change rapidly. Even if they return to the condition on which the analysis was based, the actual revenue will not be as predicted. If these considerations are taken into account, break-even analysis related to demand is an effective price selection technique, particularly when costs and demand levels are relatively stable, if only in the short term. Accurate demand is difficult to estimate and more insight is provided in Chapter 14 that deals with sales forecasting.

7.5.2 Cost-based price techniques

These have the advantage of being easier to administer than demand-based techniques. It is simple for a firm to arrive at an accurate estimation of the cost of producing something. Cost-plus pricing takes the cost of production and adds to this an amount that will provide the profit the company requires.

- 'Mark-up pricing' is a cost-plus technique that is widely used in the retail sector. The retailer takes the cost price of the product it is offering for sale and adds to this a percentage mark-up that is sufficient to cover overhead costs and provides a pre-determined percentage profit. Usually mark-up is calculated as a percentage of cost price using the following formula:

$$(100\% + \text{required \% mark up}) \times \text{cost} = \text{selling price}$$

Retailers favour mark-up pricing, because it is convenient and straightforward. Demand analysis might have been carried out by the manufacturer, who might then suggest a retail price to the retailer. This is not to say that retailers ignore demand. Usually, the faster the turnover, the lower the percentage mark-up. Retailers are also in an advantageous position of being able to experiment with sales effectiveness at varying price levels and receive quick feedback. Although mark-up pricing tends to prevail in retailing, it is common in manufacturing, because it is easier to estimate cost than demand. If a long-term view of price is taken, there is no need to make continuous demand-related pricing adjustments. In some industries, where a particular mark-up is considered 'standard', the market is correspondingly more stable, and this benefits both producers and customers alike.

- 'Target pricing' is another cost-based approach, which considers output as well as costs in determining price. The company decides on a given rate of return or 'target price' and calculates the level of output necessary to achieve this. Break-even analysis is used to determine the level of output where profits will begin. The linear rise in variable costs, as output increases, will determine the company's total costs. The company then chooses a price that will produce a revenue earning line that achieves the target profit.

Target pricing is used by skills based companies and business-to-business companies whose price philosophy is one of a 'fair return-on-investment'.

In most marketing situations, the technique has limitations. In particular, demand elasticity is ignored. Thus, although a given level of output may be prescribed which only requires a relatively low price, there is no guarantee that this volume will be bought by the market. Conversely, if the company wishes to reduce output, and still reach the target profit, a higher price must be charged which may not be acceptable to the market.

7.5.3 Psychological pricing techniques

It is the market place and not the company that exerts the greatest influence when prices are being determined. Although an individual company cannot significantly alter basic market structure, it has some influence when marketing implications are considered. Management is faced with a general level of demand for a product or service. Inside this demand level are opportunities for strategies to be developed which focus specifically on consumers. The importance that consumers attach to prestige value allows for psychological pricing techniques to be developed. Some consumers believe that price is an indication of quality; the consumer uses this perceived quality to enhance the image of his or her lifestyle.

The purchase of a 'prestige' product can then become an expression of 'self-concept'. 'Designer clothes' are a good example of prestige products; their perceived value is greater than their cost. Consumers see value in exclusivity and the ability to display that they are prepared and able to pay high prices for such fashionable items.

The influences on the consumer that make prestige pricing possible are numerous and these have been discussed in Chapter 4. In order to satisfy the consumer's psychological needs, other elements of the marketing mix, such as promotion and distribution, should support the image reflected by the price. For example, Cartier jewellery and Gucci accessories are advertised in prestige media and not in the popular press, nor would we expect to find them in our local supermarket.

Demand for prestige goods produces an unusual curve as shown in Figure 7.7. Although demand increases to some extent as prices are reduced, below a certain price further reductions can decrease the level of demand. This is because the product loses its prestigious image if price becomes too low.

Other psychological price factors concern consumer perceptions of the price itself. For some products there are price bands within which price reductions have little effect on demand. However, if price is reduced so that it falls into the next psychological price bracket, then demand will increase. This results in a step-like demand curve and is the basis of odd/even pricing (called price lining). Somehow, £4.99 appears a lot less expensive than £5.00. Similarly, for higher-priced products, an even figure reduction appears to encourage demand. The figure of £68 'appears' disproportionately less than its true difference from £70. Odd/even pricing is widely practiced in retailing, although its scientific basis is unclear, and the technique owes as much to tradition as it does to consumer analysis.

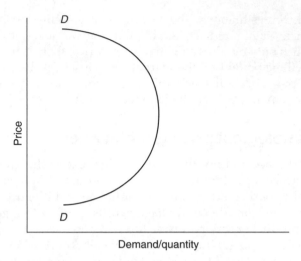

Figure 7.7 Prestige price demand curve

7.5.4 Going-rate pricing

Some companies price their products according to the going rate. Clearly, they must ensure that their cost structures and profit requirements are compatible with this, but having done so, it is a popular method when companies that are 'price leaders' feature in the market. Thus, if the main pricing objective is to meet competitive prices, going-rate pricing is appropriate. Generally, when companies collectively apply this technique in a market, prices are stabilised and price wars are avoided.

7.5.5 Price bundling

Bundling can be defined as the sale of two or more products 'bundled together' and usually sold at a discount. For example, you can buy a decorators kit 'bundled' together from B&Q which will include all the equipment you need except the actual paint. The 'bundle' is considerably cheaper than adding together the price of the individual items in the bundle if sold separately (see Stremerch and Tellis, 2002, for an excellent in depth treatment of price bundling and its rationale).

7.5.6 Pricing on the Internet

Companies such as EBay offer on-line action facilities to consumers which has turned out to be very popular indeed. Founded in September 1995, eBay is The World's Online Marketplace for the sale of goods and services by a diverse community of individuals and businesses. Today, the eBay community includes tens of millions of registered members from around the world. People spend more time on eBay than any other online site, making it the most popular shopping destination on the Internet. eBay's mission is to provide a global trading platform where practically anyone can trade practically anything. On an average day, there are millions of items listed on eBay. People come to the eBay marketplace to buy and sell items in thousands of categories including antiques and art, books, business and industrial, cars and other vehicles, clothing and accessories, coins, collectibles, crafts, dolls and bears, electronics and computers, home furnishings, jewelry and watches, movies and DVDs, music, musical instruments, pottery and glass, real estate, sporting goods and memorabilia, stamps, tickets, toys and hobbies and travel. eBay offers a wide variety of features and services that enable members to buy and sell on the site quickly and conveniently. Buyers have the option to purchase items in auction-style format or items can be purchased at fixed price through a feature called buy-it-now. For a further discussion of on-line auction pricing see the work of Massad and Tucker (2000).

7.6 Pricing strategy

Marketing management should devise a pricing strategy that is compatible with strategies attached to other elements of the marketing mix. It is not always possible to set a price and apply this rigidly to all customers in all market situations. A pricing strategy denotes how a company will price its products at particular periods of time or particular market conditions. Demand-orientated pricing sets a base price that the company must endeavour to achieve, but it assumes that price be modified in line with changes in demand. Manufacturers must realise that customers are not the same. Some will purchase greater quantities than others, or be situated in areas that are more costly to reach.

If a target-return-on-investment price is set, this may only be appropriate during the maturity stage of the product life cycle that was explained in the last chapter. During introduction or growth, it is often necessary to employ a pricing strategy that will enable the target return to be achieved over the long term.

A company's ability and willingness to formulate pricing strategies is a reflection of its willingness to adapt and modify price according to the needs of customers and market conditions.

7.6.1 Discounting

The discount structure a company employs is a major element of pricing strategy and an indicator of the firm's flexibility. If customers buy products in large quantities, they may reasonably expect to be charged a lower price than that charged to smaller purchasers. The seller may also offer discounts voluntarily in order to encourage large orders that facilitate economies of scale and assist effective production planning. Such quantity-related discounts can refer to individual orders or be based on an estimated off-take that is planned over a given period. In certain markets, price discounting is important. Day and

Ryans (1988) say that if used with imagination and creativity they can provide a firm with a strong competitive advantage.

Manufacturers can offer discounts to encourage sales of a new product or accelerate demand for a product whose stocks are high, owing to seasonal or cyclical demand variations. In the production context, it is desirable that a constant rate of output is maintained. If market conditions are not conducive to this, a price modification by means of discounting might encourage sales sufficiently to counteract variations in levels of demand.

A discounting strategy can also be applied to payment terms. It is common in industrial marketing to offer a percentage discount to firms who settle their monthly account promptly. Finance should arrive at a 'sliding scale' for discounts in relation to speed of payment that is a reflection of interest rates. The firm may then not have to wait for 30, 60 or even 90 days for settlement of many of its accounts. Discounting is a reality of pricing strategy, although it is not necessarily a standardised procedure.

The task of negotiating specific prices usually falls to sales. There are situations where the buying power of a customer gives the salesperson little alternative but to offer some discount as part of the price negotiation process. Temporary discounts should be applied with caution as they might come to be regarded as the normal price. It is easy to reduce prices, but more difficult to increase them later. When discounts are promotion-related they should have time limits defined from the outset.

7.6.2 Zone or geographic pricing strategies

In export markets a company should consider competition and local conditions prior to deciding a price level. Even within the country of manufacture, customers in some areas can be charged a price that reflects additional delivery costs. Customers, however, tend to view their location in relation to the supplier's manufacturing base as being the supplier's problem. As a result, most UK and European companies tend to be unsympathetic to arguments that the cost of transportation merits a price premium. There is almost always a competitor who is willing to supply even the furthest location at a price that is the same as locally delivered prices.

In the USA, distances are so great that producers often apply zone or geographic pricing strategies – their customer-bases being spread over an area several times larger in geographical terms than the market afforded by the entire EU. The subject of pricing for export markets is dealt with in more detail in Chapter 16.

7.6.3 Market skimming and market penetration

Chapter 6 considered marketing strategy at various stages of the product life cycle. Of specific interest were strategies for launching new products, particularly for innovative, rather than imitative, new products. In the introductory stage of the PLC, marketing management has two basic strategic pricing alternatives – market skimming and market penetration.

- *Market skimming* implies that a company will charge the highest price the market will bear, given the relative merits of the product in question. A skimming strategy is initially directed at a small proportion of the total potential market. This is likely to be made up of innovators and early adopters, who are receptive to new ideas and whose income and lifestyle makes them less sensitive to price. Diffusion theory suggests that these customer groups influence subsequent buyer categories and acceptance of an innovative product 'filters' down to a larger number of consumers. To reach this wider group of customers, the company must reduce prices progressively while, at the same time, 'skimming' the most advantageous prices from each successive customer group. The signal for each planned price reduction is a slowing down in sales. Price reductions are successively introduced until the product has ultimately been offered to the bulk of the overall target market. A variation is to launch a highly sophisticated version of a new product, and then reduce the price successively by producing cheaper, simpler, alternative or modified products at each successive stage. For a skimming strategy to be successful, the product must be distinctive enough to exclude competitors who might be encouraged to enter the market by the high prices that a company is able to charge in the earlier stages. Other elements of the marketing mix should support the skimming strategy by promoting a high quality, distinctive image. The company must also be prepared and able to forgo high volume production in the initial stages of the product's life; bearing in mind that overall the volume of sales and the price charged must be high enough to achieve profitability. The notion of market skimming is illustrated in Figure 7.8.

  In Figure 7.8 it is shown that the first to adopt a new product, as first time adopters and not replacement buyers, might be the upper middle social class 'A' (which might well be the case in high fashion). However, for a new innovative type of computer software, innovator categories might be a better indicator of a propensity to adopt. It could be that in this case 'innovators' might well be 'technical' people who may largely belong to the C2 category social class. It should also be noted in Figure 7.8 that the first price charged (P1 at T1) is the highest and as demand begins to slow at T2, then the price is lowered to P2 and so on and price P5 is the final skim.

- *Market penetration pricing*: When a company has a high production capacity that must be utilised as quickly as possible, a penetration pricing strategy is appropriate when marketing a new product. A penetration strategy relies on economies of scale to allow production to be pursued at a price low enough to attract the greatest number of buyers to the market as early as possible. This, in turn, should preclude potential competitors through cost barriers to market entry, in the form of large capital set-up costs. The longer-term goal

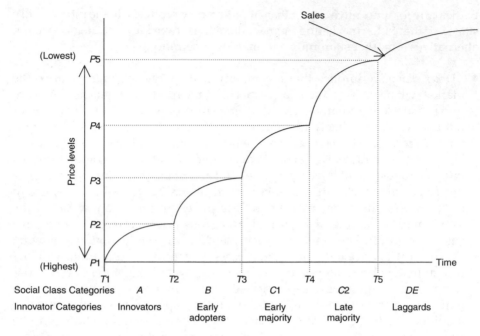

Figure 7.8 Skimming the market

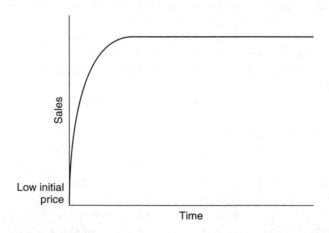

Figure 7.9 Penetration pricing

is to acquire a high market-share and to hold on to this during later stages of the product's life through further economies of scale, which might allow further price reductions to be made to fight off competition. Figure 7.9 illustrates penetration pricing where it can be seen that market share is quickly gained through the adoption of a low initial price.

7.6.4 Discriminatory pricing

Where markets are easily segmented, companies can charge different prices to each segment, even though the product on offer is basically the same. This is referred to as a price discrimination strategy. Sometimes, only minor modifications to a product can allow a discriminatory price to be charged. In other cases, discrimination may be based on non-product factors such as the time of year, customer type or location.

The term 'discrimination' does not infer exploitation, as customers can exercise choice. The manufacturer's rationale for discrimination is based on filling capacity by serving new markets. Discrimination on a customer basis can pose problems as Morris (1987) points out: 'Flexible, discriminatory pricing may generate considerable ill will amongst customers'. Volume discounting is a form of discrimination not always accepted by smaller customers. If a purchase level that qualifies for discount is 1,000 units, a customer who only needs to purchase 900 units may feel aggrieved at being excluded from the discount structure.

A popular form of customer discrimination is the variety of discounts offered to children, students and older persons for what are essentially the same services as are offered to the public at large. Apart from any altruistic aims that a company may have, it anticipates that these groups may be encouraged to participate in activities that they could not normally afford, thus increasing the company's total market.

Discriminatory prices based on time are popular with manufacturers and service industries experiencing seasonal demand. The travel industry regularly offers cheaper prices during the low season. The objective is to attract customers who might not have considered a particular holiday, if it had not been for the fact that it was offered at an attractive price. Similarly, transport operators often offer lower rates during 'off-peak' hours or to 'stand-by' passengers. If the journeys are scheduled in any case, any extra sales (at however low a price) will make a contribution to covering fixed costs.

Often only minor modifications to a product can attract a new market segment to which a company can apply a discriminatory price that is disproportionate to the added value. 'Swatch' watches are an example. The basic production cost for any watch is the mechanism. 'Swatch' watches have attractive faces and straps and they are marketed skilfully to enable a premium to be charged for what is essentially a standard production item.

When applying a price discrimination strategy, the segments chosen should be easily identifiable and separable, so they can be managed and addressed in a manner that distinguishes them from each other. This will reduce feelings of ill will that would otherwise arise from those in higher priced segments.

7.7 Summary

The usefulness of economic theory to the marketer at the beginning was qualified in relation to pricing, but a sound knowledge of basic economics is desirable for marketing practice in general. It is especially relevant to the study of demand and cost behaviour.

Price embodies more than a monetary unit that is exchanged for a product or service. It is, therefore, desirable to develop knowledge of consumer behaviour, that helps to explain why purchases are made and to this extent buyer behaviour has already explained this in Chapter 4. Although price is important, non-price competition is also effective in achieving sales. Price wars can be damaging as Miller (1989) pointed out in relation to the beer market.

Segmentation strategy, as covered in Chapter 5, is also linked to pricing. If a company's marketing mix strategy for a specific market segment is considered, the role of pricing in the context of its relationship to other marketing mix partners should become apparent.

Chapter 13 on market research includes demand analysis and forecasting in Chapter 14 deals further with the implications of pricing. Ethical considerations in relation to pricing are also discussed in Chapter 15.

References

Day, G.S. and Ryans, A.B. (1988), 'Using price discounts for a competitive advantage', *Industrial Marketing Management*, February, pp. 1–14.

Eastham, J. (2002), 'Prices down numbers up', *Marketing Week*, 20th June, pp. 22–25.

Jobber, D. (2004), *Principles and Practices of Marketing*, 4th edition, London: McGraw Hill, Chapter 11 Pricing Strategy, p. 376.

Massad, V.J. and Tucker, J.M. (2000), 'Comparing bidding and pricing between in-person and on-line action', *Journal of Product and Brand management*, 9(5), 325–332.

Miller, J. (1989), 'Anheuser-Busch, slugging it out, plans beer price cuts', *The Wall Street Journal*, October 26, p. 31.

Morris, M.H. (1987), 'Separate prices as a marketing tool', *Industrial Marketing Management*, May, 79–86.

Narayandas, D., Quelch, J. and Swartz, G. (2000), Prepare your company for global pricing, *Sloan Management Review*, Fall, 61–70.

Sherwood, B. (2003), OFT's action man takes on price fixing of toys, *Financial Times*, 20th February, p. 3.

Stremerch, S. and Tellis, G.J. (2002), Strategic bundling of products and prices: a new synthesis for marketing, *Journal of marketing*, 66, 55–72.

Tellis, G.J. (1986), 'Beyond the many faces of price: an integration of pricing strategies', *Journal of Marketing*, October, 146–160.

Further reading

Daly, J.L. (2001), *Pricing for Profitability: Activity-based pricing for Competitive Advantage*, Chichester: Wiley.

Hill, L. and O'Sullivan, T. (2004), *Foundation Marketing*, 3rd edition, Chapter 9 Pricing, Prentice-Hall, pp. 235–263.

Hollensen, S. (2003), *Marketing Management – A Relationship Approach*, Chapter 12, Pricing Decisions, Prentice-Hall, pp. 486–516.

Kotler, P. and Armstrong, G. (2004), *'Principles of Marketing'*, 10th International edition, Chapter 12 Pricing Strategies, Person Prentice-Hall, pp. 369–394.

Masterson, R. and Pickton, D. (2004), *'Marketing an Introduction'*, Chapter 10 Price, McGraw Hill, pp. 293–326.

Wright, Ray. (2004), *Business to Business Marketing – A step by Step Guide*, Prentice-Hall, Financial Times, Chapter 7, Pricing strategies for business markets, pp. 316–361.

Questions

Question 7.1

Whilst cost considerations form an essential element of the price determination process, company costs have little or not relevance to customers. Discuss in relation to an organisation's customers.

Question 7.2

Whenever possible, a company should avoid competing on the basis of price, and should instead, compete on the basis of superior value. Discuss the role of price in the price/quality relationship.

Question 7.3

What factors should be taken into consideration when pricing new products or services?

Question 7.4

How important are non-pricing factors in the marketing of an organisation's products or services? List the factors in order of importance.

Question 7.5

Under what circumstances can 'positively high pricing' or 'prestige' pricing be used effectively?

Question 7.6

Discuss the principles of market 'skimming' and market 'penetration' pricing strategies.

Question 7.7

Examine the commercial and market circumstances under which each of these pricing strategies are most likely to be used.
Discuss the nature of price and its role as an intrinsic part of the firms marketing mix.

Question 7.8

Explain the following approaches to the setting of price:

1 the economists approach,
2 the accountants approach,
3 the marketers approach.

Use specific examples to illustrate the points made.

Question 7.9

List and discuss the main business factors a firm would need to take into account when deciding to set a price for a product or service. Use specific examples where possible to illustrate the points made.

8

Channels of Distribution

8.1 Introduction

The routes marketing companies take to ensure that their goods and services reach the intended market or market segments is now examined. The term 'distribution system' refers to a complex of agents, wholesalers and retailers through which manufacturers move products to their intended markets. Marketing channels are usually made up of independent firms who are in business to make a profit. These are known as marketing intermediaries or middlemen. Distribution outlets can include combinations of owned and independent outlets or arrangements like franchising (see Ivey, 2002, p. 13).

8.2 Direct versus indirect systems

In designing a distribution system, a manufacturer must make a policy choice between selling directly to customers and employing salespeople and using intermediaries, that is, selling through agents, wholesalers and retailers. Initially, the decision is usually based on cost factors. Distribution costs are largely a function of:

1 the number of potential customers in the market;
2 how concentrated or dispersed they are;
3 how much each will buy in a given period;
4 costs associated with the practical side of the distributive operation (e.g. transport, warehousing and stockholding all of which are dealt with in detail in Chapter 9).

If the manufacturer has a large enough potential sales volume, there may be a case for selling direct and employing a sales force. Industrial goods manufacturers tend to use direct selling and often deliver direct to the customer, although in some cases wholesalers or 'factors' are used. Consumer goods manufacturers tend to use a network of marketing intermediaries because of the dispersion and large numbers of potential customers. Again, there are exceptions (e.g. Avon Cosmetics who sell direct to homes through agents). Most often, manufacturers sell to wholesalers who, in turn, break bulk, add on a mark-up and sell to retailers. However, with the increased size and power of the large food multiples, manufacturers sell direct to them and these multiples perform their own wholesaling function. Whether selling through retail chains, or wholesalers then retailers, it is important to note that the manufacturer relies on these middlemen for ultimate marketing success, as these intermediaries have the responsibility of taking the product to the ultimate consumer.

8.3 The nature of distribution

Distribution arrangements tend to be long term in nature. Because of this time horizon, channel decisions are usually classed as strategic, rather than tactical or operational ones. There are two reasons for treating channel decisions like this:

1 Channel decisions have a direct effect on the rest of the firm's marketing activities. For example, the selection of target markets is affected by, and in turn affects, channel design and choice. Similarly, decisions about individual marketing mix elements (e.g. pricing) must reflect a company's channel choice.
2 Once established, a company's channel system may be difficult to change, at least in the short term. Although distribution channels are not impervious to change and new channels emerge as old established channels diminish, few companies are able to change their channel structure with the same ease that they can change other marketing mix variables like price or advertising. Because channel arrangements are likely to change slowly over time, manufacturers need to continually monitor the distributive environment and reassess their existing channel structure to exploit and capitalise on any change. However, they should be aware of developments that are taking place so not to be caught off guard, as happened with the rapid development of the internet as a direct retailing medium, which caught many traditional distributors off balance.

Increasingly channel decisions are international in nature. Arnold (2000, p. 13) suggests distribution guidelines for manufacturers planning to enter new international markets.

1 Select distributors – the marketing firm should be pro-active and make a strategic choice of channels.
2 Look for distributors capable of developing markets, rather than those with a few obvious customer contacts. The marketing firm is looking for

a long-term partner who is willing to invest time and money and build a long lasting relationship with the manufacturing firm.

3 Treat the local distributors as long-term partners, not temporary market entry vehicles. Again the emphasis is on a long term, mutually beneficial partnership. The manufacturing firm should give channel members target to achieve and make sure they are rewarded for the achievement of goals. Channel members are independent businesses and need mentoring and looking after (see Day and Robinson, 2000, p. 25).

4 Support market entry by committing money, managers and proven marketing ideas. Many marketing firms demonstrate commitment to the distribution relationship with channel members by investing money and taking an equity stake in the channel members business. This allows them some control but more importantly demonstrates that they regard the relationship as important and long term.

5 From the start maintain control over marketing strategy. Visit the overseas distributor regularly to ensure they are meeting targets and that their performance within the channel network is in line with expectations and overall marketing strategy.

6 Make sure distributors provide financial performance data and detailed data on markets. This data will provide information for monitoring and control purposes but also provides valuable market research information on like developments in overseas markets.

7 Build links with national distributors at the earliest opportunity. After entering a new market manufacturers should endeavour to establish links with distribution channel members within the country (see Hollensen, 2003, p. 542).

8.4 Strategic elements of channel choice

An important consideration for marketing management in formulating channel policy and the number of marketing intermediaries used, is the degree of market exposure sought by the company for its products. Three distribution strategies, resulting in varying degrees of market exposure, can be distinguished.

8.4.1 Intensive distribution

Products, when viewed by consumers in their totality, are seen to be what is termed 'a bundle of attributes' or satisfactions including possession utilities and time and place utilities. Producers of convenience goods and certain raw materials aim to stock their products in as many outlets as possible (i.e. an intensive distribution strategy). The dominant factor in the marketing of such products is their place utility. Producers of convenience goods like pens, confectionery and cigarettes try to enlist every possible retail outlet, ranging from multiples to independent corner shops, to create maximum brand exposure and maximum convenience to customers. With such products, every exposure to the customer is an opportunity to buy, and the image of the outlet used is a less significant factor in the customer's mind than the impression of the product. Sometimes an intensive distribution policy can cause conflict among channel members. Usually channel conflict is to be avoided as the marketing firm want a smoothly run channel network. However a certain amount of conflict can sometimes be beneficial as it keeps channel members 'on their toes' and forces them to develop a competitive edge (see Cohen, 2000, pp. 13–14, for an interesting discussion as to how Xerox successfully uses a multi-channel approach).

8.4.2 Exclusive distribution

For some products, producers deliberately limit the number of intermediaries handling their products. They may wish to develop a high quality brand image. Exclusive distribution to recognised official distributors can enhance the prestige of the product. Exclusive (or solus) distribution is a policy of granting dealers exclusive rights to distribute in a certain geographical area. It is often used in conjunction with a policy of exclusive dealing, where the manufacturer requires the dealer not to carry competing lines. Car manufacturers have such arrangements with their dealers. With the arrangement goes a stipulation by the manufacturer that the distributor is able to uphold appropriate repair, service and warranty handling facilities. By granting exclusive distribution, the manufacturer gains more control over intermediaries regarding price, credit and promotional policies, greater loyalty and a more determined selling of the company's products.

8.4.3 Selective distribution

This policy lies between the extremes just described. The manufacturing firm may not have the resources to adequately service or influence the policies of all the intermediaries who are willing to carry a particular product. Instead of spreading its marketing effort over the whole range of possible outlets, it concentrates on the most promising outlets.

A requirement is that channel members should have certain facilities to store and market products effectively, for example, frozen food products require that intermediaries have adequate deep freeze display facilities. Specialised resources might be necessary, for example, certain ethical pharmaceutical products require that intermediaries are capable of offering advice as to the use and limitations of the product, so such products might be restricted to pharmacies. The product may have a carefully cultivated brand image that could be damaged by being stocked in limited line discount outlets where products are displayed in a functional way to reduce overheads and the final price. Selective distribution is used where the facilities, resources or image of the outlet can have a direct impact on customers' impressions of the product. An example here is 'up market' brands of perfume (see Jobber, 2004, p. 644).

8.5 Changing channel systems

Cravens (1988) stated that channels do change and manufacturers often respond too slowly to such evolution. Individual changes may be small when viewed in isolation, but cumulative change can be significant. When planning long-term channel strategy, companies need to monitor such change and attempt to anticipate future macro-environmental developments. An example of such change that happened recently has already been cited in relation to internet developments.

Change occurs at all levels in a channel system, but it has been particularly noticeable in UK retailing. Significant changes in retailing practice have occurred since the 1970s. This period witnessed an increasing polarity in the distribution turnover of retail firms. At one end of the spectrum there are large-scale operators: multiples, discount chains and the co-operative movement. At the other end there are many small shops. Some of these are completely independent retailers who purchase from wholesalers and 'cash-and-carry' outlets or who have joint purchasing agreements through 'retail buying associations'. Others are linked to wholesalers through the voluntary chain/group movement, sometimes called symbol shops (e.g. Spar) and are similar to franchises which are explained later. Numbers of shops have declined with an increased concentration of market share in the hands of a small number of large multiples that have grown at the expense of co-operatives, independents and smaller multiples.

 ## 8.6 The wheel-of-retailing: growth of multiples and 'one-stop' shopping

The 'wheel-of-retailing' concept refers to evolutionary change in retailing that can be likened to the product life cycle concept that was discussed in Chapter 5. The concept states that new retailing institutions enter the market as low-status, low-margin, low-price operations and then move up market towards higher status, higher margin and higher priced positions. New forms of retailing can be seen as going through various life-cycle stages (i.e. introduction, growth, maturity and decline). The wheel-of-retailing appears to be turning with ever increasing speed with each new retail innovation taking less time to reach the maturity stage. Evidence suggests that it took about 50 years for older-style department stores to reach the maturity (i.e. steady sales) stage; supermarkets took about 25 years and hypermarkets only 10 years. The concept is analogous to Charles Darwin's theory of evolution of plants and animals that proposed that a changing environment leads to adaptation and hence evolution. Darwin also explained that there is no need for adaptation in a stable environment; there has to be change for the evolutionary process to occur. We now look at some of the environmental changes that have taken place that have instigated adaptation and evolution in retailing over the relatively short period just described.

8.6.1 Search for economies of scale

In search for greater profits, larger retail chains devised larger scale methods of operation and supermarkets have culminated in today's hypermarkets (stores with at least 50,000 square feet of selling space) and even larger 'megamarkets'. Each new retailing mode has led to greater economies of scale and better financial return.

8.6.2 The abolition of resale price maintenance (RPM)

Until the mid-1960s, manufacturers' resale prices were protected by RPM under which retailers had to sell at prices stipulated by the manufacturers; if they sold goods below the stipulated price, further supplies could be withheld.

RPM protected small independent retailers from price competition from larger multiples because these larger operators were unable to pass on their cost economies to customers. There were some well-reported case of multiples, notably Tesco, having supplies withheld for selling below a manufacturer's stipulated price (i.e. too cheaply) which was, of course, the best publicity that could have been attained.

Because RPM restricted price competition, retailers relied heavily on non-price competition, and the level of service in many stores was arguably higher than consumers needed since they would have preferred lower prices. RPM was abolished by the Resale Prices Act (1964).

This resulted in many small shops, and a number of wholesalers who traditionally supplied such outlets, going out of business. The resultant market share that was 'freed up' fell into the hands of more efficient and powerful multiples who used their purchasing economies to compete on price and pass savings on to customers. Thus, multiples expanded at the expense of independents and the wholesalers who supplied them, as well as the co-operative movement. The latter was ideally placed to take advantage of this environmental change (because of their size) but they were too slow to react. This was largely because of their decentralised structure in terms of the movement consisting of a large number of individual retail societies whose democratically elected members (their customers) controlled them. Ironically, the co-operative movement (that was founded in Rochdale in 1844) was the first to innovate 'self-service' facilities during the Second World War. This was, however, done for social reasons of freeing up labour to help in the war effort, and at the end of the war they did not capitalise on this innovation and reverted to personal service.

8.6.3 Selective employment tax (SET)

This was a tax on 'non-productive workers' (i.e. a tax charged on selective occupations) that was introduced in 1966. Its effect was to increase shop workers' wage costs by 7%, as it was the employer, not the employee, who paid the tax. SET made labour more expensive and, relatively speaking, capital investment cheaper. This encouraged many retailers (who were the largest employers of non-productive workers) to invest in capital systems (e.g. central checkout systems) that made them less reliant on labour. This gave a further push to the widespread introduction of self-service shopping. Such large investments meant that operators demanded larger, and quicker, turnover. Quicker turnover meant that consumer goods had a shorter shelf life, so they were fresher when purchased. Thus, indirectly, SET, helped multiples to expand at the expense of smaller competitors.

8.6.4 Greater market power of multiples

As the power of multiples increased, they were able to cut out traditional wholesalers and purchase centrally, directly from manufacturers. Consumer goods manufacturers could ill afford not to be included in the multiples' product lines. Consequently, multiples were able to command advantageous discounts from manufacturers. Independents still had to purchase through traditional wholesalers, and even though some formed wholesale groups through voluntary chains/groups, they still had difficulty in matching multiples' prices. Indeed, multiples in the 1970s were dubbed with the description: 'Pile it high; sell it cheap'.

The early to mid-1980s saw the introduction of 'own label' merchandise – ranges of brands commissioned by individual multiple chains bearing their own logotype (logo). In the 1970s, multiples introduced their own 'economy brands' without any logo, the idea being that such merchandise was a cheap alternative to manufacturer branded and packaged merchandise. However, consumers quickly realised that such goods, although cheaper, were usually of inferior quality.

The first operator to bring in 'own label' merchandise was Sainsburys. Other multiple operators were quick to follow, with the result that power within food retailing channels has passed from manufacturers' brands to retailers' brands. Most food manufacturers now supply retail chains with 'own label' merchandise, with a few notable exceptions (e.g. Nestlé and Kellogg) who do not supply 'own label', as they feel that this could diminish their power within the channel (which relies on strong brands). A feature of their advertising is along the lines of: 'you will only find XXXX in an XXXX jar/pack'. This makes it clear to customers that they do not manufacture for multiples (even though their brands are often displayed alongside multiples' 'own brands' often in similar packaging). Their advertising emphasises the 'uniqueness' (unique sales proposition – USP) of their product (i.e. product characteristics that cannot be replicated).

Despite these few manufacturers who do not supply 'own label' products, in the UK the power within retail channels has switched from manufacturers to retailers (unlike many other countries where power still rests with manufacturers of strongly branded products).

Some measure of the extent of change in retailing in the UK is the fact that co-operatives had more than 25% share of the retail market in the early 1960s with independent retailers commanding over 50%. Now the Co-op share is down to less than 6%. Tesco is more than 15% and Sainsbury's is more than 12%. The total share of independents' market share, including those who belong to voluntary groups, is now down to 20%.

8.6.5 Scrambled merchandising

In an affluent country like the UK consumption of food products is relatively income inelastic. In other words, people do not buy more food when they have more money. Instead, they tend to 'trade up' and consume better quality foods. Therefore, to expand their businesses, large multiples have diversified, stocking non-food products to further their turnover and profits. Many multiples now sell items like electrical goods, garden supplies and clothing, and many no longer seem like 'food stores'. However, some of these multiples have decided to go back to their core business of food retailing, or clearly differentiate such business from their core activities (e.g. Sainsbury's Homebase), because of the confused 'scrambled merchandising' images associated with non-food retailing.

8.6.6 'One-stop' shopping

Multiples have introduced hypermarkets and megastores to capitalise on the desire for the concept of 'one-stop' shopping. As well as shopping for most of a family's needs, from gardening materials and electrical goods to food under one roof, there is an increasing tendency for customers to shop less frequently (perhaps fortnightly or even monthly instead of weekly). Payment is normally made by credit card or switch cards where the customer's bank account is debited immediately the transaction has been completed, rather than with cash. These trends have been brought about, and will continue, because of:

1 Growth in car ownership and the number of two car families. This has brought increased mobility and the ability to travel to 'out-of-town' sites. Such stores have large catchment areas, sufficient to warrant the investment in land, building and facilities. Usually, major operators are also able to attract ancillary shops such as travel agents, newsagents and florists, to open shops on the same site, so the complex becomes like a little 'town' in itself. An extension of this idea is the establishment of 'metro centres' that are usually located near large urban conurbations. Such complexes are designed for car travel as parking is easy, and these complexes are closed to the elements (e.g. covered walkways from car parks as well as the retail centre itself). The idea is not only to make shopping a more 'pleasant' experience, but to encourage larger, bulk purchases.

2 A greater proportion of married women work, meaning that family time is often at a premium, especially if there are children to look after. Time is no longer available for the luxury of 'browsing' in the shopping sense. This rise in average total family income has meant that a wife's income is often a major

contributor to the household budget, especially now that the notion of 'equal pay for equal work' has legal status.

3 Greater ownership of freezers coupled with greater car ownership means that shoppers can transport and effectively store larger volumes of food, thereby benefiting economically from bulk purchasing. In addition, universal microwave cooker ownership has boosted sales of 'instant' meals, many of which are cooked from frozen.

4 A shift in the population from urban to suburban centres has occurred (unlike poorer countries where the shift is usually toward the cities). City congestion discourages car drivers who prefer to shop in large out-of-town establishments where parking is adequate and usually free. However, this trend has recently been reversed with the 'gentrification' of some inner city areas to provide high capacity living accommodation mainly for younger people.

5 The 'division of labour' within marriage is no longer clearly defined. 'Modern' husbands, especially those in the B, C1 and C2 social categories, share roles previously regarded as being the province of their wives. They now help with shopping unselfconsciously, and share tasks like looking after children that most husbands 30 years ago would not have considered. 'Family shopping' (with a far wider range of merchandise being offered) has now become the 'norm'.

8.7 'Business format' franchising

To franchise means to 'grant freedom to do something' (derived from the French verb *affranchir* meaning 'to free'). Franchising is a system of marketing and distribution constituting a contractual relationship between a seller (franchiser) and the seller's distributive outlets (owned by franchisees). The common basic features of franchising are:

1 the ownership by an organisation (the franchiser) of a name, idea, secret process or specialised piece of equipment or goodwill;

2 a licence, granted by the franchiser to the franchisee, allowing the franchisee to profitably exploit that name, idea, or product;

3 the licence agreement includes regulations concerning the operation of the business in which licensees exploits their rights;

4 a payment by the licensee (e.g. an initial fee, royalty or share of profits) for the rights that are obtained.

Franchising is highly developed in the USA, and although it is popular in the UK, it is a relatively recent phenomenon. This has led people to believe that it is an 'imported' idea. However, its roots can be traced back to the middle-ages when important 'personages' were granted the right to collect revenues in return for various services and considerations (e.g. to carry out trades to the exclusion of others in certain areas).

The 'tied' public house (where the publican could only sells ale brewed by the brewery to which it was 'tied') is an example of franchising that has existed in Britain since the eighteenth century. This has been ameliorated since the early 1990s because monopolies legislation has compelled breweries to sell off many 'tied houses' as it was viewed as a restrictive practice. Franchising has come a long way since its early origins. It was taken from the UK to the USA, where it evolved and developed, and has been re-exported back to the UK in a more sophisticated form.

The development of franchising in the USA dates back to the end of the American Civil War (1865) when the Singer Sewing Machine Company franchised exclusive sales territories to financially independent operators. In 1898, General Motors used independently owned businesses to increase its distribution outlets. Rexall followed with franchised drugstores, and the soft-drink manufacturers Coca-Cola and Pepsi-Cola licensed bottling.

The modern American concept of the 'business format franchise' has gathered strength in Britain since the early 1960s. It contains all the components of a fully developed business system. The franchiser's brand name and business format are used for the exclusive purpose of marketing an agreed product or service from a 'blueprint', with the franchiser providing assistance in organisation, training, merchandising and management, in return for a 'consideration' from the franchisee. The 'formula' is very carefully prepared so as to minimise risk when opening the business. The basic principle that attracts new franchisees is that other people have followed the same scheme, and since they have been successful, new entrants should also be successful. The franchiser (normally a large organisation) supplies a franchisee with a business package or 'format', a trade name and specific products or services for sale to the general public. In most cases, the franchisee pays royalties and, in turn, is granted exclusive access to a defined geographical area. Some companies have a 'dual' channel of distribution system consisting of franchisees and wholly own company outlets. For example the clothing retailer Benetton still operates an international network of franchised stores but also sees a future in large 'megastores' and have now started to move into these large directly owned and operated stores (Ivey, 2002).

8.8 Growth of 'non-shop' shopping

During the past 30 years, as well as the many developments of new types of stores in retail marketing channels (e.g. supermarkets, hypermarkets, limited line discount stores) there has also been a marked increase in various forms of 'non-shop' selling.

8.8.1 'Door-to-door' direct selling

This is a relatively expensive operation, but having no wholesaler and retailer margins means that the expense is counterbalanced (e.g. Avon Cosmetics and

Betterware). It means that manufacturers' agents have to build up their clientele among customers in the local community in the expectation that they will purchase from a catalogue on a regular basis.

8.8.2 Party plan

This method of direct selling is popular for products such as cosmetics, plastic-ware, kitchenware, jewellery and linen products. A 'party' is organised in the home of a host or hostess who invites friends, and receives a 'consideration' in cash or goods based on the amount that these friends purchase. It is sometimes resented, as friends might feel there is a moral obligation to purchase.

8.8.3 Automatic vending

This form of retailing has grown dramatically since the 1960s and is now used for beverages, snacks, confectionery, personal products, cigarettes and some-times newspapers. Vending machines are placed in convenient locations (e.g. garage forecourts, railway and bus stations, colleges, libraries and factories). Automatic vending also supplies entertainment through juke boxes and arcade games.

Vending machines can also be used to provide services, as seen by the wide-spread introduction of cash-dispenser machines provided by financial institu-tions. As well as dispensing cash, these machines answer balance enquiries, take requests for statements and cheque books and receive deposits.

8.8.4 Mail order catalogues

Businesses that use mail order selling are either catalogue or non-catalogue. The former relies heavily upon comprehensive catalogues to obtain sales, but sometimes use local agents to deal with order collection and administration. Products can be purchased interest-free and extended credit terms are available for major purchases. There are also a number of specialist mail-order houses dealing with a limited range of specialist, often 'unusual' or 'exclusive' lines that are difficult to find in shops.

8.8.5 Non-catalogue mail-order

This usually relies on press and magazine advertising, and is used to sell a sin-gle product or limited range of products. 'Craft' products are often promoted in this way.

8.8.6 'Direct' marketing techniques

The use of direct mail is where a promotional letter and order form is sent through the post. Organisations using this method include book and record clubs. Television is also used, with orders being placed through a telephone call to a free phone number and the production of credit card details. Sometimes impersonality is carried to the ultimate through an answering machine. Telephone ordering is often combined with newspaper advertising, especially in colour supplements, discussed further in Chapter 10 under telemarketing and direct mail techniques.

8.8.7 Future developments

Television shopping via on-line computers is a developing medium and will become more popular alongside the internet. As opportunities for leisure activities increase (e.g. sports centres and specialist activity clubs) this kind of shopping will expand as it frees up more time to pursue such activities. This direct kind of shopping should also make goods cheaper, since orders can be placed directly with manufacturers without the high costs of intermediaries and their associated overheads. Credit facilities can be immediately available through electronic debiting. As computer systems become more sophisticated, and people become less 'afraid' of this new technology, it should become the growth area of retailing in the future.

8.9 Summary

This chapter has dealt principally with channel arrangements for consumer products and not said too much about industrial or organisational channels. For these latter routes, options are usually limited, as their preference is to deal direct. Chapter 9 provides a fuller discussion of the logistical implications of organisational channels and the notion of the decision-making unit has already been covered in Chapter 4.

Chapter 9 covers the second part of the 'place', or placement, element of the 'four Ps' and this is the subject of 'logistics'.

References

Arnold, D. (2000), 'Seven rules of international distribution', *Harvard Business Review*, November–December, 131–137.

Cravens, D.W. (1988), 'Gaining strategic marketing advantage', *Business Horizons*, Sept/Oct, 44–45.

Cohen, A. (2000), 'When channel conflict is good', *Sales and Marketing Management*, 15(4), 13–14.

Day, J. and Robinson, R. (2000), 'Drink responds to fluid needs', *Marketing Week*, August 24, 25–26.

Hollander, S.C. (1960), The Wheel of Retailing, *Journal of Marketing*, July, 37–42.

Hollensen, S. (2003), *Marketing Management – A Relationship Approach*, Chapter 13, Prentice-Hall, pp. 541–542.

Ivey, J. (2002), 'Benetton gambles on colour of the future', *Corporate Finance*, June, 13–15.

Jobber, D. (2004), *Principles and Practices of Marketing*, Chapter 17: Distribution, 4th edition, London: McGraw-Hill, p. 644.
Rosenbloom, B. (1991), *Marketing Channels: A Management View*, Orlando, USA: The Dryden Press, p. 212.

Further reading

Coughlan, A. (2001), *Marketing Channels*, London: Prentice-Hall.
Hill, L. and O'Sullivan, T. (2004), *Foundation Marketing*, Chapter 10: Distribution, 3rd edition, London: Prentice-Hall, pp. 265–298.
Masterson, R. and Pickton, D. (2004), *Marketing an Introduction*, Chapter 9: Place, London: McGraw-Hill, pp. 265–291.
McGoldrick, P. (2003), *Retail Marketing*, London: McGraw-Hill.
Sullivan, M. and Adcock, D. (2002), *Retail Marketing*, Thomson, London.

Questions

Question 8.1

Retailing: How do you account for the fact that non-shop selling has, in recent years, been one of the fastest growing areas of distribution?

Question 8.2

Channels: What should an organisation consider when it contemplates changing its channel of distribution?

Question 8.3

Distribution: In what circumstances would a company wish to adopt:

- intensive distribution,
- selective distribution,
- exclusive distribution?

Question 8.4

Channel power: How has 'power' within retail channels switched from brands to retail chains over the past 30 years?

'Ultimately, the choice of channel(s) must be based on the long term balance of the benefits and the cost of that choice,' McDonald and Christopher (2003). Discuss this statement in the context of the proposition that channel of distribution decisions are long term and strategic in nature.

What conditions might a marketing firm choose to use the following Under distribution strategies:

- intensive distribution,
- exclusive distribution,
- selective distribution?

Outline the main principles involved in each of the above channel strategies *with examples to illustrate your answer*.

Discuss current channel of distribution trends in global markets. What are the main drivers of these trends?

Outline the advantages and disadvantages of using an international, cross border, retail franchising distribution system.

What are the main marketing environmental factors impacting UK retailers at the present time.

Examine the strategic role of channels of distribution within the firms overall marketing mix.

9
Logistics

9.1 Introduction

Chapter 8 described the decisions that should be taken when a company organises a channel or network of intermediaries who take responsibility for the management of goods as they move from the producer to the consumer. For each channel member the company must decide what type of relationship it seeks. Having established such a network, the organisation must next consider how these goods can be most efficiently transferred, in the physical distribution sense, from the place of manufacture to the place of consumption.

Physical distribution management (PDM) is concerned with ensuring the product is in the right place at the right time.

Both marketing practitioners and academics have regarded 'place' as being the least dynamic of the 'four Ps' and have tended to focus on more conspicuous aspects of marketing. It is now recognised that PDM is a critical area of overall marketing management. Much of its expertise is 'borrowed' from military practice. During the Second World War and the Korean and Vietnam wars, supplies officers had to perform extraordinary feats of PDM, in terms of food, clothing, ammunition, weapons and a whole range of support equipment having to be transported across the world. The military skill that marketing has adopted and applied to PDM is that of logistics. Marketing management realised that distribution could be organised in a scientific way so the concept of business logistics developed, focusing attention on, and increasing the importance of PDM.

Marketing practice has become increasingly sophisticated and managers are more aware of the costs of physical distribution. Whilst the military must win battles, the aim of business is to provide customer satisfaction in a manner that is profitable. Business logistical techniques can be applied to PDM so that costs and customer satisfaction are optimised. There is not much point making savings in the cost of distribution if in the long run sales are lost because of customer dissatisfaction. Similarly, it does not make economic sense to provide a level of service that is not really required by the customer and leads to unnecessary costs. This cost/service balance is a basic dilemma that faces physical distribution managers.

A final reason for the growing importance of PDM or logistics as a marketing function is the increasingly demanding nature of the business environment. In the past it was common for companies to hold large inventories of raw materials and components. Although industries and individual companies differ widely in their stockholding policies, nowadays, stock levels are kept to a minimum wherever possible. Holding stock is a waste working capital for it is not earning money for the company. A more financially analytical approach by management has combined to move the responsibility for carrying stock onto the supplier and away from the customer. Gilbert and Strebel (1989) pointed out that this has a 'domino' effect throughout the marketing channel, with each member putting pressure on the next to provide higher levels of service.

Logistical issues facing physical distribution managers today is the increasing application by customers of 'just-in-time' management techniques or 'lean' manufacturing. This topic was discussed in Chapter 3, but it is re-emphasised here. Hutchins (1988) stresses that companies who demand 'JIT' service from their suppliers carry only a few hours' stock of material and components and rely totally on supplier service to keep their production running. This rigorous distribution system is supported by company expediters whose task it is to 'chase' the progress of orders and deliveries, not only with immediate suppliers, but right along the chain of supply (called 'supply chain integration' [SCI]). Lean manufacturing has been widely adopted throughout the automotive industry where manufacturers possess the required purchasing power to impose such delivery conditions on their suppliers. Their large purchasing power calls for rigorous financial controls, and considerable financial savings can be made in the reduction or elimination of stockholding costs where lean manufacturing is employed.

To think of the logistical process in terms of transportation is too narrow a view. Physical distribution management is concerned with the flow of goods from the receipt of an order until the goods are delivered to the customer. In addition to transportation, PDM involves close liaison with production planning, purchasing, order processing, material control and warehousing. All these areas must be managed so they interact efficiently with each other to provide the level of service that the customer demands at a cost the company can afford.

9.2 Definitions

This chapter considers the four principal components of PDM:

1 order processing,
2 stock levels or inventory,
3 warehousing,
4 transportation.

PDM is concerned with ensuring that the individual efforts that go to make up the distributive function are optimised so a common objective is realised. This is called the 'systems approach' to distribution management and a major feature of PDM is that these functions be integrated.

Because PDM has a well-defined scientific basis, this chapter presents some of the analytical methods that management uses to assist in the development of an efficient logistics system. There are two central themes that should be taken into account:

1 The success of an efficient distribution system relies on integration of effort. An overall service objective can be achieved, even though it may appear that some individual components of the system are not performing at maximum efficiency.
2 It is not possible to provide maximum service at a minimum cost. The higher the level of service required by the customer, the higher the cost. Having decided the appropriate level of service, a company must then consider ways of minimising costs, which should not be at the expense of a reduction of the predetermined service level.

9.3 The distribution process

The distribution process begins when a supplier receives an order from a customer. The customer is not normally concerned with the design of the supplier's distributive system or supply problems, only in its efficiency in terms of the likelihood of receiving goods at the time requested. 'Lead-time' is the period of time that elapses between placing an order and receipt of goods. This can vary according to the type of product and market and industry being considered. Lead-time in the shipbuilding industry can be measured in fractions or multiples of years, whilst in the retail sector, days and hours are common measures. Customers make production plans based on the lead-time agreed when the order was placed. Customers now expect that agreements will be adhered to and late delivery is no longer acceptable in most purchasing situations.

9.3.1 Order processing

Order processing is the first of four stages in the logistical process. The efficiency of order processing has a direct effect on lead times. Orders received by the sales team are processed through the sales department. Many companies establish regular supply routes that remain relatively stable over time providing that the supplier performs satisfactorily. Very often contracts are drawn up and repeat orders (forming part of the initial contract) are made at regular intervals during the contract period. Taken to its logical conclusion this effectively does away with ordering and leads to what is called 'partnership sourcing'. This is an agreement between the buyer and seller to supply a particular product or commodity as and when required without the necessity of negotiating a new contract every time an order is placed.

Order-processing systems should function quickly and accurately. Other departments in the company need to know as quickly as possible that an order has been placed and the customer must have rapid confirmation of the order's receipt and the precise delivery time. Even before products are manufactured and sold, the level of office efficiency is a major contributor to a company's image. Incorrect 'paperwork' and slow reactions by the sales office are often an unrecognised source of antagonism between buyers and sellers. When buyers review their suppliers, efficiency of order processing is an important factor in their evaluation.

A good data processing system for orders received allows stock levels and delivery schedules to be automatically updated, and management can rapidly obtain an accurate view of the sales position. Accuracy is an important objective of order processing, as are procedures that are designed to shorten the order processing cycle. Technological developments allow companies to cover the whole order cycle from taking the initial order to delivering the invoice via the Internet (see Hastings, 2002, p. 8).

9.3.2 Inventory

Inventory, or stock management, is a critical area of PDM because stock levels have a direct effect on levels of service and customer satisfaction. The optimum stock level is a function of the type of market in which the company operates. Few companies can say that they never run out of stock, but if stock-outs happen regularly then market share will be lost to more efficient competitors. The toy retailer 'Toys R Us' prides itself on its stock availability, but is currently working on increasing stock levels and delivery reliability to stores in order to further improve customer service (see Boyes, 2001, p. 27). Techniques for determining optimum stock levels are illustrated later. The key lies in ascertaining the re-order point. Carrying stock at levels below the re-order point might ultimately mean a stock-out, whereas too high stock levels are unnecessary and expensive to maintain. The stock/cost dilemma is illustrated by the systems approach to PDM that is dealt with later.

Stocks represent 'opportunity costs' that occur because of constant competition for the company's limited resources. If the company's marketing strategy requires that high stock levels be maintained, this should be justified by a profit contribution that should exceed the extra costs of carrying that stock. Sometimes a company may be obliged to support high stock levels because the lead-times prevalent in a given market are particularly short. In such a case, the company must seek to reduce costs in other areas of the PDM 'mix'.

9.3.3 Warehousing

American marketing texts tend to pay more attention to warehousing than do UK texts. This is mainly because of the relatively longer distances involved in distributing in the USA, where it can sometimes take days to reach customers by the most efficient road or rail routes. The logistics of warehousing is, therefore, correspondingly more complicated in the USA than in the UK. However, the principles remain the same, and indeed the EU should be viewed as a large 'home market'. Currently, many companies function adequately with their own on-site warehouses from where goods are despatched direct to customers. When a firm markets goods that are ordered regularly, but in small quantities, it becomes more logical to locate warehouses strategically around the country. Transportation can be carried out in bulk from the place of manufacture to respective warehouses where stocks wait ready for further distribution to the customers. Such a system is used by large retail chains except that the warehouses and transportation are owned and operated for them by logistics experts (e.g. BOC Distribution, Excel Logistics and Rowntree Distribution). Levels of service will increase when numbers of warehouse locations increase, but costs will increase accordingly. Again, an optimum strategy must be established that reflects the desired level of service. Many firms now use computerised warehouse management systems which runs the warehouse with a minimum of staff and even allows customers to track the progress of their order (see Nairn, 2002, p. 7).

Factors that must be considered in the warehouse equation are:

- location of customers,
- size of orders,
- frequency of deliveries,
- lead times.

9.3.4 Transportation

Transportation usually represents the greatest distribution cost. It is relatively easy to calculate as it can be related directly to weight or numbers of units. Costs must be carefully controlled through the mode of transport selected, and these must be constantly reviewed. During the past 50 years, road transport has become the dominant transportation mode in the UK. It has the advantage of speed coupled with door-to-door delivery. Many UK supermarkets such as Tesco, Asda and Waitrose offer an e-shopping service from a selection of over 20,000 items which, for a small fee, can be delivered right to the customer door (see Ryle, 2001, p. 6). Not all countries have good transport infrastructure. Carrefour the French food retailer operates in 15 Chinese cities. In France a store would receive about 10 deliveries a day from a central warehouse. In China each store gets about 300 deliveries per day direct from the producers (see Hunt, 2001, p. 36).

Patterns of retailing that have developed, and pressure caused by low stock holding and short lead times, have made road transport indispensable. When the volume of goods being transported reaches certain levels, some companies purchase their own vehicles, rather than use the services of haulage contractors. However, most large retail chains like Marks and Spencer, Tesco and Sainsbury's have now entrusted their warehousing and transportation to individual stores to specialist logistics companies as mentioned earlier.

For some types of goods, transport by rail still has advantages. When lead-time is a less critical element of marketing, or when lowering transport costs is a major objective, this mode of transport becomes viable. Similarly, when goods are hazardous or bulky in relation to value, and produced in large volumes then rail transport is advantageous. Rail transport is also suitable for light goods that require speedy delivery (e.g. letter and parcel post).

Except where goods are highly perishable or valuable in relation to their weight, air transport is not usually an attractive transport alternative for distribution within the UK where distances are relatively short in aviation terms. However, for 'round the year' food products that have traditionally only been available during the UK growing season, air freight is now popular as it is possible to get produce from growers in warmer climates onto UK supermarket shelves in a matter of days, often processed and packed in the overseas country at advantageous prices. For many classes of goods being transported over long-distance overseas routes, air freight has become increasingly popular. It has the advantage of lower insurance costs and quick delivery compared to sea transport, and without the cost of bulky and expensive packaging.

Exporting poses particular transportation problems and challenges. Chapter 16 discusses the need for the exporter's services to be such that the customer is hardly aware that goods purchased have been imported. Therefore, export transportation must be reliable.

The development of roll-on roll-off (RORO) cargo ferries has greatly assisted UK exporters who can now easily service European markets by road, once the North Sea has been crossed. 'Deep sea markets', such as the Far East, Australasia and America, are still served by traditional ocean-going freighters, and the widespread introduction of containerisation in the 1970s made this medium more efficient.

The chosen transportation mode should adequately protect goods from damage in transit (a factor just mentioned makes air freight popular over longer routes as less packaging is needed than for long sea voyages). Damaged goods erode profits, but frequent claims increase insurance premiums and inconvenience customers.

9.4 The systems or 'total' approach to PDM

A central theme of this text has been to highlight the need to integrate marketing activities so they combine into a single marketing effort. Because PDM has received insignificant attention in the past, this function has been late in adopting an integrated approach towards it activities. Managers are now more conscious of the potential of PDM, and recognise that logistical systems should be designed with the total function in mind. A fragmented approach to PDM is a principal cause of failure to provide satisfactory service and is costly.

Within a PDM structure there is potential for conflict. Individual managers striving to achieve their personal goals can frustrate overall PDM objectives. Sales and marketing management will support high stock levels, special products and short production runs coupled with frequent deliveries. Against this, the transport manager attempts to reduce costs by selecting more economical, but slower transportation methods, or by waiting until a load is full before making a delivery. Financial management will exercise pressure to reduce inventory wherever possible and discourage extended warehousing networks. Production managers will favour long production runs and standard products. It is possible for all these management areas to 'appear' efficient if they succeed in realising their individual objectives, but this might well be at the cost of the chosen marketing strategy not being implemented effectively.

Burbridge (1987) provided guidelines to how levels of service to customers can be provided at optimal cost. Senior management must communicate over-all distribution objectives to all company management and ensure they are understood. The systems approach to PDM should encompass production and production planning, purchasing and sales forecasting. Included in the systems approach is the concept of total cost, because individual costs are less important than the total cost. The cost of holding high stocks may appear unreasonable, but if high stocks provide a service that leads to higher sales and profits, then the total cost of all the PDM activities will have been effective. Costs are a reflection of distribution strategy, and maximum service cannot be provided at minimum cost.

PDM as a cost centre is worth extensive analysis as this function is now recognised as a valuable marketing tool in its own right. In homogeneous product markets, where differences in competitive prices may be negligible, service is often the major competitive weapon. Indeed, many buyers pay a premium for products that are consistently delivered on time. Similarly, the salesperson whose company provides a comprehensive service and spare parts facility has a valuable negotiating tool when discussing prices.

Distribution is not, therefore, an adjunct to marketing; it has a full place in the marketing mix and can be an essential component of marketing strategy. In terms of marketing planning, a well-organised business logistics system can help to identify opportunities as well as supplying quantitative data that can be used to optimise the marketing mix as a whole.

9.5 Monitoring and control of PDM

The objective of PDM is: 'Getting the right goods to the right place at the right time for the least cost'. This seems reasonable, and what is needed is guidance on specific measures of operational effectiveness. Management needs objectives or criteria that, in turn, allow meaningful evaluation of performance. This is the basis of monitoring and control.

9.5.1 Output of physical distribution systems

The output from a system of physical distribution is level of customer service. This is a key competitive benefit that companies can offer existing and potential

Table 9.1 An example of a simple delivery delay analysis

Delivery date	Number of orders	Percentage of total orders
As promised	186	37.2
Days late		
1	71	14.2
2	49	9.8
3	35	7.0
4	38	7.6
5	28	5.6
6	14	2.8
7	13	2.6
8	10	2.0
9	8	1.6
10–14	17	3.4
15–21	15	3.0
22–28	10	2.0
< 28+	6	1.2
	500	100.0

customers to retain or attract business. From a policy point of view, the desired level of service should be at least equivalent to that of major competitors.

Level of service is viewed as the time it takes to deliver an order to a customer or the percentage of orders that can be met from stock. Other service elements include technical assistance, training and after-sales services. The two most important service elements to the majority of firms are:

1 *delivery* – reliability and frequency;
2 *stock availability* – the ability to meet orders quickly.

Using a simple example, a company's service policy may be to deliver 40% of all orders within seven days from receipt of order. This is an operationally useful and specific service objective that provides a strict criterion for evaluation. A simple delivery delay analysis (see Table 9.1) will inform management whether such objectives are being achieved or whether corrective action is necessary to alter the actual service level in line with stated objectives. Such an analysis can be updated on receipt of a copy of the despatch note. Management can be provided with a summary, in the form of a management report, from which they can judge whether corrective action is necessary. There can, of course, be over-provision of service, as well as under provision.

9.5.2 Service elasticity

Provision of customer service is a cost that can be calculated in terms of time and money. This applies particularly in industrial markets, where potential customers often consider service more important than price when deciding to source supplies from a particular company. Service levels are a competitive marketing tool for companies supplying the automotive industry which applies lean manufacturing techniques. The concept of diminishing returns, for marketing companies wishing to raise their service levels, is illustrated in the following example:

Suppose it costs a marketing firm £x to provide 75% of all orders from stock, with 60% of all orders delivered within seven days of receipt of purchase order.

To increase either of these targets by, say, 10% may well increase the cost of service provision by 20% or 30%. To be able to meet 85% of orders out of stock, stockholding on all inventory items would have to increase. Similarly, to deliver 70% of orders within the specified time may necessitate the purchase of extra transport that might be under-utilised for a large part of the time. Alternatively, the company might use outside haulage contractors to cope with the extra deliveries, which would add to costs.

The illustration in Figure 9.1 further illustrates this point. In this example, 80% of the total possible service can be provided for approximately 40% of the cost of 100% service provision. To increase general service levels by 10% brings about a cost increase of approximately 18%. 100% service provision means covering every possible eventuality, which is extremely expensive.

In reality, maximum consumer satisfaction and minimum distribution costs are mutually exclusive, and there has to be some kind of trade-off. The degree of trade-off will depend on the degree of service sensitivity or service elasticity in the market or market segments. Two industries may use the same product and may purchase that product from the same supplier, but their criteria for choosing

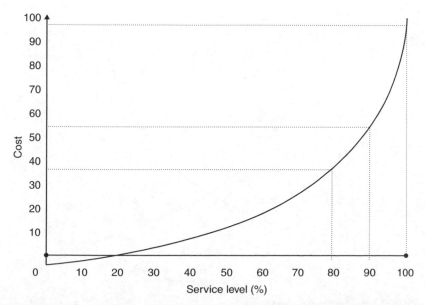

Figure 9.1 Illustration of possible diminishing returns to service level provision

a supplier may be very different. For example, both the sugar-processing and oil exploration industries use large high pressure 'on-line' valves: a sugar processing company to control the flow of its sugar beet pulp in the sugar-making process; an oil exploration company to control the flow of drilling fluids and crude oil on the exploration platform. The oil industry is highly service sensitive (or elastic) and when dealing with suppliers, price is less important, but service levels are critical. Because of the high costs of operations, and the potential cost of breakdown, every effort is made to cover every contingency. On the other hand, the sugar-processing industry is more price sensitive. Sugar processing is seasonal, with much of the processing work being carried out within two months, so as long as these critical two months are not disrupted, service provision can take a relatively low priority for the remainder of the year.

In theory, service levels should be increased up to the point where the marginal marketing expense equals the marginal marketing response. This follows the economist's profit maximisation criterion of marginal cost being equal to marginal revenue. Figure 9.2 illustrates this point and it can be seen that the marginal expense (MME) of level of service provision x_1 is Y and the marginal revenue (MMR) is Z. It would pay the firm to increase service levels, since the extra revenue generated by the increased services (MMR) is greater than the cost (MME). At service level x_2, however, the marginal expense (Z) is higher than the marginal revenue (X), so service provision is too high. Clearly, the theoretical point of service optimisation is where marginal marketing expense and marginal marketing response are equal at service level x_e.

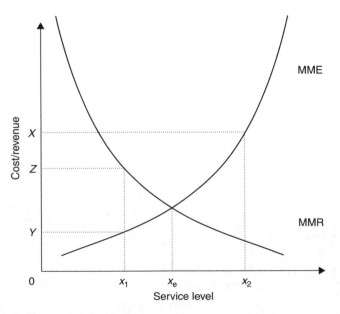

Figure 9.2 Service level versus cost/revenue

9.5.3 Inventory management

Inventory (or stockholding) is described as 'the accumulation of an assortment of items today for the purpose of providing protection against what may occur tomorrow'. An inventory is maintained to increase profitability through manufacturing and marketing support. Manufacturing support is provided through two types of inventory system:

- an inventory of the materials for production,
- an inventory of spare and repair parts for maintaining production equipment.

Similarly, marketing support is provided through:

- inventories of the finished product,
- spare and repair parts that support the product.

If supply and demand could be perfectly coordinated, there would be no need for companies to hold stock. However, future demand is uncertain, as is reliability of supply. Hence inventories are accumulated to ensure availability of raw materials, spare parts and finished goods. Generally speaking, inventories are kept by companies because they:

- act as a 'hedge' against contingencies (e.g. unexpected demand, machinery breakdown);
- act as a 'hedge' against inflation, price or exchange rate fluctuations;
- assist purchasing economies;
- assist transportation economies;
- assist production economies;
- improve the level of customer service by providing greater stock availability.

Inventory planning is largely a matter of balancing various types of cost. The cost of holding stock and procurement has to be considered against the cost of 'stock-out' in terms of production shut downs and loss of business and goodwill that might arise. These various costs conflict with each other.

Larger inventories mean more money is tied up in stock and more warehousing is needed. However, quantity discounts are usually available for large orders (e.g. of materials for production) and if fewer orders have to be placed, then purchasing administrative costs are reduced. Larger inventories also reduce the risks and costs of stock-outs.

When the conflicting costs just described are added together, they form a total cost that can be plotted as a 'U-shaped' curve. Part of management's task is to find a procedure of ordering, resulting in an inventory level that minimises total costs. This 'minimum total cost procurement concept' is illustrated in Figure 9.3.

The economic order quantity (EOQ) is based on the assumption that total inventory costs are minimised at some definable purchase quantity. The EOQ

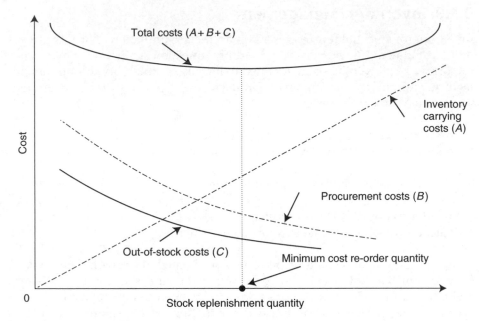

Figure 9.3 Cost trade-off model

method simply assumes that inventory costs are a function of the number of orders that are processed per unit of time, and the costs of maintaining an inventory over and above the cost of items included in the inventory (e.g. warehousing). The EOQ concept is simplistic in that it ignores transportation costs (which may significantly increase for smaller shipments) and the effects of quantity discounts. Because of these limitations, the EOQ concept has decreased in significance in the management of inventory, but the widespread adoption of business computing has allowed the use of more sophisticated versions of EOQ. An example of the traditional EOQ method is provided to give a general understanding of the principles. The economic order quantity can be calculated using the following formula:

$$EOQ = \sqrt{\frac{2AS}{I}}$$

where A is the annual usage (units), S is the ordering costs (£) and I is the inventory carrying cost as a percentage of inventory value (usually related to the current interest rate applied to the unit cost).

For example, for Annual usage = 6,000 units
        Ordering costs = £13
        Inventory carrying cost = 17% (= 0.17)
        Unit cost = £1.30

$$EOQ = \sqrt{\frac{2 \times 6,000 \times 13}{0.17 \times 1.30}}$$

$$= 840 \text{ units at £1.30 per unit.}$$

The EOQ concept and its variations basically seek to define the most economical lot size when considering the placement of an order. The order point method can be used to determine the ideal timing for placing an order. The calculation uses the following equation:

$$OP = DL_t + SS$$

where OP is the order point, D is the demand, L_t is the lead time and SS is the safety stock.

For example, for Demand = 150 units per week
Lead time = 6 weeks
Safety stock = 300 units

$$OP = (150 \times 6) + 300$$
$$= 900 + 300$$
$$= 1,200 \text{ units}$$

That is, a replenishment order should be placed when inventory levels decrease to 1,200 units. The actual size of the order placed when stock reaches this level can be calculated using the EOQ formula.

As with EOQ, the order point method incorporates certain assumptions. The order point assumes that lead times are fixed and can be accurately evaluated, which is rarely the case. However, despite the limitations of both the EOQ and order point models, the basic principles are valid and form the basis of more realistic and useful computer-based inventory models.

9.6 Summary

Discussion of PDM and logistics usually takes place from the viewpoint of the supplier. Understanding physical distribution is, however, just as important to the purchaser. In addition to understanding the distribution tasks that face the supplier, the purchasing department must also appreciate logistical techniques for inventory control and the order cycle. There is consequently a close link between PDM and purchasing.

Work study-techniques and operations management can also be linked to PDM as management is concerned with efficiency and accuracy throughout the distributive function. Whilst a logistical system should not be inflexible, if routines can be established for certain functions they will assist the distribution process.

As a function of the marketing mix, PDM is linked to all other marketing sub-functions and is an important element that plays a large part in achieving the goal of customer satisfaction.

References

Boyes, S. (2001), 'Reinventing Toys R Us', *Corporate Finance*, September, 27–28.

Burbridge, J.J. (Jr), (1987), 'The implementation of a distribution plan: a case study', International *Journal of Physical Distribution and Materials Management*, 17(1), 28–38.

Gilbert, X. and Strebel, P. (1989), 'From innovation to outpacing', *Business Quarterly*, Summer, 19–22.

Hastings, P. (2002), 'Industry seeks ways to get it together', *Financial Times IT Review*, 2nd October, p. 8.

Hunt, J. (2001), 'Orient express', *The Grocer*, 12th May, 36–37.

Nairn, G. (2002), 'More than just boxing clever', *Financial Times IT Review*, October 2nd , p. 7.

Ryle, S. (2001), '@Business: delivering the goods brings net success', *The Observer*, 12th August, p. 6.

Further reading

Brassington, F. and Pettitt, S. (2005), *Essentials of Marketing*, Chapter 8, Place, Prentice-Hall, Financial Times. pp. 243–277.

Hill, L. and O'Sullivan, T. (2004), *Foundation Marketing*, 3rd edition, Chapter 10, Distribution, Prentice-Hall, pp. 265–298.

Jobber, D. (2004), *Principles and Practices of Marketing*, Chapter 17, Distribution, 4th edition, McGraw-Hill, pp. 633–676.

Kotler, P. and Armstrong, G. (2004), *Principles of Marketing*, Chapter 13, Marketing Channels and Supply Chain Management, 10th International edition, Pearson Prentice-Hall, pp. 397–464.

Masterson, R. and Pickton, D. (2004), *Marketing an Introduction*, Chapter 9, Place, McGraw-Hill, pp. 265–291.

Questions

Question 9.1

Why has the marketing function of physical distribution management (PDM) grown significantly in importance with organisations over the past 30 years?

Question 9.2

Explain, using quantitative and non-quantitative examples, the idea that diminishing returns can sometimes be faced by marketing firms when raising the level of service provision to certain customers or market segments.

Question 9.3

Discuss the concept of service 'elasticity' and show how this concept can be applied by management when setting levels of service and how these are priced in the following sectors:

- the oil exploration sector;
- a company supplying the automotive industry.

Question 9.4

Outline and discuss the four main components of a 'systems approach' to PDM.

Question 9.5

Evaluate the importance of a fully integrated physical distribution system (business logistics system) to the successful application of the marketing concept within the firm.

Question 9.6

'Logistics management must be part of the strategic marketing plan if logistics is to play its full part in achieving marketing orientation within the firm' (Lancaster and Reynolds, 2004).

Discuss the above statement in the context of a totally integrated business logistics system and in particular pay particular attention to the contribution logistics can make to the marketing performance of the firm.

10

Advertising, Sales Promotion and Public Relations

10.1 Introduction

Advertising and sales promotion are an integral part of what is termed 'marketing communications'. The word 'communications' is derived from the Latin word *communis* meaning 'common'. Communication can be thought of as the 'process of establishing a commonality or oneness of thought between a sender and a receiver'. This definition highlights two important ideas. First, communication is a process that has elements and inter-relationships that can be modelled and examined in a structured manner. Secondly, oneness of thought must develop between sender and receiver if true communication is to occur. This implies that a sharing relationship must exist between sender and receiver.

It is a mistake to view the 'sender' (for instance, a speaker) as the active member in the relationship and the 'receiver' (a listener) as passive. Consider a person (the sender) speaking to a friend who is not really listening (the intended receiver). It might appear that communication is taking place, but no thought is being shared, and there is no communication between these friends. The reason for this lack of communication is the passivity of the intended receiver. Note that we call one of the people the *intended* receiver. Although sound waves are being transmitted, the intended listener is not receiving and sharing thought. A human receiver can be likened to a television set. A television set is bombarded by television (electromagnetic) waves from several stations. However, it receives only the station to which the channel selector is tuned. Human receivers likewise are bombarded with stimuli from many sources simultaneously, and like the television example, a person selects one source to be 'tuned to' at any moment in time (see Bayne, 2003, p. 73, for an interesting discussion of message targeting using mobile telephones). Both sender and receiver must be active participants in the communicative relationship in order thoughts to be shared. Communication is something one does *with* another person, not *to* another person. We see the relevance of this simple analogy to marketing communications as we proceed through this chapter.

10.2 Marketing communications overview

10.2.1 Models of communication

Models of the communications process may be verbal, nonverbal or mathematical. Regardless of form, they share three basic elements: 'sender', 'message' and 'receiver'.

In its simplest form, the communications process can be modelled as shown in Figure 10.1. The sender (source) is a person or group having a thought to share with some other person or group (the receiver or destination). In marketing, receivers are current and prospective consumers of the company's product. The message is a symbolic expression of the sender's thoughts. The message may take the form of the printed or the spoken word, a magazine advertisement or television commercial being examples.

Figure 10.2 shows a slightly more complex model. This model introduces 'encoding', 'decoding', 'channel' and 'feedback' elements. Encoding is the process of putting thought into symbolic form that is controlled by the sender. Similarly, decoding is the process of transforming message symbols back into thought that is controlled by the receiver. Both encoding and decoding are mental processes. The message itself is the manifestation of the encoding process and

Figure 10.1 A simple communications model

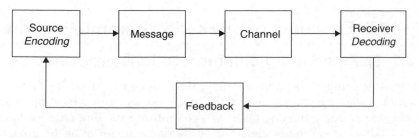

Figure 10.2 A more detailed model of the communication process

Table 10.1 Lasswell's verbal model of communication

Question	Related area of analysis
Who?	Source analysis
Says what?	Content analysis
In which channel?	Media analysis
To whom?	Audience analysis
With what effect?	Effects analysis

is the instrument used in sharing thought with a receiver. The channel is the path through which the message moves from the sender to the receiver. The feedback element recognises the two-way nature of the communications process; in reality, individuals are both senders and receivers and interact with each other continually. Feedback allows the sender of the original message to monitor how accurately the message is being received. Thus, the feedback mechanism gives the sender some measure of control in the communication process. It is acknowledged that an advertising message may not be received by customers as originally intended. Based on market feedback, the message can be re-examined and perhaps corrected.

In addition to these graphic representations, there are verbal models of the communications process. Lasswell provides us with a useful one by posing questions. Although this describes only the elements of communication, and not their inter-relationships, its real value lies in the area of research (see Hollensen, 2004, p. 559). The model identifies five key areas of analysis, as shown in Table 10.1.

Although this model is useful from the standpoint of posing critical questions for research, most verbal models are of limited use. They do not show the dynamic nature of the communication process, partly because of the static nature of words. The models presented above are general and simple. Additional complexities such as cultural factors must be added when considering an appropriate marketing communications mix for a firm operating internationally or globally (see Solberg, 2002, pp. 1–21; Harris and Attour, 2003, pp. 154–168). International aspects are considered further in Chapter 17.

10.3 Elements of marketing communications

10.3.1 The marketing communications process

Traditionally, promotion (in its broadest sense of being one of the '4Ps' of the marketing mix or one of the 7P's of the extended services marketing mix) has been viewed as being the organisation's communication link with prospective buyers. Today promotion is viewed as only one element of an organisation's overall effort to communicate with consumers (Gould, 2000, p. 22). To view it simply as promotion is to take a too narrow perspective (Schultz, 2002A, p. 11). All marketing mix variables, as well as other company actions, must be seen as part of the total integrated message the company conveys to consumers about its 'offering' which is often in the form of a brand. Communications from various sources must be integrated and coordinated to enhance and develop a unified brand image (see Robison and Rohan, 2002, p. 47).

If we consider the company and the consumer as systems, we see that they share certain characteristics. The company system might be in a position it wishes to improve (or at least maintain). For example, the company may wish to increase profits and market share; enhance its reputation among competitors, the trade, and its consumers; and/or be perceived as an innovator and leader in its field. These desires are usually expressed in the form of company goals. Thus, the company has needs to fulfil. In analogous fashion, consumers perceive their present position and personal goals they wish to attain. They also have needs to fulfil.

The common vehicle that permits each to move towards its goals is the 'total product offering'. This is the 'bundle of satisfactions' the company offers to prospective consumers. Consumers do not purchase a product for the product's sake, but for the meanings it has for them and what it will do for them in both an instrumental and a psychological sense. This is the concept that was developed in Chapter 4 relating to buyer behaviour.

Thus, the role of the marketing communications function is to share the meaning of the company's total product offering with its consumers in such a way to help consumers attain their goals and at the same time move the company closer to its own goals (see Schultz, 2002B, p. 8).

10.3.2 The marketing communications mix

Promotion in its broadest sense means 'to move forward'. However, in business, it refers to the communications activities of advertising, personal selling, sales promotion and publicity.

Advertising is a visible form of mass communications that is non-personal and paid for by an identified sponsor. Personal selling is a form of personal communication in which a seller attempts to persuade prospective buyers to purchase the company's product or service. Sales promotion relates to those short-term marketing activities that act as incentives to stimulate quick buyer action, for example, coupons, premiums and free samples. These promotional activities (advertising, personal selling and sales promotion) are variables over which the company has control. The company generally has little control over the presentation of publicity. Like advertising, publicity is a form of non-personal communication to a large group of people, but unlike advertising, publicity is not paid for by the company. Publicity is usually in the form of news or editorial comment about a company's product or service. However, companies can instigate publicity through the release of news items, thereby exercising some measure of control over the publicity component of promotion (a point discussed later in Section 10.11).

The blend of these promotional activities is referred to as the 'promotional mix', or more correctly the 'communications mix' (Jobber, 2004, p. 414). The emphasis placed on each element in the communications mix varies according to:

- product type,
- consumer characteristics,
- company resources,
- producers within the same industry who will have different promotional mixes depending on size of firm, competitive strengths and weaknesses, managerial strengths and weaknesses and managerial style and philosophy.

Other communications elements with which promotion must be coordinated are the product itself, price and choice of distribution channels. Components of product communication include brand name, package design, package colour, size, shape, trademark and aspects of the physical product itself. These product 'cues' provide the consumer with subtle messages about the total product offering. Price also has important communications value and is often used by sellers to connote quality in the product offering, and can often imply 'snob appeal'.

Retail stores (place) in which products are found have significant communications value. Stores, like people, possess 'personalities' which consumers readily perceive and often associate with the merchandise located in the stores. Two stores selling essentially similar products can project different product images to prospective consumers, particularly when the consumers are not familiar with the product category. For example, a camera sold exclusively through specialist camera shops may project an image of higher quality than one sold in a discount department store, even though the cameras may be of comparable quality. If a company has to decide whether to sell its men's 'cologne' through fashionable menswear shops or through drug stores, discount houses and supermarkets, the channel decision must be made in light of the firm's communications objectives.

Promotion is one of several activities in which companies engage to communicate their product offerings. The blend of these variables as perceived by consumers is the marketing communications mix.

10.3.3 Marketing and marketing communications

Given that the '4Ps' (7P's for services, the other three being peoples, processes and physical evidence) are important elements of both concepts, how does marketing differ from marketing communications? Some texts argue that the market mix is really a communications mix in which all activities interact, sometimes in a mutually reinforcing way, sometimes in conflict with one another, to form an image that can be favourable or unfavourable. Other texts differentiate between marketing and marketing communications by considering marketing communications as a later stage in the total marketing process.

Marketing effectiveness depends on effective communication. The market is energised or activated by information flows. The buyer's perception of the seller's market offering is influenced by the amount and type of information they have about the offering and their reaction to that information. Marketing, according to this view, relies heavily on information flows between sellers and prospective buyers. Marketing involves decision-making activities, whereas marketing communication is the process of implementing marketing decisions. Implementation of marketing decisions requires enactment of the communications process. The company's message is the combination of product, price, place and promotional stimuli it transmits to the marketplace, and communication takes place when consumers in the market interpret these stimuli.

A good marketing communications system provides for information flows from the consumer to the firm. It is a dialogue between buyer and seller and not simply a monologue from seller to buyer.

10.4 Definition of marketing communications

A formal definition of marketing communications has not yet been given, as we have attempted to describe its function to convey a 'feel' for the breadth of the area. A 'macro' definition is that marketing communications is a continuing dialogue between buyers and sellers in a marketplace. However, this is too general. A practical alternative definition defines marketing communications as the process of:

1 presenting an integrated set of stimuli to a market target with the intent of evoking a desired set of responses (Kotler and Armstrong, 2004, p. 468);
2 setting up channels to receive, interpret and act on messages from the market to modify present company messages and identify new communications opportunities.

This recognises that the company is both a sender and a receiver of market-related messages. As a sender, a firm in a competitive environment must attempt to persuade consumers to buy the company's brands in order to achieve a certain level of profits. As a receiver, the company must attune itself to its market to realign its messages to its market targets, adapt its messages to changing market conditions and take advantage of new communications opportunities. This interpretation is in line with the marketing concept. Note the word integrated used above. This is key to an understanding of modern marketing communications. Each element within the marketing communication mix interacts with all the others in some way. Hence the total communications effort must be a process of understanding these complex interactions taking place and an attempt to integrate the effects of each of the elements to bring about the desired total communications effect (see Kotler et al., 2001, pp. 627–628; Clow and Baack, 2004, p. 17) for a more detailed discussion of the integrative nature of modern marketing communications.

10.5 Message source

The nature of the source of a message as a component in the communications process can have an influence on receivers. Some communicators are more persuasive than others, and the degree to which they are more successful depends on how credible or believable the audience perceives them to be. Note the word 'perceives', for it is less important that the source is credible, and more important that the audience perceives it to be. Credibility is the sum of the set of perceptions that receivers hold in relation to a source. The audience's set of perceptions might include factors like the source's perceived trustworthiness or honesty, the potential to manipulate, its prestige, expertise, power and length of time in business. For example, the perceived degree of honesty or trustworthiness of a source depends on the audience's perception of the source's intent. If the audience believes a communicator has underlying motives like personal gain, the source will be less persuasive than one they perceive as having nothing to gain. 'Overheard conversation' has a similar effect as the receiver believes they were not the intended target of the message, so believes the communicator has no direct intent to manipulate which increases the source's credibility.

In advertising, the consumer is wary of the intentions of the advertiser. It is difficult to eliminate intent to persuade. Some television advertisements attempt to increase credibility by using 'candid' interviews with homemakers. The homemaker is asked to explain why they purchase a particular brand or asked to 'trade' their usual brand for another, for example, one box of their regular detergent for two boxes of another detergent (and the answer is always 'no'). Another approach is to ask 'consumers' to compare their brand of product with another, both in disguised form. The 'consumer' acts surprised when they learn that the sponsor's brand performs better than their regular brand. In these commercials advertisers are attempting to imply a degree of objectivity to establish credibility for their message.

If the audience perceives the source to be an 'expert' speaker, perhaps one who has appropriate education, information, or knowledge on a given subject, the source will be more successful in changing audience opinions pertaining to this area of expertise. Specialised sources of information, particularly the media, are quite often perceived as expert sources. In a study on physician's adoption of a new drug, researchers learned that physicians were more influenced by specialised technical journals than by journals aimed at the entire profession. The effectiveness of a specialised source is largely due to the fact that messages are aimed at selected audiences. In advertising, professionals are often used as promoters for brands.

Perceived status or prestige of the source affects its credibility. This can relate to a class concept, but also to the 'role' of the source in the particular situation. Everyone has several roles to play. One individual may be a corporate executive, a husband, a father, a member of the local Masonic lodge and secretary of the local Chamber of Commerce. Each role carries with it a status or level of prestige. A person usually separates these roles, adopting the one appropriate to a given situation. Generally, the higher the perceived status of a source, the more persuasive it will be. This is particularly true when the source is communicating on a topic related to role position.

When a receiver likes a source, the source will be more persuasive than if it is disliked. Evidence suggests that age, sex, dress, mannerisms, accent and voice inflection affect source credibility. These are characteristics that subtly influence an audience's evaluation of the communicator and the message.

10.5.1 The 'sleeper effect'

Sources high in credibility can cause opinion changes in receivers, but does this change endure? Evidence suggests that influence of a credible source dissipates rapidly after initial exposure to a persuasive message. Furthermore, a finding observed in several experiments is that where an audience is initially exposed to a low-credibility source, their opinion change increases over time in the higher direction suggested by that source. Figure 10.3 illustrates this phenomenon, referred to as the 'sleeper effect'.

There is another facet to the 'sleeper effect'. Evidence suggests that when a high-credibility source is reinstated (e.g. by a repeat advertisement) as one would expect, audience agreement with the source is higher after a period of time than if the source had not be reinstated. However, for a low-credibility source, reinstatement results in less agreement with the source than with no reinstatement, that is, reinstatement negates 'sleeper effect'. This phenomenon is illustrated in Figure 10.4.

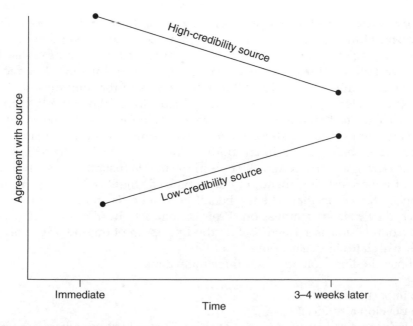

Figure 10.3 The 'sleeper effect'

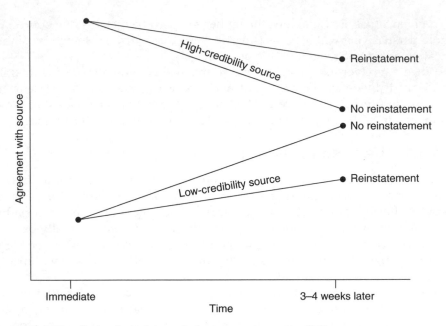

Figure 10.4 The effects of reinstatement of source on source credibility

10.6 Advertising

Advertising is paid for by a sponsor attempting to convey a message to the recipient. However, a salesperson is paid to convey the employer's (sponsor's) message to a recipient and this is not regarded as an advertisement. Another distinguishing feature is that the advertisement should be received by a large number of recipients through mass, paid-for communication. It is sometimes referred in the advertising industry to as 'above-the-line' promotion. This means that it is advertising that is paid for through the advertising industry commission system, where advertising agencies that are 'recognised' (by their professional body 'The Institute of Practitioners in Advertisers') receive a commission from the media (usually between 10% and 15% of the advertising spend, but sometimes as high as 25%) for the advertising the place on their clients' behalf. The 'line' is simply the line above which they receive commission. Promotional activity that does not receive such commission is termed 'below-the-line' promotion and this activity is dealt with later in this chapter.

Above-the-line promotion has three main aims:

1 to impart information;
2 to develop attitudes;
3 to induce action beneficial to the advertiser (generally the purchase of a product or service).

Washing detergent advertisements on television, party political broadcasts and 'situations vacant' advertisements in newspapers are examples of different forms of advertising. They are mass communications directed at an audience rather than a specific person, paid for by a sponsor (a detergent manufacturer, a political party or an employer) who desire to achieve some purpose: the sale of detergent, the winning of votes at an election or the hiring of personnel.

Advertising rarely creates sales on its own accord. Whether or not the customer buys depends on the product, its price, packaging, personal selling, after-sales service, financing and other aspects of the marketing process. Advertising is only one element of the communications mix. Advertising performs certain parts of the communications task with greater economy, speed and volume than can be achieved through other means.

The amount of the communication task performed by advertising will vary, depending on the nature of the product, frequency of purchase and price. When the product is sold through mail order catalogue, virtually the whole of the communication task is achieved by advertising and the promotional elements describing the products in the catalogue. In contrast, in the case of industrial goods, the salesperson will usually close a sale, but the task of selling the company's product is helped by the potential client's awareness of the product, achieved in part through company advertising. Here, advertising's purpose is to enhance potential clients' responses to the firm and its products.

The contribution of advertising is likely to be greatest when:

1 buyer awareness of the company's product is low;
2 industry sales are rising rather than remaining stable or declining;
3 the product has features not normally observable to the buyer;
4 the opportunities for product differentiation are strong;
5 discretionary incomes are high;
6 a new product or new service idea is being introduced.

10.7 Advertising models

Models that attempt to explain how advertising works have been drawn from various disciplines, particularly psychology, and from advertising practitioners. Early models relied on stimulus/response formula, and later ones took into account the environment in which the purchasing decision is made.

10.7.1 Starch

One of the oldest models of advertising is that of advertising practitioner Daniel Starch, who said in 1925 'for an advertisement to be successful it must be seen, must be read, must be believed, must be remembered and must be acted upon'. This model is not too useful because it takes little account of the state of mind of the consumer with respect to the product. The advertisement is assumed to be the main influence and no allowance is made for the combined or multiple effects of advertisements, implying that the effects of single advertisements on consumers are independent of each other. In reality, it is likely that the cumulative impact of repetition of one advertisement or different advertisements in a campaign will have a greater effect on the consumer than a single viewing of one advertisement. However, it still referred to in the advertising industry, but more in the context of 'starch ratings' having become a generic term relating to effectiveness ratings of advertisements.

10.7.2 The DAGMAR philosophy

This model allows for the cumulative impact of advertisements, although not in a quantitative way. Colley's defining advertising goals for measured advertising results (DAGMAR) model refers to the sequential states of mind, through which it is assumed consumers must pass:

1 from unawareness,
2 to awareness,
3 to comprehension,
4 to conviction,
5 to action.

Colley describes these levels as the marketing communications spectrum. Advertising is seen as one of a number of marketing tools (the others being promotion, personal selling, publicity, price, packaging and distribution) which, acting singly or in combination, move the consumer through successive levels of the spectrum as follows:

- *Unawareness/awareness*: People who have never heard of the product are at the unawareness level. It is possible that people buy products whose names are unknown to them, but such sales are few. At this level the advertisement is trying to make the potential customer aware of the product's existence.
- *Comprehension*: At this level the consumer is not only aware of the product, but recognises the brand name and the trademark and also has some degree of knowledge about the product – what it is and what it does. This knowledge may have been gained from the actual advertisement or gained after an information search prompted by the advertisement. For example, a potential hotel guest would be this stage recognise the names of hotels X and Y, and also know that hotel X is a three-star hotel near the airport, while hotel Y is a four-star hotel in the centre of town.
- *Conviction*: Conviction implies a firm attitude towards the product. In the hotel example, conviction may be illustrated by a consumer who says 'Hotel A is a four-star hotel in city Z where I can get good service for a reasonable price. I intend to stay there next time I visit city Z'. Colley illustrates the conviction level by examples of a woman who prefers a particular brand of lipstick and a man who prefers a particular brand of beer, where preferences are on an emotional rather than a strictly rational basis.

- *Action*: At this stage the consumer has made some overt move toward the purchase of the product. In the hotel example this will occur when the customer tried to book a hotel room. Inducing an actual purchase may be beyond the power of advertising (the hotel may be fully booked, or the room rate may be considered too expensive) but the advertisement will have been 'acted upon' which is the end point of the Starch model.

The idea that advertisements 'nudge' consumers along a spectrum that extends from complete ignorance of the product to attempting to purchase, rather than individually achieving or failing to achieve results which owe nothing to previous exposures, leads to the concept that the purpose of advertising is to bring about a change in state of mind towards the purchase of a product. Rarely is a single advertisement powerful enough to move a prospect from complete unawareness to action. Advertising effectiveness should be measured in terms of the extent to which it moves people along the spectrum.

Adoption of the DAGMAR model can lead to a clearer statement of advertising objectives and to valid measurements of success in obtaining these objectives. A study by Majaro in 1970 looked at UK and European companies and tried to answer the following questions:

1 How many companies measure systematically, if at all, the results of their advertising effort?
2 How many companies are able to express in quantitative terms the impact that a specific campaign has achieved?

Questionnaire replies revealed that 70% of firms claimed they formulated advertising objectives. Nearly all consumer goods firms selected objectives for their advertising (or said they did). Only 55% of the sample actually presented their objectives in written form. The study showed that companies formulating advertising objectives fared better in the market place than those that did not. Only 35% of the total sample reported increased market-share during a four-year period. Of these 'high fliers', 85% actively pursued an advertising-by-objectives philosophy.

The conclusions of the study promoted the value of adopting a systematic advertising-by-objectives process based on a stepwise movement through the communications spectrum, but it did not prove that success (in terms of increased market share or financial performance) is directly related to advertising.

10.7.3 The Lavidge and Steiner model

Another sequential model put forward by Lavidge and Steiner (1961) proposed a hierarchical sequence of effects resulting from the perception of an advertisement that moves the consumer ever closer to purchase. The six levels are:

1 awareness,
2 knowledge,

3 liking,
4 preference,
5 conviction,
6 purchase.

The six steps indicate three major functions of advertising: the first two, awareness and knowledge, relate to information or ideas; the second pair, to attitudes
or feelings toward the product; and the final two, conviction and purchase, produce action, or the acquisition of the product. They claimed that these three
functions (information, attitudes and action) are directly related to a classic
psychological model that divides behaviour into three components or dimensions: cognitive, affective and conative.

'Hierarchy-of-effects' models have been criticised. Joyce said: '… they are put
forward not on the basis of empirical evidence, but on the basis of an appeal to
intuition or common sense'. Although these models differ in the number and
nature of the stages in the process leading to the buying action, there is general
agreement that buying action is the culminating stage of a sequence of persuasion events. This assumes a predictable one-way relationship between
changes in a consumer's knowledge and attitudes towards a product and
changes in his or her buying behaviour towards that product.

10.7.4 Dissonance theory

This indicates that the flow of causality is not unidirectional as proposed by hierarchical models. Most decisions involve the decision-maker in cognitive dissonance or the notion that the chosen option will have some unattractive features,
while rejected options will have some attractive features. Therefore, it is predicted
that after making a decision, the decision-maker will actively seek information to
reinforce and justify the purchasing decision and will 'filter' information to
which he or she is exposed; favourable data being assimilated and unfavourable
data being discarded or ignored. Hence there is a two-way relationship, with
behaviour influencing attitudes as well as attitudes influencing behaviour.

The major implication of dissonance theory is that for existing brands in the
repeat purchase market the role of advertising is essentially defensive. It should
seek to maintain the brand within the buyer's choice portfolio and be aimed at
existing users of the brand who are aware of the brand and who have formed
positive attitudes towards it. The consumer tends to perceptually select advertisements for brands that are habitually purchased. Repetitive reassurance
advertising should, therefore, reinforce the continuation of the buying habit in
the face of competition.

10.7.5 Unique selling proposition

Models so far discussed have largely been developed by researchers drawing
on research in psychology or on experiments or observations made in the market
place. People in advertising who put forward models often have a particular

view of advertising they wish to promote. One of the best known examples is the theory developed by Rosser Reeves who reported the principles his agency had worked with for 30 years, embodied in the 'unique selling proposition' (USP). Reeves stated: 'The consumer tends to remember just one thing from the advertisement – one strong claim, or one strong concept. Each advertisement must make a proposition to the customer. The proposition must be one that competition either cannot, or does not, offer. The proposition must be so strong that it can move the masses (i.e. pull them over to your product)'. Reeves is saying that an advertisement works by making a claim for the product that is clearly related to consumer needs that will be recalled by the consumer and motivate purchasing action at the appropriate time.

10.7.6 The 'brand image' school

Alternative approaches to advertising related to the contrast between the 'USP school' and the 'brand-image school' led by the famous advertising practitioner David Ogilvy. The brand-image school concentrated on non-verbal methods of communication, evoking moods and investing a brand with additional favourable connotations that are not necessarily specifically associated with the product's properties in use e.g. connotations of prestige and quality, which Ogilvy claims 'give a brand a first-class ticket through life'. Whilst these models are intuitively feasible, there is no way of validating them. An advertisement is the carrier or channel through which the sponsor communicates a message to an audience. In 1980, Aaker and Myers used the diagram shown in Figure 10.5 to illustrate the communication process (note that this diagram is an elaboration of Figure 10.2).

The sponsor's encoded message is transmitted to recipients (by advertising or salespeople), and recipients then decode and absorb it, either in whole or in

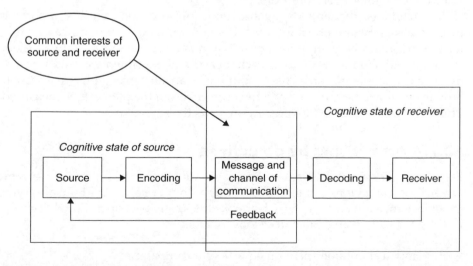

Figure 10.5 Aaker and Myers' model of communication

part. The accuracy of communication depends on the degree of correspondence between the meaning assigned to the symbols used by the source and by the receiver. Successful communication requires an area of overlap between the cognitive fields of the sender of a message and the receiver. Anything that distorts the quality of transmission, reducing the effectiveness of a message is called 'noise'. Noise can occur because the receiver does not interpret the message in the way the source intended. This can be caused by differences in the cultural backgrounds of the source and the receiver. A further example of noise is 'cognitive dissonance' that occurs when people's experience (receipt of the message) does not agree with what they previously believed.

The individual receiver may handle dissonance in a number of different ways by:

1 rejecting the message,
2 ignoring the message,
3 altering the previous opinion,
4 searching for justifications.

The first two possible reactions are negative effects from the source's point of view. Noise may also act as a message to the source (feedback) that may well change the behaviour of the source, either changing the message or ceasing communication if convinced that the particular receiver is not receptive to ideas and that further communication would be wasted.

The view that advertising works by converting people into users of a particular product or brand can be misleading. Advertising may have a positive affect, even if the level of sales is steady (or declining), by preventing loss (or greater loss) of users. In some markets, increasing the loyalty of existing users and increasing the amount they buy may be a better prospect for increasing sales than winning over non-users.

It is contended that advertising situations are so varied that it is impossible to generalise how advertising works and general model building can be misleading because every advertising campaign is a unique response to a unique situation and should generate its own measure of effectiveness. This supports the idea that a potential advertiser should have an advertising plan that sets out how the goal will be achieved and how the effects of the plan can be measured. This approach is termed 'advertising-by-objectives'.

10.7.7 Advertising by objectives

Few companies are able to express in quantitative terms the impact of a specific advertising campaign, and give little thought to precisely what they are trying to achieve through advertising. Clear objectives can assist operational decision-making for advertising. Such decisions include:

- How much should be spent on a particular campaign?
- What should comprise the content and presentation of the advertisement?

- What are the most appropriate media?
- What should be the frequency of display of advertisements or campaigns?
- Should any special geographical weighting of effort be used?
- What are the best methods of evaluating the effects of the advertising?

A classic study by Corkindale and Kennedy in 1978 suggested that systematically setting and evaluating objectives for the various elements in an advertising programme provides benefits, as long as certain conditions are met:

1 Marketing management has to consider and define in advance what each element in the programme is expected to accomplish.
2 An information system should be set up to monitor on-going performance with the nature of information required being clearly defined.
3 Marketing management will learn about the system it is operating from the accumulated experience of success (and failure) and can use this knowledge to improve future performance.

Majaro's (1970) classic research on objective setting revealed that although 70% of companies appeared to set advertising objectives, these were mostly crude and tended to be confused with marketing objectives. The question 'What are the actual advertising objectives of your company?' yielded the following in order of frequency of mention:

1 increase or support sales,
2 create or increase product or brand awareness,
3 improve image of company's products,
4 improve company's image,
5 sales promotion,
6 influence attitudes,
7 inform or educate the consumer,
8 introduce new products.

Most managers saw increasing sales or market share as a main objective, but this is a marketing objective. Unless advertising was the only element of the marketing mix that is used (as is sometimes the case in direct mail and mail-order businesses) it would not be reasonable to expect advertising alone to achieve this objective.

According to DAGMAR theory, the main objective of advertising is to accomplish clearly defined communication objectives. Thus, advertising succeeds or fails according to how well it communicates predetermined information and attitudes to the right people, at the right time, at the right cost.

Majaro's study found the following methods of evaluation were claimed to be used by companies (in rank order of frequency of mention):

1 'sort and count techniques' such as consumer mail or coupon response,
2 group interviews or panel discussions,

3 recall tests,
4 comparison of sales results (monthly, quarterly or annually),
5 psychological 'depth interviews',
6 folder tests,
7 salesmen's monthly reports,
8 annual survey by market research department,
9 reports from dealers,
10 mathematical models.

A common failure reported was that measurement methods did not dovetail with specific objectives. For instance, depth interviews were claimed to be used to measure attitude changes, although the advertising objective given on the questionnaire was 'to inform the public of a product's availability'. The overall conclusion was that relevant measures were not being used. Clear, precise advertising objectives would rectify this situation.

Majaro set out a number of advantages of the advertising-by-objectives approach to advertising:

1 It helps to integrate advertising effort with other ingredients of the marketing mix, thus setting a consistent and logical marketing plan.
2 It facilitates the task of the advertising agency in preparing and evaluating creative work and recommending the most suitable media.
3 It assists in determining advertising budgets.
4 It enables marketing executives and top management to appraise the advertising plan realistically.
5 It permits meaningful measurement of advertising results.

10.7.8 Setting objectives

It can be the case that many people in a company who influence advertising decisions do not have a common understanding of its purpose, for example:

- the Chairman may be most concerned with building a corporate image;
- the Sales Manager may regard advertising as a means of obtaining larger orders;
- the Finance Director regards advertising as an expense, chargeable to a given fiscal period;
- the Advertising Manager or the Agency Account Executive may see it as an investment directed toward building a brand image, and increasing the company's share of the market.

The main difficulty is differentiating between marketing objectives and advertising objectives. The proper sequence is to first define the overall marketing objectives and to then determine the contribution that advertising can make to each of these. An advertising objective should be one that advertising alone is expected to achieve.

The following should be considered when setting advertising objectives:

1 Advertising objectives should be consistent with broader corporate objectives.
2 Objectives should be realistic in terms of internal resources and external opportunities, threats and constraints.
3 Objectives should be widely known so people understand the goals of their work and how they relate to the broader objectives of the firm as a whole.
4 Objectives needs to be flexible, acknowledging that all business decisions, including advertising decisions, have to be made in circumstances of partial ignorance.
5 Objectives should be periodically reconsidered and redefined, not only to take account of changing conditions, but also to ensure that objectives are generally known.

Before practical work on setting advertising objectives can begin, information on the product, the market and consumers must be available. Of prime importance is a thorough assessment of consumer behaviour and motivation with particular reference to the company's target group of customers. The statement of advertising objectives should then make clear what basic message is intended to be delivered, to what audience, with what intended effects and the specific criteria that are going to be used to measure success.

Corkindale and Kennedy (1976) summarised the main considerations in setting advertising objectives under five key words:

1 *What* role is advertising expected to fulfil in the total marketing effort?
2 *Why* is it believed that advertising can achieve this role? (i.e. what evidence is there and what assumptions are necessary?)
3 *Who* should be involved in setting objectives? Who should be responsible for agreeing the objectives, co-ordinating their implementation and subsequent evaluation? Who is the intended audience?
4 *How* are the advertising objectives to be put into practice?
5 *When* are various parts of the programme to be implemented? When can response be expected to each stage of the programme?

10.8 Sales promotion

10.8.1 Introduction

Sales promotion is a dynamic and flexible sales tool that does not easily lend itself to the confines of an exact definition. Two slightly different definitions are:

- 'The short-term achievement of marketing objectives by schematic means'.
- 'Immediate or delayed incentives to purchase, expressed in cash or in kind'.

Both are accurate within their limitations although they are different. Our concern is with the function of sales promotion (what it consists of and what it does) so we shall not dwell on abstract definitions.

10.8.2 Main elements of sales promotion

Figure 10.6 shows the primary types of sales promotion and their possible uses. Other marketing elements that come within the realm of sales promotions are:

- display materials (e.g. stands, header boards, shelf strips, 'wobblers'),
- packaging (e.g. pack-flashes, coupons, premium offers),
- merchandising (i.e. demonstrations, auxiliary sales forces, display arrangements),
- direct mail (e.g. coupons, competitions, premiums),
- exhibitions.

These main types of promotions are also applicable to the industrial sector although such promotions are more likely to be closer in type to promotions mounted by manufacturers of consumer goods for retailers. In essence, they will be designed to gain optimum-sized orders over long periods.

Promotion type

Objective	Self-liquidating premium	On-pack premium	In-pack premium	With-pack premium	Container premium	Continuing premium	Trading stamps/gift coupons/vouchers	Competition	Personalities	Couponing	Sampling	Reduced price pack	Limpet pack	Related items
Product launch or relaunch						X		X	X	X	X			
Induce trial								X	X		X			
Existing produce new usage								X	X	X	X	X		
Gain new users					X	X	X	X	X	X	X	X	X	X
Retain existing users								X	X			X	X	
Increase frequency of purchase								X	X					
Upgrade purchase size	X	X		X	X							X		
Increase brand awareness								X		X				
Expand distribution								X	X			X	X	X
Increase trade stocks				X								X	X	X
Reduce trade stocks										X				X
Expand sales 'off season'						X				X		X	X	X
Activate slow moving lines										X		X	X	X
Gain special featuring in-store	X	X	X	X	X			X				X	X	X
Increase shelf display	X	X											X	X

Figure 10.6 The effective use of consumer promotions showing objectives that certain promotions might achieve

10.8.3 Sales promotion planning

There are a number of stages during the running of a particular promotion. As with any business task, a full plan should be prepared to ensure that each stage is reached. An example of a planned sequence of stages in the context of sales promotion is:

1 analyse the problem/task,
2 define objectives,
3 consider and/or set the budget,
4 examine the types of promotion likely to be of use,
5 define the support activities (e.g. advertising, incentives, auxiliaries),
6 testing (e.g. a limited store or panel test),
7 decide measurements required,
8 plan timetable,
9 present details to sales force, retailers, etc.,
10 implement the promotion,
11 evaluate the results.

10.8.4 Advantages and disadvantages of sales promotions

Advantages:

- easily measured response,
- quick achievement of objectives,
- flexible application,
- can be relatively cheap,
- direct support of sales force.

Disadvantages:

- price-discounting can cheapen brand image,
- short-term advantages only,
- can cause problems with retailers who might not want to co-operate,
- difficulty in communicating brand message.

10.8.5 Importance of sales promotion

There is often disagreement about what marketing expenditures should be attributed to sales promotion. A free plastic daffodil with every packet of washing powder is certainly a sales promotion, but price reductions can be confusing, in that '15% extra "free" ' is a sales promotion, but it might also be regarded as a price discount. Sales promotional expenditure data can easily be collected and analysed. The amount spent on sales promotion has been increasing for a long time, and this is recognition of its importance as a tool of marketing communication.

10.9 Telephone marketing

As a marketing medium the telephone derives its power from its transactional nature (i.e. one person in a controlled conversation with another). What originally began as 'ordering by telephone' soon evolved into telemarketing, a concept that can be defined as:

> Any measurable activity that creates and exploits a direct relationship between supplier and customer by the interactive use of the telephone.

The American Telephone and Telegraph Company define it as 'the marketing of telecommunications technology and direct marketing techniques'.

 ## 10.10 Direct mail

10.10.1 What is direct mail?

Direct mail is considered by some to be an advertising medium, but by others to be a separate element of the marketing communications mix. Direct mailing is the use of the postal service to distribute a piece of informative literature or other promotional material to selected prospects. A 'direct mail shot' may consist of anything from a letter to catalogues of product offerings. Well-known regular users of direct mail techniques in the UK today are Readers Digest and the Automobile Association.

Direct mail is a method of communicating a message directly to a particular person, household or firm. As such it falls under the more general heading of direct marketing that includes many other forms of direct communication. To avoid confusion, let us distinguish direct mail from related activities with which it is commonly confused. Direct mail is not:

1 *Direct advertising*: This is one of the oldest methods of reaching the consumer. It consists of printed matter that is sent by the advertiser directly to the prospect. This material is often sent by mail, but it may also be distributed house-to-house by personal delivery, handed out to passers-by, or even put under the windscreen wipers of parked cars. That portion of direct advertising that is sent through the mail is called direct mail advertising. Hence some, but not all, direct advertising is a form of direct mail.
2 *Mail order*: If the object of a direct mail shot is to persuade recipients to order the product or service by return post, the correct term is mail order or mail order advertising. Deliveries are made through mail or parcel services, or by a carrier direct from a warehouse or factory or sometimes through a local agent.

  Mail order is a special form of direct mail that seeks to complete the sale entirely by mail, while direct mail is generally supplementary to other forms of advertising and selling. Direct mail is usually a part of a company's general marketing plan, whereas mail order advertising is a complete plan in itself, and companies exist solely to conduct business in this manner. Hence, mail order is a type of direct mail, but not all direct mail is mail order.

3 *Direct response advertising*: Neither direct mail nor mail order should be confused with direct response advertising. This is the strategy of using specially designed advertisements, usually in newspapers and magazines, to invoke a direct response rather than a delayed one. The most familiar type of direct response advertising is the coupon-response press ad, in which a return coupon is provided that the reader may use to order the advertised product or service or to request further information or a sales call. Other variants involve incentives to visit the retail outlet immediately, such as special preview invitations and money-off coupons. Direct mail can also be used for direct response advertising.

10.10.2 The growth of direct mail in UK marketing

There has been a steady year on year rise in the volume of direct mail and the number of organisations using it for both business and consumer communication. A number of factors account for this increased usage and acceptance of direct mail as a major communications medium of which the most significant is the increased fragmentation of media:

- There are three UK terrestrial commercial television channels as well as satellite plus cable television being available to subscribers.
- In the print media, there has been the rapid growth of 'free sheets' alongside traditional 'paid for' local press, as well as a proliferation of 'special interest' magazines.

This fragmentation has meant that media buyers and advertisers either have to spend more money to make sure they reach as wide an audience as previously, or spread the same amount of money more thinly over a range of media.

Developments within the direct mail industry have removed many difficulties that have previously deterred large advertisers particularly in respect of the generally poor quality of large mail shots and hence such material was dubbed 'junk mail'. Information Technology advances have made it possible to 'personalise' mail shots, targeted to individuals by name. Quality has been greatly improved by increased money and creative intelligence that has been channelled into direct mail.

In order to effectively segment and target their markets and gain best value for money, organisations are increasingly opting for the benefits of direct mail – flexibility, selectivity and personal contact.

10.10.3 Uses of direct mail

The range of products or services that can be sold by direct mail is very wide as are its uses. To help define it more fully, it is appropriate to deal with direct mail to consumers and businesses separately.

Consumer direct mail

The uses of consumer-targeted direct mail are only limited by the scope of marketing imagination. Some of the more common uses are:

1 *Selling direct*: If a company has a convincing sales message, a product or service can be sold by direct mail. Direct mail is a good medium for selling a product directly to the customer without the need for 'middlemen'. The product or service can be described fully and orders can be sent straight back to the advertising company.

2 *Sales lead generation*: If a product requires a meeting between the customer and a specialised salesperson (e.g. fitted kitchens, central heating and insurance) direct mail can be a useful method of acquiring useful, qualified leads for the company's sales people. Sales calls are expensive, so anything that helps improve the call success (sale) rate is welcomed. A well-planned mail shot can act as a preliminary 'sieve', pinpointing the best prospects and ranking others in terms of sales potential. The 'warmer' the leads, the more effective will be the company's sales force with fewer wasted calls.

   Responses, indicating potential interest can be followed up by direct mail, a telephone call or a personal visit by a salesperson. One can then place a potential customer into a personal selling situation, by issuing an invitation to view the product in a retail outlet or showroom or an exhibition. This is particularly useful for products that sales people cannot take to the 'prospect' for demonstration because of its size or function.

   Direct mail creates a receptive atmosphere for the company's salespeople through 'cordial contact' mailings that build on the reputation of the company and through the 'impact' or impression created. Well-executed mailing can identify the company in a favourable light to prospects, setting up 'goodwill' or creating a latent desire that might be triggered into action by a later mailing.

3 *Sales promotion*: Direct mail can send promotional messages – 'money off' vouchers, special offers, etc. to selected targets. This can be a useful way of encouraging people to visit a shop or exhibition.

4 *Clubs*: Book clubs are perhaps the best-known example of the use of direct mail as a convenient medium of communication and transaction between a club and its members. Other items can be marketed by the club system, particularly 'collectibles', for example, record 'collections', porcelain and miniatures.

5 *Mail order*: Mail order companies use direct mail to recruit new customers and local agents as well as for direct selling.

6 *Fundraising*: One of the advantages of direct mail is the ability to communicate personally with an individual. This makes it a powerful method of raising money (e.g. for charitable organisations). It can carry the 'long copy' often needed to convince a recipient of the worthiness of the charity, and make it more likely that the reader might respond with a donation.

7 *Dealer mailings*: If a product is sold through dealers or agents, they can use direct mail to reach prospective customers in their particular catchment area just the same as a producer might do.

8 *Follow-up mailings*: The company's name can be promoted to the customer by following any kind of sales activity with a mailing e.g. checking that the customer is satisfied with their purchase or informing them that perhaps a car that they bought last year is coming up for its annual service. Customers can be kept informed of new developments, latest products and improved services. 'Exclusive' offers can be made and invitations issued. Using direct mail in this way helps to maintain contact – quickly, personally and effectively and it can increase repeat sales.

Business direct mail

Business markets are made up of closely defined, discrete groups of individuals. These groups may not be best reached by mass advertising media. Direct mail can be used to accurately identify different market sectors and provide messages appropriate to each sector (see Garber and Dotson, 2002, p. 1–17). Some of the more common uses in this context are:

1 *Product launch*: Often the launch of a new industrial product or business service entails getting the message across to a small, but significant, number of people who will influence buying decisions (e.g. catering managers and car fleet managers).
2 *Sales lead generation*: As in consumer markets, direct mail can effectively reach qualified sales leads for a company's sales force.
3 *Dealer support*: Direct mail makes it easy to keep dealers, retail outlets, franchise holders, etc, more fully informed of tactical marketing promotions and plans.
4 *Conferences and exhibitions*: Business and trade conferences and exhibitions are well-established means of communicating with potential customers and business colleagues. Direct mail can be used to invite delegates, who may be attracted if the event relates to a specific theme of direct interest to them.
5 *Follow-up mailing using the customer base*: Much business takes the form of repeat sales to the existing customer base. Since these are existing clients it can be worthwhile mailing them regularly, as long as the content of the mail-out relates to something that is new or of specific interest rather than simply being 'junk mail'.
6 *Marketing research/product testing*: Direct mail can be used for marketing research, especially amongst existing customers. Questionnaires can be used as part of a regular communication programme, with levels of response being increased by some kind of incentive. Small-scale test mailings can be made to sample a target market. The results can give a quick and accurate picture of market reaction, with minimum risk. A marketing approach that is successful in a 'test mailing' can later be mailed to the full list.

10.10.4 Direct mail as part of the promotional mix

In both consumer and business markets, direct mail must fit in with a company's other promotion efforts. For example, a television or press campaign can reach a broader audience, and raise the level of general awareness of the company and its products. If such a campaign is added to a direct mail campaign aimed specifically at groups of people or companies most likely to buy, or to people particularly wanted as customers, the effectiveness of the overall campaign might be significantly raised.

List of respondents to direct response techniques in other media (e.g. 'couponed' press advertisements or television or radio commercials which give a 'phone-in' number or a contact address) can be used as mailing lists for direct mail approaches.

10.11 Public relations

10.11.1 Definitions

There are a number of definitions of public relations (PR), each emphasising a different approach. The difficulty in developing a single definition reflects its diversity. Two definitions are useful. First, that of the Institute of Public Relations (IPR):

> 'Public Relations practice is the deliberate, planned and sustained effort to establish and maintain mutual understanding between an organisation and its publics.'

Note that the definition refers to an organisation's 'publics' in the plural, since PR addresses a number of different audiences.

An alternative is provided by Jefkins (1988):

> 'Public Relations consists of all forms of planned communication, out-wards and inwards, between an organisation and its publics for the pur-pose of achieving specific objectives concerning mutual understanding.'

This modified version of the IPR definition adds an important element, 'specific objectives', making PR a tangible activity, that is, it can be measured and evaluated.

10.11.2 Communications and PR

The purpose of PR is to establish a two-way communication to resolve conflicts of interest by seeking common ground or areas of mutual interest. The implication is that PR exists whether an organisation wants it or not. Simply by carrying out its day-to-day operations, an organisation necessarily communicates certain messages to those who interact with the organisation and they will form an opinion about the organisation and its activities. The task of the PR function is to orchestrate those messages in order to help the organisation project a corporate identity or corporate personality.

10.11.3 Corporate identity or personality

PR activity should be carried out within the framework of an agreed and understood corporate identity or personality. This personality should reflect the style of top management, since they ultimately control the organisation's policy and activities. A corporate personality can become a tangible asset if it is managed properly and consistently.

Managers do not necessarily consciously consider the role of personality when they make decisions. Therefore, the PR executive needs to be placed so that he or she is aware of all issues, policies, attitudes and opinions that exist in the organisation, and which might have a bearing on how it is perceived by outsiders who form part of the organisation's 'publics'.

The use of the word 'personality', rather than 'image', is deliberate. An image is a reflection or an impression which may be a little too polished, or a little too 'perfect'. True PR is more than superficial. This is important, because in journalistic parlance, a 'PR job' implies that somehow the truth is being hidden behind a glossy, even false, facade. Properly conducted, PR emphasises the need for truth and full information. The PR executive, as manager of corporate personality, can only sustain a long-term corporate identity that is based on truth and reality.

Despite the inclusion of 'specific objectives' in the definition of PR, it remains difficult to evaluate because of the abstract nature of 'personality' and the practical implication of the time lag between initial costs and derived benefits.

10.11.4 PR planning

Like other aspects of marketing communications PR has a planning sequence as shown in Figure 10.7

The PR audit is a study that is carried out to establish the current image of the company using desk research, interviews, observation, monitoring of media and other marketing research techniques.

This is followed by definitions of objectives. Here, although PR is usually associated with marketing, full PR deals with production, finance, human resources and other internal departments as well as external customers in addition to the adjacent community who might be located next to a manufacturing plant, external planning agencies, local and national government interests, etc. Each will demand a share of the PR budget, so budget constraints might mean that PR objectives have to be reduced.

These internal and external interests or 'publics' will hold opinions and will probably know less than they should know about the organisation. They will need to be targeted using a variety of media and techniques. PR deals mainly with editorial and programme people and to a lesser extend with media people who sell advertising space. PR uses a broader variety of media than advertisers including the use of house journals, videos, PowerPoint presentations, CD ROMS, websites, seminars, exhibitions as well as paid-for advertising. PR is able to tackle communications in a more personal manner than advertising.

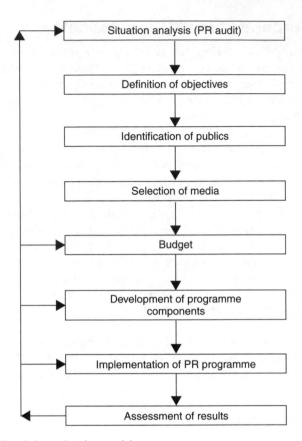

Figure 10.7 Public relations planning model

Furthermore, it normally carries the weight of editorial comment through the news media that has been generated through press releases generated through PR, and this is more 'believable' than 'paid for' advertising.

The budget for PR includes labour, materials and expenses and this can be quite substantial if PR is carried out by an external PR agency, so it is essential that this is agreed beforehand. Results of the PR programme should be related to the original research and the objectives and this is usually measured by the amount of editorial coverage that was gained afterwards in terms of standard column centimetres of coverage, TV and radio coverage.

10.12 Summary

The theme of communication that has been specifically dealt within this and the next chapter is linked with most other aspects of the text. In particular, Chapter 1 described marketing orientation. It is principally through above- and below-the-line promotion that marketing orientation is communicated to consumers. Chapter 3 outlined the overall marketing mix of which promotion is a principal component. Chapter 11 covers personal selling and the promotional aspects of communications that have been covered in this chapter are an essential back-up to the selling function.

Effective communication is only possible with an understanding of buyer behaviour that was the subject of Chapter 4. Communication is one of the more contentious areas of marketing, especially in the light of consumerism and the broader social dimensions of marketing, which are aspects that are examined in Chapter 15.

References

Aaker, D.A. and Myers, J.A. (1982), *Advertising Management*, 2nd edition, Englewood Cliffs, NJ: Prentice-Hall, Inc., pp. 233–236.

Bayne, K.M. (2003), 'Marketing without wires: targeting promotions and advertising to mobile device users', Info, *The Journal of Policy, Regulation and Strategy for Telecommunications*, 5(3), 73.

Clow, K.E. and Baack, D. (2004), *Integrated Advertising, Promotion and Marketing Communications*, 2nd edition, New Jersey: Pearson Prentice-Hall, p. 17.

Colley, R.H. (1961), *Association of National Advertisers*, New York, USA.

Corkindale, D.R. and Kennedy, S.H. (1976), *The Process of Advertising*, Bradford, UK: MCB Publications.

Garber, L.L. and Dotson, M.J. (2002), 'A method for the selection of appropriate business to business integrated marketing communications mixes', *Journal of Marketing Communications*, 8, 1–17.

Gould, S.J. (2000), 'The state of IMC research and applications', *Journal of Advertising Research*, September–October, 22–23.

Harris, G. and Attour, S. (2003), 'The international advertising practices of multinational companies: A content analysis study', *European Journal of Marketing*, 37(1), 154–168.

Hollensen, S. (2004), *Global Marketing, A Decision-Oriented approach*, 3rd edition, Financial Times, Prentice-Hall, p. 559.

Jefkins, F. (1988), *Public Relations*, 3rd edition, London: Pitman Publishing.

Joyce, P. (1967), 'What do we know about how advertising works? *Advertising Age*.

Jobber, David, (2004), *Principles and Practices of Marketing*, 4th edition, McGraw-Hill, p. 414.

Kotler, P. and Armstrong, G. (2004), *Principles of Marketing*, 10th International edition, Person Prentice-Hall, p. 468.

Kotler, P., Armstrong, G., Saunders, J. and Wong, V. (2001), *Principles of Marketing*, 3rd European edition, Pearson Education, Ltd., p. 627.

Laswell, H.D. (1948), *Power and personality*, New York, USA: W. W. Norton, p. 104.

Lavidge, R.J. and Steiner, G.A. (1961), 'A model of predictive measurement of advertising effectiveness', *Journal of Marketing*, 25, October, 59–62.

Majaro, S. (1970), 'Advertising by Objectives', *Management Today*, January.

Ogilvy, D. (1961), *Confessions of an Advertising Man*, New York, USA: Atheneum.

Reeves, R. (1961), *Reality of Advertising*, New York, USA: A.A. Knopf Inc.

Robison, F. and Rohan, R. (2002), 'Developing a Brand', *Black Enterprises*, May, pp. 47–48.

Schultz, D.E. (2002A), 'Summit explores where IMC CRM meet', *Marketing News*, March 4th, 11.

Schultz, D.E. (2002B), 'Marcom model reverses traditional pattern', *Marketing News*, April 1st, 8.

Solberg, C.A. (2002), 'The perennial issue of adaption or standardisation of international marketing communication: organisational contingences and performance', *Journal of International Marketing*, 10(3), 1–21.

Further reading

Blyth, J. (2002), 'Using trade fairs in key account management', *Industrial Marketing Management*, 31, 1–9.

Kanso, A. and Nelson, R.N. (2002), 'Advertising localisation: overshadows standardisation', *Journal of Advertising Research*, January–February, 79–89.

Kissan, J. and Richardson, V.J. (2002), 'Free cash flow, agency costs, and the affordability method of advertising budgeting', *Journal of marketing*, January, 94–107.

Kotler, P. (2003), *Marketing Management*, 11th edition, Upper Saddle River, NJ.: Prentice-Hall, pp. 583–584.

Proctor, J. and Richards, M. (2002), 'Word of mouth marketing: beyond pester power', *International Journal of Advertising and Marketing to Children*', 3(3), 3–11.

Smith, P. (2001), *Marketing Communications: An Integrated Approach*, London: Kogan Page, Chapters 1 and 2.

Tharp, M. and Jeong, J. (2001), 'Executive insights: The Global Network Communications Agency', *Journal of International marketing*, 9(4), 11–31.

Questions

Question 10.1

Explain, using illustrations, what is meant by:

- the 'source effect';
- the 'sleeper effect'.

as concepts that can be applied in marketing communications theory.

Question 10.2

'The evaluation of advertising effectiveness is not worth the effort and cost involved'.

Critically evaluate this statement.

Question 10.3

What are the advantages to an organisation of systematically evaluating the effectiveness of sales promotion expenditure with reference to clearly defined communication objectives?

Question 10.4

What form should a marketing communications evaluative procedure take? Outline a scheme for such an evaluation programme.

Question 10.5

Explain how direct mail can be used to:

- generate sales leads;
- 'follow-up' a sales visit.

Question 10.6

Define the term marketing communications mix and examine the integrated nature of all of the communications elements within the mix.

Question 10.7

Examine the role of direct marketing within an overall marketing communications campaign targeted at customers in:

- consumer markets,
- business to business markets,
- if possible use examples to illustrate the points made.

Question 10.8

Outline three conceptual advertising models of your choice and briefly discuss their practical use to marketing management.

Question 10.9

Explain why it is necessary for marketing management to set clearly defined, operationally measurable objectives when planning an advertising campaign.

11

Selling and Sales Management

11.1 Introduction

An obvious function of selling is to make a sale and this remains true despite recent additions of many ancillary functions. Much background work of selling can be done remotely, for instance, by e-mail, but personal selling is a specific task involving face-to-face contact on a personal basis. This means suitably skilled and trained professionals should carry out this function. Selling tasks differ, depending on the type of goods and services. Some salespeople are simply order-takers, whilst others employ more sophisticated arts of prospecting, negotiating and demonstrating to close a sale.

Personal selling is the primary communication vehicle in organisational marketing, but in industrial marketing in particular (buying situations were discussed in Chapter 4) and here sometimes over 80% of total marketing costs relate to sales force costs. Personal selling is less important in most retail situations, especially in FMCG markets like grocery products. Selling to end-users increasingly uses non-personal forms of communication like packaging, advertising, merchandising and sales promotion discussed in Chapter 10. Communications mix elements are not normally used in isolation; they complement each other.

11.2 Nature of selling

Everyone lives by selling something as each time we engage in conversation, we are exchanging views and ideas. In a sense, when we attempt to persuade others to accept our viewpoint, we are attempting to 'sell' our ideas. Without selling as a commercial activity, many transactions would simply not take place. Personal selling plays a vital role in the exchange process in any advanced economy.

11.2.1 Importance of personal selling to individual organisations

The importance of personal selling varies, for example, goods and services requiring low-involvement decisions like FMCGs are usually sold through retail stores on a 'self-service' basis. Salespersons are, however, needed to 'sell' these products in bulk to the retail trade. The degree of selling skill required for this task depends on the reputation of the manufacturer and the popularity of the brands involved. It is not really necessary to 'sell' well-known brands of grocery products such as Heinz beans, Nescafe coffee or Bovril to the trade, as these are stocked in any case because of their popularity with customers. In such situations, the salesperson's role is one of re-ordering, ensuring stock replenishment and rotation, merchandising advice and customer liaison. Indeed, when servicing supermarket chains, they monitor stocks themselves, and head office central buyers simply perform a negotiating role with manufacturers' representatives.

With goods and services requiring high-involvement decisions, the role of personal selling is more complicated. Negotiating the sale of expensive consumer durables like cars usually requires a personal approach, a high degree of product knowledge and a certain amount of selling skill. Selling in business-to-business situations presents a challenge and requires a high degree of selling skill. Expensive capital equipment like machine tools, are usually purchased after much negotiation. In such circumstances that involve appraising technical complexity there is a high degree of perceived risk. The buyer (or people who form the DMU who are involved in the purchasing decision process) need detailed knowledge of goods or services being considered. The salesperson must identify prospective purchaser's key requirements, not only in terms of product performance, but also their price ceiling, delivery, credit and after-sales service requirements (see Clow and Baack, 2004, p. 17).

11.2.2 Importance of personal selling to the national economy

The UK is a trading nation that earns its living in the world by selling goods and services abroad. In terms of the national economy, the most important role of personal selling is its contribution towards promoting the sale of UK produced products and services overseas. Exports are needed to compensate for goods and services that are imported and this is fundamental to the maintenance of a healthy balance of trade.

Since the UK joined the European Economic Community (EEC) in 1973, which is now the EU markets have become increasingly important to UK firms. As discussed in Chapter 2, the intention of the EU was to create a completely 'free' market between member states meaning that even that greater competition faces UK companies. It also provides an exciting business environment. The role of the UK's professional selling capability in this context is of great importance, and the ability of UK organisations to capitalise on the opportunities offered by this free market depends largely on the calibre of the UK selling profession. Some research sources that the total number of personal sales personnel will decline in Europe and the USA over the next 10 years due to advances in indirect selling technologies especially those of the Internet. Some estimates put this decrease as a much as 50% (see Blankenhorn, 2000, p. 29). Improvements in direct mail and other direct marketing techniques such as 'digital direct-to-press' technology which allows marketers to send tailor made message generated from a computer and customised to the prospect's needs by mail has also contributed to this trend (see Totty, 2000, p. 36). Those that will be left will be those that industry and commerce simply cannot do without. This is likely to enhance the professional standing of the profession.

11.2.3 Cost-effectiveness of personal selling

As an element of an organisation's marketing communications mix, the relative importance of personal selling depends on the overall objectives, the type of industry in which the company is involved and general conditions of the marketplace. Personal selling might be particularly effective, but it can also be expensive and a salesperson's salary is not the only selling cost. Other add-on costs like a company car, expense account, extra travelling costs, administrative support and share of general overheads, often exceeds the salary cost of the individual salesperson. Personal selling is typically the most expensive form of communication available to a company when calculated on a straight cost-per-contact basis. Because of this cost, personal selling should be used only when it can achieve results more cost-effectively than other marketing mix elements such as advertising or direct mail.

11.3 Situations requiring a personal approach

11.3.1 Situations of high perceived risk

The purchase of products that are radically new, expensive or technically complex are often viewed with some perceived risk by prospective buyers. A salesperson uses professional skill to identify the customer's areas of concern and takes steps to lower the concern or eliminate the perceived problems. Perceived risk is one of the most common barriers to the achievement of a sale. Without a clear understanding of consumer and organisational buying behaviour, the salesperson would lack the necessary psychological tools to be effective.

11.3.2 Technically complex products

Products like new robotic machine tools or a new computer system can cause confusion to potential customers particularly if they are not experts. Such products need careful explanation if the potential customer is to fully grasp the capabilities of the product or system being sold. These tasks can best be carried out in face-to-face situations by salespersons with a high level of product knowledge.

11.3.3 Commercially complex negotiations

Financial arrangements, maintenance contracts, spare-parts availability and responsibility for staff training can make the commercial details of many transactions complicated. The complexity of the buying situation contributes to the degree of perceived risk experienced by potential purchasers and such situations require negotiation and explanation that are most effectively conducted on a personal basis.

11.3.4 Industrial/organisational markets

It has already been mentioned that around 80% of the total marketing budget of firms operating in industrial markets can be spent on personal selling. The reason is that the goods and services sold are often technically complex, expensive and innovative, and are perceived by prospective purchasers to be potentially risky, so much personal reassurance is needed and this can only be provided on the face-to-face basis that is provided through personal selling.

11.4 The expanded role of the modern salesperson

The primary responsibility of a salesperson is to achieve a successful sale, but for marketing orientated salespersons, selling is only one facet of the task. There are other functions undertaken in the course of customer contact including:

11.4.1 Servicing

The salesperson often provides various services to customers such as consultancy, technical advice, arranging after-sales service, arranging finance and expediting delivery from the factory to the customer's premises.

11.4.2 Prospecting

Although many companies supply their salespeople with qualified sales 'leads', a certain amount of a salesperson's time must still be devoted to obtaining and developing their own leads. Some will result from the salesperson 'cold calling'. Existing satisfied customers are a productive source of leads and new prospects can be obtained by asking satisfied customers if they know of anybody who might have a need for the type of goods and services on offer. This technique is successful in industrial selling, but is also applicable to cold-calling situations like sales of life assurance.

11.4.3 Information gathering

Salespeople are in personal contact with customers and potential customers most working days. They are in an excellent position to collect market information and intelligence. By talking to customers and keeping alert, they should be able to gather information that might be useful to marketing management in a number of areas:

- *Marketing plans* – salespeople can make a valuable contribution to marketing plans by offering advice on customer preferences and requirements in such matters as price, credit, discounts, promotions, market segmentation and timing of marketing efforts.
- *Sales forecasting* – whereby the sales-force composite method is an established method of subjective forecasting (see Chapter 15).
- *New product development* – existing customers can provide salespeople with ideas for new products or improvements to existing products.
- *General marketing research* – salespeople can provide information about market conditions, competitive developments and customers. Customers may have a multi-sourcing policy and by probing, the salesperson may be able to gain information about competitors' activities. Chapter 4 outlined the need for a marketing intelligence system, which is a crucial component of the organisation's overall marketing information system.

11.4.4 Communicating

Salespeople use many forms of communication with customers in addition to verbal communications, for example, reports, charts, models, diagrams video, laptop computer and slide presentations. They use these skills when they visit customers and when addressing potential customers at exhibitions and other venues. The aim of communicating may not specifically be to make a sale; it may be to communicate the message of the company's image.

11.4.5 Allocating

There are times when the salesperson may have to perform an allocating role. During times of product shortage (perhaps resulting from an industrial dispute, shortage of raw materials, production problems, political problems or unexpected excessive demand) salespeople may have to evaluate customer loyalty and future sales potential and allocate stocks accordingly.

11.5 The salesperson as a communicator

The salesperson uses many forms of communication, but in the final analysis, the most effective form is voice communication. Many elements of sales courses are concerned with what a salesperson should say, when they should say it and how they should say it. Effective communication is a two-way process, because important as it is for the salesperson to talk, it is just as important to listen. Listening skills should be taught and developed. It is easy to 'switch off' when someone is talking a lot and think about something else. The hallmark of a sales professional is to actively listen to what customers have to say. This requires a conscious effort on the part of the listener that can be mentally exhausting.

Salespeople often work within one industry, or for a single firm, for a considerable period. Over the years they develop not only selling skills, but also technical expertise. When one is an expert, it is sometimes difficult to communicate with non-experts. When talking to a fellow expert, a person often skips over elementary points. When a potential customer is discussing something new with a salesperson there is a temptation for the salesperson to think: 'I wish they would get to the point'. Simple points that the salesperson may have heard from other customers many times are nonetheless new and important to this potential customer. The professional salesperson should actively listen and use the extra mental time not needed for comprehension to interpret what is being said and plan his or her reaction.

A salesperson deals with a finite range of products, but often with a large number of customers. Many customers' problems are likely to be similar. To the customer, the situation probably appears unique, but the salesperson may well think 'I've heard it all before!'. Many sales situations are similar, but rarely are they exactly the same and such thinking is bad sales practice. During customer contact, the professional salesperson not only makes sure they are listening to everything the customer has to say, but actually shows the customer that they are listening through non-verbal forms of communication, such as eye contact, facial expressions, hand and head movements and other forms of body language. Such non-verbal cues enable the salesperson to signal understanding or, indeed, non-understanding of what the customer is saying. A salesperson can use non-verbal communication to regulate the speed, depth and detail of the customer's discussion without verbal interruption. Such non-verbal exchange encourages customers to 'open up' and discuss points in greater detail. It also helps to build rapport between the salesperson and the customer and this is important factor in making the sale.

Attempting to understand a complicated topic takes mental effort and concentration. The speaker takes non-verbal response as an indication that the listener has understood the problem. If the topic being discussed is too technical or complicated, the professional salesperson should say so and tell the buyer that it is beyond his or her area of knowledge and obtain technical assistance from head office, rather than attempting to bluff and pretend that the discussion has been understood.

11.6 The sales sequence

The most important part of a salesperson's job is the sales interview and as already discussed many other tasks have found their way into the itinerary. A good deal of time is also taken up in travelling – often on average 30% of the working day. Such a diverse range of activities and travelling means that careful planning must be done to ensure that face-to-face contact with customers is maximised. This can be achieved by adopting a general plan for all sales interviews and specific tactical plans for individual interviews.

The general sales plan used for sales interviews is called the sales sequence. It should be flexible and be adapted to suit individual sales situations. The salesperson should listen to what the prospect has to say, and interpret non-verbal clues then adjust the sales message and approach to fit with the requirements of the situation. Figure 11.1 shows the sequence of a general plan for this activity.

This sales sequence is a formula. Each stage is now examined in more detail.

11.6.1 Preparation

Company knowledge

Includes knowledge of the company's systems, procedures, price, terms and general policy on matters like complaints and returned goods. The salesperson needs to update such information on a regular basis. For example, if the company decides to extend credit terms or alter its quantity discount structure it is important that the salesperson knows about such changes immediately.

Product knowledge

This includes knowledge of existing and new products or services and it is an opportunity for the salesperson to demonstrate technical skills. Limitations of the company's range should also be known, as making exaggerated claims will lead to resentment. Salespeople paid on low salary (or no salary) and commission are more likely to make exaggerated claims to advance personal remuneration.

Market knowledge

The salesperson needs an up-to-date awareness of the state of the market and must be knowledgeable about new developments. Such knowledge includes activities of competitors. Chapter 2 emphasised the importance of market intelligence, part of the organisation's overall marketing information system. Salespeople are well placed to act as 'intelligence providers'. For instance, if the salesperson finds that competitors are giving special trade discounts or some other incentive, they should report this to their marketing department.

Customer knowledge

Knowledge is needed about the size of the customer's company, affiliation to other companies, bargaining power, markets they serve, etc.

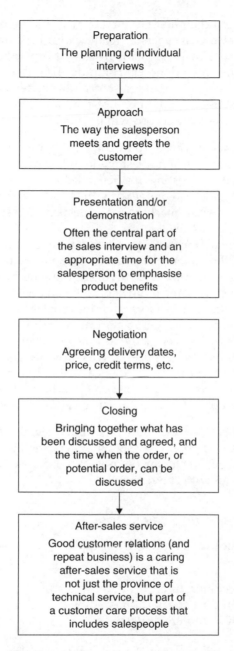

Figure 11.1 The sales sequence

Specific preparation for individual interviews includes having personal knowledge about customers (even down to idiosyncratic behaviour) so the interview can be conducted at a more personal level. For example, knowledge of the buyer's family circumstances – perhaps gained at the last sales interview, for example, a son or a daughter getting married, can help provide a personal touch and show that the salesperson really cares. Preparation for individual interviews can be made easier by using a straightforward aid known as a customer record card, but now done via computer. The salesperson should keep such a file for every live account. It is also useful keep records for potential customers and lost customers in the hope of winning them over or back in the future. Information on such a record will include:

1 A record of previous purchases (particularly the most recent purchase).
2 Any particular comments of interest made by the prospect, for example, 'We might be interested in investing in a new machine if and when our new USA venture takes off'. Such a comment, with details of the date it was made, would be useful to say a machine-tool salesperson, especially if American interests have started to develop.
3 Personal details including basic issues like the customer's name, including Christian name if the buyer operates on a personal rather than formal basis. The salesperson should make a point of introducing him or herself by both Christian name and surname (both should be on a visiting card) then let the buyer choose whether to use a formal or informal style of address. Names of other people in the purchasing or technical departments should be similarly logged (assistant buyers eventually become chief buyers). Customer family details and special interests are useful. This provides good background information that can be used to 'break the ice' at the beginning of an interview (e.g. 'Did you manage to reduce your golf handicap after all?').
4 The best and worst days to call (from the customer's point-of-view).

By referring to such data before making a call the salesperson can be better prepared e.g. if interest was previously shown in a particular product range, then prices, delivery, discounts, etc. for the possible order can be prepared beforehand and talked about with conviction.

Equipment, samples and sales aids

The following is indicative, and which are appropriate or useful will depend on the sales situation:

- sales brochures and literature,
- handbooks and product specifications,
- up-to-date price lists and credit details,
- samples,
- demonstration kit, for example, PowerPoint/videos/spreadsheet,
- graphs, models and supporting material,
- trade directories,
- order book,
- pens, calculator and stationery,
- credit card – not a sales aid, but useful for settling fuel and entertainment bills and possession of a company card confers 'seniority'.

Journey planning

The salesperson should have an organised plan for appointments and other calls on a daily basis. Planning should consider both current customers and prospects (people to whom the company does not sell, but wishes to in the future).

Because face-to-face sales time is at a premium and so much of a salesperson's time is spent travelling it is important that itineraries are well planned. One method is known as differential call frequency. In many industries it is common for more substantial customers to receive a higher frequency of personal calls other than clients. In the illustration, the salesperson's overall call cycle is eight weeks and the overall territory can be divided into four approximately equal areas. Customers are then classified in terms of their relative importance, with Group A, the most frequent purchasers and Group C, the least frequent. The frequency of personal calling is related to the customer type:

Group A (20 customers) – call every two weeks
Group B (50 customers) – call every four weeks
Group C (130 customers) – call every eight weeks

On this basis a differential call frequency plan can be drawn up. A typical plan for such a situation is shown in Table 11.1.

The differential call frequency plan shows, for example, that in Week 4 the salesperson calls on all 'A' group customers in Areas 4 and 2, and all 'B' group customers, and half of 'C' group customers in Area 4. In Week 8, the salesperson calls again on all 'A' group customers in Areas 4 and 2, on 'B' group customers and the other half of 'C' group customers in Area 4. If this plan is followed, the salesperson's objectives will be achieved in that all 'A' customers receive a call every 2 weeks, 'B' customers every 4 weeks and 'C' customers every 8 weeks, thus completing what is termed the sales journey cycle.

There are some factors that complicate the operation of this system, for example: type of area (urban or rural); one area being more difficult to plan than

Table 11.1 Differential call frequency plan for different areas

Week no.	Customer type		
	A	B	C
1	1 + 3	1	½ of 1
2	2 + 4	2	½ of 2
3	3 + 1	3	½ of 3
4	4 + 2	4	½ of 4
5	1 + 3	1	other ½ of 1
6	2 + 4	2	other ½ of 2
7	3 + 1	3	other ½ of 3
8	4 + 2	4	other ½ of 4

another; ease of obtaining appointments (in certain industries [e.g. the licensed trade] there are times of the week or day when visits are not convenient to the customer); unequal distribution of customers; sales visits taking longer than expected perhaps because a protracted negotiating process; seasonal factors (e.g. the clothing trade is dictated to by seasonal demand, so buyers will purchase at certain times of the year in readiness for 'spring' or 'autumn' collections).

There are a number of suggestions that can help the salesperson in this respect:

1 Make firm appointments to avoid being kept waiting unnecessarily.
2 Adhere as closely as possible to the allotted time for each visit.
3 Budget time for contingencies.
4 Budget time for prospecting new accounts.
5 Use a customer record card or computer for recording important 'background' information.
6 Personal preparation prior to going into the interview (e.g. composure and pausing beforehand so as not to give the impression of 'rushing' which may give the buyer the impression that he or she is simply being 'fitted in' between 'more important' meetings). Such preparation also includes appropriate dress, general grooming and personal hygiene.

11.6.2 Approach

The manner in which the salesperson approaches a prospective customer (the prospect) is a fundamental skill of professional selling. To be able to evaluate a situation quickly and judge the mood and type of personality of the prospect are valuable skills. Some pointers are:

- First impressions are important and the salesperson should be prepared, alert and of good disposition.
- The opening of the sales interview should be pleasant and businesslike. This is important if it is the first interview. In such a situation, opening remarks should be considered carefully.
- The salesperson should discuss the business at hand quickly to avoid wasting selling and prospecting time.
- If the prospect sets a time limit the salesperson should strictly adhere to this.
- If another appointment is made, the salesperson should enter this in a diary and note relevant conversational details on a record card.
- The salesperson should ask relevant questions and 'actively' listen to the answers.
- If the buyer's debts need to be discussed, it is advisable to do this at the beginning of the interview. The salesperson then feels that the debt has been acknowledged and dealt with, and new negotiation can take place without the complication of previous dealings.

11.6.3 Presentation and/or demonstration

The first stage was 'preparation' and this and subsequent stages depend on good foundations. The salespersons should have cast him or herself in the role of the buyer and established the level of explanation that will be required. Presentations are much more effective when the needs of potential customers are studied beforehand and such information should be available from customer record cards.

During a sales presentation and/or demonstration, the role of the salesperson is to communicate specific product or service benefits of interest to the potential customer. Products or services have many features, and 'customers buy benefits, not features'. A salesperson should examine the product range and list the major selling points of each product. Important selling points are those that are unique to the product or service and give some sort of advantage over similar products offered by competitors. An important and unique selling point is referred to as a unique proposition (USP).

The salesperson should have identified product benefits required by the customer during the preparation stage. People buy for a variety of different reasons and the sales professional must quickly assess the customer's buying motives, which may be economic, social or psychological. The most common ones revolve around performance, economy and price, durability, appearance, safety, comfort and adaptability, and Chapter 4 discussed these motives in detail.

Such a presentation can help overcome buying objections. If dialogue is carried out on a 'to-and-fro' basis, the seller may find it worthwhile to encourage objections, in the knowledge that they can be dealt with adequately.

Whenever possible, the salesperson should refer to needs of the prospect and talk in a language that the prospect can readily understand. For example, when householders purchase a new central-heating boiler, they do not always want to know about technical details of the equipment. It is generally sufficient for the prospect to know how many litres of water the boiler will heat, how many baths or showers it will provide, that it will heat all radiators needed to warm the house and for how long it will be guaranteed. However, if the boiler is being sold to the building trade, technical information is likely to be a major part of the presentation.

Sales are lost because the salesperson over-presents too much technical detail. If the prospect gives the salesperson buying signals, an attempt should be made to close the sale (a trial close) that is dealt with shortly.

11.6.4 Negotiation

Raiffa (1982) claimed that negotiation goes to the heart of the selling process; in effect, it is the key element. This process usually involves two parties who wish to bring about an agreement that is favourable or acceptable to both sides. One party, usually the seller, makes a presentation and an offer in terms of price, credit, delivery, etc. The other party evaluates the points the seller has made. Each party knows what they would like to achieve from negotiation and how

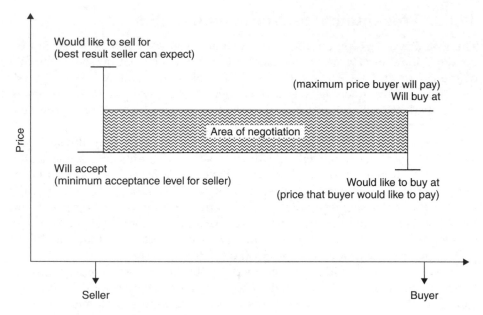

Figure 11.2 The 'room for manoeuvre' concept in negotiation

far they are prepared to go in offering concessions. Hence, sales negotiation is a process of presentation, evaluation, counter-proposal and concession. Each party has an optimal result in mind, but concedes that the achievement of this goal is rarely possible and that they must be prepared to compromise. The 'gap' between the 'optimal' result and the 'minimum acceptable limit' gives each party 'room for manoeuvre'. This important concept in the sales negotiation process is illustrated in Figure 11.2. The example given concerns price, but the concept is equally valid for any area that is open to negotiation like credit terms, delivery or quality.

11.6.5 Closing

The fundamental objective of the selling process is to obtain an order to make a sale. It is, therefore, essential that a salesperson has detailed knowledge of appropriate closing techniques. Perhaps even more important is an appreciation of when and under what circumstances to use each technique, and this comes with experience.

Some of the more common closing techniques are:

Basic close

When the salesperson sees buying signals from the prospect the salesperson starts filling in the order form. If there is no objection, a successful sale is achieved. The techniques that follow are variations of this basic approach.

Alternative choice

When the salesperson has received buying signals from the prospect, he or she attempts to close by offering the prospect an alternative choice, for example, a prospect is showing serious interest in purchasing a new car and asks about delivery and this is taken as a buying signal. The salesperson might then ask: 'What would be your preferred colour?' If the prospect states a preference, a sale is made. This a method of 'trial close' (i.e. a method of 'fishing' for a definite closing signal from the prospect).

'Puppy dog' technique

If you give a family a puppy to look after for two weeks, they are likely to grow fond of it and will be reluctant to part with it at the end of the period. The same principle can be applied to a product that might be loaned for a period. This technique is used by companies who offer their machines free or at a greatly reduced rental for a 'trial period'. It is hoped that the prospect will get used to having the machine and that at the end of the trial period there will be resistance to sending it back.

Summary question

This technique is used when the salesperson experiences sales resistance. The salesperson has discovered the main cause of resistance through a process of elimination. For example:

'Is it the price?' 'No!'
'Is it the colour?' 'No!'

Each time the prospect says 'No', they are eliminating potential causes of resistance. This allows the salesperson to concentrate on the most important area of resistance.

Similar situation

This method is best illustrated by an example: imagine a salesperson selling security devices 'door-to-door'. Upon meeting resistance, he could point to a similar situation: 'The Lewis family in Winchester Avenue said the same as you. They thought the product rather expensive and wanted more time to think about it. A week later they were burgled as well as being underinsured!'

The selling implication is obvious, and this technique can be powerful in influencing a prospect's decision, especially if the prospect can easily relate to the analogy.

Sharp angle

When a prospect requests information, the salesperson uses the reply to ask for a sale. For example,

Customer: 'Do you have it in green?'
Salesperson: 'If we have it in that colour do you want it?'

Final objection

This is a mixture of 'summary question' and 'sharp angle'. If the prospect shows resistance, the salesperson uses summary questions to ascertain the most important objection and refutes that one.

Imagine a potential customer in a showroom considering purchasing a new built-in kitchen:

Salesperson: 'Is it the price?'
Customer: 'No, the price is fine and it seems good value.'
Salesperson: 'Is it the credit terms, then?'
Customer: 'No, those seem fair.'
Salesperson: 'You mentioned earlier that you were concerned about its size. Is this still troubling you?'
Customer: 'Well yes, it is really. You see on Sundays my family all come to lunch and I need to be able to cook a meal to feed 10 people. I need to cook a really large joint or a turkey.'
Salesperson: 'So, what you are really concerned about is oven capacity?'
Customer: 'Yes.'

The salesperson then demonstrates to the prospect's satisfaction that the oven has the capacity to cook a roast meal for 10 quite adequately by reference to the instructional manual and envisioning food in the oven.

The techniques mentioned are not exhaustive. The skill is in knowing which technique is appropriate in specific situations.

11.6.6 After-sales service

It is part of a salesperson's task to provide or to offer advice and information after a sale has been made. Where appropriate, the salesperson should encourage the customer to take out a service contract and provide information about service centres. Good after-sales service is vital in securing post-purchase satisfaction and repeat business, especially in the case of a major purchase. It is well known that 'cognitive dissonance' often follows, and this phenomenon was discussed in Chapter 10. It is in the salesperson's own interest to ensure that the customer is entirely satisfied after a major sale, and part of this process should ideally include after-sales service arrangements. This is now so important that a relatively new concept of marketing has been introduced called 'customer relationship management' (CRM) and this is the subject of Chapter 13 (but see also Anonymous, 2000a,b,c, pp. 3–4, for a discussion of the application of customer data to the sales process, also Anderson, 2003, p. 133, for a more international perspective).

11.7 Sales management

11.7.1 Setting sales force size

Factors that should be taken into account by sales management in reaching a decision on sales force size are:

1 the company's financial resources,
2 numbers of customers to be reached,
3 average number of calls required per customer, per week, per month, etc.,
4 average number of calls that can be made by a salesperson in a given period,
5 distribution policy of the firm, dependent on company policy in relation to exclusive, selective or mass distribution (Chapter 8 detailed these categories).

Some companies use bespoke formulae for calculating optimum size of a sales force taking the above criteria into account (see Ligos, 1998, p. 15, for an interesting discussion of sales force size considerations). Many companies are now using sales teams rather than individual sales people, particularly for large complex accounts. Each member of the team will bring a particular skill and the sales team usually hold meetings with the 'prospect' team (see Jackson et al., 1999, p. 15). The use of sales teams is also particularly prevalent in complex international selling negotiations (see Govindarajan and Gupta, 2001, p. 63).

11.7.2 Evaluating sales force performance

Looking at individual salesperson performance in terms of sales volume relative to their sales colleagues is simplistic and can be misleading. Comparative sales performance measures are meaningful only if there is little variation from territory to territory.

There may well be differences in market potential and workload (e.g. Birmingham with its high population density profile will clearly differ in market potential from Cornwall which is largely rural. In terms of workload, travelling around Cornwall will involve greater distances between calls, but driving and parking will be less of a problem than in Birmingham). There may also be differences in promotional support, competition, length of time the company has operated in a particular area and the degree of goodwill that the company has built up.

Measures of individual evaluation

Such measures can be qualitative or quantitative, for example:

- *Qualitative*:
  degree of product knowledge,
  quality of sales presentation and demonstration,
  self-organisation (use of time, journey planning, etc.),
  intelligence,
  patience,
  tenacity,
  enthusiasm, motivation and ambition,
  grooming and general appearance.
- *Quantitative*:
  sales volume,
  number of orders secured,
  number of new orders,
  number of customers/orders lost,
  number of sales calls made,
  number of service calls made,
  expenses incurred,
  amount of market intelligence gathered.

Sales forecasts can also be used as a basis for evaluation. Once potential sales in relation to each area and then each salesperson's individual territory have been forecasted, these are translated into sales targets or sales quotas that each salesperson is budgeted to sell (this is sometimes referred to as the 'sales budgetary' process). These area-by-area forecasts represent the potential contribution to the company's net profit. Actual contribution can then be compared to potential contribution once the forecasted period has been reached. A ratio of 1:1 would mean that the salesperson had exactly obtained all the forecasted potential business in a particular area and he or she would have exactly reached their agreed sales target or quota.

11.7.3 Remuneration of salespeople

Salespeople are paid by one of the following methods:

- salary only,
- salary plus commission or sales-related bonus,
- commission only,
- percentage of profits from a given territory.

There is much disagreement as to whether sales force compensation should be linked to what they actually sell. Day and Bennett (1964) carried out the first piece of extensive research in this area in the United States.

Straight salary offers the least incentive for salespersons to sell more, but it offers stability and security of earnings. Sales management should expect any reasonable task to be performed. It is particularly appropriate when salespersons have to consider customers' interests in terms of aspects of customer care they have to perform to retain customers. This is increasingly important within lean manufacturing situations where it is acknowledged that customer retention is often more important than winning new customers. In some circumstances, straight salary can be linked to a group bonus whereby all members of a team share a bonus relating to profitability during the previous period.

Salary plus commission (or sales-related bonus) is the most popular method of compensation. Some companies use escalator commission/bonus schemes where the higher the sales, the higher the commission/bonus pro rata. The ratio between fixed basic salary and commission differs from company to company. Generally, the salary element provides a living basic wage, with the commission element acting as a sales incentive. In most cases this commission is linked to a sales target or quota system. Once a salesperson sells above an agreed target or quota, then some kind of escalator commission structure is sometimes applied. This escalator sometimes works on the basis of increasing commission percentages once certain levels of sales have been reached within a given period.

The commission only method is usually used for self-employed agents. Some organisations like life assurance companies and home improvement organisations often employ part-time salespeople on this basis. The method can be advantageous to the company as the cost of each salesperson is directly related to their sales achievement. There is also a big incentive for salespersons to be successful as the level of income is determined by individual effort. The main disadvantage is that such salespersons feel less a 'part' of the organisation, so after-sales service relationships with customers may suffer, and many such sales tend to be 'one off' purchases.

Today many sales managers have moved away from straight commission compensation because many believe it drives the sales person to try and sell too aggressively to try and close the sale. As long term relationships are now the name of the game in many sales situations, especially in business to business situations, commission plans are increasingly being based on the success of building and maintaining long term relationships (see Peppers and Rogers, 1999, p. 20).

11.7.4 Recruitment and selection of salespeople

The sales job and a suitable salesperson will vary according to the product or service being sold. The following hypothetical job description and evaluation checklist is only a guide.

- *Responsibility*: The representative will be responsible directly to the sales manager.

- *Objective*: Achieve an annual sales target across the product range in the area for which he/she is responsible, as economically as possible and within company policy.
- *Planning*: Become familiar with company policy and plan how to achieve defined objectives within the limits of that policy. Submit this plan to higher management.
- *Implementation*:
  - Act as an effective link between customers and head office;
  - organise own travel itinerary;
  - develop a comprehensive skill in selling;
  - maintain and submit accurate records;
  - gather market intelligence and report this to Head Office;
  - assess the potential of the area in terms of:
    - visits,
    - outlets for company products,
    - activity of competition;
  - protect and promote the company image;
  - avoid unnecessary expense;
  - achieve harmony with fellow staff by setting a good example and maintaining loyalty towards superiors.
- *Evaluation*: The following is a general checklist for evaluating prospective candidates for a selling position:
  - age and marital status,
  - health,
  - interests,
  - education,
  - previous employment and experience,
  - location,
  - clean driving licence,
  - references,
  - appearance/demeanour,
  - intelligence,
  - integrity,
  - motivation.

This list is not exhaustive and criteria are not in any order of importance. These criteria can be incorporated into a rating matrix using an evaluation scale (e.g. excellent, very good, good, fair, poor).

Possible sources of recruitment are:

- inside staff, that is, current employees
- salespeople from outside the company i.e. in many cases from the company's competitors
- advertising in the press, on websites and other media
- specialist recruitment agencies

11.8 Summary

Personal selling is a highly effective but expensive marketing communications tool. The cost of employing an additional member of the sales force is not simply remuneration. It also includes 'add-on' costs of vehicle depreciation, overhead allocation and support services like sales administration. Personal selling and other forms of non-personal communication, for example, sales promotion, direct mail, exhibitions and trade fairs complement each other.

Selling encompasses a range of situations and activities. Some sales tasks are no more than 'order taking', whereas other situations involve complex activities. Some salespeople specialise in selling in consumer markets and others in selling in industrial or public sector markets. Whatever the industry and sales setting, there is a common theme running through all situations relating to professionalism and ethical practice.

The modern salesperson has a far more expanded role than was the case 25 years ago. Selling is still the primary function of the task, but modern sales activity involves many other marketing tasks like attending exhibitions, gathering market intelligence, contributing to marketing plans, and helping to formulate sales forecasts and engaging in professional customer relationship management, which is the subject of Chapter 13.

References

Anderson, P.H. (2003), 'Relationship marketing in cross-cultural contexts', in Rugimbana, R. and Nwankwo, S. (eds.), *Cross Cultural marketing*, London: Thomson, p. 133.

Anonymous (2000a), 'A crash course in customer relationship management', *Harvard Management Update*, 5(3), 3–4.

Anonymous (2000b),'CRM metrics', *Harvard management Update*, 5(3), 3–4.

Anonymous (2000c), 'The technological underpinnings of CRM', *Harvard Management Update*, 5(3), 3–4.

Blankenhorn, D. (2000), 'E-mail use shifts from prospects to closures', *Advertising Age's Business Marketing*, 85(1), 29–30.

Clow, K.E. and Baack, D. (2004), *Integrated Advertising, Promotion and Marketing Communications*, 2nd edition, New Jersey: Pearson Prentice-Hall, p. 17.

Govindarajan, V. and Gupta, A.K. (2001), 'Building an effective global business team', *MIT Sloan Management Review*, Summer, 63–71.

Jackson, D.W., Widmier, S.M., Giacobbe, R. and Keith, J.E. (1999), 'Examining the use of team selling by manufacturer's representatives: a situational approach', *Industrial Marketing Management*, March, 155–164.

Ligos, M. (1998), 'The incredible shrinking sales force', *Sales and Marketing Management*, December, 15.

Peppers, D. and Rogers, M. (1999), 'The price of customer service', *Sales and Marketing Management*, April, 20–21.

Raiffa, H. (1982), *The Art of Science of Negotiation*, Cambridge, USA: Harvard University Press, p. 10.

Totty, P. (2000), 'Direct mail gets a new lease on life', *Credit Union Magazine*, 66(4), 36–37.

Further reading

Hollensen, Svend. (2004), *Global Marketing, A Decision-Oriented Approach*, 3rd edition, Financial Times, Prentice-Hall, pp. 621–642.

Jobber, D. and Lancaster, G. (2003), *Selling and Sales Management*, 6th edition, London: Prentice-Hall.

Masterson, R. and Pickton, D. (2004), *Marketing an Introduction*, McGraw-Hill, Chapter 8, pp. 226–263.

Pickton, D.W. and Broderick, A. (2004), *Integrated Marketing Communications*, 2nd edition, Englewood Cliffs, NJ: Prentice-Hall.

Reed, D. (1999), 'Field Force', *Marketing Week*, 23rd September, pp. 55–57.

Wilson, K. and Millman, T. (2003), 'The global account manager as political entrepreneur', *Industrial Marketing Management*, 32, 151–158.

 Questions

Question 11.1

Planning is an essential part of the selling process. What should be included in the weekly calling plan, and what information should be recorded after each visit is made?

Question 11.2

The primary task of a sales representative is to sell the company's products or services. What additional tasks could a sales representative be expected to undertake and how might they affect their selling role?

Question 11.3

In order to determine how well or how badly each salesperson is performing, a sales manager needs an appraisal system. Why is this important, and what questions should such an appraisal system be able to answer?

Question 11.4

How can the field sales force contribute to the process of achieving long-term relationships with customers through relationship marketing and customer care? Give specific examples.

Question 11.5

Examine the role and importance of personal selling within the 'promotions' mix of the modern marketing firm.

Question 11.6

Give examples of marketing situations where the use of personal selling is likely to be particularly effective and important.

12

Direct Marketing

12.1 Direct marketing explained

Direct marketing is a collection of techniques that enables organisations to market goods and services directly to customers (business-to-customers or B2C). It is a pro-active approach to marketing that takes the product and/or service to potential customers rather than waiting for them to come to a store or other point of access. It is a form of 'non-shop' shopping and is sometimes referred to as 'precision marketing' or 'one-to-one' marketing. Rather than the marketing firm sending out a general communication or sales message to a large group of potential customers, even if these constitute a well-defined market segment; direct marketing tends to target specific individuals or households. In a business-to-business (B2B) context this would be an individual or a specific organisation or firm. Direct marketing is not just concerned with marketing communications. It is also concerned with distribution. In using direct marketing, the firm is making a choice to cut out the use of marketing intermediaries and sell the product or service direct to customers. This has implications for both channels of distribution and logistical decisions.

Direct marketing comes in a variety of forms. It is one of the fastest growing areas of marketing and is being propelled by technical advances, particularly in the field of computer technology and the Web (see Totty, 2000, p. 36). Academics and consultants have taken up direct marketing with enthusiasm, and have helped to drive the subject forward both intellectually and practically.

12.1.1 Direct marketing is not new

Direct marketing is not new, as many companies have sold products direct to the public for years, for example, Kleeneze and Avon who have sold products door to door for many years. Direct mail through the post and mail order catalogues have been utilised for a long time and all are forms of direct marketing. Direct marketing originated in the early 1900s and the Direct Marketing

Association (DMA) was established in the USA in 1917. Direct marketing became an important force in the UK in the 1950s, but at this stage of its development it was generally concerned with direct mail, mail order and door-to-door personal selling. Today the scope of direct marketing has expanded dramatically largely due to the use of the telephone and in particular the use of the Internet. Direct marketing includes all marketing communications elements that allow an organisation to communicate directly with a prospect. This includes direct mail, telephone marketing, direct response advertising, door-to-door personal selling and the Internet.

Party plan companies have been selling products direct to customers in people's homes for many years. The telephone has been used for B2B sales for a long time particularly for the regeneration of 'routine' orders and for making sales appointments. It is now being used increasingly in domestic direct marketing programmes often to 'follow up' a posted personalised mail shot. Motoring organisations, such as the RAC and AA in the UK, have used direct personal selling for years to sell membership of their organisations and today use direct mail extensively to keep members informed about product and service benefits. However, as already mentioned, direct marketing has evolved with the advances in computer technology. The use of computers to store, retrieve and manipulate customer information has revolutionised the way direct marketing firms operate. Direct marketing firms can make use of the Internet and computer databases which allows them to access data 'warehouses' and gives them the capability to sort and aggregate or 'fuse' data to increase its value as a marketing resource.

12.1.2 Not all direct marketing is 'IT' driven

There is still the opportunity for 'old fashioned' methods that are well proven. Some of the more traditional direct marketing methods like door-to-door selling are employed and are effective and widely used by many companies. Traditional direct mail and telephone marketing techniques are widely employed by a range of direct marketing companies. Technology, especially computer technology, continues to develop at a rapid pace and ideas are changing constantly. It will be interesting to see what the world of direct marketing will look like in 10 or 20 years time. Figure 12.1 illustrates its development.

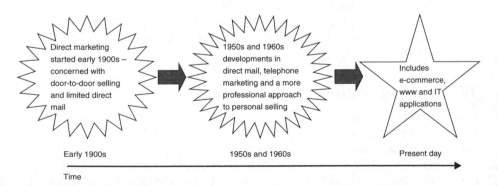

Figure 12.1 Development of direct marketing

12.2 Objectives of direct marketing

Much direct marketing activity is intended to result in a sale. However, in some situations a direct sale might be unlikely or inappropriate. In such cases some other form of measurable response might be used. For example, a direct mail campaign and a telephone-marketing programme may be used in the engineering industry to invite and encourage buyers to attend a machine tool exhibition. A leaflet drop for double-glazing might contain a free phone number for the prospect to request a brochure or estimate. The result may not be a sale, but some specific, measurable action that will hopefully contribute to an ultimate sale. Although a sale may not be the immediate objective of a direct marketing campaign, some form of direct response on behalf of the recipient of the message will be. This, in turn, will contribute to the eventual sale. Hence, direct marketing is not necessarily the same as direct sales. It might be used to keep customers informed of new product developments or to send them specific discount offers.

12.2.1 Strategic role of direct marketing

Direct marketing should not be used as a mere tactical marketing communications tool, but should be integrated with the rest of the communications mix. All marketing communications elements interact to some extent. Direct marketing is likely to form a major part of communications strategy of many companies and not simply form a kind of tactical adjunct. Other forms of communication are likely to be used in conjunction with direct marketing programmes even if these are only general corporate advertising programmes. Many firms use direct marketing predominantly, but not to the exclusion of other communication methods. Direct marketing is often used as part of integrated customer relationship management (CRM) programmes, which we discuss in the next chapter. CRM programmes are by their nature long term and strategic in nature.

12.2.2 Definition of direct marketing

Direct marketing is broadly defined as any direct communication to a consumer or business recipient that is designed to generate a response in the form of a direct order, a request for further information (lead generation), or a visit to a store or other place of business for the purchase of a specific product or service (traffic generation). The emphasis is on direct marketing communication. A leading trade magazine, Direct Marketing, goes further and defines direct marketing as a process that is:

> 'An interactive system of marketing that uses one or more advertising media to affect a measurable response and/or transaction at any location, with this activity stored on a database.'

Dibb and Simkin (2001, p. 545) defines direct marketing as:

> 'a decision by a company's marketers to select a marketing channel that avoids dependence on marketing channel intermediaries, and to

focus marketing communications activity on promotional mix ingredients that contact directly targeted customers.'

Fill (2002, p. 667) defines direct marketing:

'Direct marketing is a strategy used to create a personal and inter-mediary free dialogue with customers. This should be a measurable activity and it is very often media based, with a view to creating and sustaining a mutually rewarding relationship.'

The goal is to provide the customer with information relative to their needs and interests. A profile on the direct and interactive marketing industry offers a useful way of looking at it as a cyclical process with six distinct phases:

1 The creative stage and design phase, where the marketing plan is constructed and appropriate media channels are selected.
2 Data compilation where both internal data, such as customer lists and outside data from a database company or list broker is assembled in preparation for the next stage in the programme.
3 Database management, where information is 'mined', 'fused', aggregated or disaggregated, enhanced and standardised for use in the programme.
4 Database analysis, or fine tuning the database which further focuses on an optimal target market.
5 Execution and fulfilment where customer inquiries and orders are acted upon and information on response rates are collected for final post programme analysis.
6 Response analysis where the results of the campaign are examined for effectiveness before the cycle begins again.

12.3 The Direct Marketing Association

The DMA is the oldest and largest trade association for users and suppliers in the direct, database and interactive marketing fields. Founded in 1917, the DMA has more than 4,700 member organisations, commercial as well as not-for-profit, from the USA and over 50 nations on six continents. Reflecting the revolutionary impact of the WWW and e-commerce on the industry, The DMA has acquired two e-commerce trade associations, the Association for Interactive Media (AIM) New York and the Internet Alliance (IA) Washington, D.C. The DMA shapes the way organisations apply direct/interactive-marketing meth-ods to marketing, sales and customer service activity. Their mission is to encourage growth and profitability of their members and adherence to ethical standards. To achieve this the DMA:

1 Provides strong leadership in government and public affairs representation, public relations and communications, adherence to established ethical

guidelines, self-regulation and the identification and promotion of new and best practices to project and grow the business.

2 Promote an environment in which users of direct/interactive marketing and their suppliers will develop the necessary skills to prosper.

3 Assist members to understand consumer and business customer needs and concerns regarding direct/interactive marketing and confirm that member's respect and act on those needs and concerns.

12.4 Uses of direct marketing using different media

We have examined the nature of direct marketing and its role in the communications mix, and now discuss the main areas of direct marketing. The discussion that follows is not exhaustive, but it covers the main direct marketing tools and examines their application in different marketing situations. We start with the use of telephone or telemarketing, which has been used particularly in industrial and B2B marketing. We then examine developments and the use of direct mail, which has seen enormous growth as a direct marketing tool over the past 30 years. Telemarketing and the use of direct mail were two of the main pillars of the direct marketing industry when the DMA was established in the USA (see Dipasquale, 2002, p. 16, for a detailed account of expenditures on telephone marketing and direct mail).

Direct mail examines some of the revolutionary developments in the use of the Internet in direct marketing. Topics here include database marketing and techniques of data mining and data fusion, which are central to the direct marketing revolution when using this medium. Direct personal selling is well established as a direct marketing tool and formed the 'bedrock' of the direct marketing industry at the time of the establishment of the DMA in 1917. We finally examine direct response, concentrating mainly on television direct response advertising, but also covering newspapers and radio applications.

12.4.1 Telephone marketing

Telephone marketing has been used as a direct marketing tool for many years, although mainly in B2B situations. Much routine reordering can be handled over the telephone without the need for an expensive personal visit. The telephone is used to keep in touch with customers between visits. It can be used to make 'cold call' appointments and re-appointments with established clients. It is extremely versatile and can be used in many ways as a marketing tool. In consumer markets it is now used extensively and has grown in importance as a marketing tool. Services like banking are offered over the telephone and customers can give instructions to pay bills and receive a balance on their account using special access codes. Many companies use the telephone as part of a direct marketing programme. They may start first with a direct response press advertisement, which gives a free number to call. This starts the direct marketing process going.

The telephone derives its power as a marketing medium from its transactional nature (i.e. one human being in a controlled conversation with another). What originally began as 'ordering by telephone' evolved into telemarketing, a concept defined as:

> 'Any measurable activity that creates and exploits a direct relationship between supplier and customer by the interactive use of the telephone (Roncoroni, 1986, p. 26).'

The American Telephone and Telegraph Company (AT&T) define it as:

> 'The marketing of telecommunications technology and direct marketing techniques (Nash, 1984, p. 156).'

Telephone marketing is divided into incoming and outgoing call telemarketing. With incoming call telemarketing the prospect makes the call to the marketing firm, usually in response to a direct mail advertisement or direct response television advertisement giving a free phone or toll free telephone number. Hence, telemarketing is often used with other direct marketing tools as a part of an integrated programme. The caller may wish to sign up to a service such as insurance, apply for a loan over the telephone, order a product seen on the television or in a direct response advertisement or ask for further details. The call is logged and often recorded. The caller is then followed up with an outgoing telephone call sometime later, or sent information through the post. A personal visit might be arranged, for example, from a kitchen surveyor. Outgoing telephone marketing may simply be the return of an incoming call. Often existing customers are telephoned to ask if they want to take advantage of a special offer. For example, if a loan has been taken out with a finance company by a good customer, the firm may ring that customer to offer another loan at a special discount rate. A bank may ring a customer to ask if they would like to make an appointment at the branch to have their mortgage reviewed or discuss house insurance.

Companies can exploit the telephone as a marketing tool in a number of ways:

- *Cost savings*: Telephone selling provides a customised means of communications. Greater sophistication in telemarketing equipment and services, new marketing approaches and developments in applications have turned the use of the telephone into 'telemarketing'. The telephone may not have the quality of a personal sales call, but it is significantly cheaper. Sometimes in the initial stages of a direct marketing programme a personal visit is not necessary or appropriate anyway.
- *Supplement to a personal visit*: Professional salespeople use a system of differential call frequency to plan their visits to customers. Salespeople may have

to prioritise their calls on a key account basis. Although they may not be able to visit less important customers with the same frequency as more important customers, they can make a telephone call on a regular basis to keep customers informed and build and maintain relationships.

- *Gaining marketing intelligence*: Marketing firms can speak to customers on a regular basis, not only to maintain relationships, but also to ask questions about their needs and wants and purchasing intentions. This information can be recorded and fed into the firms marketing information system (MkIS) for future use. Buying intentions can be used to produce sales forecasts for future planning. On establishing customer needs, telephone marketers can introduce new products to clients and use the call to sell further products.
- *Supplement to direct mail and other advertising*: Many direct mail and other forms of direct response advertising, on television, press or radio, for example, will carry a free phone message. This enables the prospect to make telephone contact at no cost. Prospects can make an immediate commitment to purchase whilst the advertising message is still fresh in their minds. If they do not ring to make a purchase, they may telephone for further information, which in turn produces a qualified lead for further marketing action.

The above list is not exhaustive, but it serves to demonstrate how versatile the telephone can be as a direct marketing tool. The use of the telephone is still growing as a marketing tool and further advances in technology and the linking of the telephone to television and the Internet will bring further developments in the future making it an even more important marketing medium.

12.4.2 Direct mail

Direct mail explained

Direct mail is considered by some to be an advertising medium, but by others to be a separate element of the marketing communications mix. Direct mailing is the use of the postal service to distribute informative literature or other promotional material to selected prospects.

A direct mail shot may consist of anything from a letter to weighty catalogues of product offerings. Regular users of direct mail techniques in the UK are the Readers Digest and the Automobile Association.

Direct mail is a method of communicating a message directly to a particular person, household or firm. As such it falls under the more general heading of direct marketing, which includes many other forms of direct communication. We now distinguish direct mail from related activities with which it is commonly confused:

Direct mail is not:

1 *Direct advertising*: This is one of the oldest methods of reaching consumers. It consists of printed matter that is sent by the advertiser direct to the prospect. This material is often sent by mail, but it may also be distributed house-to-house by personal delivery, handed out to passers-by, or put under the windscreen

wipers of parked cars. The portion of direct advertising that is sent through the mail is called direct mail advertising.

2 *Mail order*: If the object of a direct mail shot is to persuade recipients to order the product or service by return post, the correct term is mail order or mail order advertising. Deliveries are made through mail or parcel services or by carrier direct from a warehouse or factory or sometimes through a local agent. Mail order is a special form of direct mail. It seeks to complete the sale entirely by mail, whilst direct mail is generally supplementary to other forms of advertising and selling. Direct mail is part of a company's general marketing plan, whereas mail order advertising is a complete plan in itself, and companies exist solely to conduct business in this manner. Mail order is a type of direct mail, but not all direct mail is mail order.

3 *Direct response advertising*: Neither direct mail nor mail order should be confused with direct response advertising. This is the strategy of using specially designed advertisements, usually in newspapers and magazines, to invoke a direct response rather than a delayed one. The most familiar type of direct response advertising is the coupon-response press advertisement, in which a coupon is provided which the reader may use to order the advertised product or service or request further information or a sales call. Other variants involve incentives to visit the retail outlet immediately, such as preview invitations and money-off coupons. Direct mail can also be used for direct response advertising.

Growth of direct mail in UK marketing

Post Office/Royal Mail statistics show a continuing rise in the annual volume of direct mail and in the number of organisations using it for business and consumer communication. A number of factors account for this increased use and acceptance of direct mail as a communications medium. Of the most significant is the increased fragmentation of media:

- There are now three UK terrestrial commercial television channels as well as a wide choice of satellite and cable television available to subscribers,
- In the print media, there has been the rapid growth of 'freesheets' alongside traditional local press, as well as a proliferation of special interest magazines.

This fragmentation has meant that media buyers and advertisers either have to spend more money to ensure they reach as wide an audience as previously, or spread the same amount of money more thinly over a range of media. Developments within the direct mail industry have removed many difficulties that have previously deterred large advertisers particularly in respect of the inferior quality of large mail shots and hence such material being dubbed 'junk mail'. IT advances have made it possible to 'personalise' mail shots, targeted to individuals by name. Quality has been improved by increased investment that has been channelled into direct mail. There have been tremendous technical strides in all areas of direct mail, including computer aided design of direct mail material and use of mail merge software that produces results that look like letters. Materials can be produced and addressed exclusively for individuals. Data storage and customer profiling, targeting of direct mail shots to individuals and organisations are possible. In order to effectively segment and target markets and gain best value for money, organisations are increasingly opting for the benefits of direct mail – flexibility, selectivity and personal contact.

Uses of direct mail

The range of products or services that can be sold by direct mail is wide, as are its uses. To define it more fully, it is appropriate to deal with direct mail to consumers and businesses separately.

Consumer direct mail

The uses of consumer-targeted direct mail are only limited by the scope of imagination. Some of the more common uses are:

1 *Selling direct*: Direct mail is a good medium for selling to customers without the need for middlemen. Product offerings can be described fully and orders can be sent straight back to the advertising company.
2 *Sales lead generation*: If a product requires a meeting between the customer and a specialised salesperson (e.g. fitted kitchens, central heating and insurance) direct mail is a useful method of acquiring good, qualified leads for the company's salespeople. Sales calls are expensive, so anything that improves call success rate is welcome. A well-planned mail shot can act as a preliminary sieve, pinpointing the best prospects and ranking others in terms of sales potential. The 'warmer' the lead, the more effective will be the sales discussion with fewer wasted calls.

   Responses, indicating potential interest can be followed up by direct mail, a telephone call or a personal visit by a salesperson. Potential customers can be placed in a personal selling situation by issuing an invitation to view the product in a retail outlet, showroom or exhibition. This is useful for products that salespeople cannot take to prospects for demonstration because of its size or function.

   Direct mail creates a receptive atmosphere for the company's salespeople through 'cordial contact' mailings that build on the reputation of the company and through the impression created. Well-executed mailing places the company in a favourable light to prospects, setting up goodwill or creating a latent desire that might be triggered into action by a later mailing.
3 *Sales promotion*: Direct mail can send promotional messages – money off vouchers, special offers, etc. to selected targets. This is a useful way of encouraging people to visit a shop or exhibition.
4 *Clubs*: Book clubs are the best-known example of the use of direct mail as a convenient medium of communication and transaction between a club and its members. Other items can be marketed by the club system particularly 'collectibles', for example, record collections, porcelain and miniatures.

5 *Mail order*: Mail order companies use direct mail to recruit new customers and local agents, as well as direct selling.

6 *Fundraising*: An advantage of direct mail is ability to communicate personally with an individual. This makes it a powerful method of raising money. It can carry the 'long copy' often needed to convince recipients of the worthiness of the charity, and make it more likely that the reader might respond with a donation.

7 *Dealer mailings*: If a product is sold through dealers or agents, they can use direct mail to reach prospective customers in their particular catchment area just as a producer might.

8 *Follow-up mailings*: The company's name can be promoted to customers by following any kind of sales activity with a mailing , for example, checking that the customer is satisfied with their purchase or informing them that perhaps a car they bought last year is coming up for its annual service. Customers can be kept informed of new developments, latest products and improved services. 'Exclusive' offers can be made and invitations issued. Using direct mail in this way helps maintain contact quickly, personally and effectively and can increase repeat sales.

Business direct mail

Business markets are made up of closely defined, discrete groups of individuals. These groups may not be best reached by mass advertising media. Direct mail can be used to accurately identify different market sectors and provide messages appropriate to each sector. Some of the more common uses are:

1 *Product launch*: Often the launch of a new industrial product or business service entails getting the message across to a small, but significant, number of people who will influence buying decisions (e.g. catering managers and car fleet managers).

2 *Sales lead generation*: As in consumer markets, direct mail can effectively reach qualified sales leads for a company's sales force.

3 *Dealer support*: Direct mail makes it easy to keep dealers, retail outlets, franchise holders, etc. more fully informed of tactical marketing promotions and plans.

4 *Conferences and exhibitions*: Business and trade conferences and exhibitions are well-established means of communicating with potential customers and business colleagues. Direct mail can be used to invite delegates, who may be attracted if the event relates to a specific theme of direct interest to them.

5 *Follow-up mailing using the customer base*: Much business takes the form of repeat sales to existing customers. Since these are existing clients it can be worthwhile mailing them regularly, as long as the content of the mail-out relates to something that is new or of specific interest rather than simply 'junk mail'.

6 *Marketing research/product testing*: Direct mail can be used for marketing research, especially amongst existing customers. Questionnaires can be used as part of a regular communication programme, with levels of response being increased by some kind of incentive. Small-scale test mailings can be

made to sample a target market. The results can give a quick and accurate picture of market reaction, with minimum risk. A marketing approach that is successful in a 'test mailing' can later be mailed to the full list.

Direct mail as part of the promotional mix

In both consumer and business markets, direct mail must fit in with an organisation's other promotion efforts, for example, a television or press campaign can reach a broader audience and raise levels of awareness of a company. If such a campaign is added to a direct mail campaign aimed specifically at groups of people or companies most likely to buy, or to people particularly wanted as customers the effectiveness of the overall campaign can be significantly raised.

Lists of respondents to direct response techniques in other media, for example, 'coupon' response press advertisements or television or radio commercials that give a 'phone-in' number or contact address can be used as mailing lists for direct mail approaches.

12.4.3 Use of the Internet as a direct marketing tool

Customers now have more products and services to choose from and more information available to them to help them make purchasing decisions. Conventional communications, principally media advertising, is not as effective as it used to be. This is partly because there is more for consumers to digest, and partly because people have learned to ignore it. The rise of the Internet means that companies can go further than conventional communications would allow them to in the past.

There is a new group of products and services that relies on customers registering their interest in them with the company. Amazon.com for example, encourages customers to review books and publishes their comments on the website so both the firm and other users can read and make use of them. A US airline invites customers to register their preferences for last minute offers via its web site, and then emails potential customers with details of weekend breaks at their preferred resorts. These are examples of the precision that can be achieved with direct marketing (see Marsh, 2001, p. 29, for a discussion on how FedEx uses its database to create highly targeted direct marketing campaigns to 5 million customers in over 200 countries).

The Internet has the potential to be the most powerful direct marketing tool ever. In 10 years owning a computer workstation that is wired to the Internet will be as common as owning a TV is today. Children being taught at school using new technology today and playing computer games at home will take the use of the Internet as a shopping medium for granted. The Internet is not a fad; it is a major technological development that will continually evolve. We are at the beginning of the next business revolution that will affect the way we live, work and play. The technology involved in setting up the Internet has demonstrated that it will significantly change the way people interact with each other, particularly in the sphere of direct marketing. The Internet crosses boundaries of geography, politics, race, sex, religion, time zones and culture. Some areas of marketing are almost totally underpinned by technology and its application, for example, the use of e-marketing based on Internet technology and variations that have been developed from original Internet concepts such as the Intranet and Extranet, which connects and links employees, customers, suppliers and partners. The Internet has reduced the planet to a global village, accelerated the pace of technology, opened up tremendous possibilities for direct marketers and altered the way they think about doing business. It has started the new revolution in direct marketing; some say the most important revolution since the invention of commercial advertising, the 'e-commerce revolution'. It is the revolution people can no longer ignore anymore.

It is contended that the e-commerce revolution will rebuild the existing economy and change the way marketing and business is conducted. Doubters say the likely effect of this new technology is over-blown and many people will stop using it once the novelty has worn off.

Database marketing

Improvements in database software and related computer technology have revolutionised the direct marketing industry. Nothing has driven the direct marketing industry forward more than IT developments, especially in the development of database software and applications. Database marketing is a marketing and sales system that continually gathers, refines and utilises information and data that drives relevant marketing and sales communications programmes. It is used extensively, but not exclusively, in direct marketing. Examples are sales calls, direct mail and advertising to selected companies to acquire new customers, retain customers, generate more business from existing customers and create long-term loyalty. The Internet, e-commerce, rising costs of direct marketing and more emphasis on customer retention over customer acquisition are only a few salient factors affecting the way firms carry out business today. Firms have to move quickly and keep up with latest developments and trends, and invest in relevant software and systems to stay ahead of the competition (see Blakenhorn, 2001, p. T16).

Database marketing is more than a data retrieval system. Whilst direct marketing describes a collection of marketing communication tactics like direct mail, telemarketing and direct response advertising, database marketing describes a way of organising a company's total marketing and sales processes. It is broad and can impact market research and product development through to customer service. Accurate information about customers that is readily available to everyone in the marketing company can transform the company's marketing ability (see Davenport, 2001, p. 63).

Strategic and tactical implications

Database marketing aims to focus and target and take guessing out of marketing programmes. Perfect accuracy is never possible, but it allows for significant improvements in accuracy and efficiency if used properly. Some companies engage in 'hit-or-miss' marketing. This means management often makes decisions based on intuition or instinct rather than on hard facts based on scientific evidence, so instead for predicting target audiences on hard facts they make best guesses about who their target audience is and what they want. This can be expensive in terms of wasted direct mail shots and other forms of communication.

It allows you to take information you already have in your customer databases, analyse it to find any patterns like purchasing associations and relationships, and use information that has been gained to produce and instigate better marketing and sales programmes. This means targeting specific groups with specific messages about products that are important to them, rather than giving irrelevant information. This means that more resources can be spent on prospects that are most likely to buy, increasing the return on marketing and sales investment.

Proper use of databases gives marketing better tools to operate more professionally and improves the effectiveness of marketing campaigns, allowing for the more effective allocation and utilisation of marketing resources. Database marketing is sometimes referred to as precision marketing. Directing a marketing programme from a well constructed and managed database is analogous to shooting a rifle at a target using a precision telescopic sight rather than a conventional sight. Developments in database marketing over the past 20 years, has probably done more to drive the direct marketing industry forward than any other single development.

Principles of database marketing

Some illustrations are provided of applications and basic principles of database marketing. This is not an exhaustive or definitive list, but it serves to illustrate the main principles:

- Consider characteristics your best customers have in common so you can target your next programmes to prospects with similar characteristics. Evaluate which market segments buy from your firm. You might think you know this, but analysis could uncover market segments you have sold a significant amount of product to, but did not realise it. This process enables the firm to improve its segmentation by refocusing and redefining existing segments or it may highlight unexpected new segments.
- Ascertain whether different market segments buy different products from you. This will allow you to spend marketing and sales resources more effectively by marketing each of your products to the best potential industries, firms or prospects. Study which market segments bring most revenue and which ones bring highest average revenue. This is the application of differentiated marketing, which divides the total market into segments, and then has a slightly different marketing strategy for each segment.
- Find out what types of industries, firms or individuals respond to which types of marketing communication, so you can decide where to spend advertising

and marketing resources next time. Ascertain that they not only respond to your programmes, but also actually buy, and which buy from you repeatedly. These might have been different demographic profiles or different in some other way, which might be commercially exploitable, and you may then decide to modify your targeting tactics and only market to segments that buy more frequently.

- Calculate the average lifetime value of customers. This can be done using discounted cash flow procedures (discussed in Chapter 10). This information can be used to find out which customers are not achieving their potential. Marketing and sales programmes can then be devised to encourage more purchases. Reward the most frequent buyers and buyers that bring the highest revenue. The concept of lifetime value is central to the idea of customer retention and long-term relationship marketing.

12.4.4 Direct personal selling

Marketing communications can be classified into personal and impersonal methods. Conventional advertising is classified as impersonal and of course selling is personal and involves some form of interaction with a prospect, referred to as a dyadic relationship. This interaction can be at a distance, over the telephone for example. However, most personal selling is carried out on a face-to-face basis and this dimension is a key strength of personal selling. Selling was the focus of the previous chapter, and it was discussed that it is more expensive on a cost per contact basis, but sometimes there is no substitute for a personal approach. Consumers benefit from direct selling because of the convenience and service it provides, including personal communication, demonstration and explanation of products to a higher standard than in conventional stores or through printed media. Home delivery by the salesperson who took the order provides even further satisfaction. This is different from conventional shopping, and cuts out the need for marketing intermediaries, thereby saving customers money.

The task of selling differs according to products or services being marketed. In some situations the task of selling is more a matter of keeping customers satisfied and the task then calls for more skills of personality and caring. In other situations, contractual negotiations might be the main emphasis of selling where skills of prospecting, negotiating, demonstrating and closing a sale will be greater criteria of success. In organisational marketing, reliance is placed on personal communication. For FMCGs, emphasis is placed on above- and below-the-line communication. In organisational selling the proportion of selling within the total market budget usually outweighs all other marketing expenditure. Direct selling is a specific form of selling. Not only is it personal, but it is direct and constitutes an expanding channel of distribution. Moreover, direct selling provides a channel of distribution for companies with innovative or distinctive products not readily available in traditional retail outlets. It may be that products on offer are produced by a relatively small firm that cannot afford to compete through advertising and promotion, because of the costs associated with gaining space on retail shelves of major outlets. Hence, customers gain by being able to purchase products that would have been unavailable had the marketing company to operate through conventional retail outlets. Direct selling enhances the retail distribution infrastructure. It can serve customers with a convenient source of products that may not be available elsewhere.

Direct selling is described as marketing products and services directly to consumers face-to-face generally in their homes, at their workplace and other places away from permanent retail locations. It typically occurs through explanation or personal demonstration by a direct salesperson, or direct seller.

Products and services sold by direct sellers are varied as are people involved in the direct selling industry, particularly insurance, financial services, cosmetics, skin care products, personal care items, home appliances, household cleaning products, nutritional products, toys, books, clothing, jewellery, fashion accessories, etc. Sometimes, such products are sold in the context of group presentations (party plan). Tupperware produce a range of products, especially kitchenware and food and drink storage boxes. The company is an example of a party plan selling strategy used successfully. In this approach, the direct salesperson demonstrates products to a group of guests, invited by a host in whose home or other location the direct selling demonstration takes place. By contrast, other types of direct selling often explain and demonstrate the products being offered to customers in the comfort of their homes at a time that is convenient for them on a personal one to one basis rather than in a group. Avon Cosmetics uses freelance agents to visit people in their own homes and demonstrate and explain the use of a range of beauty products.

Direct selling provides benefits to individuals who desire an opportunity to earn income and build their own business. It also offers an alternative to consumers who want something different from traditional shopping.

Multi-level marketing

Multi-level Marketing (MLM), like many innovative business systems, was developed in the USA and exported to other parts of the world. Some suspicion surrounds MLM as there is confusion with pyramid selling. This was an unethical business practice that is banned in the UK. An important component of the direct selling industry is multi-level marketing. It is also referred to as network marketing, structure marketing or multi-level direct selling, and has proved to be a successful and effective method of compensating direct sellers for marketing and distributing products and services direct to consumers. Unlike 'pyramid selling' MLM is an ethical business practice that uses the principle of 'team building' in terms of stimulating salespeople to aspire to better levels of performance to sell products. Direct salespersons are usually self-employed people working on a freelance basis for commission on sales. Figure 12.2 explains how it is structured.

Salespersons normally start by selling goods and services to the public, often in the first instance, to people they know such as friends and work colleagues.

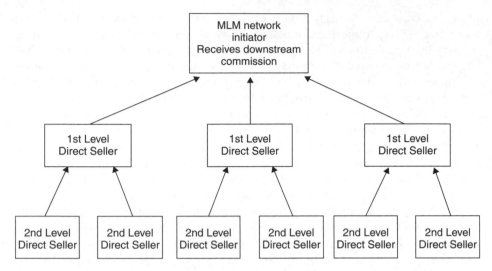

Figure 12.2 Principle of MLM showing team originator receiving downstream commissions from those lower in the network

They then move up the hierarchy to not only sell products themselves, but to recruit other direct sellers to sell as part of their own team. They not only receive commission on the goods they sell themselves, but also earn 'downstream' commission on products the people they have recruited have sold. Eventually they may move from selling direct themselves, and concentrate on managing others in their team. As the team grows so does the 'downstream' commission that accrues to the original team organiser. Eventually the end the team leader may have a network of many direct selling staff at different level in the hierarchy. Some will be content to sell some product direct on a part time basis. Some may want to recruit a small team. Some may want to be senior team leaders and put in effort to lead a whole networking team of direct personal selling staff and reap the rewards of commissions based on the selling effort of their team combined with their own motivational, leadership and managerial skills.

World Federation of Direct Selling Associations

Founded in 1978, the WFDSA is a non-governmental, voluntary organisation representing the direct selling industry globally as a federation of national Direct Selling Associations (DSAs). The United States Direct Selling Association serves as the Secretariat for the Federation and is based in Washington, D.C. The mission of the WFDSA is to support direct selling associations in the areas of governance, education, communications, consumer protection and ethics in the marketplace and to promote personal interaction among direct selling executives regarding issues of importance to the industry. There are over 50 national DSAs represented in its membership, and in 2001 it was estimated that worldwide retail sales by its members accounted for more than $US95 billion through the activities of more than 25 million independent salespersons. The World Federation and its national DSAs understand the necessity for ethical conduct in the marketplace and as such the WFDSA has developed a World Code of Conduct for Direct Selling that all national DSAs have approved and implemented in their national codes. All direct selling companies agree to be bound by these codes as a condition of membership in a national DSA. The WFDSA regularly publishes a newsletter, World Federation News, with an international focus on direct selling for distribution to member DSAs and companies.

12.4.5 Direct response advertising

This area has witnessed an enormous growth over recent year's particularly direct response television advertising. Direct response advertising is a major part of those communication activities classified as direct marketing. Direct response advertising uses carefully crafted marketing communications to generate a response directly from advertising itself. This could be a telephone call to you asking for an appointment to provide further information or an order in the post or request for a brochure. A coupon presented for a discount or free sample can also be used. Credit cards as convenient charging platforms over the telephone have helped to expand this type of business. Many product are advertised on television that cannot be purchased elsewhere, and the only way to obtain the product is to telephone a free phone or toll free number given in the advertisement order within a short period of time (see Tedeschi, 2001, p. C4, for an excellent discussion of the interactive nature of television direct marketing).

Since the firm is generating and monitoring responses, management can measure the contacts and income produced by each individual advertisement or mailing. Conventional advertising is difficult to evaluate in terms of sales response, where it is more appropriate to evaluate the communications effect rather than the sales effects following advertising. Management can test different forms of advertising in consecutive issues of the same publication, and see which is most effective or schedule the same advertisement in different publications and learn which publication is most effective in producing the desired response. Direct response is the only type of advertising that allows evaluation of the effectiveness of operations in relation to specific, measurable objectives.

It is difficult for a firm to evaluate specific sales response from conventional advertising because of 'multiple causation'. An advertisement is only one of a number of communications being used by firms simultaneously. It is difficult to separate out the effects, particularly the sales effects, in respect of each of these forms of promotion. As they do not have any response generator or tracking mechanism in place for quantifying sales results, it is difficult to ascertain which medium is working and which is not. Lord Lever of household detergent fame once said: 'I know that half my advertising is wasted, but I don't know which half'.

Direct Response Advertising relies on compelling and persuasive material to bring about a specified response. Its objective is not merely to inform, but to bring about a desired specific response, that can be objectively measured. With Direct Response Advertising, creative writers use artwork copy, page layout, plus carefully crafted text, to explain salient reasons to purchase a product or service.

 ## 12.5 Summary

Direct marketing is a branch of marketing that has gone through rapid growth and technological change over the past 30 years. It is an important marketing process and some organisations base their entire marketing strategy on direct marketing methods. Worldwide, the direct marketing industry is huge. As firms seek ways of obtaining more value from marketing budgets, direct marketing is likely to become even stronger in the future. Direct marketing refers to a collection of methods that allows companies to communicate with, and obtain a direct response, from prospects. It allows firms to target customers more precisely than conventional non-direct marketing techniques and is referred to as precision marketing.

Direct marketing techniques are constantly being improved and developed and new innovative media are likely to be developed in the future. At present, the main methods employed within the direct marketing industry are the use of the telephone, direct mail, the internet, direct 'face-to-face' personal selling and direct response advertising using television, radio and newspapers, trade journals and magazines. The industry is being driven by a desire for greater accuracy and economy in marketing operations and by developments in IT that can be applied to direct marketing. Database marketing in particular has revolutionised the way organisations use direct marketing and has increased efficiency in areas like direct mail and telephone marketing. Direct marketing is not solely driven by IT. Some traditional methods that were used in 1917 when the Direct Marketing Association was founded in the USA are still being used successfully, particularly face-to-face direct personal selling. However, these techniques have benefited from the information revolution in terms of retrieval of customer information and improved targeting. Direct marketing is a major force within marketing and is likely to increase in future.

 ## References

Blakenhorn, D. (2001), 'Marketers hone targeting', *Advertising Age*, June 18th, T16.
Davenport, T. H. (2001), 'How do you know their customers so well?', *MIT Sloan Management Review*, Winter, 63–67.
Dibb, S. and Simpkin, L. (2001), *Marketing Briefs: A Revision and Study Guide*, Oxford: Butterworth-Heinemann, p. 545.

Dipasquale, C.B. (2002), 'Direct mail sector staying the course', *Advertising Age*, March 11th, 16.

Fill, C. (2002), *Marketing Communications: Contexts, Strategies and Applications*, Chapter 28: Direct Marketing, Financial Times, Prentice-Hall, p. 667.

Marsh, H. (2001), 'Dig deeper into the database goldmine', *Marketing*, January 11th, 29–30.

Nash, E.L. (1982), *Direct Marketing*, McGraw-Hill, p. 156.

Roncoroni, S. (1986), 'Direct marketing', *Financial Times*, April 15th, 26.

Tedeschi, B. (2001), 'Television shopping channels may become the big winners in the competition for online sales', *New York Times*, April 16th, C4.

Totty, P. (2000), 'Direct mail gets a new lease on life', *Credit Union Magazine*, 66(4), 36–37.

Further reading

Miller, R. (2001), 'Marketers pinpoint their targets', *Marketing*, January 18th, 40–41.

Kotler, P. and Armstrong, G. (2004), *Principles of Marketing*, 10th edition, Chapter 17: Personal Selling and Direct Marketing, Prentice-Hall, Inc., pp. 524–563.

Betagnoli, L. (2001), 'E-marketing tricky in Europe', *Marketing News*, July 16th, 19.

Bird, D. (1999), *Common Sense Direct Marketing*, London: Kogan-Page.

The Grocer (2002), 'Tesco link with suppliers for personalised online appeal', *The Grocer*, February 16th, 4.

Godin, S. (1999), *Permission Marketing: Turning Strangers into Friends, and Friends into Customers*, New York, NY: Simon & Schuster Publishing Company.

McAlevey, T. (2001), 'The Principles of Effective Direct Response', *Direct Marketing*, April, 44–47.

Hafner, K. and Lyon, M. (1996), *Where Wizards Stay Up Late: The Origins of the Internet*, New York, NY: Simon & Schuster.

Hardaker, G. and Graham, G. (2001), *Wired Marketing: Energising Business for e-Commerce*, New York: John Wiley and Sons.

Meller, P. (2001), 'DM industry welcomes EU spam decision', *Marketing Week*, November 15th, 8.

Plamer, A. (2000), *Principles of Marketing*, Chapter 20: Direct Marketing, Oxford: Oxford University Press.

Questions

Question 12.1

Using examples, explain the role of direct response advertising within the overall marketing communications mix.

Question 12.2

Explain how the use of 'incoming call' telephone direct marketing differs in its role and use from 'outgoing' telephone direct marketing. Use examples to illustrate the points made.

Question 12.3

Trace development in the direct marketing industry from the beginning of the twentieth century to the present day.

Question 12.4

Demonstrate how direct mail can be used with other direct marketing tools to form a cohesive and fully integrated direct marketing programme.

Question 12.5

Explain the term 'multi level marketing' and give the main reasons for its success as a direct marketing business process over the past 20 years.

Question 12.6

Outline selling situations where direct personal selling is likely to be more effective than other direct marketing techniques. Justify your views by reference to specific examples.

Question 12.7

Discuss how the Internet is likely to develop as a direct marketing tool over the next 10 years.

13
Customer Relationship Management

13.1 Introduction

Customer relationship management (CRM) and associated tactical issues of customer care have evolved and developed substantially over the past 20 years. The subject of integrated CRM has evolved out of the earlier, but related, topic of relationship marketing (RM). As with e-commerce, some observers feel that CRM is just the latest hunt for a more ideal business philosophy, or more unkindly, the latest 'management fad'. Others see CRM as a change in business philosophy, one that incorporates and consolidates many earlier areas of new thinking such as total quality management, internal marketing and relationship marketing. It is to the topic of RM that we next turn, followed by a discussion of the related subject of 'internal marketing', because organisations need to market the concept of marketing to their own staff and others, the so-called 'internal customers'. Organisations need to create the right spirit and internal culture before they can expect success in long-term external relationships. It has been discovered that employees behave toward customers in much the same way as the management behaves toward them. If they are treated badly they are more likely to treat customers badly. If they are treated well they are more likely to treat customers well. We then examine the nature and importance of customer care. Both internal marketing and relationship marketing aim to provide a better internal and external business framework to enable the better care of customers. Finally, the principles of complete CRM system including computer software applications are examined.

13.2 The changing face of marketing

Marketing has been characterised by dynamic change. Many people who trained in marketing in the 1970s and 1980s find that their knowledge is now out of date. Much of this change has to do with the adoption of new computer-based technology such as the Internet, Extranet, Intranet, database marketing, data warehousing and the World Wide Web. Today, marketing management must show appreciation of the commercial possibilities of new marketing technologies. As discussed in Chapter 12, management does not necessarily have to be technical experts themselves, as specialist technical staff can be employed to do technical aspects of the work. They do, however, need to be able to understand the strategic implications and possibilities of the new technologies and be able to advise others how the technology can be employed to gain a strategic advantage over the competition and to improve marketing performance. Not all of these dramatic changes in marketing thinking have been due to technological advances, and many have been more philosophical in nature, although the application of new Internet-based marketing technologies may have facilitated some of these changes. Until recently, for example, the concept of totally integrated CRM systems remained an idealised concept that was confined to textbooks and academic papers, but difficult to put into practice in the business world, especially for the smaller enterprise (see McCaig, 2000, p. 30, for a discussion on the application of CRM to the smaller firm). The development of sophisticated computer software products and increase in memory available to systems to enable them to store, manipulate and retrieve large amounts of customer data has made the 'idealised' concept a reality for more progressive business firms (see Brassington and Pettitt, 2005, p. 47, for a discussion on how fast, complex data processing of customer information has helped firms establishing workable relationship marketing polices).

The very nature and direction of modern marketing has altered. The basic definition of marketing as a business process concerned with satisfying customer needs and wants more effectively than competition remains the same, and the basic marketing concept is still valid today. However, the process used to accomplish this has changed. Marketing textbook from the 1970s and 1980s contain far less information than current texts, with modern ones containing topics like Internal Marketing, Relationship Marketing, e-marketing, Green Marketing and Customer Relationship Management which are all recent additions to marketing literature. There has been a paradigm shift in the way marketing firms view their customers, look after them, nurture them and establish the long-term relationships (see Keller, 2002, p. 14, for a discussion on the true life time value of customers). Basically, the focus of marketing has shifted from the short-term, transactional, view of customers to seeing customers as a long-term income stream over many years, or the relationship marketing approach. Long-term relationships are achieved by firms meeting or exceeding customer's expectations of service, quality, price and delivery (see Hatch and Schell, 2002, p. 32, for a discussion on the importance of delighting customers). Industrial companies have practised this relationship building and management approach for some years in B2B marketing, but it is a relatively new concept in B2C marketing.

 ## 13.3 Relationship marketing

RM is a business concept that developed as a result of dissatisfaction with conventional transactional marketing. This applies particularly in B2B marketing where shortcomings of conventional marketing were first recognised. In 1954 Drucker said: 'There is only one valid definition of business: to create customers. It is the customer who determines what the business is (p. 65)'. Hence, customers are central to business and the underlying theme behind RM is the acquisition, satisfaction and retention of customers (note the importance of the word 'retention' see McMaster, 2001, p. 55). In a sense it is the marketing concept developed into a format in which it can be applied operationally, rather than merely being a concept.

The concept of RM was introduced into literature by early researchers in customer care such as Berry (1983, pp. 25–28). The subject of marketing had been developed largely from the experience of US firms and business researchers involved in consumer markets. These principles and theories seemed to have almost universal applicability in consumer markets of developed economies, especially Europe, and were only applied as an overriding business philosophy much later. The principles and practices of modern marketing developed in the US consumer market sector did not work quite so well in B2B environments or for the service sector. As western economies were reconstructed after the war, agriculture and manufacturing became less important and shared only a smaller proportion of these countries' GDP. Such countries are described as being in the post-industrial phase of development. In a post-industrial economy many jobs are of an intellectual type. Services then become the predominant economic activity that is carried out. Marketers looked to the conventional wisdom in marketing literature and found it no longer fitted the new 'service-based' economies and new thinking was required. In the growing B2B sector of the economy, there developed dissatisfaction with conventional 'one sale ahead' transactional marketing approach. It had been recognised in industrial markets for some time that commercial relationships between buyer and seller organisations required a more long-term interaction approach rather than the short-term philosophy of the next sale. This new thinking resulted in the development of relationship marketing (see Sullivan, 2001, p. 50).This has now been accepted by most firms, not just those involved in marketing services or industrial products.

Gronroos (1990, pp. 3–11) proposed a marketing strategy continuum ranging from transaction marketing, which was regarded as more appropriate to B2C marketing particularly in the field of FMCG's through to RM. This approach was seen as more suitable for B2B and services marketing. RM is now used in all markets. Copulsky and Wolf (1990, pp. 16–20) used the term RM to identify a type of database marketing. In their model, the database is used by marketing firms to select suitable customer targets for promotion of products and services. The message sent to customers is tailor made to fit their particular needs and wants. The response is monitored and used to produce various measures including the projected lifetime value of the customer. McKenna (1991, pp. 1–10) linked RM to the organisational structure of a business. The whole business was organised to produce a RM approach rather than it merely being a business process. The major concern amongst practitioners with the conventional marketing approach was that it was too short-term and transactional in focus. This may have worked well over the years in a predominantly B2C environment, but less so for service marketing, industrial and other forms of B2B marketing where the creation and maintenance of long-term relationships with customers was crucial for long-term commercial success. The modern usage of the term RM describes a situation where the creation, satisfaction and retention of customers are at the very centre of marketing strategy (again please note the importance of the word 'retention' and the importance of keeping the customer coming back, for more see Stout, 2002, p. 51).

13.3.1 TQM: the starting point

In the 1970s W. Edwards Deming (see also Deming, 1993, pp. 1–35 for an update), a world expert on quality issues, formulated a seminal theory of quality based upon his intimate knowledge of Japanese manufacturing, specifically with Toyota, concerning 14 key quality points. This revolutionised many aspects of production management. His ideas on quality were termed 'total quality management'. TQM philosophy now permeates thinking throughout entire organisations that adopt this philosophy. TQM is a structured system for satisfying internal and external customers and suppliers by integrating the business environment, striving for continuous improvement, and searching for breakthrough in development and maintenance cycles as well as changing organisational culture. A key to implementing TQM can be found in this definition, and this is the idea that TQM is a structured system. Describing TQM as a structured system meant that it is a strategy derived from internal and external customer and supplier wants and needs that have been determined by management. Pinpointing internal and external requirements allows management to continuously improve, develop and maintain quality, cost, delivery and morale. TQM is a system that integrates all of this activity and information.

13.3.2 Reverse marketing

Since the 1980s many firms have recognised that the way forward for business success is to change from an emphasis on cost and price as key marketing elements, to one of providing superior service through personal interaction and the formation of long-term relationships. Hence, there has been a change from a transactional focus in marketing towards a long-term relationship approach.

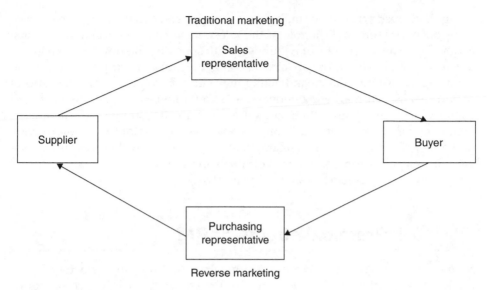

Figure 13.1 The notion of reverse marketing

The traditional role of the salesperson was seen as one of initiating commercial transactions by visiting buyers with the objective of securing orders, or being considered about the next tendering round. However, with the development of 'lean manufacturing' (formerly termed 'just-in-time manufacturing' or JIT) where deliveries are tightly scheduled and quality must presuppose 'zero defects', there has been a move in this commercial emphasis and it is now common for buyers to actively source their suppliers with a view to the establishment of long-term 'comakership' partnerships. This idea is called 'reverse marketing' and is illustrated in Figure 13.1.

The implication for sellers is that they must build on these partnerships in the knowledge that sales will continue so long as they supply goods of the right quality, at the right time and at an agreed price. Relationship marketing is the term used to describe this technique. This has led to the modern notion of 'customer care', which involves a range of tactics to ensure that customers are permanently satisfied in terms of meeting and exceeding their expectations. TQM that is driven from the marketplace and total manufacturing quality (zero defects) are the realities of such partnership agreements. The tactics of RM mean that companies should sense changes in the marketplace, which is where the quality chain is based.

In a properly lean manufacturing system, demands from customer are met and operating costs reduced through a reduction in inventories, raw materials and component parts. Holding stock is an unproductive resource that has to be financed, so lean manufacturing through its practice of reducing stocks to an absolute minimum is an efficient means of making cost savings. In such systems relationships must be formed between customers and suppliers. This means a reduction in the number of suppliers and long-term relationships being developed with a key small group of suppliers, usually only one for each component or material. The role of the salesperson changes from one of transactional salesperson to one of relationship salesperson who devotes time to acting in a trouble shooting capacity, keeping the flow of supplies secure and ensuring consistent quality, and acting more in a liaison capacity. The concept of RM means that marketing endeavours should be based on many customer contacts over time, rather than single transactions. It also involves the idea of 'team selling' where non-marketing people like accountants and production personnel all form part of this relationship team who actively meet and associate with major customers in terms of nurturing the relationship and ensuring that the partnership (partnership sourcing) works.

13.4 Practical effects of RM

Many companies bring marketing and new product development together at earlier stages in the development process. Project teams include people from a number of departments led by a project or product 'champion' to see through the entire development process. This process can start when the idea is being tested out through techniques like brainstorming through to the research and design stage to when the product is finally launched. Such a process means there is continuity of involvement by the project champion.

An adaptation of this idea is termed 'best practice benchmarking' (BPB) where multifunctional personnel co-operate similarly to the process described above, and the team's duty is to acquire data on products and companies in their industry that have higher performance and activity levels to that in their own companies. From this study, ways are then suggested from which improvements can be made. Because of the multi-functional nature of the team, it is acknowledged that benefits that accrue from BPB exercises should drive team members to establish better standards of performance.

13.5 Supply chain integration

In 1994 a study was undertaken in the UK by A T Kearney, consultants. This investigated the supply chain from end of line manufacturers, right back up the supply chain, to sources of raw materials. Its conclusions were that business improvements could be effected not by viewing dealings between purchasers and sellers as isolated transactions, but by seeking to involve everybody down the supply chain, hence the term: 'supply chain integration (SCI)'.

Different supply chain relationships should be possible, with some members merely being content to act as manufacturers and fabricators and supplying to a specification (i.e. seeing their task as being good producers at the right quality and at the right time) but others might like to become more involved in end-use applications and even proffer suggestions for improvement, although they may be towards the beginning of the supply chain. By considering the entire supply chain, new opportunities would present themselves and benefit everybody in the supply chain. This should improve overall effectiveness in the supply chain in terms of the elimination of waste and suggesting better ways of operation, thus reducing overall costs.

The result should be that it is then possible to propel service standards to final customers to superior levels by concentrating the complete supply chain in this direction through mutual co-operation, rather than weakening the attempts of individual elements of the chain through conflicting objectives. The outcome means a necessity for closer relationships between suppliers and customers. The task is not easy because of problems of such integration, and the task of ascertaining measures of sophistication that individual members of the supply chain want or expect.

13.6 A new paradigm

Considering the dialogue relating to RM and SCI it is appropriate to reflect on views put forward by Gronroos (1990, pp. 3–11) who argued that traditional views of marketing are unsatisfactory in a modern business environment. He emphasised the shortcomings of McCarthy's 'four Ps' and went on to articulate that more 'Ps' like 'people' and 'planning' should be added as new marketing viewpoints. The basic concept of supplying customer needs and wants in target markets has always had relevance, but he contends that this still views the firm as supplying solutions and not receiving its ideas from the marketplace. He attempts to redefine marketing in a way that applies the principles of RM:

> 'Marketing is to establish, maintain and enhance long-term customer relationships at a profit so the objectives of parties involved are met. This is done by a mutual exchange of promises.'

13.7 Internal marketing

As we have explained earlier in the text, good internal marketing can be viewed as a pre-requisite for good, effective external marketing polices. It would be difficult to have one without the other. In a very real sense the internal marketing is actually an intrinsic part of the relationship marketing process. However the mass adoption of the internal marketing ethos by firms could be regarded as 'macro' issue. The principles of internal marketing is being widely adopted by all kinds of firms as they strive to create a truly customer orientated culture within their organisations. More than in any time before, today good marketing is seen just as much of an internal process as an external one.

Internal marketing is an interface between marketing and human resource management and involves each discipline. The application of internal public relations has a salient role to play in the overall process of achieving an internal marketing 'culture' because it too embraces both of these areas of management. The impetus is for organisations to become more 'customer focused' or 'marketing oriented', but how does is work in reality? Whether a firm wishes to employ relationship-marketing policies, engage in social marketing activities, or practice 'green marketing' polices, those working for the organisation will still need the right spirit, ethos and internal culture. This is where internal marketing is relevant (see Roehm *et al.*, 2002, p. 202, for a discussion on the importance of company training to secure good relationship-marketing outcomes). Increasingly, firms are embracing the notion of internal marketing and its widespread adoption as a 'micro' issue in marketing. Trends in marketing now pay more attention to getting the 'spirit' or the 'culture' right before attempting to improve the external marketing performance of the organisation. Internal marketing is now an important and intrinsic part of what is considered to be conventional marketing 'wisdom'. The term 'internal marketing' refers to the process of applying the general principles of marketing inside the firm. Marketing as a business philosophy is concerned with producing an appropriate internal company culture or 'internal spirit' that will result in the firm becoming truly marketing orientated and customer focused. The process of internal marketing involves more than simply applying internal public relations inside firms, although as we discussed earlier, internal public relations is of paramount importance.

13.8 Customer care

High levels of customer care are essential to firms operating in today's increasingly competitive market environment, and this is the key to achieving many business objectives confronting competitive firms like:

- minimising loss of customers,
- attracting new customers,
- improving profitability,
- enhancing company image,
- improving customer and employee satisfaction.

High quality customer care is relative. With new operators and competitive forces constantly coming into play, no firm can stand still. Regular customer care 'health-checks' have become an essential part of operating strategy for existing firms and new firms will need to ensure that they enter the market as high up the customer service ladder as possible. The cost of replacing customers is much greater than the cost of keeping them. If those lost include customers a firm can least afford to lose – the most profitable ones – then the impact on profitability is significant. Reichheld and Teal (1996, pp. 44–46) provides data supporting this view; a 5% increase in retention can lead to profit improvements of up to 85%. But he warns of what he calls the 'satisfaction trap', particularly for marketing researchers carrying out customer service appreciation surveys. His research showed that 60–80% of customers who defected from firms said in a satisfaction survey just prior to defecting, that they were 'satisfied' or 'very satisfied' with the service provided by the company. Customer purchase patterns themselves seem to provide a more accurate basis for measuring satisfaction than customer surveys (see also the work of Schulze, 2000, p. 21).

13.9 Customer relationship management

CRM has developed from a synthesis of RM; internal marketing and customer care to form a fully integrated system. The ability of firms to use such a system owes much to the availability of appropriate computer-based technologies as discussed in Chapter 12. However, CRM is much more than just a Web-based customer care programme, or an enhanced database marketing programme (see Rigby *et al.*, 2002, p. 101, for an interesting discussion on how not to design a CRM program). CRM has evolved from a technology-centred scheme to a business-value activity as firms move from viewing customers as exploitable income sources to important assets that have to be looked after and developed. CRM is a comprehensive approach that provides total integration of every area of business that impacts on the customer – namely marketing, sales, customer service and field support, through the integration of people, process and technology, taking advantage of communication possibilities of the Internet. CRM creates a mutually beneficial relationship with customers (see Kotler and Armstrong, 2004, p. 15). Figure 13.2 explains this view.

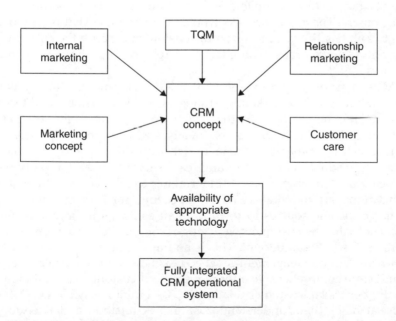

Figure 13.2 Factors contributing to development of CRM concept and practical implementation

Society is changing at an ever-increasing rate, with more choice and less time to choose and to enjoy the results. There seems to be less time, even though it was predicted only a few years back, stated that new technology would provide more time and lead to the 'leisure society'. Customers have more products and service to choose from, and more information available to help make purchasing decisions, for example, the task of purchasing a new mobile telephone: these are so sophisticated; there are so many different models and information available on the capabilities of each model in magazines, Internet and in conventional advertising is enormous and it is difficult to know where do you start. Consumers can now shop at all hours including Sundays and national holidays. It is possible to go to the supermarket during the night. People can bank via mobile telephones, research house purchases on the Internet and book air tickets through the Internet or through television using teletext. Godin (1999, p. 17) said the average consumer sees 3,000 marketing messages a day. To reach its audience, a message has to be relevant and well targeted. He argues that conventional media advertising is not as effective as it was. This is partly because there is so much more of it for consumers to see and digest, and in part because people have learned to ignore it. Additionally, the rise of the WWW means that companies can go further than conventional communications.

Building high value, loyal, lifetime relationships is the most powerful competitive tool a firm possesses. Management should reward staff for doing it right and make sure they ask the customers if they are satisfied with the service they receive and then check purchasing behaviour to see if they remain loyal. Jeff Bezos (CEO of Amazon.com) has said: 'I encourage everyone who works at Amazon to wake up terrified every morning. They should be afraid of our customers. Those are the folks who send us money. That is why our strategy is to say; heads down, focus on the customer, because the customer needs change at a slower rate'. The control of relationships lies in the hands of customers.

CRM is a major part of many companies' e-commerce strategy and their long-term 'relationship marketing' strategy. CRM is a business and technology discipline that helps firms in the acquisition and retention of their most important and profitable customers. Ideally, CRM systems help firms provide start to finish customer care, from initial acquisition of the customer, right through to product delivery and after-care service. CRM is rapidly evolving from being a technology-centred undertaking to a business-value endeavour. Organisations are moving away from seeing their customers simply as exploitable income sources to treating them as assets to be valued and nurtured. The value of customers is a long-term concept and lifetime value of customers is what is important. This is an important trend that represents the use of knowledge-management practices, such as the use of databases to capture and store comprehensive information about customers to build long-term, mutually beneficial, customer relationships. Companies need a CRM strategy because it helps them understand customer-acquisition and retention goals, which is the basis of relationship marketing practices. CRM also helps companies retain customers and increase profitability. CRM strategy helps companies co-ordinate the management of customer relationships across systems and strategic business units.

CRM software can bring together data from disparate systems and business units to provide a holistic view of customers and a company's relationship with them. It can help co-ordinate customer contact and relationships across channels (e.g. retail or WWW) by presenting a unified message regardless of the contact point. CRM strategies can be a defence against being the same as every other supplier and can allow the marketing firm to differentiate itself through superior service, for example, if a company manufactures a 'commodity' product like welding rods it can differentiate itself through better CRM and customer service. CRM is most effective when companies use proactive strategies to support the sales process through acquisition, retention, and development. Many businesses are moving to Web-based CRM, but this does not obviate personal interaction that is so crucial. Active CRM technology means that customers contacting a Web site for information can be followed up immediately by telephone or some other form of communication. A mixture of communications can be used from the Internet, telephone, direct mail and personal contact.

CRM projects are important and managers must have clearly defined objectives for such programmes. Measuring return on investment is an important first step in determining criteria against which success of the programme will be appraised. The quality of any set of measures must be to tell management if each project requirement was achieved. Some common CRM measures include numbers of new customers, cost of acquiring these new customers, customer satisfaction, customer attrition, the cost of promoting products, profit margins, incremental revenue and inventory turnover. Firms need to consider ways in which Web-based CRM will enhance relationships with their customers and where the service and information provided will be excellent, but also where the relationship management teams really utilise data available to cement and nurture the relationship with their clients. At this point, the e-communication and e-interaction between a firm and its external customers will be in harmony.

13.10 Summary

The nature and direction of modern marketing has altered. The basic definition of marketing as a business process concerned with satisfying customers' needs and wants more effectively and efficiently than competition reminds the same. The marketing concept is as valid today as it has always been. However, the processes used to accomplish this have changed. If you examine a standard marketing textbook from the 1970s or even the 1980s and one from today and compare them, you will see a number of topics in the current version, which were not even mentioned earlier. Topics such as 'Internal Marketing',

'Relationship Marketing', 'e-marketing', 'Green Marketing' and 'Customer Relationship Management (CRM)' are all recent additions to marketing literature. In particular there has been what can only be described as a complete paradigm shift in the way the management of marketing firms view customers, look after them, nurture them and establish relationships with them over the long term. Basically, the focus of marketing has shifted from the short-term view of customers as the next 'transaction' to seeing customers as a long-term income stream over many years, or a 'relationship' marketing approach.

The concept of RM was introduced into the literature by early researchers into customer care such as Berry (1983, pp. 25–28). The subject of marketing had been developed largely from the experience of firms and researchers involved in consumer markets, mainly based in the USA. Marketing as a subject and business discipline was developed in the USA. These principles and theories seem to have almost universal applicability in consumer markets of developed economies throughout the world.

CRM is a major part of many companies' e-commerce strategy and their long-term 'relationship marketing' strategy. It is a business and technology discipline that helps firms in the acquisition and retention of their most important and profitable customers. CRM systems help firms provide start to finish customer care, from initial acquisition of the customer right through to product delivery and aftercare services. CRM is rapidly evolving from being a technology-centred undertaking to a business-value endeavour. This is an important trend that represents the use of knowledge-management practices such as use of databases to capture and store comprehensive information about customers to build long-term, mutually beneficial, relationships. Companies cannot succeed or grow unless they serve their customers with a better value proposition than the competition. This is what the marketing concept has always advocated. Measuring customer loyalty can accurately measure the weaknesses in a company's value proposition and help formulate improvements. Providing customers with ongoing value, satisfying their individual needs, and ensuring that they get what they want when and where they want it, is critical in today's dynamic and competitive market. If a company fails its customers, there are rivals waiting to take over.

References

Berry, L.L. (1983), 'Relationship marketing', in: Berry, L.L. *et al.* (eds), *Emerging Perspectives on Services Marketing*, Chicago: American Marketing Association, pp. 25–28.

Brassington, F. and Pettitt, S. (2005), *Essentials of Marketing*, Prentice-Hall, Financial Times, p. 47.

Copulsky, J.R. and Wolf, M.J. (1990), 'Relationship marketing: positioning for the future', *Journal of Business Strategy*, July–August, 16–20.

Deming, W.E. (1993), *The New Economics for Industry, Government, Education*, Cambridge, MA: Massachusetts Institute of Technology Center for Advanced Engineering Study, pp. 1–35.

Godin, S. (1999), *Permission Marketing*, Simon and Schuster, p. 17.

Gronroos, C. (1990), 'Relationship approach to marketing in service contexts: the marketing and organisational behaviour interface', *Journal of Business Research*, 20, 3–11.

Hatch, D. and Schell, E. (2002), 'Delight your customers', *Target Marketing*, April, 32–39.

Johnson, L.K. (2002), 'The real value of customer loyalty', *MIT Sloan Management Review*, Winter, 14–17.

Kotler, P. and Armstrong, G. (2004), *Principles of Marketing*, 10th International edition, Pearson Prentice-Hall, p. 15.

McCaig, M. (2000), 'A small retailer uses CRM to make a big splash', *Apparel Industry*, 31(10), 30–34.

McKenna, R. (1991), *Relationship Marketing*, London: Century Business, pp. 1–10.

McMaster, M. (2001), 'A Lifetime of Sales', *Sales and Marketing Management*, September, 55.

Reichheld, F.F. and Teal, T. (1996), *The loyalty effect: The Hidden Force Behind Growth, Profits and Lasting Value*, McGraw-Hill, pp. 44–46.

Rigby, D.K., Reichheld, F.F. and Schefter, P. (2002), 'Avoid the four perils of CRM', *Harvard Business Review*, 80, 101–108.

Roehm, M.L., Boman Pulins, E. and Roehhm, H. (2002), 'Designing Loyalty-building programs for packaged goods brands', *Journal of Marketing Research*, 39(2), May, 202–213.

Schulze, H. (2000), 'Where has all the service gone?', *Strategy & Leadership*, 28(5), 21.

Stout, E. (2002), 'Keep them coming back for more', *Sales & Marketing Management*, February, 51–52.

Sullivan, B. (2001), 'Winners focus on customers', *Computerworld*, 35(24), 50–51.

▍ Further reading

Anonymous (2000a), 'A Crash Course in Customer Relationship Management', *Harvard Management Update*, 5(3), 3–4.

Anonymous (2000b), 'CRM metrics', *Harvard Management Update*, 5(3), 3–4.

Anonymous (2000c), 'The technological underpinnings of CRM', *Harvard Management Update*, 5(3), 3–4.

Clow, K.E. and Baack, D. (2004), *Integrated Advertising, Promotion and Marketing Communications*, 2nd edition, New Jersey: Pearson Prentice-Hall, Chapter 12, pp. 366–399.

Drucker, P. (1954), *The Practice of Management*, New York: Harper and Row, p. 65.

Hill, L. and O'Sullivan, T. (2004), *Foundation Marketing*, 3rd edition, London: Prentice-Hall, pp. 7 and 26.

Jobber, D. (2004), *Principles and Practices of Marketing*, 4th edition, New York: McGraw-Hill, pp. 117–122.

Masterson, R. and Pickton, D. (2004), *Marketing an Introduction*, New York: McGraw-Hill, pp. 17–18.

Peppers, D. and Rogers, M. (1999), 'The price of customer service', *Sales and Marketing Management*, April, 20–21.

Questions

Question 13.1

Explain the historical development of the relationship marketing concept from the end of the Second World War to the present day.

Question 13.2

Compare and contrast the concept of 'reverse marketing' with the traditional marketing concept.

Question 13.3

What are the main component parts of a fully integrated customer relationship management system?

Question 13.4

Explain how the development of Internet-based technologies has facilitated the adoption and application of the customer relationship management (CRM) concept.

Question 13.5

Discuss the contention that the customer relationship management (CRM) concept is more of a step change in fundamental marketing philosophy than simply the application of computer database techniques to consumer profiles.

Question 13.6

What do you understand by the term 'life-time' value of customers and how can this concept be used to evaluate the efficiency of a relationship marketing program?

Question 13.7

Do forms really want to keep all of their customers for life? Discuss.

Question 13.8

Fully explain the concept of 'Internal' marketing?

Question 13.9

Explain the relationship between internal marketing and external 'relationship' marketing.

Question 13.10

Explore the main ethical aspects of implementing a full customer relationship management (CRM) scheme within a firm.

14

Marketing Information and Research

14.1 Introduction

The American Marketing Association (AMA, 1961, p. 1) defines marketing research as: 'the systematic gathering, recording and analysing of data relating to the marketing of goods and services'. Kotler (1994, p. 257) defined it as: 'systematic problem analysis, model building and fact finding for the purpose of improved decision-making and control in the marketing of goods and services'. Doyle (1994, pp. 39, 124) stated that marketing management consists of five tasks, one of which is marketing research and explains: 'Management has to collect information on the current and potential needs of customers in the markets chosen, how they buy and what competitors are offering'.

Research attempts to find reliable and unbiased answers to questions. Marketing research provides information in a systematic way about the markets for goods and services and probes people's ideas and intentions on many issues. As explained in Chapter 2, in a complex consumer society, there is little direct contact between producers and consumers. Marketing research can, by the collection, analysis and interpretation of facts, find out what it is that people want and ascertain why they want it. The application of techniques and methodology of marketing research are as applicable in the not-for-profit sector as in profit-making organisations.

14.2 Marketing information systems

Effective marketing decisions are as good as the information on which they are based. Decision-making underlies the management process at every level and the terms 'managing' and 'decision-making' are synonymous. Marketing management is the process of making decisions in relation to marketing problems. Marketing research is utilised by marketing management when planning the marketing strategy of an enterprise. A disciplined and systematic approach to research methodology to the area of investigation is needed and a series of steps should be taken in developing, planning and executing research with a view to solving specific problems (Demirdjian, 2003, pp. 218–223).

Marketing research is part of the marketing information systems (MkIS) that collects, processes and coordinates information from a wide range of sources. The MkIS is a computer-based decision support system and has a number of inputs and one output as shown in Figure 14.1.

Three inputs can be seen: marketing research, market intelligence and the internal accounting system (see Chowdhury, 2003, pp. 576–580, for a discussion on the use of databases and 'data mining'). MkIS output is used for strategic marketing planning that formulates marketing plans and implements them, but what is planned does not always match what happens. Deviations from what was planned are fed back into the MkIS represented by a double-headed arrow. Inputs from the Internal Accounting System relate to factors like sales analyses by time, by product group, by region and by customer type. Market intelligence relates to information that has been obtained principally from the field sales force that, in the course of their work, obtains information about customers, competitors, distributors, etc. and feed this into the MkIS. Sales forecasting is a marketing responsibility and from the forecast company (corporate) plans are prepared. The material for sales forecasting is obtained from all three inputs to the system and the forecast also outputs into strategic marketing plans. The MkIS is a component part of an organisation-wide management information system (MIS).

Market intelligence is generated principally by the field sales force. The internal accounting system relates to sales and financial data that can be located in the financial information system that is part of the MIS. This chapter concentrates on the areas of marketing research that form a major part of an MkIS.

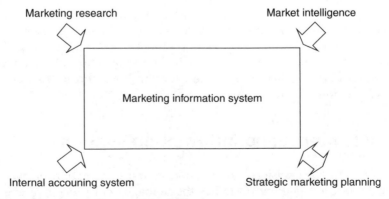

Figure 14.1 Marketing information system (MkIS)

14.3 Main areas of marketing research

The underlying concept is an appreciation of the fact that to manage a business well, is to manage its future. Marketing research has a contribution to make in decisions involving any area of an organisation's marketing mix (see Birn, 2004, p. 7). Management needs information about its markets, competitors and changes and developments in the external environment to aid marketing decisions, whether these are operational, tactical or strategic (see Hague *et al.*, 2004, p. 7, for a discussion on the scope of market research).

14.3.1 Product research

This is concerned with aspects of design, development and testing of new products, as well as the improvement and modification of existing products. Activities include:

- comparative testing against competitive products,
- test marketing,
- concept testing,
- idea generation and screening,
- product elimination/simplification,
- brand positioning.

This last point is particularly important as heavy competitive pressures make it important that brand positioning strategies be effectively developed.

14.3.2 Communications research

FMCG companies in particular spend a lot on marketing communications. The communications mix (including personal selling, direct mail, exhibitions, sponsorship and advertising) can be more effectively planned as a result of research information. Communications research activities include:

- pre- and post-testing of advertising,
- media planning research,
- readership surveys,
- testing alternative selling techniques,
- exhibition and sponsorship evaluation.

14.3.3 Pricing research

Pricing research can be used to:

- assist in establishing a more market-orientated pricing strategy,
- see what kind of prices consumers associate with different product variations (e.g. packaging),
- establish market segments in relation to price.

14.3.4 Corporate planning

Research activities that can assist corporate planners include:

- evaluation of companies for acquisition,
- assessment of an organisation's strengths and weaknesses,
- portfolio analysis,
- corporate image studies.

14.3.5 Distribution research

Techniques like retail auditing can monitor the effectiveness of different types of distribution channels and detect regional variations.

This list is not exhaustive, but it illustrates the range of areas in which marketing research can aid decision-making. Other areas include industrial market research and international market research.

 ## 14.4 Evaluating information

Marketing information can be expensive to obtain (e.g. a national ad hoc survey commissioned from a large agency). Information is vital to successful marketing in terms of its generation, processing and circulation. Extraneous information can be a problem in marketing research, as it is often the case that unnecessary information is collected which is expensive and time wasting. The information function needs to be managed and controlled like any other area of the company's operations so information needs to be:

- reliable,
- relevant to users' needs,
- adequate for the type of decisions being made,
- timely,
- cost-effective to obtain.

 ## 14.5 Marketing research as a problem-solving process

The solution of a marketing problem requires a systematic approach. This permits better application of available resources to the key elements of the problem with minimum loss of time (see Severson, 2002, pp. 17–35). Every marketing problem has three vital dimensions.

1 *Time*: This determines the urgency of the situation. It is significant, because some research approaches that might otherwise be suitable may be impossible within the time before a decision must be reached.

2 *Profit*: This determines the relative importance of the particular problem given the financial situation of the company. It is helpful in assigning priorities to different problems competing for attention.
3 *Facilities*: This is concerned with availability of personnel and other facilities required for a successful solution of the problem.

A problem-solving approach to marketing research planning involves six steps:

1 *definition* of the marketing problem in specific terms;
2 *refinement* of the marketing problem, and its subdivision into individual marketing research problems;
3 *development of a plan* for securing the facts or information needed;
4 *execution of the plan* by collecting facts or information;
5 *Analysis and interpretation* of the facts in terms of the problem;
6 *Summary* of the results in a report.

The objective of this problem-solving process is identify and isolate problem elements, for example, in a complex marketing problem, such as an unexplained sales decline, this can be sub-divided into competitive, market and company elements. Hypotheses are developed and explored in the search for problem elements. Sometimes research is necessary, even in this diagnostic stage, to help define the problem. Marketing research is more effective and makes its maximum contribution when it is integrated into the problem-solving process at the marketing problem level, than when the research function is simply assigned portions of the problem for exploration without consideration of the background to the problem.

14.6 Marketing research methods

Information sources may be primary or secondary. Primary data is information that is collected at first hand for a specific project, normally generated from external sources through sample surveys or experiments. This work is described as fieldwork or 'ad hoc research' if it is a one off research project.

The starting point should be desk research using secondary data. This information is historical, and if it has been researched on a continuous basis it can indicate trends and tendencies. Analysis can highlight areas in need of further research. Company records are the raw material of sales analysis. The main approaches are product, area or territorial, customer and time analyses. External publications are the next source to investigate. There are three principal sources: government/official publications, trade association publications and specialist publications.

When data for solving a marketing problem cannot be found from secondary sources, the company must then generate primary information, usually through a survey that involves four major steps:

1 setting objectives for the survey,
2 developing the survey method and sample design,

3 collection of data,
4 interpretation of data.

The first is important in cost terms, for without a clear statement of objectives, much interesting, but irrelevant, information might be obtained. There are several methods of obtaining information:

14.6.1 Personal interviews

These may be structured or unstructured and direct or indirect. Direct interviews are used to obtain descriptive information – getting at the facts. Unstructured direct interviews are used for exploratory work to make sure that the final questionnaire will be well structured and relevant to the problem. In structured interviews a set of predetermined questions is asked; in unstructured interviews the questions are put as the interviewer sees best during the course of the interview.

When an unstructured indirect interview is used to establish motives it is known as a depth interview. Indirect interviews have developed into a specialised area called motivation research. Direct questions are of less value for diagnostic purposes. Most motivation research techniques employ the principle of 'projection', for example, the 'third-person' technique, word association tests, sentence completion tests, thematic apperception tests (TAT) in which 'themes' are described by the perceptual/interpretative use of pictures, often cartoons. The main problem with motivation research relates to sample selection and size considerations.

Advantages of personal interviews are:

- good sample control,
- more reliable answers,
- allows longer questionnaires,
- greater flexibility,
- observation is possible.

Disadvantages are:

- cost is high,
- there might be bias owing to personal contact,
- difficulty in obtaining cooperation from respondents.

14.6.2 Telephone interviews

These are useful when information is sought quickly and it is relatively inexpensive. So long as not too detailed information is sought, cooperation can be obtained relatively easily, especially during evenings. Sample bias is a problem as telephone lists only include respondents whose numbers are included in telephone directories and will not include those who are ex-directory. In addition, the sample can be biased as it only includes co-operating respondents. A recent problem is that an increased use of the telephone to canvass for sales approaches has made respondents wary. There might also be difficulties is personal data is required.

14.6.3 Postal questionnaires

These can be sent to as many respondents as required and the method offers cheapness, wide distribution and speed. If respondent anonymity is possible, it will lead to candid answers and interviewer bias is eliminated. However, there is usually a high non-response rate. The questionnaire cannot be too long, and risks of ambiguity are increased if more than dichotomous questions are asked. It might also be difficult to classify respondents as personal questions might be viewed as being intrusive.

14.6.4 Panel surveys

In the field of consumer goods are retail audits like those provided by AC Nielsen Co. and Retail Audits Ltd. who provide surveys on a continuous basis. There are also consumer panels, usually on a continuous basis, like those provided by the Attwood Consumer Panel (mainly for food products) or Audits of Great Britain (AGB) mainly for consumer durables. Consumer panels may be conducted through co-operating respondents keeping a diary, filling in a questionnaire or allowing the researcher to conduct a home-audit.

14.6.5 Marketing experiments

An experiment is a method of gathering primary data in which the researcher is able to establish causation of effect amongst the variables being experimentally tested. Experiments can be carried out in artificial 'laboratory' type settings or as field experiments like 'test marketing' where researchers choose a 'representative' geographical area or at least one where they can statistically adjust data to make them representative of a wider market area such as the UK as a whole. The test market then becomes a 'model' of the total market. Seelig (1989) stated that test markets are expensive, but being a field experiment they have the advantage of realism or 'external validity' over laboratory experiments. Schlussberg (1989) advocated 'simulated test markets' as a means of reducing costs. These are not full test markets and involve surveying a small sample of consumers and showing them pictures or samples of product and ascertaining their preference as if they were really shopping.

Other techniques include 'extended user tests', 'blind' and 'simple placement' tests. In addition, there are the techniques used in the pre- and post-testing of advertising themes and copy, like split-run copy testing. 'Group discussions' or 'focus groups' (as opposed to interview questioning) can escape from the notion of 'rational' thinking.

14.6.6 Sampling

Although this is not a method of marketing research, it is appropriate to consider it under this heading as it underlies the validity of research. The sample design is a plan that sets out who is to be sampled, how many respondents are to be surveyed and how they are to be selected. Sampling procedures may be probability (or random) or on a non-probability basis, usually a quota sample. In a probability sample, every member of the population has a known probability of being included and their selection is random. These probabilities are taken into account when making estimates from the sample. The following sample methods involve probability:

- simple random sample,
- systematic sample (e.g. every nth name on a list),
- cluster sample (blocks selected randomly),
- area sample (blocks are geographic),
- stratified sample (sampling within strata, for example, different family sizes),
- multi-stage sample (random sampling within random clusters).

For a true random sample to be taken from a complete national sampling frame, costs would be prohibitive so the usual method is to take a quota sample. The characteristics required of respondents are determined in advance (usually to represent the demographics of the population as a whole). Interviewers are then required to obtain specific quotas of people to make up the sample they interview, but using their own resources to do this rather than through any other statistical method.

We need to be aware of the difficulties in obtaining information from a sample of respondents. The sample itself may be a source of error if it is not representative. It may start by being representative, but may cease to be so as a result of non-response and possible substitution of other respondents. There may also be errors in responses. Inaccurate information may result from an inability or unwillingness of respondents to help. Unwillingness is a complex area that may be due to a perceived loss of prestige, a resentment of invasion of privacy or a personal reaction to the interviewer.

14.7 The research brief

This is the process through which management conveys the nature of marketing problems or information needs to market researchers working in the company or in a research agency. Research briefs should be expressed in writing, but more typically they are given verbally. This is the start of the overall market research process (see Callingham, 2004, p. 136).

Translating a marketing problem into a comprehensive research study can be difficult and much depends on the ability of marketing personnel and researchers to effectively communicate with each other. The following are some typical problems that prevent a thorough brief being achieved:

- some marketing problems are difficult to define;
- the marketing person knows little about research or its limitations;
- researchers often have a low status in the company so a full and frank discussion of the problem is not possible for security reasons;
- the researcher is often seen as a 'fire fighter', brought in on an ad hoc basis with no continuous understanding of the product/market;
- marketing people might find it difficult to ascertain how accurate the data has to be (this affects costs and sample sizes) and often lack statistical skills necessary to understand the relationship between accuracy, sample sizes and costs.

The task of the brief is to effectively bring the two parties together. A good brief (usually achieved after detailed discussion) should ensure that irrelevant information is not requested and it should:

- state the population(s) to be surveyed/sampled (e.g. consumers not buyers, car owners not car drivers);
- state the appropriate variables to be measured;
- by and large, not pre-empt the design of the research; many marketing personnel think they know how to do research, but in practice few can do it properly.

Once the researcher has a brief, it is then possible to prepare a research 'proposal'.

14.8 Exploratory research

Whatever the purpose of a research exercise (e.g. exploratory or descriptive) it is costly in terms of time and money. The company should 'explore' the situation before investing in the production of more conclusive research. In exploring the market, all available sources of facts and ideas should be consulted so that a picture of the market can be built up before conclusive research is commenced. Sound exploratory research gives a clearer idea of the situation and highlights possible areas of investigation.

Before being able to design a cost-effective survey, it is necessary to be informed about the market, the population and the topics of interest in a particular area as most full surveys are sample surveys rather than census surveys. Exploratory data is needed about population parameters (e.g. sex, age, socio-economic and geographical characteristics of the population) to be able to design an appropriate sampling scheme. The sample may have to be broken down into quotas based on such characteristics.

Exploratory research is essential because the research methodology used in a sample survey is usually a questionnaire. Before a meaningful questionnaire can be designed (one with relevant questions that people can understand, arranged in a sensible order) it will be necessary to have an idea of consumer behaviour and attitudes towards various products including competitors' products and substitutes. This information will include brands available in the market and consumer attitudes towards them, the relative popularity of brands and the context in which the products/brands are used.

Exploratory research thus indicates which areas need to be investigated, in what depth and the type of information required (e.g. qualitative or quantitative) as well as the amount of data to be collected. It allows the researcher to arrive at a set of assumptions on which to base the research. The more thought that is put into this stage the less is the opportunity to make subsequent mistakes. The Internet is an excellent starting point. Using a search engine such as Google provides you with information to at least get you started on a project. The Internet can also be used to contact people, experts, for example, for further background information on a new topic area (see Grossnickle and Raskin, 2001, pp. 9–13, for a discussion on the use of the Internet in marketing research and also Scholl *et al.*, 2002, pp. 210–223, for an interesting examination of collecting qualitative research on the Internet).

14.9 Stages in the research process

14.9.1 Problem definition

This leads to a preliminary statement of research objectives – usually to provide information, that is, this stage is an identification of information needs:

- What information is needed?
  Motivations – values, beliefs, feelings, opinions;
  Evaluations – attitudes, intentions;
  Knowledge – facts, behaviour, actions;
  Demographic – socio-economic, etc. (on/from people, stores, companies, brands, products).
- Why is information required?
  For exploration, description, prediction or evaluation.
- Where does information come from?
  Secondary data sources, both internal and external to a company,
  primary data sources (i.e. from fieldwork).

14.9.2 Review of secondary data sources

- Company records, reports, previous research,
- trade associations, government agencies, research organizations,
- advertising/marketing research agencies,
- books, periodicals, theses, statistics, conference proceedings, etc.

14.9.3 Select approach for collection of new/primary information

- Experimentation,
- observation,
- surveys – mail, telephone, personal,
- motivational research techniques – depth interviews, group interviews, projective techniques.

14.9.4 Research design

- Methods,
- sampling issues,
- design.

14.9.5 Data collection

14.9.6 Analysis and interpretation

14.9.7 Evaluation

Conclusions are drawn from the evaluation of results and suggestions and recommendations are made to management.

14.10 Methods of collecting data

14.10.1 Experimentation

Experimentation can be used to test or assess the effect of some element(s) in the marketing mix, for example, product, package, price change, advertising, promotion, type of outlet. There are two types:

1 *Field experiments* are controlled experiments, where a change in an experimental variable(s) is related to a resulting level of sales, advertisement recall/recognition, or attitudes, for example, coupon trials, split-run advertisements and test-markets. Possible problems are:
   - 'contamination' of control units,
   - influence of uncontrolled variables,
   - short-run response (evaluation of the results must consider carry-over effects and present sales being at expense of future sales).
2 *Laboratory experiments* involve using individual consumers or consumer groups/juries/panels. The researcher has a high degree of control and can introduce and exclude stimuli to create laboratory type testing of real-life situations to measure attitudes towards products, prices, packages, advertising or promotion, as well as preferences and intentions to buy. The problem is that situations are artificial and it must be questioned as to the extent

information collected will reflect actual future reaction and behaviour in the market place.

14.10.2 Observation

This method is used to describe rather than explain. Observations are selective and can be of people or physical phenomena, observed by people or by mechanical devices.

1 *People observing people*: This includes watching people in shops, children with toys. Only overt behaviour is measured. There is no interviewer or response bias, but because motivations, preferences, intentions or attitudes cannot be observed, problems can arise in the interpretation of observations.
2 *Mechanical devices observing people*: Such devices include:
   - eye camera: changes in pupil size measure interest (e.g. in response to advertisements);
   - tachistoscope: a projection device to present visual stimuli for a very short and then increasing periods of time (e.g. to measure brand-name awareness);
   - psycho-galvanometer: a device that measures galvanic skin response (e.g. to measure response when exposed to different types of advertisement);
   - tape-recordings (e.g. of sales people with customers);
   - photographic cameras and video recorders.
3 *Physical phenomena observed by people*:
   - analysis of documents (e.g. content analysis of advertisements),
   - observation of physical characteristics,
   - inventories: store/retail audits, information on brand/stock levels,
   - 'pantry' audits of products/brands on hand (many consumer audits/ panels are comprehensive and also include diaries on product consumption, media exposure, purchasing habits and even opinions).
4 *Physical phenomena observed by mechanical devices*:
   - traffic counters,
   - television (and radio) audiometers.

14.10.3 Surveys (using questionnaires)

Surveys can be conducted by mail, e-mail, telephone, e-mail or personal interview (see Brown *et al.*, 2001, pp. 425–440); Questionnaires can be self-administered or used in a personal interview situation (see Brace, 2004, p. 2). The choice is determined by:

- cost,
- timing,
- type of information needed,
- amount of information needed,
- ease of questioning,
- accuracy required.

Consideration should be given to:

- using pilot surveys,
- sample size(s),
- method of analysing results.

Issues that should be considered under each of the survey methods include:

Postal and e-mail surveys

- Who is the respondent? – industrial buyer? middle/lower class consumer? doctor?
- Nature of the survey: Will motivation to respond be high?
- Questions: How simple must they be?
- Length of the questionnaire: What is the limit?
- Response bias (there should be none from interviewers, only from the sample).
- To what extent do respondents differ from non-respondents?
- Sample selection: Size may be related to expected response rate.
- Is a 'list' (of potential respondents compiled by/bought from an external source) being used? How accurate is it?
- Should respondents be provided with prepaid reply envelopes?
- Response rate: This will affect cost/value of the survey. If relatively slow, it may be appropriate to send reminders to follow up non-respondents.
- Importance of cover letter, request for cooperation and/or instructions.
- Cost: Should be relatively low per response.

Telephone surveys

- Who is the respondent? Are telephone subscribers who are not ex-directory representative of the required population?
- Telephone contact is impersonal. How important is credibility of the interviewer?
- Questions should be short and simple.
- The interviewer can only talk to one person at a time (usually). Is it the right one?
- The respondent cannot consult other people, company records, etc.
- This method is relatively cheap and fast.

Personal interviews

- Who is the respondent?
- Where is the respondent: in the home/office? in the street? in a cinema queue?
- Factors affecting motivation to participate in an interview are indicated in Figure 14.2 that outlines the problems of personal interviews.
- Response bias in reaching the sample – non-contact, interviewer error, refusal to be interviewed.
- Bias in responses – incorrect and/or untruthful answers, omissions, interviewer's perception of the interviewee.

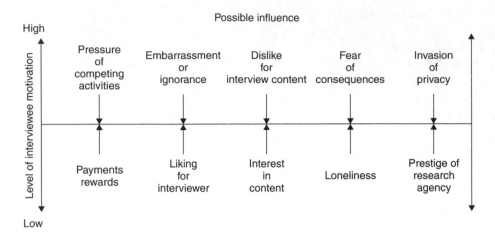

Figure 14.2 Factors affecting interviewee participation

- Who is the interviewer: Salesperson? Housewife? Freelance researcher? – What qualifications and training do they need?
- The cost of this method is usually high.

Questionnaires

- Types of questions – open ended or structured – yes/no, multiple-choice, rankings, paired comparisons, checklist (e.g. 'which of these . . .')
- Wording of questions
  - Avoid ambiguity: the question must have the same meaning for all respondents.
  - Respondents' ability to answer will relate to their level of education and the language used as part of the questionnaire. Questions should be self-exploratory and fully understood.
  - Respondents' willingness to answer: They may be reluctant, for example, to answer questions on personal matters such as income.
  - Avoid influencing the answer (e.g. 'Do you brush your teeth every day?').

- Sequencing of questions (and alternatives within questions):
  - initial questions should provide motivation (and encourage further cooperation);
  - questions should follow a logical order – from general to the specific;
  - rotate questions/sub-questions to eliminate bias;
  - place personal questions at the end, or 'bury' them in the middle.

- Scaling techniques for attitude measurement:
  These usually determine content and direction of attitudes rather than intensity. More commonly used techniques are:
  - paired comparisons;
  - Likert summated ratings (agreement on a five-point scale);

- ○ Thurstone's equal appearing intervals (paired comparisons);
- ○ Osgood's semantic differential: a bipolar scale used to measure opinions about ideas, products, brands, stores, companies, etc.;
- ○ Guttman's scalogram;
- ○ Stephenson's sort technique.

- Other considerations:
  - ○ length of questionnaire;
  - ○ use of cue cards (e.g. rotating lists of alternative responses);
  - ○ aids to recall (e.g. pictures of advertisements);
  - ○ presentation (especially if the questionnaire is to be self-administered);
  - ○ methods of coding and analysis of data will affect design and structure of questions.

14.10.4 Motivational research techniques

Motivational research techniques aim to discover underlying desires, emotions and motives of consumers that influence their behaviour. These techniques often penetrate below the level of the conscious mind and uncover motives of which consumers are unaware or attempt to conceal.

There are two approaches to motivational research: *the psycho-sociological approach* relies on group behaviour of consumers and the impact of culture and environment on their opinions and reactions; and *the psychoanalytic approach* which relies on information drawn from individual respondents in depth interviews and projective tests. Freudian interpretations dominate such analysis (see McPhee, 2002, pp. 53–70).

Techniques used include:

- *Depth interviewing* which employs interviewing and observational methods. The interviewer chooses topics for discussion and through non-structured, indirect questioning leads the respondent to free expression of motives, attitudes, opinions, experiences and habits in relation to advertisements, products, brands, services, etc.
- *Group interviewing* where the interviewer is responsible for moderating and stimulating group discussion, to encourage freedom of expression and interaction between individuals.
- *Projective techniques* may help to reveal what the respondent might cover up in direct questioning. Examples of such techniques include:
  - ○ verbal projection, for example, asking 'Why do you think people do. . . .?', that is, asking about someone else with the expectation that answers will actually apply to respondents themselves;
  - ○ word association tests;
  - ○ sentence completion exercises (e.g. 'People buy on credit when . . .', 'Prices are high because . . .');
  - ○ response to pictures (thematic apperception tests [TAT] – respondents give a description of a pictured situation based on their own experience and attitudes);
  - ○ interpretation of ink blots (Rorschach tests).

14.11 Problems in research exercises

The practical problems encountered in planning and executing a sample survey can vary with the type of material and nature of the information required. Investigations can be broken down into four phases: planning, execution, analysis and the report.

14.11.1 Planning

Aspects requiring consideration in the planning stage include:

1 *Specification of the purposes of the survey*: It is important to be clear as to what the problem is in the first place and then determine which aspects of it are appropriate to a solution using survey techniques. A basic question must be asked: Is a sample survey the best way of solving the problem? If the advice of a statistician is to be sought, then this should be done as early as possible.
2 *Definition of the population*: The categories or types of respondents to be included in a survey, its scope, etc, are largely determined in broad outline by the purposes of the survey. However, marginal categories require special consideration because:
   - excluding them can simplify the survey (cheapen its cost) without materially affecting the outcome;
   - the inclusion of certain marginal categories can be valuable where relationships are discovered between sub-groups of the population and variables being measured;
   - In many situations multi-phase sampling would answer any doubts on this matter.
3 *Determination of the details of information to be collected*: List information required to solve the original problem. This list can be expanded by contacting people in the company who might find results of the survey useful. The list should be as extensive as possible at this stage so no omissions are made. A selection then has to be made within the practical limitations of the survey (expense, time, etc).
4 *Practicability of obtaining the required information*: Each item of information selected should be considered in terms of how practical it is to obtain, given the level of accuracy required. For example, it should be asked:
   - Do the respondents have the knowledge required to answer the questions?
   - Will it involve them in a lot of effort?
   - If the information is to be obtained by observation, can it be observed or measured accurately?
   Considerations like these may lead to further modifications.
5 *Methods of collecting the information*.
6 *Methods of dealing with non-response*: Unless non-response is confined to a relatively small proportion of the whole sample the results cannot claim any general validity. This problem becomes particularly acute in postal surveys and in random samples from human populations where response can be

very low. In such cases, follow-up letters/calls can increase the response. However, the results of the sample can be weighted for non-response by identifying the characteristics of the initial non-respondents who reply on follow-up.

7 *The sampling frame*: The structure of a survey is determined by a sampling frame, and until its details have been obtained, no planning of the survey can be undertaken. Care should be taken to ensure that the frame is accurate, complete, not subject to duplication and is up-to-date.

8 *Pilot surveys*: The practicability of any survey is best checked by a pilot survey(s). They are designed to check:
   (a) The questionnaire:
      ● Use a broad quota sample (e.g. representative of all socio-economic groups).
      ● Good investigators should be used with instructions to follow up diversions, check the meanings of words, verify respondents' trains of thoughts, and as far as possible, record all that is said.
      ● The last pre-test should use the final approved questionnaire.
   (b) The sample:
      ● Check the ease of getting the smallest sub-group wanted.
      ● Check the number of interviews possible in the time allowed.
      ● Check that the selection process and the call-back/substitution procedure are feasible.
   (c) The survey contact:
      ● Check additional fields of enquiry shown up by (a) and also the appearance and 'feel' of the pilot results. Sometimes results obtained in the field will reorient the basic approach to the survey.

14.11.2 Execution of a survey

After the planning stage, the execution of a survey involves:

1 administrative organisation to cover the supervision of the field operations, the investigations, follow-ups, check calls, etc. and the central task of collation, tabulation and computation;
2 selection, training and supervision of field investigators;
3 briefing conference;
4 control and accuracy of the field work;
5 editing of schedules;
6 coding of answers to open-ended questions;
7 data analysis.

14.11.3 Analysis of results

Numerical accuracy during the analysis should be verified by repetition, by cross checks or by using different methods of computation to arrive at the same result. If the sampling procedure is defective in some way, the result can sometimes be adjusted to compensate for the defect, for example, if the sample contains incorrect proportions of certain classes of the population, this can be overcome by weighting the results of the sample.

14.11.4 The report

The following features should be included in a survey report:

1 A general description of the survey:
   - statement of purpose of the survey,
   - description of material covered,
   - nature of information collected,
   - method of collecting of the data,
   - sampling method,
   - accuracy,
   - period of time of the survey,
   - cost,
   - who is responsible for the survey,
   - references.
2 Design of the survey:
   - Sampling design aspects of the survey should be specified.
3 Methods of selecting sampling units.
4 Personnel and equipment used.
5 Findings of the survey.

14.12 Questionnaire design

The objective of a questionnaire is to design questions that have the same meaning to everybody. There are basic rules in questionnaire design that are now elaborated.

14.12.1 Physical layout

The general layout of a questionnaire is shown in Figure 14.3.

- Each question should be numbered.
- Use capital letters for the main sections.
- Instructions to be given to the investigator concerning the conduct of the interview (alternative routes in the questionnaire) should be in bold face, capital letters and underlined.
- Arrange answer codes, boxes, etc. as near to the right-hand side as possible.
- Lines drawn at suitable intervals can bring clarity to the design of the questionnaire.
- Arrows can be used to indicate the routes through 'skip' questions.

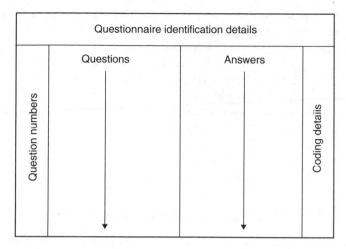

Figure 14.3 A specimen questionnaire layout

14.12.2 Types of questions

There is no general rule that can be used to decide which type of question is most suitable to elicit particular types of information. The following are the types of questions most commonly used:

1 *Open-ended questions*: This can provide clue as to what answer might be expected from the respondent, for example, a question which begins 'What do you think of . . .?' will bring forth comments over a full range of opinion. With a large sample, the mass of diverse data collected cannot be statistically analysed since verbatim answers (and they must be so recorded) can only be hand-summarised and then not always satisfactorily. However, open-ended questions are useful in the pilot stage of a survey to show the range of likely answers.

2 *Unaided recall questions*: The basic rule here is not to mention the nature of the answer material and to avoid asking leading questions like: 'How did you travel to the station to catch this train?'

3 *Dichotomous questions*: A dichotomous question offers two answer choices, basically 'yes' and 'no'. A third possible answer ('don't know') is implicit in this type of question. It has been found that as long as the researcher does not mention this alternative, then people who understand the question will simply choose one of these two alternatives.

4 *Multiple-choice ('cafeteria') questions*: The informant is given a graduated range of possible answers from which to choose a preferred response. The possibilities should be listed in rank order from one extreme to the other. It may be necessary to reverse the order on half of the questionnaires in order to prevent listing bias. In general, an even number of items is preferred, because where an odd number of potential answers are offered there sometimes a tendency for respondents to select the middle (or neutral) choice.

5 *Thermometer questions*: This is an evolution of multi-choice questions that seeks to minimise disadvantage of a discrete classification. Informants are asked to rate their feelings on a numerical scale, for example, 0–10 or 0–100. It is presumed that errors in this type of question cancel each other out.

6 *Checklists*: A checklist is the standard way of prompting a respondent's memory without the interviewer biasing him or her in relation to any item on the list. Care must still be taken to avoid bias, as too many items can lead to 'fatigue' on the part of the respondent and a preference for the earlier items. This bias can be avoided by rotating the items during the survey. A further problem is that brand leaders may be selected more frequently because of the weight of advertising rather than the criterion that is being investigated.

14.12.3 General rules for question design

- Use simple words that are familiar to everyone, for example, shop – not outlet; shopkeeper – not retailer
- Questions should be as short as possible
- Don't ask double-barrelled questions, for example, 'Have you a PC and a laptop?'
- Don't ask leading questions, for example, 'Do you buy instant coffee because it is the quickest way to make coffee?'
- Don't mention brand names, for example, 'Do you consider "Hitachi" to be the best audio equipment?'
- Don't ask questions that might offend, for example, 'When did you last wash your hair?' 'Do you work or are you a housewife?'
- Avoid using catch phrases or colloquialisms
- Avoid words that are not precise in their meanings, for example, 'Does this product last a reasonable length of time?' 'Are there sufficient comedy shows on TV?'
- Direct questions will not always give the expected response. Perhaps not all possible answers have been foreseen, for example, 'Are you married?' does not cover the possibilities of divorce, separation, etc.
- Questions concerning prestige goods may not be answered truthfully. Careful rewording can avoid this, for example, 'Have you a television capable of receiving teletext transmissions?' might be better asked by: 'How many hours per week do you watch television?' followed by: 'Do you watch teletext transmissions?'
- Only questions that the respondent can answer from knowledge or experience should be asked, for example, It would be pointless to ask a housewife if she prefers cooking by gas, if she has never experienced cooking by other means
- Questions should not depend on the respondent's memory
- Questions should only allow one thought to be created in the respondent's mind; where multiple thoughts are created, confusion can result and an inappropriate answer may be given, or one that does not accurately represent the respondent's opinion (where the respondent has to choose between possible answers). This particularly applies to questions commencing 'Why . . .?'

- Avoid questions or words with an emotional bias, for example, use Conservative/Labour; not Tory/Socialist.

14.12.4 Positioning of questions

The first question asked should be easy to answer to gain the interest of the informant if possible; it should require a factual answer. Generally, the questionnaire should begin with easier questions and proceed to the more difficult ones, but the questions of the greatest importance should be about one third of the way through the questionnaire.

Information about the respondent (age, address, full name, occupation, etc.) should appear at the end of the questionnaire unless it is necessary to obtain it at the beginning of the interview, for example, as in quota sampling, in order to eliminate non-pertinent respondents prior to commencement of the interview.

The transition from question to question should be smooth and logical. Any 'jumps in thought' should be introduced before the next question is asked.

14.12.5 Miscellaneous information

A questionnaire should have a title to identify it. Standard information can include the respondent's name, home address, sex, age (usually asked for in groups, for example, 20–25, 26–30, . . .) income group and occupation, interviewing district identification, place and date of interview and interviewer's name.

14.12.6 Recording answers

If possible, ensure that the investigator or respondent uses one of the following methods to record the respondent's answers:

- writing a number,
- putting a cross (×) or a tick (✓) in a box,
- underlining correct answers,
- crossing out incorrect answers,
- writing in a predetermined symbol,
- ringing a number or letter.

When open-ended questions are used, enough space should be allowed for answers to be recorded verbatim.

14.12.7 Questionnaire length

A questionnaire should be as short as possible in relation to the data to be secured. For a standard questionnaire investigation among householders in their own homes, a typical limit is what can be reasonably printed on both sides of an A4 sheet. For interviewing people in the street, one side of an A4 sheet is a reasonable limit. If the schedule is lengthy, interview appointments should be made, and in such a case then interviews of up to one hour are reasonable.

14.12.8 Questionnaire evaluation

The following are a list of basic questions that should be asked about any questionnaire:

1 Is each question clearly worded?
2 Does it break any of the rules of question design?
3 Is each question concerned with one single factor?
4 Are the questions ones that will elicit the answers necessary to solve the research problem?
5 Is each question unambiguous and will both the investigator and the informant have the same understanding of the question?
6 Are all the possible answers allowed for?
7 Are recording arrangements foolproof?
8 Will the answers to each question be in a form in which they can be cross-tabulated against other data on the same or other questionnaires?
9 Will the answers be in a form that will allow at least some to be checked against established data?

14.13 Summary

Marketing research is the starting point of the business process in a marketing orientated organisation and it is the principal component of the organisation's MkIS. Information can be collected internally and market intelligence can be gathered from employees like as sales staff. Information collected from formal marketing research can be enhanced by computer modelling etc. Hence marketing research provides a valuable source of input data to the overall MkIS.

References

Birn, R.J. (2004), *The Effective Use of Market Research*, London: Kogan Page Ltd., p. 7.
Brace, I. (2004), *Questionnaire Design*, London: Kogan Page Ltd., p. 2.
Brown, J., Culkin, N. and Fletcher, J. (2001), 'Human factors in business to business research over the Internet', *International Journal of Market Research*, 43(4), 425–440.
Callingham, M. (2004), *Market Intelligence*, London: Kogan Page Ltd., p. 136.
Chowdhury, S. (2003), 'Databases, data mining and beyond', *Journal of American Academy of Business*, March, 576–580.
Demirdjian, Z.S. (2003), 'Marketing research and information systems: the unholy separation of the siamese twins', *The Journal of American Academy of Business*, 3(1/2), 218–223.
Doyle, P. (1994), *Marketing Management and Strategy*, London: Prentice-Hall International (UK), pp. 39, 124.
Grossnickle, J. and Raskin, O. (2001), 'What's ahead on the Internet: new tools, sampling methods, and applications help simplify Web research', *Market Research*, Summer, 9–13.
Hague, P., Hague, N. and Morgan, C.A. (2004), *Market Research in Practice*, London: Kogan Page Ltd., p. 7.

Kotler, P. (1994), *Marketing Management, Analysis, Planning, Control and Implementation*, London: Prentice-Hall International, p. 257.

McPhee, N. (2002), 'Gaining insight on business and organisational behaviour: the qualitative dimension', *International Journal of Market Research*, 44(1), 53–70.

'Report of the Definitions Committee of the American Marketing Association' (1961), AMA, Chicago, p. 1.

Schlossberg, H. (1989), 'Simulated vs traditional test marketing', *Marketing News*, October 23, 1–2, 11.

Seelig, P. (1989), 'All over the map', *Sales and Marketing Management*, March, 58–64.

Severson, J. (2002), 'What every manager needs to know about consumer research', *Management Quarterly*, Summer, 17–35.

Scholl, N., Mulders, S. and Drent, R. (2002), 'On-line qualitative market research: interviewing the world at a fingertip', *Qualitative Market Research: An International Journal*, 5(3), 210–223.

Further reading

Aaker, D.A., Kumar, V. and Day, G.S. (2000), *Market Research*, 7th edition, Chichester: John Wiley.

Bains, P. and Chanarker, B. (2002), *Introducing Market Research*, Chichester: John Wiley.

Birn, R. (ed.) (2002), *The International Handbook of Market Research Techniques*, 2nd edition, London: Kogan Page.

Craig, C.S. and Douglas, S.P. (2000), *International marketing Research*, Chichester: John Wiley.

Hague, P. (2002), *Marketing Research*, 3rd edition, London: Kogan Page.

Hollensen, S. (2004), *Global Marketing, A Decision-Oriented Approach*, 3rd edition, Financial Times, London: Prentice-Hall, pp. 135–165.

Kumar, K. (2000), *International Marketing Research*, Englewood Cliffs, NJ: Prentice-Hall.

McGiven, Y. (2002), 'The Practice of Market and Social research: An Introduction', Financial Times, London: Prentice-Hall.

Nancarrow, C., Pallister, J. and Brace, I. (2001), 'A new research medium, new research populations and seven deadly sins for Internet researchers', *Qualitative Market Research: An International Journal*, 4(3), 136–149.

Peterson, R.A. (2000), *Constructing Effective Questionnaires*, Thousand Oaks, CA: Sage Publications.

Smith, D.V.L. and Fletcher, J.H. (2001), *Inside Information: Making Use of Marketing Data*, Chichester: John Wiley.

Wright, L.T. and Crimp, M. (2000), 'The marketing Research Process', 5th edition, Harlow: Pearson Education.

Questions

Question 14.1

Use examples to illustrate how marketing research can aid marketing decision making.

Question 14.2

Exploratory research has a specific role to play in the overall marketing research process. Examine this role and outline research techniques that might be utilised at the exploratory stage.

Question 14.3

Under what circumstances would qualitative research techniques be more appropriate to use than quantitative research techniques? Give specific examples.

Question 14.4

List the advantages and disadvantages of using a telephone survey compared to a postal survey. Under what circumstances might a telephone survey be more appropriate?

Question 14.5

Compare and contrast probability sampling with non-probability sampling. Under what conditions might a market researcher have no other choice but to use a non-probability sampling procedure?

Question 14.6

Examine the role and importance of 'marketing research' within the firms over-all marketing mix.

Question 14.7

Outline and discuss the stages within the marketing research planning process.

Question 14.8

Examine the nature and role of a fully integrated marketing information system (MkIS) within the modern marketing firm.

Question 14.9

Describe the concept of a modern, integrated 'marketing information system' (MkIS) and examine its usefulness in marketing decision making.

15

Sales Forecasting

15.1 Introduction

The act of preparing for the future implies forecasting. In our personal lives, such predictions are usually made on an informal, subjective basis. If they turn out to be wrong we can usually adjust our personal circumstances. The same degree of flexibility does not generally exist in our working lives as decisions are usually of a more formal nature and of greater consequence.

The nature of managerial decision-making involves forecasting future conditions which might be for an important 'one-off' decision e.g. the company may be considering expanding by acquisition, diversifying into a totally new market or modernising its production processes. Such decisions tend to be long-term and strategic, rather than operational. In such situations, because of the importance of decisions being made, forecasting should receive careful consideration, meaning an investment of resources in the forecasting process (see Wright, 2004, p. 97).

Managerial decisions are not always strategic and much of a manager's time is taken up with day-to-day operational issues, which although not of the same magnitude as strategic decisions, are nonetheless important to the manager because of the proportion of time they occupy. Management requires forecasting information to assist when making operational decisions, although the required time horizon for such forecasts is shorter than for strategic decisions. For example, for the marketing manager to set monthly sales targets, operational expense or advertising budgets, he or she may require regular short-term forecasts for each product, broken down according to product type, size, colour, salesperson's territory, channel of distribution and even by individual customer.

Whatever type of decision is being made, forecasting is required. Forecasting is a key to success, but poor forecasting can lead to high inventories and associated stockholding costs which must be paid for out of working capital, or under-production and unrealised market potential.

The recognition of the importance of forecasting was first illustrated by the results of a major research exercise carried out in the USA by Ledbetter and Cox

(1977, pp. 84–92). They found that forecasting techniques were used by 88% of the 500 largest industrial companies in the USA. It was also established that no other class of planning techniques was used as much as forecasting.

Although forecasting is important in most functional areas of a firm, the forecasting of sales is particularly important. The sales forecast is the foundation on which company plans are constructed and for this to be sound, the forecast must be built on firm scientific foundations (see Hollensen, 2004, pp. 158–161).

The central issue facing businesses is not whether to forecast, but how to forecast. The forecaster can choose 'subjective' or 'objective' methods or a mixture of each.

15.2 Forecasting terminology

Terminology used to describe forecasts make a distinction between 'prediction' and 'forecasting' using 'forecast' to refer to objective, quantitative techniques and 'predict' to denote subjective estimates.

The availability of appropriate data is of central importance to the development of a forecasting system. Depending on the degree of accuracy required, most forecasting techniques require considerable amounts of data to be collected and analysed in terms of usefulness and validity before it can be used in the forecasting process.

Selection of the most suitable forecasting method from the choice of techniques available depends on the availability of existing data and/or the company's ability to acquire relevant data, for example, a technique requiring a long historical time series would be of little use, if data were only available for the past 2 years. If accuracy or validity of data were questionable, it would not be worthwhile or cost-effective to spend time and effort using a sophisticated technique known for its precision. The principle of 'garbage in/garbage out' applies and a forecast will only be as good as the data used in its compilation.

15.3 Data collection

Once the company has decided how much time, energy and money is to be spent on data collection, it must determine where it will obtain data. The most promising sources depend on the specific situation.

There are two main categories of existing data:

1 'Internal data' generated within the organisation, for example, previous company plans, sales statistics and other internal records. For certain situations this may be sufficient.
2 'Secondary data from external sources', for example, Government and trade statistics and published marketing research surveys.

These are important, and in many forecasting situations it is necessary to utilise both.

A third category of data is that generated specifically for the forecasting task through some form of marketing research such as a sample survey, a test-marketing experiment or an observational study. This can be an expensive source of data, so before commencing, a full study should be made to see if this is available from other sources.

15.3.1 Internal data sources

In immediate and short-term forecasting used for operational decision-making and control purposes, much data can be gathered from internal sources. There may be questions that can only be answered by a detailed investigation of the firm's own data, so it is essential that internal data is collected, recorded and stored as part of routine administrative procedures. Desk research into internal company records is a useful and economic source of data and should be a starting point for data collection in a forecasting exercise. An advantage is that the departmental manager concerned can give an indication of the accuracy of data and its relevance to the forecasting situation. A disadvantage is that although the company's internal system may contain useful information, it may be difficult for the forecaster to obtain it in an appropriate form as it has been compiled for different purposes.

Success in obtaining past data from within the firm will depend to a great extent on knowing the firm and its staff. Obtaining access to information may sometimes be a problem so it is important that such exercises have the authority of top management to obtain maximum cooperation.

The first stage is to take a systems analysis approach and trace the documentary procedures of the firm. The forecaster should look carefully at what records are kept and how data is obtained, altered, processed and circulated throughout the firm. Every document should be recorded, possibly using some form of flow chart. The type of document as well as the function it serves should be noted as well as its origin and destination.

Administrative and documentary procedures vary, but most company systems start with a customer enquiry and end with the customer's invoice. With detailed analysis, it is possible to identify the main steps in the procedure within each department. The idea is to build up a picture of the overall system from individual employees to the total departmental system and ultimately the company. Unofficial records are sometimes kept for contingency purposes. Such sources may be useful to the forecaster and can be discovered by probing.

15.3.2 Data from the sales department

The sales/marketing department is the main point of commercial interaction between the company and its customers. Consequently, it is the chief source of information including:

1 *Sales volume by product and by product group*: This information can be combined to give total sales volume, but it also allows each product or product

group in the overall product mix to be evaluated in terms of its contribution to total volume.

2 *Sales volume by area*: This may be divided according to salesperson territories, standard media areas as used by the Joint Industry for Television Advertising Research (JICTAR) or other geographical areas (e.g. countries).

3 *Sales volumes by market segment*: The basis for segmentation may be regional or, especially in industrial markets, by type of industry. Such information will indicate which segments are likely to remain static, which are in decline and which show growth possibilities. Where the firm deals with a few large customers, segmentation may be by individual customer, and any change in demand from any of these may be significant in terms of forecasting sales.

4 *Sales volume by type of channel of distribution*: Where a company has a multi-channel distribution policy, it is possible to calculate the effectiveness and profitability of each type of channel. It also allows for trends in the pattern of distribution to be identified and taken into account in forecasting future channel requirements. Channel information by geographical area may indicate a difference in the profitability between various types of channel in different parts of the country, allowing for geographical differentials.

   Information gathered by types of retail outlets, agents, wholesalers and distributors can contribute to a more realistic forecast. Such information allows marketing to identify and develop promising channel opportunities, resulting in more effective channel management.

5 *Sales volume over time*: In terms of sales and units sold, this allows seasonal variations to be identified and inflation and price adjustments can be taken into consideration.

6 *Pricing information*: Historical information relating to price adjustments by product types allows forecasters to establish the effects of price increases or decreases on demand. The forecaster is then able to judge the likely effects of future price changes.

7 *Communication mix information*: The effects of previous advertising campaigns, sponsorship, direct mail or exhibitions can be assessed. Various levels of expenditure in marketing communications can be evaluated. This information will act as a guide to the likely effectiveness of future communication mix expenditures.

8 *Sales promotional data*: The effectiveness of past promotional campaigns such as reduced-price pack, coupons, self-liquidating offers and competitions can be assessed. Trade incentives aimed at distributive intermediaries can also be assessed in terms of their individual influence on sales.

9 *Sales representatives' records and reports*: As discussed in Chapter 11, sales representatives should keep files on 'live' customers. Often these records are kept in considerable detail, ranging from information on customer interests to detailed personal information as well as information about the customer's firm, its product range, diversification plans and likely future purchases. Even what the customer last said to the salesperson may be recorded. Sales representatives normally make reports to the sales office on matters like orders lost to competitors, customers holding future purchasing decisions in

abeyance and information on quotations that never materialised in orders. This information is potentially useful to the forecaster.

10 *Enquiries received and quotations sent*: Customers submit enquiries asking for details of price, delivery, etc., and records should be kept of verbal enquiries. Enquiries lead to a detailed quotation being submitted to the customer. This information can be useful to the forecaster, especially if patterns can be established in the percentage of enquiries that mature into orders, and the time between a quotation being submitted and an order being received. The number of requests for quotations can provide a guide to economic activity in the market place, and as firms are likely to request quotations from a number of sources, the number of quotations successfully converted into orders gives an indication of the firm's market share.

15.3.3 Data from other departments

Accounts department

The management accountant will be able to provide accurate cost data. Other useful information can be gained from previous management reports (see Cravens *et al.*, 2002, p. 12). Management information requirements differ between firms, but such reports may contain accurate information on such matters as:

- number of new customers in a given period,
- number of withdrawals,
- number of items sold by product in volume and monetary terms,
- total sales by salesperson, area, division, etc.

Management accounting reports give information on staff matters such as absenteeism. Such information can be useful when attempting to accurately forecast production capacity. Past budgets with variance analysis will show budgeted figures against actual figures.

Finance will also keep statistics on current operations like orders received, orders dispatched and orders on hand. Such information is kept for internal management information needs and to fulfil legal requirement when presenting accounts. This information may duplicate information held elsewhere, but may be most easily accessible in the accounts department. Since such information has been collected independently, it can be used as a 'check' on information gathered from other sources.

Purchasing department

Copies of purchase orders, material lists, requisitions, material status schedule reports, information on suppliers (e.g. reliability of delivery, lead times, prices) can be useful. Purchasing will also be able to provide stock control data relating to reorder levels, buffer and safety stock levels, economic order quantities and stock-turn by inventory item. The forecaster may need to take such information into account. Stock availability and short lead times are part of general levels of service offered to customers. Depending on the service sensitivity of the market, service levels can have a significant influence on demand. Present and future service levels will have a bearing on both sales and materials management as an increase in the level of service would mean more stock and a greater variety of materials being held.

Despatch department

The despatch department will have its own information system detailing goods despatched and transportation methods as well as advice notes and other delivery documents. Such information may be useful for forecasting in its own right or act as a check on information gathered elsewhere (see also Hollensen, 2003, p. 700).

Production department

The production department should be able to supply documentation relating to production control, for example, copies of works orders, material lists and design information. Information should be available on orders placed on the company's own factory, requisitions for materials to stores, orders subcontracted to other suppliers, manufacturing times, machine utilisation times and order completion dates.

15.3.4 Departmental plans

Not only should historical and current internal information be available to the forecaster, but this should also include short-, medium- and long-term plans relating to individual departments.

Activity and changes in company policy or methods of operation already planned can have considerable bearing on a forecast. For instance, plans to expand the sales department or to increase promotional activity will affect a sales forecast. Investment in capital equipment such as new machine tools or a new material handling system may significantly affect both materials requirements and future sales.

The sources mentioned are not an exhaustive list of all types of internal information available to the forecaster. Other departments, for example, human resource management, research and development, purchasing, etc. may hold useful information. Choice of sources will depend on the type of forecast required.

15.4 Forecasting methods

15.4.1 Subjective methods

Subjective methods of forecasting are generally qualitative techniques that rely largely on judgment rather than numerical calculations. They are sometimes called 'intuitive' or, unkindly perhaps, 'naïve' techniques, and are applied through a mixture of experience and judgment. Subjective techniques include:

Executive opinion (or jury) method and sales force composite

This method involves the sales or marketing manager making an informed subjective forecast. This is sometimes done in conjunction with the field sales force (in which case it is termed the 'sales force composite' method) and then consulting other executives in production, finance and elsewhere. The group forms a 'jury' that delivers a 'verdict' on the forecast. The final forecast is thus based on the collective experience of the sales force and the group and has the backing and input of experienced executives in the company. Proponents claim that the informed opinions of such people provide as valid a prediction as any other method. Such panels are often used in the final stages of the development of a forecast. Where subjective forecasts have been obtained from various sources, there is a need to assess and evaluate each one before consolidating them into a final forecast.

Advantages

- The forecast is compiled by people who have experience of the industry.
- The final forecast is based on the collective experience of a group, rather than on the opinion of a single executive.
- Because the final forecast is based on consensus of opinion, variations in individual subjective estimates are 'smoothed out'.
- Because of the status of individuals contributing to the forecast, the figures are perceived to have a high level of source credibility by people who make use of the forecasting information.

Disadvantages

- If salespersons know that the resulting sales quotas or targets are linked to bonus payments or commission rates, they may deliberately produce pessimistic forecasts in order to be in a better earning position.
- As forecasting is only a subsidiary activity of the salesperson, the forecast may often be based on guesswork rather than on careful reasoning. Salespeople are often too concerned with everyday events to devote sufficient time to produce realistic forecasts. Chapter 11 explained that the modern salesperson has a much wider role than 15 years ago. They are expected to attend exhibitions, contribute to marketing plans, provide market intelligence and carry out numerous other related activities. Add to this time spent travelling and waiting to see clients, and there is little time available for close reflection on forecasting activity. This particularly applies if a large number of product forecasts were required on a regular basis.

Customer-use projections

This method uses survey techniques to ascertain purchase intentions of customers and/or users. Such surveys range from the sales representative merely talking to existing and potential customers and reporting back to head office to more formal market research surveys. In consumer markets, where the population is large, a sample survey is usually undertaken. Such a survey can be at two levels: customer intentions to buy, or the distributive intermediary's intention to stock and promote the product(s). In organisational markets, where numbers of customers may be relatively few, sampling may not be necessary. This method is seldom used on its own, but more often in conjunction with other forecasting methods. Test marketing is also used to produce forecasts and is similar to surveys. A small representative area is used and the results form the basis of a forecast. Seelig (1989, pp. 58–64) proposed using simulated test marketing, that is, a test market in a laboratory.

Advantages

- The information on which the forecast is based comes from prospective purchasers and the rationale is that only they really know what and how they are likely to purchase in the future.
- The technique utilises proven marketing research methodology such as sample surveys, projective techniques and questionnaires to elicit information.
- The task of producing sales forecasts can be subcontracted to professional research agencies which is useful if time is at a premium.

Disadvantages

- Sample surveys, particularly if they involve face-to-face contact with customers and potential customers, can be time-consuming and expensive. Costs must be compared with those of alternative methods of producing a forecast using a cost-benefit approach. If forecasts are required regularly, then such methods are likely to be expensive particularly if forecasts are required in a disaggregated form (e.g. product line by product line over time).
- There may be a difference between what respondents say they are going to purchase and their actual purchases.
- There is a limit to how often the same people (e.g. purchasing managers) can be approached and expected to participate in such a fact-finding study.

Where subjective forecasting techniques are used, the 'jury of executive opinion' and 'sales-force composite' methods have greater application than customer-use projections. This is true in industrial markets as the success of these techniques depends on a close relationship between the supplier and customers.

15.4.2 Bayesian decision theory

The methods of subjective forecasting described are not an exhaustive list. Some other methods are variations on the techniques described. The main exception is Bayesian decision theory that is a mixture of qualitative and quantitative techniques (see Buck and Sahu, 2000, pp. 424–440). The method is named after Reverend Thomas Bayes (1702–61), a statistician. Despite the fact that it was developed in the eighteenth century, it has only recently been widely adopted (see Bayes, 1736, p. 1).

The method incorporates the firm's estimates at data inputs for the statistical calculation of sales forecasts. It uses network diagrams showing the probable outcome of each decision alternative considered. These are shown together with expected values and associated probabilities, initially derived on a subjective basis (see Bayes, 1764, p. 6).

One of the problems of using probabilities in statistical model is in ascertaining initial probabilities to commence the forecasting process. Bayesian statisticians differ from 'purist' statisticians in the respect that 'purists' view the concept of probability as the relative frequency with which an event might occur. The Bayesian view is that probability is a measure of our belief and that we can always express our degree of belief in terms of probability. Although initial probabilities are derived subjectively, that is, the figures are based on judgmental opinion, rather than on objective calculation, proponents of Bayesian theory believe that such probabilities are perfectly valid and acceptable as initial starting points in an extensive quantitative forecasting process. It is the subjective nature of arriving at the initial probabilities that makes the Bayesian approach useful in solving business problems for which initial probabilities are often unknown and are difficult or impossible to calculate using objective methods.

To use the Bayesian approach, the decision-maker must be able to assign a probability to each specific event. The sum of the probabilities of all events considered must be unity (one). These probabilities represent the magnitude of the decision maker's belief that a particular event will take place.

In business situations such decisions should be delegated to people who have knowledge and experience to assign valid initial subjective probabilities to the occurrences of various business events. These initial probabilities are based on previous experience of information (such as published secondary data) acquired prior to the decision-making process. For this reason, the initial subjective probabilities are referred to as 'prior probabilities' (see Buck, 2001, pp. 695–702).

When making business decisions, the financial implications of actions must be taken into account. For example, when a manager is considering investing a firm's surplus cash, he or she must consider the probability of making a profit (or loss) under different economic scenarios and also assess the probability of such scenarios or events occurring. Applying Bayesian decision theory involves selecting an option and having a reasonable idea of the economic consequences of choosing a particular course of action. Once the relevant future events have been identified, the decision-maker assigns prior subjective probabilities to them. The expected pay-off for each act is then computed and the act with the most attractive pay-off is then chosen. If pay-offs represent income or profit, the decision-maker usually chooses the act with the highest expected pay-off (see Smith and Faria, 2000, pp. 525–544). To illustrate the theory just described, a practical example is now discussed:

Highburton Textiles produce high quality Axminster carpets made from 80% wool and 20% nylon (for strength). In the UK the product retails for approximately £22 per square metre. Axminster carpets are very popular among higher income households in Australia where only small quantities are produced. The product is perceived by Australian higher social groups as being a luxury purchase. For Highburton Textiles to gain economies in freight charges, export consignments need to be relatively large and it is planned that the first consignment will be worth £3,000,000. Because of its high-status image in Australia, the carpet can command a premium price (about £ sterling 36 per square metre equivalent). However, such a product is a deferrable purchase and demand is only likely to remain high if the Australian economy remains strong. Management can foresee a possible decline of the Australian economy as the main risk factor in this venture. The first 12 months are particularly important, as this is the time the first consignment is expected to be sold given the present economic climate. Economists have predicted an economic downturn over this period if monetary conditions tighten in response to rising domestic inflation and poor trade figures.

The decision facing Highburton Textiles management is whether to risk going ahead with the Australian centre now, when present demand for their product is likely to be high, or to postpone the decision, waiting for the economic outlook in Australia to become more stable. If the decision is postponed, fashion tastes may change away from this type of product in the interim.

The management of Highburton Textiles assesses the Australian economy is likely to go in one of three directions over the next 12 months:

1 stay the same,
2 slight deterioration,
3 significant deterioration.

Management assigns subjective initial probabilities to each of the possible economic scenarios (Table 15.1). (Note that the sum of probabilities of the three possibilities considered is unity [1]).

The direction of the Australian economy is an event (E) that is outside the control of the company. Management decides on three possible courses of action (A):

1 Export now while conditions are relatively good.
2 Delay six months, in which time the direction of the Australian Government's economic strategy is likely to become clearer.
3 Delay one year to observe the longer-term economic trends.

Table 15.1 Subjective prior probabilities of alternative future economic scenarios

Event	Probability
Economic conditions remain the same	0.4
Slight deterioration in the economy	0.3
Significant deterioration in the economy	0.3
Sum of probabilities	1.0

Management then forecasts expected profit for each course of action under different economic conditions (Table 15.2).

The prior probabilities are now incorporated into a decision tree (Figure 15.1). This is made up of 'nodes' and 'branches', with the decision point represented by square and chance events by circles.

The expected value (EV) is now calculated for each forecast and then totalled for each alternative course of action (A). This is done using pay-off tables where the expected profit for each event is multiplied by its assigned probability and the resulting products summed (see Table 15.3).

Table 15.2 Expected pay-offs for different decisions under different economic conditions

Events (E)	Actions (A)		
	1	*2*	*3*
	Export now	*Delay 6 months*	*Delay 1 year*
(a) Economic conditions remain the same	1,600,000	1,200,000	1,000,000
(b) Slight deterioration in economy	900,000	740,000	400,000
(c) Significant deterioration in economy	−648,000	100,000	160,000

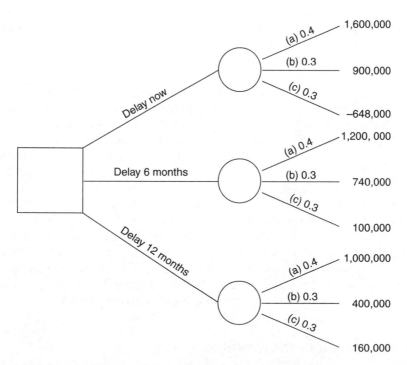

Figure 15.1 Decision tree for Highburton Textiles Ltd. (a) Economy remains same; (b) slight deterioration; (c) significant deterioration

Table 15.3 Expected value (EV)

Event (E)	Probability	Expected Profit (£)	Expected Value (£)
A1 – Export now			
(a)	0.4	1,600,000	620,000
(b)	0.3	900,000	270,000
(c)	0.3	−648,000	−194,400
Total EV			695,600
A1 – Delay 6 months			
(a)	0.4	1,200,000	480,000
(b)	0.3	740,000	222,000
(c)	0.3	100,000	30,000
Total EV			732,000
A1 – Delay 12 months			
(a)	0.4	1,000,000	400,000
(b)	0.3	400,000	120,000
(c)	0.3	160,000	48,000
Total EV	568,000		

By examining total values for each of three possible actions management sees that A2 (i.e. delay action for 6 months) gives the maximum expected pay-off (£732,000). Since the action is selected under conditions of uncertainty, the EV is referred to as the 'EV under uncertainty' and the action chosen as the 'optimal action'.

In the Highburton Textiles example, the probabilities assigned to events were prior probabilities. They were subjective, largely based on the decision-makers' beliefs in the probability that certain events will occur. Such an analysis, carried out using prior probabilities, is called a prior analysis.

After prior analysis, the decision maker has two choices – to go ahead with the optimal action indicated by the prior analysis or to collect additional primary data, re-evaluate the probabilities in the light of further information and carry out new calculations. Additional information may be obtained by carrying out a market research survey or some other form of primary data collection procedure (as described in Chapter 13). If additional information is gathered and another analysis carried out, the term for these new calculations is 'posterior analysis'. Clearly, it is going to cost the decision-maker time and money to collect further information. A decision must be made as to whether the better-informed decision will be worth the extra cost or not.

15.4.3 Objective methods

Objective methods of forecasting are quantitative in nature. Historical data are analysed to identify a pattern or relationship between variables, and this pattern is then extended or extrapolated into the future to make a forecast. Objective methods fall into two groups: 'time series' and 'causal' models.

Time series models

Time series analysis uses the historical series of only one variable to develop a model for predicting future values. The forecasting situation is treated like a 'black box', with no attempt being made to discover other factors that might affect behaviour.

Because time series models treat the variable to be forecast as a function of time, they are most useful when other conditions are expected to remain relatively constant, which is most likely true of the short-term rather than the long-term. Hence, such methods are particularly suited to short-term, operational, routine forecasting – usually up to 6 months or so of current time.

Time series methods are not very useful when there is no discernible pattern of demand. Their whole purpose is to identify patterns in historical data, model these, and extrapolate them into the future. Such methods are unlikely to be successful in forecasting future demand when the historical time series is erratic. Because it is assumed that future demand is a function of time only, causal factors cannot be taken into consideration. For example, such models would not be able to incorporate impact of changes in management policy.

Causal models

Causal models exploit the relationship between the time series of the variable being examined and one or more other time series. If other variables are found to correlate with the variable of interest, a causal model can be constructed incorporating coefficients that give the relative strengths of the various causal factors, for example, the sales of a product may be related to the price of the product, advertising expenditure and the price of competitors' products. If the forecaster can estimate the relationship between sales and the independent variables, then the forecast values of the independent variables can be used to predict future values of the dependent variable (in this case, sales).

Such techniques are illustrated by two of the simpler models, 'moving averages' and 'exponential smoothing' that are discussed here. More sophisticated time series models include decomposition models and auto-regressive moving averages (Box–Jenkins) techniques that are the subject of more advanced study.

Moving averages (time series)

Simple moving average

The simple moving or 'rolling' average is a useful and uncomplicated method of forecasting the average expected value of a time series (see Birn, 2002, p. 90). The process uses the average individual forecasts (F) and demand values (X) over the past n time periods.

A suffix notation is used, which may seem complicated, but is quite simple: the present is referred to as time t and one period into the future by $t + 1$, one period into the past by $t - 1$, two periods by $t \pm 2$, and so on. This is best appreciated with reference to a time diagram:

The simple moving average process is defined by the equation:

$$F_{t+1} = F_t + \frac{1}{n}(X_t - X_{t-n})$$

where F_{t+1} is the forecast for one period ahead, F_t is the forecast made last time period for the present period, n is the number of time periods considered in the calculation, X_t is the actual demand at the present time, and X_{t-n} is the actual demand for period $t - n$.

Weighted average

The simple moving average has the disadvantage that all data in the average are given equal weighting, that is,

$$\frac{1}{n}$$

More recent data may be more important than older data, particularly if the underlying pattern of the data has been changing, and, therefore, should be given a greater weight. To overcome this problem and increase the sensitivity of the moving average, it is possible to use 'weighted averages', with the sum of the weights equal to unity, in order to produce a true average. In decimal form, a weighted moving average can be expressed as:

$$F_{t+1} = 0.4X_t + 0.3X_{t-1} + 0.2X_{t-2} + 0.1X_{t-3}$$
(notation as defined for the simple moving average)

Problems common to all moving average procedures are that a forecast cannot be made until n time periods have passed, because it is necessary to have values available for the previous $n - 1$, etc. periods. The sensitivity or speed of response of moving average procedures is inversely proportional to the number of periods n included in the average. To change the sensitivity, it is necessary to change the value of n which creates problems of continuity and much additional work.

The methods of simple and weighted moving averages discussed so far are only suitable for reasonably constant (stationary) data – they are unable to deal with a significant trend. An example of a 'stationary time series' is shown in Figure 15.2. It can be seen from the graph that over a period of nine months the time series fluctuates randomly abut a mean value of 200 units that is not increasing or decreasing significantly over time.

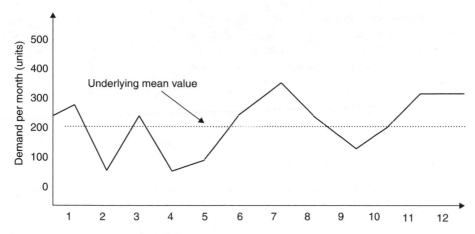

Figure 15.2 Example of stationary time series

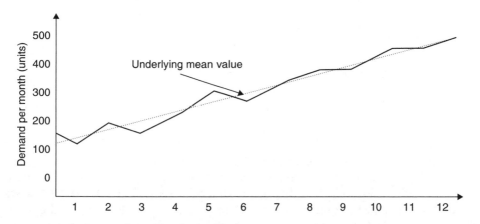

Figure 15.3 Example of time series with a linear underlying trend

In the times series shown in Figure 15.3 the underlying mean value of the series is not stationary. If a line of best fit is drawn through all of the points, you can see that while the actual values are fluctuating randomly, the underlying mean value is following a rising linear trend.

Double (linear) moving average

A method of moving averages designed for a reasonably stationary time series cannot accommodate a series with a linear trend. In such situations, the forecasts tend to lag behind the actual time series, resulting in systematic errors. To counter such error factors, the method of 'double' (or 'linear') moving averages has been developed. This method calculates a second (or double) moving average that is a moving average of the first one. The principle is that a single moving average (MA_t^1) will lag behind the actual trend series X_t and the second moving average (MA_t^2) will lag behind MA_t^1 by approximately the same amount.

The difference between the two moving averages is added to the single moving average MA_t^1, to give the level (a_t). The difference between MA_t^1 and MA_t^2 can then be added to the level (a_t) to produce a one- or m-period-ahead forecast.

The 'double moving average procedure' is summarised as follows:

1 The use of a simple moving average at time t (denoted as MA_t'').
2 An adjustment, which is the difference between the simple and the double averages at time t ($MA_t'' - MA_t'$).
3 An adjustment for trend from period t to period $t + 1$ (or to period $t + 1$ (or period $t + m$, if the forecast is for m period ahead).

The updating equations for the double moving average are as follows:

Single moving average:

$$MA_t'' = \frac{X_t + X_{t-1} + X_{t-2} + \cdots + X_t - N + 1}{N}$$

Double moving average:

$$MA_t' = \frac{MA_t'' + MA_{t-1}'' + MA_{t-2}'' + \cdots + MA_t'' - N + 1}{N}$$

Level component $\quad a_t = MA_t'' + (MA_t'' - MA_t') = 2MA_t'' - MA_t'$

Trend component $\quad b_t = \dfrac{2}{N - 1}(MA_t'' - MA_t')$

Forecast $\quad\quad\quad\quad F_{t+m} = a_t + b_t m$

The general principle of the double moving average is shown in Figure 15.4.

Although the double moving average has the advantage of being able to handle data with a trend, it has the disadvantage of requiring extra data. N data points are required to update each MA_t'' and MA_t', that is, $2n$ or twice the number required for the simple moving average must be stored. The necessity for substantial data storage makes the double moving average less attractive in practice than other techniques which provide similar results from less data. This is particularly so if short-term forecasts are required on a routine basis (e.g. weekly) for a large number of items.

Exponential smoothing (time series)

Exponentially weighted moving averages overcomes some of the shortcomings and limitations of the moving average method.

Simple exponential smoothing

When using simple exponential smoothing, weightings used in the averaging process decrease exponentially over time, allowing greater weight to be given to more recent values. This is achieved by means of a smoothing coefficient, the value of which can be chosen to give the required weight to each piece of

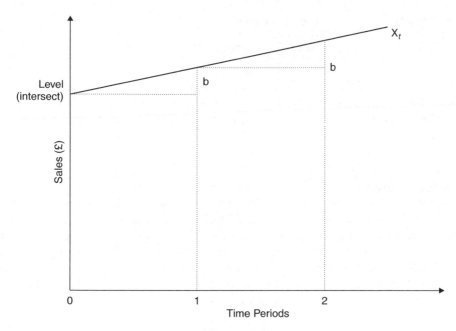

Figure 15.4 Diagrammatic representation of principle of double moving average

historical data used in the calculation of the forecast. To illustrate the principle, we let the weighting function used to smooth the random fluctuations from the time series, be denoted by α (alpha). A series can be constructed:

$$\alpha + (1 - \alpha) + \alpha(1 - \alpha)^2 + \alpha(1 - \alpha)^3 + \alpha(1 - \alpha)^4 + \cdots + \alpha(1 - \alpha)^n$$

For $0 \leq \alpha \leq 1$, as n gets larger the sum of the series will approximate to one. For example, if $\alpha = 0.4$ and $n = 15$, the series will sum as follows:

$$0.4 + 0.24 + 0.144 + 0.0864 + 0.0518 + 0.0311 + 0.0187 + 0.0112 + 0.0067$$
$$+ 0.004 + 0.0024 + 0.0015 + 0.0009 + 0.0005 + 0.003 = 0.995$$

Rounded up, this is 1.0.

To illustrate how the technique is used in forecasting, we use the notation discussed earlier for simple moving averages (i.e. the one-step-ahead forecast produced in current time is denoted by F_{t+1} and the actual current demand value by X_t). Using the weighting coefficient series, we produce the following equation:

$$F_{t+1} = \alpha X_t + \alpha(1 - \alpha)X_{t-1} + \alpha(1 - \alpha)^2 X_{t-2} + \alpha(1 - \alpha)^3 X_{t-3} + \cdots$$
$$+ \alpha(1 - \alpha)^n X_{t-n}$$

Transcribing this equation to an expression for F_t (by subtracting one from all the subscripts) we obtain:

$$F_t = \alpha X_{t-1} + \alpha(1 - \alpha)X_{t-2} + \alpha(1 - \alpha)^2 X_{t-3} + \cdots + \alpha(1 - \alpha)^{n-1} X_{t-n}$$

The equation for F_{t+1} can be written as follows:

$$F_{t-1} = \alpha X_t + (1 - \alpha)[\alpha X_{t-1} + \alpha(1 - \alpha)X_{t-2} + \alpha(1 - \alpha)^2 X_{t-3} + \cdots + \alpha(1 - \alpha)^{n-1} X^{t-n}]$$

The expression in the square brackets is exactly the same as that derived for F_t. Substituting F_t, we obtain the basic equation defining a simple exponentially-weighted moving average from which all other models or exponential smoothing are derived:

$$F_{t+1} = \alpha X_t + (1 - \alpha)F_t$$

(More correctly, the process is a geometrically weighted moving average, the exponentially weighted moving average being its analogue in continuous [series] form).

The technique of simple exponential smoothing is historically very important, as it was the first 'adaptive forecasting' method to be proposed. It is adaptive in the sense that the current forecasting errors are used to update the model: A more compact form of equation can be achieved by noting that $X_t - F_t$ represents the value of the current forecasting error, e_t' and that the equation for simple exponential smoothing could be written as:

$$F_{t+1} = F_t + \alpha(X_t - F_t)$$
$$F_{t+1} = F_t + \alpha(e_t)$$

Therefore, the previous forecast is updated by a proportion (α) of the current error (e_t).

An example is given where the one-period-ahead forecast (weeks, months or years) for a hypothetical product is calculated using this last equation. Different values of smoothing coefficient have been used in the calculation ($\alpha = 0.1, 0.5$ and 0.9). In the first period, no earlier forecast is available to use as an F_t value. The normal convention of using the observed value X_t for F_t in the first calculation has been followed:

Time period	Observed demand (X_t)	Exponentially smoothed forecast values (units) (F_t)		
		$\alpha = 0.1$	$\alpha = 0.5$	$\alpha = 0.9$
1	2000	–	–	–
2	1350	2000	2000	2000
3	1950	1935	1675	1415
4	1975	1937	1813	1897
5	3100	1941	1894	1967
6	1750	2057	2497	2987
7	1550	2026	2124	1874
8	1300	1978	1837	1582
9	2200	1910	1569	1328
10	2775	1939	1885	2113
11	2350	2023	2330	2709
12	–	2056	2340	2386

Double exponential smoothing

Simple exponential smoothing is only appropriate for a relatively stationary time series. In particular, the method will perform badly if the series contains a long-term trend. Like simple moving average, if simple exponential smoothing is applied inappropriately to a time series with a trend, the forecast will continually lag behind the actual value of series X_t.

The method of 'double exponential smoothing' is technically known as 'Brown's one parameter linear exponential smoothing'. This method introduces additional equations to those of the simple exponential smoothing to estimate a trend. The method uses the same principle as the double or linear moving average, that is, that if simple exponential smoothing is applied to a time series with a significant trend it will lag behind. If single exponential smoothing is applied again to the first smoothed series, the second smoothed series (S_t^2) will lag behind the first (S_t^1) by approximately the same amount as the first smoothed series (S_t^2) lagged behind the original time series (X_t). This is illustrated in Figure 15.5.

Brown's method accepts that after initial transients have died down, S_t^1 will lag behind X_t by amount A. A second single exponentially weighted average (S_t^2) will lag behind the first (S_t^1) by the same amount, A. At time t, the difference between S_t^1 and S_t^2 is added to the S_t^2 to give the level component at. A proportion of the difference between S_t^1 and S_t^2 is then used to provide a trend component, b_t, which is multiplied by the number of periods ahead to be forecast, m, and the product added to the level at to produce a forecast for m steps ahead.

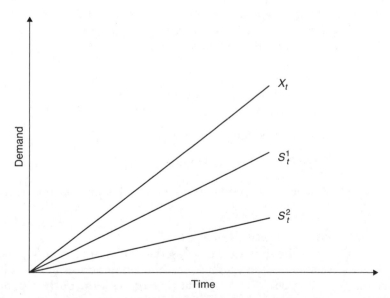

Figure 15.5 Lagged response of simple exponential smoothing model applied to a series with a linear additive trend

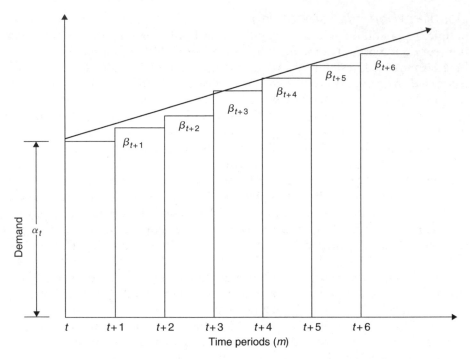

Figure 15.6 The level (α_t) and trend $(\beta + m)$ components of Brown's double exponential smoothing

Brown's model of double exponential smoothing is made up of two components: a level component (or intercept) (α) and a trend component (β). These components are combined to provide a forecast, as illustrated in Figure 15.6. The updating equations for Brown's model are:

Single smoothing $S_t^1 = \alpha X_t + (1 - \alpha)S_{t-1}^1$

Double smoothing $S_t^2 = \alpha S_t^1 + (1 - \alpha)S_{t-1}^2$

Level component $\alpha_t = S_t^1 + (S_t^1 - S_t^2) = 2S_t^1 - S_t^2$

Trend component $\beta_t = \dfrac{\alpha}{1 - \alpha}(S_t^1 - S_t^2)$

Forecast $F_{t+m} = \alpha_t + \beta_t m$

where m is a multiplier of the trend component, that is, the periods ahead to be forecast.

Winter's trend and seasonal model

The exponential smoothing models discussed so far cannot deal with seasonal data. When seasonality does exist, these methods may perform poorly, because the seasonality will produce a systematic error pattern. Such a data series requires the use of a seasonal method to eliminate the systematic pattern in the errors. 'Winter's trend and seasonal model' is based on three smoothing equations – one for stationary series, one for trends and one for seasonality. The updating equations for this model are as follows:

$$\text{Overall smoothing} \quad S_t = \alpha \frac{X_t}{I_{t-L}} + (1 - \alpha) I_{t-L}$$

$$\text{Trend} \quad Z_t = Y(S_t - S_{t-1}) + (1 - Y)(Z_{t-1})$$

$$\text{Seasonality} \quad I_t = \beta \frac{X_t}{S_t} + (1 - \beta) I_{t-L}$$

$$\text{Forecast} \quad F_{t+m} = (S_t + mZ_t) I_{(t-L+m)}$$

where L is the length of seasonality (e.g. the number of months or quarters in a year), Z_t is the trend component, I_t is the seasonal adjustment factor, F_{t+m} is the forecast for m periods ahead, X, Y and β are the smoothing coefficients for overall smoothing, trend and seasonal components, respectively.

15.5 Summary

Forecasting is the starting point for business planning, so if the forecast is incorrect then all strategic and tactical plans will be affected. It follows that the most important link is with marketing planning and control that is the theme of final Chapter 19. Forecasting draws for its application on other areas, especially marketing research in relation to products that are new to the market, and this was the subject of the Chapter 14.

References

Bayes, T. (1736), 'An Introduction to the Doctrine of Fluxions, and a Defence of the Mathematicians Against the Objections of the Author of The Analyst', published anonymously but discussed at the *Royal Society of London* in 1742 when Bayes was elected a Fellow of the Royal Society.

Bayes, T. (1764), 'Essay towards solving a problem in the doctrine of chances', *Philosophical Transactions of the Royal Society of London*.

Birn, R. (ed.) (2002), '*The International Handbook of Market Research Techniques*', 2nd edition, London: Kogan Page p. 90.

Buck, C.E. (2001), 'Applications of the Bayesian statistical paradigm', in *Handbook of Archaeological Sciences*, Brothwell, D.R. and Pollard, A.M. (eds), Chichester: Wiley pp. 695–702.

Buck, C.E. and Sahu, S.K. (2000), 'Bayesian models for relative, archaeological chronology building', *Applied Statistics*, 49(3), 423–440.

Cravens, D.W., Lamb, C.W. Jr., Crittenden, V.L. (2002), *Strategic Marketing Management Cases*, 7th edition, London: McGraw-Hill, p. 112.

Hollensen, S. (2003), *Marketing Management – A Relationship Approach*, London: Prentice-Hall, p. 700.

Hollensen, S. (2004), *Global Marketing, A Decision-Oriented Approach*, 3rd edition, Financial Times, Prentice-Hall, pp. 158–161.

Ledbetter, W.N. and Cox, J.F. (1977), 'Operations research in production management: and investigation of past and present utilization' *Production & Inventory Management*, 18, 84–92.

Seelig, P. (1989) 'All over the Map', *Sales and Marketing Management*, March, 58–64.

Smith, J.Q. and Faria, A.E. (2000), 'Bayesian Poisson models for the graphical combination of expert information', *Journal of the Royal Statistical Society*, B 62, 525–544.

Wright, R. (2004), '*Business to Business Marketing: A Step-by-step guide*', Financial Times, London: Prentice-Hall, p. 97.

Further reading

Brennan, Ross, Baines, Paul and Garneau, Paul, (2003), *Contempory Strategic Marketing*, London: Palgrave Macmillan, p. 15.

Kotler, P. (2000), *Marketing Management: The Millennium Edition*, London: Prentice-Hall, p. 118.

Kotler, P. Armstrong, G. Saunders, J. Wong, V. (2001), '*Principles of Marketing*', 3rd European edition, Pearson Education, Ltd., pp. 292–298.

Hill, L. and O'Sullivan, T. (2004), *Foundation Marketing*', 3rd edition, London: Prentice-Hall, pp. 84, 418–420.

Questions

Question 15.1

What are the advantages and disadvantages of the various qualitative forecasting methods available to a market researcher wishing to forecast sales up to one year ahead of current time.

Question 15.2

'Good forecasting becomes a key factor in company success. Poor forecasting can lead to overly large inventories, costly price markdowns, or lost sales due to being out of stock' (Kotler). Critically evaluate the above statement, using examples to illustrate the points being made.

Question 15.3

What is the difference between sales forecasting up to one year ahead of current time and the annual sales budget? Show how each contributes to the marketing planning and control process.

Question 15.4

What advantages do exponential smoothing forecasting techniques have, if any, over the method of moving averages techniques?

Question 15.5

Discuss the type of decision making that involve either subjective or objective forecasting.

Question 15.6

Discuss the main principles of Bayesian forecasting. Demonstrate how it can be used in a practical way by marketing management.

Question 15.7

What forecasting methods might be useful for long-term strategic planning?

Question 15.8

What are the main differences between moving averages and exponential smoothing?

Question 15.9

What internal sources of information might be useful in helping to produce short term sales forecasts? Give examples.

16

Societal Marketing

16.1 Introduction

Marketing practice is the subject of criticism and debate that essentially revolves around two themes:

1 Aspects of business malpractice are frequently associated with, or grouped under the umbrella of marketing. This is due to a misconception of marketing's true meaning. Added to this is the fact that marketing orientation, which puts customers at the centre of business activity, grew out of sales orientation. Sales orientation puts production at the centre, and its philosophy is the 'sharp practice' of selling excess production by forceful means as discussed in Chapter 1.
2 Social commentators question the ethics of marketing and its place in our social system. In a world of finite resources, they query whether we might be devoting too much to the gratification of materialistic wants to the detriment of the social good. It is suggested that marketing creates artificial wants and resources channelled into competitive advertising; branding and packaging are a waste of money and might be better employed elsewhere.

It is, however, acknowledged that marketing is not merely a business practice, but a social influence that can be used to improve the quality of life in its widest sense. This influence should not be patronising; rather it should be exercised in cooperation with the individuals and groups who are consumers of marketing's offerings.

Linked to the idea of marketing as a beneficial social force, is the extension of functional marketing into non-commercial activities. The pursuit of customer satisfaction is a valid aim irrespective of the profit motive. Marketing as a discipline is appropriate to the not-for-profit sector, because its practice obliges managers to think and act efficiently with end user needs in mind. Marketing is a style and philosophy of management that is not restricted to business. It also has social consequences. Implicit in true marketing-orientation is a recognition that business responsibility extends beyond a company's immediate customers.

This chapter examines the validity of criticism aimed against the marketing system and we must then develop our own opinions and consider marketing from these perspectives. The issue of 'consumerism' is meant to assist this process. The chapter also extends the marketing concept into issues of social marketing and marketing for non-profit making organisations.

16.2 Common criticisms of marketing

16.2.1 Customer dissatisfaction

The marketing system functions in an environment that seldom operates as theory predicts. This does not negate the value of theory, but one should be aware that the world of reality is not perfect and at best theory can only predict what is likely to happen. The marketing concept is often criticised when customer satisfaction is not achieved, but the concept at least provides a clear objective against which performance can be measured and necessary remedial action taken. The fact that companies acknowledge the marketing concept and pursue a customer-orientation does not excuse shortfalls in efficiency, but for many, 'marketing' has become a generic term for 'business activity'. Amongst those active in business are firms that pursue a short-term 'sales-orientated' approach. Thus, as well as genuinely marketing-orientated companies who are at times not too efficient, consumers must contend with companies whose short-term goal is profit and for whom customer satisfaction is sublimated. Criticisms levelled against such companies include:

1 poor product quality;
2 misleading packaging and labelling;
3 unreliable delivery;
4 poor after-sales service;
5 uninformative or offensive advertising.

Consumers have a right to be protected from such practices (see uninformative or offensive advertising see Pickton and Broderick, 2005, pp. 192–193). This protection is particularly necessary when the product or service is complicated (e.g. insurance and credit). Governments and consumer bodies have taken steps to enforce protective measures. It must be noted that consumer sovereignty is a powerful safeguard against malpractice and whilst it is not always the case, it is likely that companies that consistently fail to provide customer satisfaction will ultimately exhaust their supply of customers and go out of business (see Crane and Desmond, 2002, pp. 548–569). Customer pressure and legislation has decreased opportunities for companies to exploit consumers, and has increased marketing orientation by companies that act in their favour.

The main debate about marketing is not concerned with customer satisfaction. Criticisms are voiced by philosophers and social, economic and political commentators who question the ethos of the marketing system, looking at issues like the manipulation of society, efficient resource utilisation and the social effect of marketing on lifestyles and value systems. Brownlie and Saren (1992) have even argued that marketing has now outlined its usefulness.

16.2.2 Monopolies and limitation of consumer choice

The notion that marketing creates monopoly and limits consumer choice is a common criticism. The idea that some companies might become powerful enough to dictate what, how and where consumers buy is an issue. In reality, it is rare and temporarily the case that consumers have only one source of supply. The existence of Anti-trust laws in the USA and the Monopolies and Mergers Commission in the UK is evidence of official concern over monopolistic practices.

For the most part, laws and commissions have been established to curtail monopoly by acquisition. A state of monopoly that is reached by continued increase in market share is, to a great extent, a reflection of consumer choice. In a capitalist system, marketing allows companies that are successful to tend towards monopoly. Marketing's critics suggest that 'pure competition' affords consumers more varied choice. This argument has a sound theoretical basis, but one of the conditions for a state of pure competition is that all buyers and sellers have perfect knowledge, and buyers are 'economic' and 'rational' consumers. Studies of consumer behaviour show that this is rarely the case. Moreover, companies that tend towards monopoly are subject to competition from firms that attempt to differentiate and improve their products and services to gain market share through customer satisfaction. This is a powerful safeguard against risks of consumer exploitation.

This 'tempering' of power was aptly illustrated during the 1970s and 1980s:

1 At one point it seemed that a few large bakeries (in a powerful oligopoly) had begun to 'restrict' UK consumer choice to processed sliced bread. This product was initially adopted because it reflected consumer preference. The few companies involved in manufacture felt powerful enough to ignore market segments that preferred other varieties of bread, and made their manufacturing task easier by limiting consumer choice. After some time these large bakeries encountered powerful consumer resistance. Today supermarkets have 'in-store' bakeries and specialist independent bakers have experienced a revival.

2 Major breweries reduced their number of product lines and produced what was convenient and profitable, namely 'keg' beer. Breweries now provide beer whose selling points are traditional recipes and regional specialisation. These examples illustrate the power of consumer choice and sanction against companies who have neglected the marketing concept.

3 In the late 1970s in the UK major banks dominated the consumer market. They have been obliged to revise their product offerings because of legislation

and new initiatives taken by smaller banks, building societies and the Post Office.

It is argued that companies will gain power only as long as they fulfil the essential criteria of the marketing concept.

16.2.3 Inefficient utilisation of resources

A common criticism of marketing is that the marketing system is wasteful. Could not the enormous sums spent on advertising be better used in product development or simply reducing costs to consumers? It is not wasteful for companies to transport basically similar goods all over the country, when these companies could concentrate on their immediate locality at a reduced cost? In other words, it is proposed that scarce resources should be deployed on producing goods rather than marketing them.

There is a case to answer where advertising is purely competitive. In some countries, advertising which relies solely on direct comparison with competitive products is not permitted. In the UK, the Advertising Standards Authority (ASA) 'watchdog' body requires advertisements to be 'legal, decent, honest and truthful'. The existence of such a body is evidence that some companies abuse the power which media expenditure allows them.

Ideally, advertising should be an informative form of promotion. Creative and informative advertising plays a valid role in assisting consumer choice. Although it seems wasteful to devote large sums to the promotion of essentially similar products, several products would not exist were it not for the fact that consumers themselves demand product differentiation. Any interference in this process would limit consumer choice rather than promote consumer welfare. Moreover, the situation is self-regulating as companies cannot devote infinite sums to advertising. Advertising expenditure is an extra cost that is ultimately governed by the price the consumer is willing to pay.

Distribution costs are also criticised. Goods must be transported from manufacturer to user, but critics believe that marketing extends this transportation needlessly because many goods are generically similar. In fact, these goods are usually highly differentiated with respect to style, price and design.

As discussed in Chapter 8, the past 30 years has witnessed the retail structure in the UK alter significantly and we are now served essentially by national chains. This phenomenon is noticeable in 'do-it-yourself' supplies. Companies set up on the periphery of towns in so-called 'sheds' that are factory-type constructions. The result is that small hardware stores are rare today. Such distribution patterns are certainly efficient and the success of the 'superstores' would indicate that consumers are being satisfied. In the long term, consumers must decide whether convenience outweighs the potential disadvantage of choice restriction. Whilst a complicated distributive structure may appear wasteful in the 'macro' sense, the right of consumers to 'vote through the purse' is also important.

Distributive intermediaries are also criticised, and many retailers boast lower prices because they have 'cut out the middleman'. In many cases such claims are justified, but marketing intermediaries do perform valuable specialist functions that serve both consumers and manufacturers.

Critics of marketing must continually refer their arguments back to the issue of consumer choice. There is no evidence to suggest that in centrally planned economies, the distributive systems used to supply goods and services brings about greater consumer satisfaction. As was witnessed after the break-up of the Soviet Union, the converse might well be the case. The concept of 'marketing' enables consumers themselves to apply sanctions against inefficiency and waste.

16.2.4 Social effects of marketing on lifestyles and values

The idea that marketing promotes materialism and creates artificial needs and values is perhaps one of the most difficult concepts to debate. Marketing has been accused of creating a 'dependence effect' by creating and satisfying wants that do not originate with the consumer. There is no doubt that a great deal of marketing activity caters to materialism. It is considerably less certain that this is wrong in itself and if so, where blame should lie. A defender of marketing would maintain that the marketing system merely reflects society's values. But who should determine our values and material ambitions? It is true that as consumers we surround ourselves with possessions that we do not 'need' to sustain life. Psychologists argue that many material goods satisfy hidden inner needs and anthropologists point out that even amongst primitive societies, value is placed on many functionally useless possessions.

Another factor in the 'materialism' debate concerns quality of life or standard of living. Many consumer goods can be deemed materialistic, but most also provide a more comfortable way of life, reduce labour and release time to pursue other interests. At an individual level, many firms market goods and services whose value to society is questionable. At the macro level, marketing has done much to improve the quality of life generally, even though the perceived value is likely to differ between different sectors of society.

16.3 Consumerism

Arguments have been outlined for and against the marketing system in a socio-economic context at a 'macro' level. The modern day consumer movement, which had its roots in the 1970s, is mainly involved in specific issues. However, consumerism has macro dimensions and is responsible for much of the social awareness displayed by many business organisations today. Such companies do not view consumerism as a threat, but as a movement that can be responded to positively, so as to serve their customers and society more effectively. There are, however, companies that have neglected the marketing concept and their social responsibilities and such customers have a right to consumer protection and advice (see Brassington and Pettitt, 2005, pp. 42–45).

The organised 'consumer movement' had its origins in the USA. At first, its actions were sporadic in response to specific events in the early part of this century. The consumerist phenomenon really began to be noticed in the late 1950s. Social commentators such as Vance Packard and Rachael Carson began to alert the American public to the idea that the business community was more concerned with its own welfare than that of its customers. Vance Packard's book *The Hidden Persuaders* (1957) challenged the advertising industry and Rachael Carson's *Silent Spring* (1962, re-published 2002) attacked the business community for its neglect of, and disregard for, the environment. The idea that individuals could combat the power of huge corporations had been unimaginable until Ralph Nader published his indictment of the automobile industry, *Unsafe at any Speed: The Designed-In Dangers of the American Automobile* (1965), which was particularly aimed at General Motors. This, and other campaigns, signified the foundation of organised consumerism.

In the UK, the movement gained momentum more slowly, and its roots can be traced back to the magazine *Which*, published by the Consumers' Association which was established in the 1960s. The magazine selects, tests and classifies products and services according to their relative performance. Such information was initially received with great interest, as the idea was totally new to British consumers. Perhaps more important than the specific information that *Which* provided, was the conceptual breakthrough of the idea that consumers need not accept the offerings of manufacturers without question and had a right to express their opinions about what was offered for sale. It was no coincidence that companies began to adopt the marketing concept as a business orientated philosophy at the same time as consumers began to realise the potential of their influence.

Consumerism can be defined as 'a social movement seeking to augment the rights and power of buyers in relation to sellers'. Consumerism, therefore, accepts that both parties have rights.

Buyers have the right:

1 not to buy products offered to them,
2 to expect the product to be safe,
3 to expect that the product is essentially the same as the seller has stated.

Sellers have the right:

1 to introduce any product in any style or size, provided it is not injurious to health and safety, and provided potentially hazardous products are supplied together with appropriate warnings;
2 to price products at any level, provided that there is no discrimination amongst similar classes of buyers;
3 to say what they like in the promotion of their products, provided that any message is not dishonest or misleading in content or execution;
4 to spend any amount of money they wish in order to promote their products and to introduce any buying incentive schemes, providing that are not deemed to be unfair competition.

The idea of 'consumer sovereignty' or 'consumer veto' is central to arguments used to defend marketing. This power should never be underestimated and is the consumer's chief weapon against business malpractice. A serious problem is the fact that if companies deliberately set out to deceive customers, the consumer is distinctly disadvantaged. Consumerists, therefore, rightly emphasise that the obligation is on business organisations to provide satisfactory goods in the first place. Why should customers only be able to veto goods and services after having been initially disappointed? The consumer movement augments the basic 'buyers' rights' just described, by specifically stating what should be expected of the seller.

In 1962, President John F Kennedy, in keeping with the mood of that era in the USA, made a classic declaration on consumer rights that still forms the basis of modern day consumerism. He proposed:

1 *The right to safety*: The consumer should be able to expect that there are no 'hidden dangers' incorporated into the product. Companies must seek safe alternatives to additives and components that are known to be harmful. In particular, the pharmaceutical industry can make consumers vulnerable if adequate testing is not carried out. The drugs Thalidomide and Opren have provided test cases in this respect. The suitability of polyurethane foam in upholstery, which can be a fire hazard, was a poignant *cause célèbre* of consumerism. Unfortunately, it is true that in many cases, legislation is necessary before positive steps are taken to reduce risks. Some manufacturers argue that consumers are unwilling to pay the higher prices that product improvements would require. Consumerists can at least alert buyers to potential risks before they make a choice between economy and safety.

2 *The right to be informed*: Whilst consumerists can increase consumer knowledge for many product categories, they might argue that the 'typical' consumer does not have the time, skills or specialist knowledge with which to make choices or understand product information if it is couched in technical jargon. Consumers have the right to expect sellers to provide the maximum relevant information about their products in an understandable manner (see Cates *et al.*, 2004, pp. 67–84, for an interesting discussion on the need for labelling information in the food industry). Consumers can only make reasoned purchase decisions after having received comprehensible information. Misleading product information can be conveyed in guarantees, product labelling, advertising and 'small print'. The travel industry is often criticised in this respect (see Webster, 2001, p. 18).

3 *The right to choose*: Closely linked with need for protection of the customer against misleading information is the right of safeguard against confusing information. In order to make a reasoned objective choice consumers should be able to distinguish 'real' competition in manufacturers' promotions. Products should be presented in such a way that is relatively simple for consumers to relate quality and quantity to cost before making purchases.

4 *The right to be heard*: Consumers have the right to express dissatisfaction not only to suppliers, but to other parties so attention can be focused on poor

service and product performance. This right implies the existence of a mechanism for redress should a product prove unsatisfactory. The need for a mechanism that is organised and watched over by an external body is important as manufacturers and consumers have become more distanced from each other. In the case of faulty goods, consumers sometimes find it confusing and difficult to discover to whom a complaint should be addressed. In the UK, the Consumers' Association and 'watchdog' TV programmes fulfil this role. However, for the vast majority of goods and services on sale today, there is never any need for recourse to such measures.

In addition to Kennedy's rights, two more rights can be added that reflect modern day circumstances:

5 *The right to privacy*: With the information revolution has come an increase in direct marketing through database management (see Fletcher, 2001, pp. 128–41). Much of the promotional material that is distributed in this way is beneficial to consumers and it is possible to make more directly targeted approaches to potential customers that are more likely to fit recipients' social class and consumption profiles. However, some people take the view that use of their details in databases is an invasion of privacy and view such approaches as invasive 'junk mail'. They now have the right to be able to remove their details from such mailing lists through the 'Data Protection Act' (see Chaffey *et al.*, 2003, pp. 87–88).

6 *The right to a clean and healthy environment*: Ecological awareness is a significant issue nowadays. Organisations like 'Greenpeace' and 'Friends of the Earth' have shed their eccentric image and achieved 'respectability' that they did not possess twenty years ago (see Laschefski and Freris, 2001, pp. 40–43). Indeed, it is through many of the issues with which they have been associated that environmental legislation has followed and environmental polluters have been prosecuted. Recently, the government has introduced a voluntary 'environmental initiative' in which companies are subject to inspection and 'certification' that their manufacturing processes does not pollute the environment. At the time of writing there is fierce debate in relation to GM crop trials.

The consumerist movement has come a long way in obtaining a 'fair deal' for consumers. Companies are now more 'consumer aware'. In the early 1960s many companies actually believed that customers' needs and wants were being adequately satisfied. Consumerism has been an education process, as well as a 'policing mechanism'. Whether consumers are better served today because companies have made voluntary changes, or because they have been coerced, is not important; the fact is that individual consumers do receive a far better treatment from manufacturers and service providers.

Companies should develop their own customer orientation and concern for consumer welfare. Unfortunately, in order to protect consumers from companies who have not accepted this challenge, it has been necessary for governments to take action. Whilst UK Governments and the legal system have always taken an interest in 'fair trading', the 1970s in particular witnessed the Government's increasing concern for consumer affairs – spurred on by the consumer movement. The following list of statutes allows some insight into the nature of this development.

Some examples of statutory instruments for consumer protection:

Aerosol dispensers (EEC requirements) regulations (1977)
Babies dummies (safety) regulations (1978)
Business advertisements (disclosure) order (1977)
Consumer credit (credit reference agency) regulations (1977)
Consumer Credit act (1974)
Consumer Protection Act (1987)
Consumer Safety Act (1978)
Cooking utensils (safety) regulations (1972)
Cosmetic products regulations (1978)
Electric blankets (safety) regulations (1971)
Fair Trading Act (1973)
Hire Purchase Act (1973)
Mail order transactions (information) order (1976)
Nightdresses (safety) regulations (1967)
Price marking (bargain offers) order (1979)
Pyramid selling schemes regulations (1973)
Resale Prices Acts (1964 and 1976)
Supply of Goods (Implied Terms) Acts (1973, 1982)
Toys (safety) regulations (1974)
Unsolicited Goods and Services Acts (1971 and 1975)

In the UK there is no single 'consumer law' or specific code for consumer protection. In broad terms, the two most pertinent statutes relating to the consumer are the 'Sale of Goods Act (1979)', one in a series of Sale of Goods acts since 1893, and the 'Trade Descriptions Act (1972)'. In addition to these and other legal measures, the Government established the 'Office of Fair Trading' and appointed a Minister for Consumer Affairs. The 'Office of Fair Trading' was established in 1973 and together with the 'Consumer Protection Advisory Committee' was designed to monitor the activities of the business world, investigate and publish information in consumers' interests. In liaison with industry, the Office encouraged self-regulatory activities and helped to establish Trade Associations.

All local authorities have 'Trading Standards Departments' that oversee the proper execution of the 'Weights and Measures' and 'Food and Drugs Acts' as well as acting in an advisory capacity to consumers in cases of dispute, a task which was supported and developed by 'Consumer Advice Centres' since 1972. These were, however, abolished in 1980 on the premise that consumerism was beginning to protect consumers too much, to the commercial detriment of manufacturers.

When the impact of the consumer movement was first felt, many companies felt threatened by the apparent restrictions that the movement sought to impose. In truth, consumerism helped business to identify its own shortcomings as well as the real needs of its customers. Many companies benefited by adopting a positive stance, and instead of attempting to hide product defects, made safety, honesty and service product 'features' including initiatives in areas of labelling, pricing and credit agreements. Such features enabled companies to appeal to the psychological, as well as physical needs of buyers.

Consumerism is now a permanent feature of society as there is always a need for vigilance against opportunist sellers. Consumerism is involved with broader socio-economic issues as well as basic aspects of consumer protection. Many consumers now feel positive about environmentalism, ethical treatment of animals (see *The Grocer* 2001, p. 23) and firer trade with developing countries (see Watson, 2001, pp. 38–39). They are also concerned with pricing issues at macro, in addition to micro, levels. Consumer bodies now discuss these issues with governments. To this extent, consumerism has graduated from involvement in specific issues that affect small sections of the population to an interest and involvement in those issues that affect society as a whole.

Marketing has undergone a similar evolution. A new perspective on the marketing concept must be adopted if firms are to prosper in a way that is acceptable to society. The essence of the marketing concept is still customer satisfaction and this must be achieved through a social as well as customer orientation (see Wright, 2004, pp. 146–148, for a discussion of business ethics in a business to business context).

16.4 Social marketing

Marketing, as defined by the marketing concept, is a management system with customer satisfaction being the object of marketing effort. Any extension to this definition simply adds to marketing's remit, but the basic tenet of customer orientation remains unchanged. The concept of social marketing holds that business activity should satisfy and be acceptable to 'society' as well as to targeted customer groups; it refers to the study of markets and marketing activity within a total social system.

The requirement that marketing be socially acceptable is not new; it has existed as long as organised trading has been practiced. The recognition of the role of social marketing has, however, gained momentum and crystallized in the past 30 years. Two factors have accelerated this development:

1 Sociologists and economists identified the phenomenon of the post-industrial society. During the twentieth century, the major thrust of business activity centred on the provision of basic commodities. Compared with the previous decade in the nineteenth century, disposable income was severely limited. Even during the 1950s and 1960s, the aftermath of the Second World War restricted the availability and the means to obtain gods and services that could be described as luxury items. Although poverty has not been entirely

eliminated in developed nations, during the past two decades living standards have improved to such an extent that the basic needs and wants of a large proportion of their populations have been fulfilled. This has led to more people being able to choose how to spend an augmented disposable income and increased leisure time in what has been described as the 'affluent society'. Marketing management has been efficient in catering for the affluent society, and in fulfilling society's so called 'meta-needs'. The affluence of the post-industrial society has brought with social costs that are linked to profound changes in society's value systems. Perhaps it is not the task of marketing to dictate what is good or otherwise for society. It is certainly the remit of 'social marketing' to question whether products and services on offer have a detrimental effect on society. This social awareness should also be used in an attempt to ascertain whether consumers are really receiving satisfaction and whether the products on offer provide long-term benefits to the quality of life, or whether they are merely for short-term gratification. Critics of marketing hold marketing partially responsible for 'cultural pollution'. Social marketing does not imply acceptance of 'guilt', but its existence implies that such views should be respected and considered seriously.

2 The second spur to the development of social marketing concerns scarcity of the earth's basic resources relative to the abundance of manufactured goods as well as the way in these goods are produced. Marketing's success in providing for our material needs and wants has also contributed to their existence. The environmentalist is concerned with issues like pollution, waste, congestion and ecological imbalance. Social marketing recognises that it is not enough to provide customer satisfaction if, in doing so, society as a whole is adversely affected. The social marketer's task is to find new products or new production methods that do not pollute damage or deplete scarce resources.

Two important and complex questions face today's marketing practitioners:

1 The debate can be simplified by considering the obviously harmful results that can be directly attributed to marketing action. The causes of industrial pollution are usually easy to identify and quite often an alternative process can be devised which reduces or eliminates the problem. Such remedies can, however, be costly, and the question that is posed is whether the consumer is prepared to pay for a safer environment, or whether this cost should be borne by the producer? The issue of 'lead in petrol' provides an example of social marketing in action. The help of the Government (which has kept the price of unleaded petrol lower than that of leaded petrol) combined with an open-minded attitude by consumers, has enabled a compromise to be reached that provides a needed product at a reduced social cost. Oil companies have been prepared to invest in research into unleaded petrol, in return for which consumers have been asked to accept modifications in their product usage.

2 The second question deals with a philosophical issue that cannot be easily answered. How much, for example, should governments or religious bodies

influence our lives? Certainly consumers (in the form of society as a whole) are largely responsible for their own social and moral welfare. What steps do individual consumers take in order to minimise pollution or reduce wasteful consumption of energy? Usually, some external, organised body coordinates such actions. Consumerists call for social responsibility in business, but say little about the need for consumers to also accept a share of the responsibility.

Marketing is a social force that not only transmits a standard of living, but it reflects and influences cultural values and norms. Marketing can use its influence and expertise to work for the 'social good' in areas where it is popularly accepted that there is scope for improvement. For example:

1 automobiles (pollution, congestion and safety),
2 foodstuffs (additives, preservatives and pesticides),
3 packaging (non-biodegradable materials),
4 manufacturing (pollution, noise and safety).

Social marketing addresses these problems by seeking ways to provide customer satisfaction at a reduced 'social cost'. Consumerism and government legislation have, to some extent, coerced companies into a more socially responsible approach to their activities. Many companies have made voluntary moves towards social orientation. Manufacturers are putting more thought into packaging design by providing their goods in less wasteful packages that can be disposed of more easily. Aerosol manufacturers have discontinued use of a propellant that damaged the earth's ozone layer. While acknowledging that product costs and performance will always be keys to success, producers have been urged to take on responsibility and liability for the products they sell.

Marketing's critics argue that such examples of a social orientation are attempts to gain popular appeal. We cannot always be sure of the motivation behind moves towards social marketing, but this is not really the issue. Whatever the motives behind such a shift in a company's business orientation, it is good that such movements are occurring. Whether these initiatives originate from within the company or are prompted by external pressure is irrelevant to consumer satisfaction. In the long term, however, it is preferable that social initiatives in marketing are made by the companies involved. Progress in social orientation is likely to be more beneficial and enduring if business is the voluntary initiator of social change, than if change is imposed through external agents like government legislation.

Although social orientation benefits consumer, marketing practitioners face considerable problems in implementing socially orientated strategies. In particular, many socially desirable modifications to products and marketing strategy involve extra costs for which the consumer is not prepared to pay. Automobile production is an example of an industry that is able to provide added safety features, such as anti-lock braking systems, where price is less sensitive, but they cannot easily incorporate such modifications into the sensitive lower price ranges.

The onus is on marketing to find ways of improving products at minimum extra cost, but consumers should be prepared to make some financial contribution towards their own welfare.

Our concerned is not with matters that are 'functional' in the marketing sense. Marketing's social responsibilities imply a transition from a pure 'management' orientation. However, this added dimension does not suggest that profit is unimportant. Profit is the essential element of a company's survival, and companies cannot implement social programmes without financial security.

16.5 Marketing in not-for-profit organizations

There is a distinction between 'managerial' or 'systems' marketing and the wider remit of a 'societal' or a socially orientated approach to marketing. Non-profit-making organisations are an example of a reverse of the marketing transition that should be made by progressive companies. For the most part, non-profit organisations already perform roles designed to cater for social, rather than commercial, needs. To this extent, their social orientation is already established and what is required is the adoption of managerial marketing techniques to accomplish their tasks.

It may seem strange that services like the Health Service, Public Libraries or the Police Force should consider that marketing has anything to offer them. On further investigation, many parallels can be drawn between the functions of the 'profit' and 'not-for-profit' sectors.

Non-profit organisations have 'products' (usually services) and 'consumers' (users) and they function through organisational structures of purchasing, production and personnel. A parallel for 'selling' is not so readily apparent. For example, in a public hospital 'customers' have little opportunity to exercise choice because of scarce resources and the fact that one hospital is not really acting in competition with another. Marketing implies customer satisfaction and in this respect, those who are directly involved with consumers in non-profit organisations have roles similar to those of sales personnel. This is not to suggest that doctors or nurses perform a 'sales function' in the accepted sense. They are, however, the last link between the organisation and the user, and in this sense they represent the organisation and influence consumer attitudes towards its service/product. In addition to the physical similarities of profit and non-profit organisations they both have marketing problems, although this fact is not generally declared. To a certain extent the government has attempted to address this in respect of health care with the introduction of General Practitioner 'fund-holder' status and 'Hospital Trusts' with the object of making them more accountable in financial and marketing terms.

The business sector is often criticised for poor marketing. Ultimately, unless companies resolve their marketing problems, consumers have the sanction of placing their custom elsewhere. The public sector receives criticism that is often frustrated and aggravated by the fact that in most cases the sanction of choice does not exist. Not-for-profit organisations, whose customer-orientation is poor, are still able to function, but when criticism develops into resentment, the task becomes increasingly difficult.

If we recognise that not-for-profit organisations have marketing structures and marketing problems, we can then use marketing functions as tools for more effective action. The most important element of marketing for non-profit organisations is 'communication'. Commercial enterprises find customers and communicate with them in order to make sales. In the non-commercial sector it is easy to lose touch with customers. The idea that non-profit organisations can take their users for granted can be likened to sales-orientation.

In non-profit situations, marketing-orientation involves defining what the organisation is attempting to supply or achieve which is similar to defining the market in the commercial sector. A public library does more than provide books. It also serves as a meeting place, a support to local schools and a source of information for a wide range of commercial activities. When seen through a marketing orientation, libraries are involved in providing 'leisure' and 'information'.

Not-for-profit organisations should fulfil their functions through the marketing mix. Apart from 'price', the mix elements are no different to those for commercial product or service marketing. The emphasis in the marketing mix varies according to the task. A local police force may place emphasis on public relations in order to foster a favourable image of the police within their community to facilitate the functional tasks of policing. The police visit schools so children can get to know them better and understand their place in the community. Police forces hold 'open days' and run public relations campaigns and view their task as a far wider one than catching criminals.

16.6 Quality and marketing

Quality should be integrated at all levels in a company and for this to have meaning; marketing must be integrated throughout the company. This means that designers must fully understand customer requirements that must be translated to the production process with the final link being to produce the product when the customer wants it, and at the right price. Engineering, without a true understanding of customer needs, can result in customer dissatisfaction. Equally, a marketing team, cut off from its technological base, is impotent and cannot hope to accurately interpret the capabilities of the company in relation to customer requirements. There must be a balance between these disparate functions and remove the exclusivity of the 'marketing' label, because marketing is what everybody does and gives rise to the notion of the 'part-time marketer' (PTM) where everybody in the organization is responsible for satisfying customer needs. Similarly, the concept of total quality management (TQM) holds that every member of the organisation is responsible for the image and service that the company puts forward. These two aspects are inseparable in helping to provide customer satisfaction.

TQM is a powerful tool if it is introduced to each audience in the right way. This is due to the differences in 'mind set' between marketing and manufacturing. By careful selection of methods of introduction it is possible for all to embrace the process so that it can interface between marketing and manufacturing and between other functions effectively. In order to break down departmental barriers so that staff from different departments can work together to tackle problem solving (known as 'continuous improvement processes') many companies have set up quality improvement teams so that synergy exists and interfaces between marketing, production, quality, purchasing and human resource management and this theme was elaborated in Chapter 13. The role of marketing in quality improvement teams is to be assured that the organisation is doing the right things in terms of building customer valued quality products.

Taeger (1992) reported that the 3M Document Systems Group have formed a corrective action team to introduce improvements involving members of sales, marketing and other departments to look at the distribution of camera cards. By a process of communicating with each other, and reaching a consensus opinion about the important areas of business and how well the group was performing in these areas, the team has substantially improved the operation of the business.

Best practice benchmarking (BPB) as defined by the DTI (1993) involves the formation of a project team comprising people from multifunctional areas such as marketing production, quality and purchasing. The team's task is to obtain information on products or companies that have a higher level of performance or activity and to identify areas in their own organisation that need improving. The team needs to be given the facility for research on product development and quality. Because of the benefits of shared knowledge in this multifunctional team, companies that implement BPB should find that this will drive members of the team to meet new standards or even exceed them.

16.7 Summary

16.7.1 The macro dimension

Research by Sheth (1992) has shown that four macroeconomic forces are shaping global marketing strategies:

1 regional integration;
2 technology advances (e.g. the adoption of information technology in business [Stalk *et al.*, 1992]);
3 emergence of an ideology free world and the role of the market economy policy;
4 borderless economies due to global sourcing and competition (Schill and McArthur, 1992).

To seek dominant market share organisations may want to expand their marketing and manufacturing efforts to other geographical areas and attain economies of scale through increased systemisation and interconnection between the process operations. Flexibility becomes a greater component of manufacturing systems that allows relatively small batches to be produced on a mass production bases.

Unisys Corporation's flexible manufacturing system enables it to assemble up to 2,500 printed circuit boards per week in 64 different configurations, having 1,327 components. The system enables time to market to be reduced significantly because the components can be assembled in any sequence and even in lot sizes of one. Market segmentation is of course an important issue here. Willigan (1992) has reported that even high-powered marketing companies such as Nike have continued 'slicing up' their product ranges to add diversity. Kasturirangan *et al.* (1993) state that mature industrial markets have resorted to trade-offs, tailoring the mix for particular homogeneous needs, and so leading to better use of resources.

There is recognition that there must be a change from a production/cost-dominated strategy towards one of servicing the diverse needs of global customers through marketing. This process of inter-dependence formation has led to the development of relationship marketing that involves building long-term relationships with customers through the practice of 'retention economics'. As the strategic geographical perspective of companies has changed from domestic to international marketing, then the marketing paradigm has transformed from a transactional focus to a relationship focus. Customer focused quality is also important as it involves a move towards customer targeted activity. As we move towards a global economy customers demand even better quality and place increasing importance on reliability, durability, ease of use and service.

16.7.2 From competitive strategy to strategic marketing

Schill and McArthur (1992) contend that a new thinking emanated in the 1980s known as the 'competitive strategy' era. An integrated/functional role within the overall task of formulating and implementing corporate competitive strategy, led marketing theorists to take on a new dimension known as 'strategic marketing'. This attempted to integrate manufacturing, finance, human resource and other functions with marketing to support a cohesive competitive strategy focusing on such matters as cost leadership and product differentiation. The notion was established that company-wide solutions were necessary in providing solutions to customers' problems.

Manufacturing supports overall business objectives through the design and utilisation of suitable manufacturing resources and capabilities. Alignment of manufacturing and marketing strategies will contribute significantly to the overall success of the organisation. Marketing led strategies are usually based on the principles of growth throughout the product range. The relationship between marketing objectives and manufacturing strategies appears to be a critical factor affecting the success of the organisation, but the nature of this relationship is not well defined. Piercy (1991) refers to the 'strategic internal market' that should have the goal of developing a marketing programme aimed at the internal marketplace in a company that parallels and matches the marketing programme aimed at the external marketplace of customers and competitors. This model comes from a simple observation that the implementation of external marketing strategies implies changes of various kinds within organisations – in the allocation of resources, in the culture of 'how we do things here' and even in the organisational structures needed to deliver marketing strategies effectively in customer segments.

The role of marketing should be seen as one of co-ordination across the company's functional units. This is critical because each department is likely to have different views of customers. Sheth (1992) summarises it when he says:

> It will become increasingly important for the left hand to know what the right hand is doing, especially in the market boundary of front line personnel in procurement, manufacturing, selling and service market offerings.

The social, ethical and economic issues of marketing look at managerial systems from a 'bird's eye' viewpoint. If we are to broaden our marketing scope further we must turn to other disciplines to gain an objective view of marketing's place in society. The role of profit in marketing assumes a capitalist economic system. A study of politics and economics allows the student to consider other systems. The ethical and moral questions raised by marketing can also be considered with reference to sociology that can help us understand how and why the population reacts to marketing activity.

It is contended that quality as well as marketing must permeate the entire manufacturing operation and this has given rise to the notion of TQM and the PTM. As marketing becomes central to all business activity so its role changes from being a function of management to that of a company wide philosophy that has total quality as its driving force.

References

Brassington, F. and Pettitt, S. (2005), *Essentials of Marketing*, Financial Times, London: Prentice-Hall, pp. 42–45.

Brownlie, D. and Saren, M. (1992), 'The four P's of the marketing concept: prescription, polemic, permanent and problematical, *European Journal of Marketing*,' 26(4), 34–47.

Carson, R. (1962), *Silent Spring*, Boston, USA: Houghton Mifflin (original edition).

Carson, R. (1965), *Silent Spring*, Harmondsworth: Penguin Books, ISBN: 0-14-013891-9.

Cates, S.C., Carter-Young, H.L., Puro, E.L., Post, R.C. and Manka, A. (2004), 'Consumer attitudes towards and preference for food standards of identity', *Journal of Food Products Marketing*, 10(1), 67–84.

Chaffey, D., Mayer, R., Johnson, K. and Ellis-Chadwich, F. (2003), *Internet Marketing, Strategy, Implementation and Practice*, Financial Times, London: Prentice-Hall, pp. 87–88.

Crane, A. and Desmond, J. (2002), 'Societal marketing and morality', *European Journal of Marketing*, 36(5–6), 548–569.

DTI, (1993), *Best Practice Benchmarking*, London: Department of Trade and Industry.

Fletcher, K. (2001), 'Privacy: the Achilles heel of the new marketing', *Interactive Marketing*, 3(2), 128–141.

Kasturirangan, V., Moriaty, R.T. and Swartz, G.S. (1992), 'Segmenting customers in mature industrial markets', *Journal of Marketing*, 56(2), 89.

Kotler, P. and Andreasen, A.R. (1991), *Strategic Marketing for Non-Profit Organisations*, Englewood Cliffs, NJ: Prentice-Hall.

Laschefski, K. and Freris, N. (2001), 'Saving the wood', *The Ecologist*, July–August, 40–43.

Nader, R. (1965), Unsafe at any Speed; the Designed-in Dangers of the American Automobile (Unknown Binding), ISBN B00005X2CK, *Published personally by Ralph Nader*.

Nader, R. (1991), *Unsafe at any Speed; the Designed-in Dangers of the American Automobile*, Reprint, 25th Anniversary edition, MA: Knightsbridge Pub Co, ISBN: 1561290505.

Packard, V. (1957), *The Hidden Pursuaders*, New York: Random House.

Piercy, N. (1991), *Market-led Strategic Change*, London: Thorsons, p. 367.

Pickton, D. and Broderick, A. (2005), *Integrated Marketing Communications*, Financial Times, London: Prentice-Hall, pp. 192–193.

Schill, R.L. and McArthur, D.N. (1992), Redefining the strategic competitive unit: towards a new global marketing paradigm, *International Marketing Review*, 9(3), 5–23.

Sheth, J. N. (1992), Emerging marketing strategies in a changing macroeconomic environment: a commentary, *International Marketing Review*, 9(1), 57–63.

Stalk, G., Evans, P. and Schulman, L. E. (1992), Competing of capabilities: the new rules of corporate strategy, *Harvard Business Review*, April, pp. 57–69.

Taeger, D. (1992), 3M's got it taped, *Total Quality Management*, December, pp. 1–5.

The Grocer (2001), 'Reassuring consumers', *The Grocer*, 5 May, p. 23.

Watson, E. (2001), 'Blind tasting', *The Grocer*, 9 June, pp. 38–39.

Webster, B. (2001), 'BA faces claim for "failing to warn" health danger', *The Times*, 31 July, p. 18.

Willigan, G. E. (1992), 'High performance marketing', *Harvard Business Review*, July, p. 104.

Wright, R. (2004), *Business to Business Marketing: A Step by Step Guide*, Financial Times, Harlow, UK: Prentice-Hall, pp. 146–148.

Further reading

Buxton, P. (2000), 'Companies with a social conscience', *Marketing*, 27 April, pp. 33–34.

Carroll, A. (1991), The pyramid of corporate social responsibility: Toward the moral management of organizational stakeholders, *Business Horizons*, 34, 39–48.

Challener, C. (2001), 'Sustainable development at a cross-roads', *Chemical Market Reporter*, 16th July, pp. 3–4.

Kolah, A. (2002), *Essential Law for Marketers*, Butterworth-Heinemann.

Post, J.E., Lawrence, A.T. and Weber, J. (2001), '*Contemporary Issues in Business with Readings*', New York: McGraw-Hill.

Slevin, J. (2000), *The Internet and Society*, Cambridge, MA: Polity Press.

The Economist (2000), 'The politics of whaling', *The Economist*, 9th September, p. 42.

Zugelder, M., Flaherty, T. and Johnson, J. (2000), 'Legal Issues Associated with International Internet Marketing', *International Marketing Review*, 17(3), 253–271.

Questions

Question 16.1

Use of marketing by non-profit organisations
Marketing is increasingly being used by non-profit organisations such as colleges, libraries and political parties. What is the relevance of the marketing concept to the non-profit organisation and why are such organisations making more use of the techniques of marketing?

Question 16.2

Consumerism
Discuss the notion that in a society that has embraced the concept of free enterprise, business should be allowed to get on with its wealth creating activities without interference from consumerists.

Question 16.3

Ethics
Marketing has been criticised both on economic and ethical grounds. Discuss these criticisms, indicating how far you think they are justified.

Question 16.4

Quality
How is marketing involved in the company wide process of total quality management?

Question 16.5

Strategic marketing
How do you view the scenario as put forward by Sheth that marketing should be viewed as one of co-ordination across an organisation's functional units? How can it be implemented?

Discuss the recent developments which collectively have become known as 'green marketing' (i.e. sympathetic to environmental, ecological and related issues) and the likely importance of such issues to marketing firms over the next decade.

Do marketing firms really care about ethical and moral issues or are their actions in this direction simply a cynical exploitation of customers fears?
Is the notion of free market profit maximising forms compatible with business ethics?

17
International Marketing

17.1 Introduction

People have traded surplus goods and produce for centuries. The framework for international trade was laid down at the turn of the nineteenth Century trading although this was 'one-sided' in favour of Britain. During the twentieth Century, as the British Empire in particular diminished, trade between nations evolved on a fairer and more meaningful buyer/seller basis. Some nations possess natural resources in excess of their needs which have a value placed on them by other nations and this forms the basis of trading.

Since the advent of industrialisation the concept of 'trading' has become more complicated. Human expectations have risen such that people are no longer content with the basic essentials of life. Manufacturers have responded by producing goods designed to fulfil these higher expectations. In order for economies to grow and develop, they must earn revenue that comes from outside their own countries. Governments have a vested interest in promoting international trade and to attempt to ensure that their balance of trade is not adverse.

The marketing concept has developed and been accepted as a way of business management that is valid internationally. The pursuit of customer satisfaction that is demanding in home markets requires additional skills when operating in internationally. A new marketing mix that caters for differences in language and culture is often developed to suit foreign markets. International marketing involves precise documentation, and is often frustrating when dealing with problems not normally encountered in home-based marketing, but it can be very rewarding. The late John F. Kennedy contended: 'world trade leads to world peace'.

17.2 Defining sub-divisions of international activity

Confusion exists between the terms 'global', 'multinational marketing', 'international marketing' and 'exporting'.

The term 'global' refers to organisations with a presence on every continent of the world with the possible exception of Antarctica. Multinational marketing refers to a relatively small number of companies whose business interests, manufacturing plants and offices are spread throughout the world. Although the overall strategic headquarters and control may be based in an original 'parent' country, multinational company presences operate alongside their national counterparts so they are not immediately distinguishable from them. Multinational companies are not principally exporters; they actually produce and market goods within the countries they have chosen to develop (see McAuley, 2001, pp. 4–5).

The difference between exporting and international marketing is less clear-cut. A company that engages in simple exporting considers it to be a peripheral activity. Most firms have some export involvement, and the term 'exporting' is commonly applied to firms whose export activity represent less than 20% of total turnover. This implies that their international activities are sporadic and lacking in commitment to the degree of modification they should be prepared to make to their products and marketing mix strategy to sell successfully in overseas markets (see Fillis, 2002, pp. 912–927, for a discussion on barriers to internationalisation among smaller enterprises and also Knight, 2000, pp. 12–32, for a further discussion of international marketing in a small firm context).

A company's overseas activities can be described as international marketing once overseas sales account for more than 20% of turnover, at which point it is reasonable to assume that a company has made a firm strategic commitment to overseas involvement. The term implies:

1 a strategic decision has been taken to enter foreign markets;
2 the necessary organisational changes have been carried out;
3 product and marketing mix adaptations for these markets have been made;
4 the company has made 'mental' and 'attitudinal' adjustments appropriate to an international marketing strategy.

In essence, international marketing is concerned with any conscious marketing activity that crosses national frontiers. Multinational corporations and exporters (as just defined) represent extremes on the international marketing scale. Between these two extremes are firms who market overseas and who are involved in some way in distributing their products from home manufacturing bases.

Many companies have developed their overseas activities by means of licensing agreements or joint ventures. Such forms of distribution are discussed later and the concepts of marketing are as pertinent to them as to home manufacturer/overseas customer arrangements. International marketing is not separate from national marketing: the underlying marketing concept is still valid.

It is considered separately here because of the frequent, and often essential, requirements for modifications to the marketing approach (see Fletcher, 2001, pp. 25–49, for a discussion of such an approach). The product may need to be physically modified, and international marketing might require that a firm modifies its internal organisation. Even when products are left physically unchanged, to be successful overseas, it may be necessary to employ completely different marketing mix strategies from those in operation in the domestic market.

The 'rules' for international marketing are no different from those applied to home-based marketing. Management must set objectives that its international strategy should achieve. This strategy must be implemented through the marketing mix being organised in a way that is appropriate to the market being considered. It is likely that an individual marketing mix strategy will need to be developed for each market. Marketing research, advertising and promotion, packaging or sales management all possess the same rationale in both market types; what differs is the way these functions are performed.

The design and implementation of an advertising campaign or a marketing research survey is often more difficult in international markets. Language and culture are the principal areas of difficulty. Physical communication can sometimes pose additional problems for international marketers. 'Face-to-face' contact is the best way of conducting negotiations, but even in a firm that has a large-scale international commitment, day-to-day international communication can be limited compared to domestic activities.

The Internet offers unique international marketing opportunities for companies and customers to communicate with each other via a mass medium on a new mediated environment. Business firms and customers are now in positions to build relationships with one another effectively and cost efficiently (see Chaffey et al., 2003, pp. 71–72, for a discussion on the number of UK and other international firms with access to the Internet). They can learn on an individual basis how to satisfy needs and wants of their customers by using Internet technologies. At the same time, the new medium also challenges business, because the Web and its relationship-marketing 'business model' may conflict with more established marketing methods. Using a hypermedia computer mediated environment (HCME), which is what the Internet and the WWW actually is, is very different from conventional marketing media and ways of carrying out the marketing task.

Firms will need to redefine their businesses in terms of organisational structure, production, marketing, communications, sales, after sales services and overall strategic planning processes. Successful web strategies can only be achieved by embracing the medium proactively and from a complete organisational point of view. It should be part of overall and comprehensive corporate strategies formulated by the top management. Internet marketing strategies should be integrated within the entire organisation and it should not be viewed as simply an additional marketing and advertising channel. It has opened the immense opportunities for business people to reach the global sourcing. The Internet will be the most cost effective business place.

Whatever market is considered, the underlying marketing concept does not change. International marketing can be demanding and companies considering international markets should be aware that additional and different demands are made in fulfilling what is already a difficult task.

17.3 Why enter international markets?

Some firms originate with the intention of seeking international involvement. The products or services they offer may be so specialised that the domestic market alone will not provide sufficient sales. This is commonplace in industrial markets where, for example, specialist machinery manufacturers make relatively few sales because the rate of repeat purchase is low. Although the value of each sale may be high, the interval between repurchasing dictates that as wide a market as possible must be sought. Other firms may start out on the basis of having identified a buoyant foreign market (see Segal-Horn, 2002, pp. 8–19, for a detailed discussion on reasons for internationalisation and globalisation.

The majority of companies, however, begin their overseas involvement from the basis of a well-established home market. The decision to 'go international' can be due to a variety of reasons:

1 *Saturation of the home market:* Many companies in mature markets find that the scope for growth is limited. Competitive action may be threatening their market share. Overseas opportunities must be sought to maintain the viability of existing production capacity. This action might also extend the life cycle of a product.

2 *To facilitate growth:* The actions of competitors might mean there is pressure on a company to increase production capacity and sales volume. Growth markets might present a situation in which a company that does not grow with market trends becomes relatively smaller in relation to competition and is then less able to compete in terms of lower costs and innovation. Access to overseas markets facilitates growth by providing new outlets for increased production.

3 *To achieve lower unit costs:* The core business may remain in the domestic market whilst new markets abroad afford the opportunity to increase production and lower overall unit costs. Such cost advantages allow a company to keep pace with market expansion and even permit the company to expand its domestic market share, provided that returns on overseas activity are sufficient to make a contribution to fixed costs and cover the variable costs of increased production.

4 *Depressed demand in the home market:* Some companies regard overseas markets as marginal cost areas. At times of depressed demand in the home market, exporting can maintain production capacity and make a contribution to fixed costs. The ability to pursue such a 'hit and run' strategy depends on the type of market in which the company is involved. For price-sensitive commodity markets this is a viable strategy. However, international marketing is usually dependent on long-term involvement. Companies that turn to export

markets in times of need and return to the home market when it is convenient are usually unsuccessful.

An indirect advantage of international marketing is that the company gains a new perspective on its activities. Involvement in foreign markets gives the firm a yardstick by which to measure its efforts at home and reduces the likelihood of complacency. It also follows that risk is spread more widely with each new market that is successfully entered.

17.4 How does international marketing begin?

Implicit in the earlier definition of international marketing activity is the idea that simple exporting is a pursuit that accounts for only a small part of a company's overall affairs. The implication is that exporting does not involve the company in any major modifications to its home-based marketing. The term 'international marketing' is used to describe the activities of firms that have made a positive decision to enter overseas markets and are prepared to implement whatever is required to achieve success in such markets.

Many firms begin exporting in a passive way. Whilst being exclusively involved with the home market, they may receive unsolicited enquiries for their products from abroad. These could be as a result of a press or magazine article or simply through 'word-of-mouth'. Such extra business is likely to be welcomed as long as it can be undertaken without making any alterations to the existing marketing structure. Requests for modifications to the product or payment terms are unlikely to be considered because these would detract from the company's main marketing effort. Such action may also involve financial commitment which the company feels could be better employed elsewhere.

When a company's capacity is not being fully utilised export orders will probably be welcomed. As long as marketing strategy is home-based, these orders will tend to take second place when the home situation begins to improve. Such sporadic commitment can continue for a long time, and is a viable policy as long as customers are prepared to conduct business in this manner. However, it is likely that the overseas customer will look for some kind of security of the supply route. In the long term it is in the interests of both buyers and sellers to establish such a working relationship.

This sporadic type of exporting can provide the basis for further export involvement. At some point in a company's life, a decision has to be made on whether to develop exporting or not. Clearly, a strong relationship exists between the level of exports and how far a company is prepared to change in response to this. As the level of exports grow, a company is more likely to adopt an international marketing philosophy. As export growth increases, the company will become less passive and more actively involved in exporting, thus taking on an international marketing orientation. The company can initiate this growing commitment gradually by making small changes, but at some stage a conscious decision should be made to devote more marketing effort to exports.

The gradual evolution towards export commitment may be punctuated by the following actions:

1 allocation or engagement of employees with specific responsibility for internal aspects of exporting such as export documentation, shipping and basic customer liaison;
2 minor modifications to payment terms and conditions;
3 involvement in export marketing research;
4 engagement of overseas agent(s) and/or distributor(s);
5 engagement of export sales personnel;
6 decision to carry out product modification to suit individual overseas markets;
7 involvement in overseas promotion, including participation in international trade fairs and exhibitions.

Although a gradual evolution of export activity is common, some companies make a single decision to become involved in international marketing without prior involvement. This may represent a major element of an expansion strategy that might be achieved by selling directly to overseas markets or entering into some form of joint venture.

17.5 The international decision – a strategic commitment

An undertaking to become involved in international marketing is strategic in nature. As with all aspects of strategic decision-making, information is needed and careful preparation is essential. The decision will involve financial outlay and organisational change.

The company's first step should be to examine the strategic alternatives. It may be that some other option is easier to implement and carries less risk. If an international strategy is the chosen route, profitability and accessibility to the market should be thoroughly considered and markets with the greatest profit potential should be identified. Some markets might appear to be highly profitable, but have features that might increase risk. Such influences may be physical, cultural, government and market-related. Some markets might be well served by domestic suppliers or existing exporters, that the level of competition might be a barrier to entry.

The key to making the correct decision is adequate research. Desk research should identify potential markets that should then become the subject of extensive field research. Marketing research and subsequent market selection represent one side of the company's strategic preparation process.

As well as looking 'outward' to the marketplace, the company should prepare and organise its internal structure to meet the challenges that international marketing will present. Production and transport should be organised to meet additional demands and new commercial procedures might be needed. If the new export business can be accommodated within existing office procedures this will be more cost effective, but inevitably new procedural systems must be devised. It is an error to try to 'fit exporting in' with existing office systems as this approach treats exporting as a subsidiary activity. To be successful, overseas business must be considered as an entity in its own right and not just an adjunct to domestic marketing arrangements. Such commitment involves adjustments in attitudes as well as physical adjustments.

17.6 The international mentality

An 'international mentality' is an intangible attribute and it is unlikely that a firm will succeed in international markets without it. Just as an understanding and acceptance of the marketing concept should permeate a firm, those involved in export activity should extend the concept overseas with a committed approach to their markets.

Too often overseas markets are afforded second-class treatment whilst the domestic market receives priority. When export markets are less profitable than those at home, such an attitude might be understandable, but it cannot be condoned. Once the 'international decision' has been taken, overseas customers should expect the best service the firm can offer. It is only by providing service at least as good as local suppliers that the international marketer can hope to succeed.

The mentality required means a genuine interest in overseas customers and their countries plus a willingness to adapt, as well as a high degree of patience and tolerance. This is an indispensable characteristic in higher management and international sales personnel, and it is the task of managers to encourage and develop this amongst their staff, through training and explanation.

17.7 Organisation for international marketing

17.7.1 Internal organization

Once a company begins to operate internationally, organisational changes should be made. Export documentation is complicated and requires specialist expertise. Some firms manage their own freight forwarding that demands specific skills. As export activity increases, it might be necessary to establish a complete export administration department.

Communication between the company, its customers and intermediaries might seem to be a basic observation, but the speed of response to electronic mail, fax, postal and telephone messages is a measure of the firm's efficiency.

When communication is efficient, it denotes a business-like attitude; rapid response to requests for samples or technical information demonstrates that the company is interested in its customers. The fact that a customer is on the other side of the world often has the effect of decreasing the urgency of any request. The company should implement systems and procedures to ensure that communication, in the sense of customer liaison, is rapid and efficient.

17.7.2 External organisation – the method of supply

How the company organises its sales force (i.e. people who are directly concerned with customers and intermediaries), and how agents and distributors are selected and managed, is an important practical consideration. Some firms approach their overseas markets directly whilst others employ commercial agents and distributors to act in conjunction with, and on behalf of, the supplier.

Overseas agents are often nationals of the country concerned. They can be individuals or companies. Their role, supported by the supplier, is to identify customers and provide 'on-the-spot' representation for the supplier. They are normally paid on a commission basis. Distributors operate by purchasing from the manufacturer and then reselling after a mark-up has been added for their services. The market for industrial goods lends itself more to agency agreements than consumer goods where distributorships are more common.

The agent/principal relationship is vital to the success of any overseas operation. Whilst agents are not direct employees they should be afforded the attention and cooperation that company employees might expect. The agent should be able to demonstrate to customers that a positive relationship has been established with the principal in the form of a true 'partnership'.

Apart from financial reward, agents can be motivated by regular contact and sales support, prompt replies to their queries and requests, invitations to the principal's premises and regular updates on company developments. The agent should respond by providing constant feedback and information about the marketplace. Agents should develop long-term objectives that will benefit both themselves and their principals in the form of a true partnership that normally implies territorial exclusivity in relation to the product or service being represented.

The initial criteria for agent selection are similar to those applied to the appointment of any new employee. Most agents have more than one principal and their existing activity should complement, but not compete with, what is proposed.

The agent search process is often carried out through commercial contacts, but can also include advertising or the employment of consultants to prepare a short-list of potential agents. Government agencies such as the British Overseas Trade Board (BOTB), Chambers of Commerce and British Consulates in relevant countries can also be a useful source of contact.

The appointment of distributors is a similar process. The firm requires an overseas distributor who has relevant experience and contacts and whose existing activities are in harmony with the proposed product range. The principal differences are related to the fact that, unlike an agent, the distributor actually purchases the goods from the supplier. They usually contract to maintain agreed minimum stock levels. Although the distributor reduces risk and financial outlay for the supplier, losing 'title' to the goods reduces the control the supplier has over the marketing of their products.

Direct investment is a further organisational option, and this is dealt with later in this chapter.

◼ 17.8 International marketing strategy

The decision to become involved in overseas markets is 'strategic'. The decision should be informed, and can only be implemented after adequate preparation (see Westhead *et al.*, 2002, pp. 51–68, for treatment of appropriate marketing strategies for the smaller enterprise specifically). The implementation of international marketing strategy is particularly affected by the influences and constraints of the international marketing environment (see Gupta and Govindarajan, 2001, pp. 45–56). Political, economic, socio-cultural and technological (PEST) factors may differ and home and overseas markets can exhibit wide environmental differences.

International strategy formulation should thus take the following course:

1 *Investment analysis* – can resources be better employed by adopting a strategic alternative, say in the home market?
2 *Market selection* – which markets appear most likely to fulfil the company's overall strategic objectives?
3 *Broad-based functional decisions* – how will the marketing mix be employed in order to implement the strategy?

The chosen strategy should possess specific objectives to permit subsequent measurement of results. These objectives must be realistic and within the capabilities of the firm and take account of the environmental factors of the market. They should also be consistent and not conflict with each other. Typical objectives include a specific return on investment (ROI) a specific market share percentage and a specific time scale.

Only through a strategic approach can the company objectively assess its situation and plan a modified international marketing strategy. Related to the decision about how much of a company's turnover should be allocated to overseas markets, is how much the company is prepared, or can afford, to spend to attain this goal. The amount or 'level' of investment is a key strategic issue that is governed by the method of entry into the market and the way in which the international marketing mix is employed.

Issues of environment have been dealt with in Chapter 2 and the nature of strategy and control is the concern of the final Chapter 19. Features that distinguish international strategy from that of the home market are:

1 environmental issues are more wide ranging and complex;
2 there is a higher level of risk;
3 the level of investment is usually higher, involving not only the commitment of financial resources, but additional organisational burdens.

17.9 The international marketing mix

Once overall strategy has been formulated, the company must develop a 'mix strategy' to achieve the strategic objectives that have been set. The marketing mix is, therefore, the 'tool' of strategy. The essential elements are the same, whether the market is international or domestic. Any home-based mix strategy is likely to require modification for international marketing.

17.9.1 Product

In order to achieve economies of scale, companies attempt to streamline their organisational systems and standardise production. This can only be achieved when it is acceptable to the customer. The company must be willing to make changes. Basic, physical changes to the product are not normally the major source of problems to a company that has serious international intentions. More problematic are intangible factors like image and product positioning.

Packaging is a major element of the product that can be affected by both legal and cultural aspects of the international market. For example, package sizes produced for the home market may not correspond to those in another country. In some countries certain colours have religious significance, and it would be offensive to associate such colours with material goods. Climate can also be an important factor when considering package type. For instance, in warmer more humid climates, chocolate bar manufacturers put an extra layer of wrapping around the silver foil to prevent the product from melting. In industrial markets, some countries may be unable to handle goods packed in their existing form because of lack of appropriate materials handling equipment.

Labelling is a product-related area where local mandate or convention can dictate modifications. The information required on pharmaceutical products differs throughout the world, and specific package sizes might be required by law. In some countries the level of literacy may require that important information be related graphically. Language presents an obvious need for label modification. Firms with a wide international involvement tend to repeat the information required in a variety of languages relevant to their major markets in a positive move to accommodate these markets as well as reducing the number of label modifications. A brand name that sounds innocuous in the home market may have a different significance in another language. Even a logo can possess a connotation that might be negative.

Dealing in many markets allows the company to pursue a variety of product policies. At any one time it is likely that a single product's life cycle position will vary in different markets and countries. This implies that the marketing mix and product decisions should be adapted accordingly.

A feature of the past 25 years has been a consistent effort by internationally orientated firms to standardise their products. Although life cycle positions may call for differing strategies, a goal has been to provide an internationally accepted product image. Whilst individual markets might require an individual mix strategy, product decisions can be simple and Coca Cola and Levi jeans are specific high profile examples.

17.9.2 Promotion

Promotional tools and strategies for international markets are similar to those available domestically, but they are not equally appropriate to both situations. The greatest opportunities for simplifying the communications task exist when:

1 all media are available;
2 there are no governmental restrictions on the type of advertising allowed;
3 advertising and promotion can be developed centrally;
4 the product is not affected by cultural variables.

A combination of all these circumstances is not common and is least likely in developed markets like those of Western Europe. Despite similar economic circumstances, these markets have significant cultural variables, whose influence only diminishes when marketing industrial commodities. The Americans have been criticised for their failure to recognise this, as they often regard Europe as a single, homogeneous market.

In addition to the obvious problem of language, most advertising must be otherwise modified to suit its target market. Cultural attitudes to family life, behaviour, good manners and sexual equality vary widely between nations. Legal restrictions may also forbid comparative advertising or restrict broadcasting time. This compounds the issue of copy translation and message. Unless it is carefully conceived and checked out by nationals of a country, the message and advertising copy might be totally misdirected.

Whilst media available can vary between countries, the major criterion for media selection is universal. The appropriate medium is that which reaches the highest number of prospects within the target market at the most cost-effective rate, taking into consideration the specific task that the advertising is designed to achieve.

Sales promotional strategies also need to be 'tailored' to the market. Although standard techniques can be employed, where the product is readily distinguishable as 'imported', the promotional emphasis is normally centred around some form of joint effort organised by an agency of the exporting country (e.g. a Trade Association or a Chamber of Commerce). Large retailers in the target country might be persuaded to host in-store promotions that feature a variety of products from a particular country.

In industrial markets, trade fairs or exhibitions are valuable promotional tools. Companies can participate individually or through some co-operative venture. Participation in such events is often made more attractive by government aid or sponsorship. The benefits derived from attendance at exhibitions are sometimes difficult to measure. Exhibitions provide the company with an international meeting point for seeing a large number of customers in a short space of time. Naturally, the company should set clear objectives, but often 'orders taken' is the only clear yardstick of success. Other measures can include the number of enquiries. If the product is technical, it may be some time before enquiries are converted into orders.

17.9.3 Distribution

International distribution involves wide-ranging decisions. As well as physical distribution and logistics, the company must consider whether to use agents and/or distributors or to sell directly to the overseas customer.

In general, transportation decisions are clear and can be refined as the company gains experience. Clearly, perishable products should be despatched by the fastest means. An expensive mode like air freight would not, on the other hand, be appropriate for bulky, low value products.

The idea of 'total distribution' or the systems approach as discussed in Chapter 9, is particularly applicable to international marketing. In commodity markets, or where there is local competition, service is frequently the major competitive tool. A company that consistently delivers on time will build up a level of loyalty that may never be achieved by promotional means. The organisation of the distribution mix is a function of the product and market type and where international markets are concerned, distribution is a high profile element of the overall marketing mix.

17.9.4 Price

The price element of the marketing mix in international markets is complicated by transportation costs and currency fluctuations. However, basic pricing strategies still apply. Unless the company is merely seeking to 'off load' excess capacity, research carried out before the market entry decision is made should establish that it is possible to make some level of profit given the cost structure of the company. Important questions are how much is the company is able to change, and how much price is a function of the product and of the market situation?

Depending on the product/market relationship, the company can adopt one of three basic pricing strategies that have already been considered in Chapter 7:

1 market penetration pricing,
2 market skimming,
3 market (competitor) based pricing.

When market conditions permit, opportunities for 'skimming' should be taken and innovative products lend themselves to this approach. A market penetration strategy should be considered carefully before being applied to export markets. The relatively volatile nature of overseas markets and the associated risks can bring about a change in the market situation before the company has had the opportunity to recoup its investment through a low penetration price policy. Possible market changes include currency fluctuations, government action and aggressive competitive reaction from within the target country. Whilst opportunities for product and price differentiation in overseas markets are apparent, it is a feature of the twenty-first century that, in general (and especially in consumer markets), product standardisation is increasing. This means that a company often has little option than to charge a price established by competitors. In such situations it is essential that cost structures have been thoroughly examined and that the expected return on investment is considered to be acceptable before market entry. Where the company is obliged to operate within a predetermined price framework, it should attempt to differentiate its products by other means.

Procter & Gamble is an example of a company that is successful internationally and obtains high market share through an emphasis on promotion rather than price. International markets can offer special opportunities for obtaining high prices due to the prestige or novelty associated with the country of origin. Burberry clothes have a 'Britishness' sought after throughout the world. The French have a reputation for high quality cosmetics. International sales of some brands of whisky are probably due as much to their Scottish origin as to their taste.

Apart from how much to charge is the question of how prices are to be applied. It has been stated that exporters should modify their approach to customers so as to minimise possible complications. Importers are not concerned with the problems of foreign suppliers and simply require goods and services under conditions that are as similar as possible to those existing through normal purchasing channels. Modifications in price application might be necessary for successful international marketing and this is the responsibility of the supplier. The main issues of international pricing are the price quotation where the main terms used in export/import transactions are:

1 'Ex-works' – here the importer is solely responsible for transport and insurance from the supplier's premises.
2 'FOB (free on board)' where the supplier is responsible for the costs of transport and insurance until the goods are loaded immediately prior to export. Once loaded onto a ship or aircraft, the customer assumes responsibility for further costs.
3 'CIF (cost, insurance and freight)' is where the supplier's quotation includes all costs of delivery to a port convenient to the customer. A typical quotation may read 'CIF local port', but often the port of destination is specified.
4 'C&F (cost and freight)' is where insurance is not included in the price. This might be because the government of the importer insists on using the

country's own insurance facilities. Sometimes the government of the importing country might specify the shipping line that the exporter must use.

5 'Delivered client's warehouse' (sometimes termed 'rendu' or 'free delivered') is a typical quotation used in trading within Europe where lorries can deliver 'door-to-door'. The supplier is responsible for all costs, including customs clearance, but excluding any local duties or taxes.

6 More specialist quotations include 'FAS (Free-alongside)' and 'FOW (Free-on-wagon)'.

Payment terms and conditions vary from country to country. Thirty-, sixty- and ninety-day credit terms are common within Europe. Discounts for prompt payment also vary.

'Letters of credit' are a normal trading condition in more distant markets. They provide protection for both parties because funds are not transferred until conditions are met. Once they are fulfilled the supplier is guaranteed payment by the bank. In some countries, especially those with balance-of-payments problems, payment can be deferred by as much as two years. Financial institutions exist that are able to factor payments to suppliers for a percentage of the cost involved. Means of payment must, therefore, be carefully considered before sales are negotiated.

Currency is an important consideration and 'hard' currencies like the US dollar, the Euro and the pound sterling are 'universal' currencies, but they are not always the most convenient means of exchange for most international trade. From a marketing perspective, it can be preferable to make quotations in the customer's local currency as long as it is readily convertible and stable in international terms. This shows a commitment to the overseas customer. Where local competition is strong, quotations made in local currency can remove one of the distinctions which competition might use to argue against international sourcing. Financially, trading in foreign currencies carries an element of risk that can be offset by buying the currency 'forward'.

17.9.5 International sales management

Given the complexity and variety of international sales management, systems should be devised that are effective in each market being served. Export sales staff are often recruited from outside the firm, but it is not uncommon for home-based sales personnel to be given overseas responsibilities. The latter option might be feasible where a clear interest and commitment to international activity is evident. It is a mistake to transfer successful domestically based sales staff to overseas markets as their effectiveness is often reduced. An 'international mentality' is a prerequisite and this should ideally be supported by linguistic ability, or at least willingness to learn the local language as this can foster goodwill.

Many organisational options are available. An international sales team can be home-based and be made up of nationals of the exporting country. Each salesperson will be responsible for one or more territories workloads being divided between home-based liaison and follow-up, and actually visiting the markets. The amount of time spent abroad will depend on the market and product. Apart from the practical side of visiting customers to conduct business, such visits reinforce the commitment of the company to its overseas customers. It is essential when making visits that the salesperson has sufficient authority to take important business decisions 'on the spot'. This increases the salesperson's credibility and raises the tone of the meeting from what might otherwise appear to be a courtesy visit. The need to make such decisions whilst abroad requires a level of managerial ability not always needed for domestic sales staff. International sales personnel should, therefore, be able to work with minimal supervision that requires self-discipline and determination.

Expatriate sales personnel (nationals of the exporting country) can be domiciled in the target country. Although the business rationale for such a system is sound, management problems can occur. Maintaining an expatriate sales force is expensive and complex. The company might feel that control over its salespeople is reduced and salespersons may feel personally isolated from the home country. Morale amongst staff living abroad for long periods can be difficult to maintain.

When a high level of sales is achieved in a particular country it might be appropriate to engage a national sales managers and sales personnel. They have the advantage of familiarity with the language, customs and culture, which expatriate sales staff might never achieve. On the other hand, customers might consider a sales force of locals as 'once-removed' from the company and less directly involved in the marketing process. The company may also find that control measures are more difficult to apply.

17.10 International intelligence and information

The expense of entry into international markets places a burden on a company's MkIS (marketing information system) that must provide accurate information for strategic decision-making. The MkIS should function as it would for domestic purposes, but the breadth of information required is greater and information can be more difficult to obtain. Some companies employ specialist international agencies.

Field research is sometimes frustrated by language problems, in which case it may be necessary to engage local research agencies. In developing nations, organised data collection might not exist; levels of literacy can be low and media available for promotion limited.

At the secondary stage the research process should relate to:

1 international trade directories and magazines,
2 government statistics and reports,
3 embassies and consulates,

4 published surveys,
5 'on-line' data services accessed directly or through specialist agencies,
6 international banks and other financial institutions.

As well as supplying information for marketing preparation, the intelligence system has a vital role to play in monitoring the international environment once business has begun. In the 'home' country, much information available through the media is taken for granted. The intelligence system should ensure a regular flow of information from the countries being monitored. It is part of the role of agents, distributors, sales personnel and other locally based employees to contribute information.

17.11 Cultural variables

As 'culture' is intangible and unwritten it is assimilated rather than learned. Cultural variables can pose problems when devising marketing strategy. Advertisers need to be aware of differences in such aspects as humour, morality and the role and status of women. Colours have religious significance or can signify good or bad luck. As mentioned already, care must be taken in package design and labelling. Sales personnel must observe rules of etiquette that are part of the socio-cultural context of an international market. International marketers should obtain assistance and advice from nationals before applying their own cultural and business values to marketing activities (see Svensson, 2001, pp. 6–18).

Culture is an 'ethnic' rather than 'geographic' factor. A country may contain groups of people with radically different cultures; the Germans and the French recognise distinct cultural differences between the north and the south of their respective countries that are not be immediately apparent.

17.12 Government and political activity

International marketers must consider the influence of governments on their activities. In recent years, some emerging economies in Africa have been politically unstable. Countries that have emerged following the break up of the Soviet Union have displayed volatility. Governments can also frustrate the efforts of international marketing in developed economies. A country might need to redress a balance-of-trade problem and to do so might impose duties on imported goods that can effectively bar attempts to export to that country. Another reason for such action in developing countries is to protect local industries from foreign competition. Governments might subsidise certain industries to maintain employment, thereby changing the basis of competition.

The EU has encouraged free trade between member nations and this culminated in the 'harmonisation' accord at the end of 1992 that covers matters like customs procedures and differing legal requirements for labelling and product safety.

17.13 Direct international investment

'Investment' has been used to describe resource allocation (financial or human) used to enter an overseas market. 'Direct investment' also implies a semi-permanent diversion of funds and expertise so the company is no longer transporting finished goods from the home base to export markets, but is manufacturing outside the home country or engaging in cooperation with foreign manufacturers.

17.13.1 Direct investment

This is normally considered when the firm's level of international involvement has reached a point where it is no longer practical or convenient to continue the physical transfer of goods from one country to another. Sometimes direct investment provides a method of entry into overseas markets that bypasses the export evolution process. By purchasing a foreign company, or by entering into a licensing or industrial cooperation agreement, a company gains immediate market access and revenue from abroad without necessarily having had prior international involvement.

17.13.2 Licensing

This involves one company allowing another to use a trademark or patent, or a manufacturing process, design or recipe, for which the user company makes a payment. It is a relatively easy method of entry into foreign markets and it provides immediate revenue.

Licensing is much favoured by Japanese companies, although some have been criticised for using this as a 'back door' method of entry and once the product has become established, they can take over the licensee and with it, a ready-made marketing system for the original product.

17.13.3 International cooperative ventures

These involve the sharing of technology or manufacture between two companies from different countries. As well as sharing knowledge and expertise to mutual advantage, both companies benefit from sharing costs.

17.13.4 Joint venture

These operations involve two companies joining together to manufacture and market their products as one. They differ from cooperative ventures in that the companies are effectively merging, rather than sharing, their expertise. Often a new company is formed in which neither party has an overriding shareholding. The maintenance of a 50:50 holding interest helps to ensure that conflict between the two parties is minimised, although in some countries there is an insistence that the 'local' partner has a controlling interest (i.e. 51% or more).

In markets where there is not scope for licensing or joint manufacture, it might be possible to establish local sales and distribution centres overseas. Although costs are usually high compared with those of maintaining such centres at home, this system has the advantage of allowing the company to retain control over its activities. It is often a precursor to establishing the company's own manufacturing facilities overseas, which represents the sophisticated degree of international investment. Risk is associated with any large investment, but by installing its own capacity in a foreign country, control is retained and the opportunity exists to build up goodwill with both the community and the government.

17.14 Multinational and global marketing

Companies such as Ford, IBM, McDonalds, Shell and Mitsubishi can be described as multinational companies. Although they have their 'roots' in a single country, whose office may still hold overall strategic power, they are multinational in nature because their activities are worldwide, and in particular, because they have established themselves in countries on an equal footing with indigenous companies. They operate as national companies in everything but name.

If such companies decide to divert their resources from one country to another, the consequences for local communities in which their operations decrease or cease can be severe. Their size and power can also tend towards monopoly, and it is the responsibility of governments and trading blocks to ensure that this power is not abused.

If trend towards worldwide standardisation of products (whether it be cars, hamburgers or clothes) continues, and cultural groups grow increasingly alike in their tastes as societies become more 'cosmopolitan', the importance of multinationals is likely to increase. The rise of multinationals means that in product terms certain goods have 'global' appeal. These goods are successfully marketed in all countries with little or no attention to product or image modification. This is the phenomenon of global marketing.

In most countries one is able to see local people wearing Levi jeans, driving Ford or Toyota cars, drinking Coca Cola and listening to Sony personal stereos. Companies that achieve such standardisation simplify their marketing task and create effective competitive barriers. This is a trend that seems likely to increase with growth in multinational activity.

Keegan (1969) put forward a theory that is now regarded as seminal and central to strategic thinking when considering international marketing. He considered the mix elements of product and promotion and identified five possible strategies that are described in Figure 17.1. Explanations follow in relation to each of these strategies.

1 *Straight extension*: The product or service and the type of communication message is the same for overseas and home markets (e.g. Coca Cola).

Products

		No change	Adapted	New product
Marketing Communications	No change	Straight extension	Product adaptation	
	Adapt	Communication adaptation	Dual adaptation	Product invention

Figure 17.1 Keegan's five strategies for international marketing

2 *Communications adaptation*: The promotional theme is modified and the product or service remains unchanged (e.g. bicycles are promoted as basic means of transportation in developing countries whereas in developed countries they are promoted as a means of recreation).

3 *Product adaptation*: The product or service is different for home and overseas markets; whereas the promotion is the same for both (e.g. petrol has a different 'formula' for colder climates than for warmer climates).

4 *Dual adaptation*: The communication message and the product or service are altered for each market (e.g. clothing products where designs and structure are different for each market and promotion can emphasise functionality or fashion).

5 *Product invention*: The above strategies are appropriate where product needs and market conditions are similar to the home market, but in developing countries this may to be true. New product development might be required to meet customer needs at an affordable price (e.g. a 'hand cranked' washing machine is an example of 'backwards invention' to suit the needs of countries where there is an uncertain power supply and washing is done by hand).

17.15 Help to UK exporters

For small and medium-sized enterprises (SME's) and large companies who are new to international markets, the UK government offers a wide range of services to assist and promote marketing efforts (see also Forsman *et al.*, 2002, pp. 1–12 who examine international marketing issues from a small and medium sized firms perspective).

17.15.1 Statistics and market information

The BOTB is able to supply a wide variety of information on specific markets throughout the world on request. The Export Intelligence service provides regular information on specific markets for a subscription. Such information can be augmented by direct application to British consular offices throughout the world through commercial officers who have detailed local knowledge of particular industries. These services include the preparation of shortlists of potential agents and distributors.

The BOTB sometimes provides direct financial assistance for market research projects aimed at export markets. Financial support, from the BOTB, is available to exporting companies.

Trade fairs and exhibitions

Companies wishing to participate in overseas trade fairs and exhibitions can do this through their Trade Association or local Chamber of Commerce. The BOTB also organises and subsidises trade delegations to selected overseas markets.

Market entry guarantee scheme

This is effectively a loan of up to 50% of the costs involved in entering a new export market. If the venture is unsuccessful, the loss is shared by the exporter and the BOTB. The scheme is aimed at small to medium-sized firms.

Export Credits Guarantee Department (ECGD)

This is a Government organised insurance scheme that extends normal insurance cover to include non-commercial risks like war, expropriation and balance-of-payment crises in countries to which goods have been sent.

 ## 17.16 Summary

This chapter has described the operation of companies engaged in exporting at various levels of activity. The subject encompasses all topics within marketing. To be an international marketer, there should be no distinctions between countries: the only differences should be in terms of how the marketing mix is employed for different markets/countries.

The decision to enter overseas markets is an important strategic consideration that cannot be effected without considerable preparation and willingness to adapt. International marketing is not a quick remedy for companies who find themselves in difficulty on the domestic front. An international strategy should be preceded by close examination of the available alternatives in the home market. Increasing sales volume through overseas markets may only be possible by means of extensive product and marketing mix modifications, the cost of which may negate the expected advantages. Similarly, an investment in a product life cycle extension strategy aimed at overseas markets might be better utilised in the development of new products for the home market.

 ## References

Chaffey, D., Mayer, R., Johnson, K. and Ellis-Chadwick, F. (2003), 'Internet Marketing, Strategy, Implementation and Practice', Financial Times, London: Prentice-Hall, pp. 71–72.
Fillis, I. (2002), 'Barriers to internationalisation: an investigation of the craft microenterprise', European Journal of Marketing, 7–8, 912–927.

Fletcher, R. (2001), 'A holistic approach to internationalization', *International Business Review*, 10, 25–49.

Forsman, M., Hinttu, S. and Kock, S. (2002),'Internationalisation for an SME perspective', paper presented at the 18th Annual IMP Conference, September, Lyon, pp. 1–12.

Gupta, A.K. and Govindarajan, V. (2001), 'Converting global presence into global competitive advantage', *Academy of Management Executive*, 15(2), 45–56.

Keegan, W.J. (1969) 'Multinational product planning: strategic alternatives' *Journal of Marketing*, 33, 58–62.

Knight, G. (2000), 'Entrepreneurship and marketing strategy: the SME under globalisation', *Journal of International Marketing*, 8(2), 12–32.

McAuley, A. (2001), *International Marketing, Consuming Globally, Thinking Locally*, Chichester, UK: John Wiley & Sons, Ltd., pp. 4–5.

Segal-Horn, S. (2002), 'Global firms: heroes or villains? How and why companies globalise', *European Business Journal*, 14(1), 8–19.

Svensson, G. (2001), ' "Glocalisation" of business activities: a "glocal strategy" approach', *Management Decision*, 39(1), 6–18.

Westhead, P., Wright, M. and Ucbasaran, D. (2002), 'International market selection strategies selected by "micro" and "small" firms', *Omega – The International Journal of Management Science*, 30, 51–68.

Further reading

Ali, A.J. (2001), 'Globalisation: the great transformation', *ACR*, 9(1), 1–9. Usinier, J.C. (2000), *'Marketing Across Cultures'*, Financial Times London: Prentice-Hall.

Bartlett, C.A. and Ghoshal, S. (2000), 'Going Global; lessons from late movers', *Harvard Business Review*, 78(2), 132–142.

Cateora, P.R., Graham, J.L. and Ghauri, P.N. (2000), *'International Marketing'*, European Edition, London: McGraw-Hill.

Chetty, S. and Holm, D.B. (2000), Internationalization of small to medium sized manufacturing firms: a network approach', *International Business Review*, 9(1), 77–93.

Fletcher, R. (2001), 'A holistic approach to internationalisation', *International Business Review*, 10, 25–49.

Harvey, M., Nocicevic, M.M. and Kiessling, T. (2001), 'Hypercompetition and the future of global management in the twenty-first century', *Thunderbird International Business Review*, 43(5), 599–616.

Simon, H. and Otte, M. (2000), 'The new Atlantic economy', *Harvard Business Review*, 78(1), 17–20.

UNCTAD (2000), 'World Investment Report', United Nations Conference on Trade and Development, Geneva.

World Economic Forum (2000), *The Global Competitiveness Report*, Geneva: World Economic Forum.

Questions

Question 17.1

Definitions
Explain how overseas marketing differs from overseas trading?

Question 17.2

International involvement
How can firms begin to increase their involvement in international markets? Discuss the relative merits of the methods you describe.

Question 17.3

Information sources
Outline the statistical and other International Market Research Information that is provided by the Government in order to assist potential exporters. What limitations or problems are apparent when preparing to use such sources?

Question 17.4

Financial implications
Why does the acceptance of a foreign order usually impose a proportionately heavier financial burden on the supplier than for a similar home market order? What steps can be taken to reduce this effect?

Question 17.5

Examine the proposition that marketing internationally in emerging markets is so different from any other international marketing situation that it is insufficient for Western firms to develop the traditional practice of having country-focused strategies, such as a "China strategy" and an "India strategy," and to begin to consider the firm's "emerging market strategy."

Question 17.6

What is the role and contribution of the sales force to the success of the firm involved in international marketing?

Question 17.7

What are the main factors management must consider when planning and organising a sales force capability for the firm in an overseas market?

Question 17.8

What is the meaning of globalization for marketing and what are the principle arguments for and against it?

Question 17.9

Many consumer markets in the developed world are fragmented and consumer product firms develop programmes to consolidate these markets. It is argued that the natural convergence in these markets facilitates consolidation. Discuss.

Question 17.10

Discuss the main reasons for firms moving from serving purely domestic markets to becoming international or even multi national marketing organisations. Use specific examples if possible to illustrate the points being made.

Question 17.11

Is it necessary to adopt a specific business outlook for success in international markets? Is such an outlook a prerequisite for the motivation in firms to internationalise?

Question 17.12

Discuss the commonly held belief that there is no single market entry strategy which is appropriate in all circumstances.

Question 17.13

Why does channel conflict occur? Is conflict more likely to occur in international marketing?

Question 17.14

What role has innovation in international channel management? How can a firm maintain or gain market share by innovating in the channel of distribution?

Question 17.15

What is culture? Why is an understanding of culture important in international marketing?

Question 17.16

Outline and discuss the principle elements of culture as they affect the behaviour of the international firm.

Question 17.17

The world market is really a series of market segments, each with different needs and wants. Successful international market segmentation requires a careful selection of country markets, regions and customers. Discuss.

Question 17.18

Before the firm can take a decision to enter a specific foreign market there must be an awareness of opportunities in the market. How does the firm become aware of such opportunities?

18

Internet Technology and Marketing

18.1 Introduction

Computer-based technology is all around us and influences every area of our lives. In this chapter we look at developments such as the World Wide Web (WWW), the internet, e-commerce in general, databases and their application such as data mining and data fusion and the way these new developments and techniques have changed the face of marketing practice over the past 10 years. The internet (the net) is a vast and continually growing web of computer networks that link computers around the world. The web or WWW is a development of the internet where accessing information is user friendly. 'Electronic commerce' is a general term for the buying and selling process that is supported by electronic means. Advances in technology are having a tremendous impact on all areas of business, including marketing. There has been an explosion of information on the subject, and the aim of this chapter is to impart an appreciation of the main issues involved with the use of electronic commerce. Key technological advances are discussed in terms of how they affect the marketing firm and their impact on marketing activities both now and in the future.

The twenty-first century should witness incredible advances in the application and development of technology. The product life cycle of many products is moving ever faster as technological advances supersede existing product types and forms. The task of marketing is to capitalise on and exploit the business opportunities this new technology brings. Organisations must adapt this new technology in order to survive.

In particular we examine the use of the net and the WWW that has formed the platform for the new e-marketing revolution, and begin by analysing and assessing some of the more salient technological developments that are taking place with respect to marketing and business. This discussion focuses on the impact, applications, and implications of these technologies with regard to marketing practices and processes rather than an analysis of the technologies themselves. Many of the technological developments, which follow are interrelated, for example, development of databases and growth of e-commerce are underpinned by advances in technologies in computing such as 'data mining' and 'data fusion'.

18.2 Importance of electronic commerce

Business in general and marketing in particular has become increasingly affected by, and dependent upon, technology. Furthermore, technological progress itself is accelerating exponentially. The rate of development increases as scientists and technologists learn from what has happened in the past, for example, the digital computer was developed in a laboratory in the UK at Manchester University and since then others have developed the basic technology in to what we see today. We examine some of the salient changes and advances in technology as they affect the marketer. At this stage, advances in technology are beginning to change the nature of marketing and other business and commercial activities. In as little as ten years the process of marketing will change significantly. Some say that the traditional marketing paradigm is no longer applicable in the world of the internet and that new concepts are called for. Certainly the modern-day marketer needs to be familiar with the key advances in technology that are impacting on the marketing process (see Curry, 2001, pp. 114–128 for a discussion on interactive television and its integration with other technologies such as the Internet). A summary of the reasons are listed below:

- Advances in technology enable the marketing process to be carried out not only more effectively but also more efficiently and computer-aided questionnaire design for marketing research is a case in point. The computerisation of measuring instruments for advertising research is another good example. Advances in technology allow the marketing professional to do more things and to do tasks better.
- New technology increasingly facilitates the ease with which information, so vital to effective marketing planning and decision making, can be collected, analysed and used. Marketing Information Systems and the ability to 'tap' into internal and external databases has revolutionised the planning process in marketing in terms of detail and speed. Data mining and data fusion are techniques that allow marketing research professionals to 'engineer' information from a wide variety of sources and even create 'virtual' consumer models from such information.
- Competitive success is increasingly based on the application of advances in technology. If we take mobile telephones, for example, it is no longer enough to produce a product that is capable of making a telephone call. Today people

want telephones that send text messages, answer e-mails, play computer games and provide video clips.

- Developments in business related technology contributes to the growth of the international company and a move towards the global market and consumer. Smaller firms in particular benefit from internet based business technologies as it reduces their size disadvantage. Electronic commerce has no geographic boundaries; it is as easy to interact with customers in New Zealand from the UK, as it is to interact with consumers in the UK. Many companies, in order to differentiate their products and reduce costs, are increasingly using computer-based technology. 'Just-in-time' ordering and stock holding systems saves firms huge inventory and logistics costs compared with traditional systems. Computers have facilitated the use of these new systems and processes.
- Developments in business related computer technology allow marketers to be more customer focused, for example, faster and more flexible responses to customer needs. The use of database marketing and data mining has improved the accuracy and efficiency of many marketing operations, particularly communications like direct mail.

The examples provided demonstrate that marketing management must understand advances in technology that are taking place, otherwise they will not perform effectively. Some marketing firms even contribute to these changes, for example, Napster.com pioneered the marketing of music on the net and Amazon.com leads the way in the marketing of books and CDs. These two companies are example firms making use of the new technology and who contribute to the development of the net as a mainstream commercial medium. These companies are similar to Procter & Gamble Limited as they were in the 1950s and 1960s when they pioneered many fast moving consumer goods marketing techniques used today in the field of branding and sales promotions.

Marketing means staying ahead of the competition. Marketers must have the required skills to use the technologies of today and tomorrow to assist the marketing process. The marketing manager of the future will need an understanding of the use of technology within the discipline and be able to factor in the use of new technology into all aspects of their marketing plans and operations. There has been a significant change in the technological environment of marketing firms; this is not a minor 'ramp' technological change but a huge 'step' change in the way marketing firms do business. If they do not react and adapt to this new environment they will become extinct. Figure 18.1 explains this graphically.

18.3 Database marketing

18.3.1 Database marketing defined

The internet, e-commerce, the continuing rise of direct marketing and increasing emphasis on customer retention over customer acquisition are only a few of the

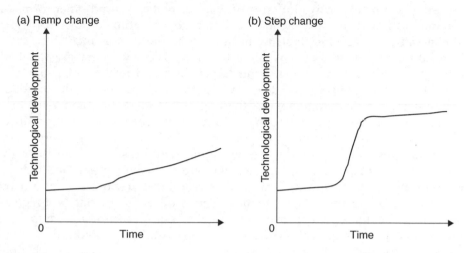

Figure 18.1 Example of (a) ramp and (b) step changes in effects/impact of technological development

factors affecting the way firms carry out modern day business. Firms have to move fast, keep up with the latest developments and trends and invest in the most relevant software and systems to stay ahead of competition. 'Database marketing' is two words. The first word implies that data is organised and stored in a computer system. The second implies that firms use this data in their marketing and sales programmes.

Database marketing is a marketing and sales system that continually gathers, refines and utilises information and data that then drives relevant marketing and sales communications programmes. Examples of this are sales calls, direct mail pieces and advertising to selected companies to acquire new customers, retain customers, generate more business from existing customers and create long-term loyalty. Database marketing is more than just a data retrieval system. While 'direct marketing' describes a collection of marketing communication tactics such as direct mail, telemarketing, response advertising, etc., database marketing describes a way of organising a company's total marketing and sales process. It is very broad and can have impact from market research and product development all the way through customer service. Information about customers that is accurate and available to everyone can transform a company's market capacity.

Database marketing is about focusing and targeting. Databases take the 'guess' out of marketing programmes. They do not provide perfect accuracy, but they do allow for significant improvements in both accuracy and efficiency if used properly. Many companies operate 'hit-or-miss' marketing meaning that management often makes decisions based on intuition or instinct rather than on hard facts based on clear scientific evidence. Hence instead of predicting target audience based on hard facts they make best guesses about who their target audience is and what this audience wants. This process of 'best guessing' can be expensive in terms of wasted mail shots and other forms of communication. As already mentioned, database marketing lets us work more intelligently, and provides tools to make more accurate assessments. It lets us take information that is already in customer or sales-lead databases analyse it to find patterns such as purchasing associations and relationships, and use the information gained from this analysis to produce and instigate better marketing and sales programmes. Running better marketing and sales programs means targeting specific groups with specific messages about products that are important rather than giving irrelevant and uninteresting information. If we can target the right industries with the right messages about the right products, we will spend less resources marketing to companies or individuals who are never going to buy. This will release more resources to spend on prospects that are most likely to buy. The proper use of databases gives marketing the tools to improve the effectiveness of marketing campaigns saving time and money. It allows for more effective allocation and utilisation of marketing resources. Database marketing is referred to as precision marketing. Directing a marketing programme from a well constructed and managed database is analogous to shooting a rifle at a target using a telescopic sight rather than using a shotgun.

18.3.2 Principles of database marketing

Below are illustrations of possible applications and basic principles of database marketing. They are not exhaustive or definitive, but serve to illustrate the main principles:

- First, find out what characteristics the best customers have in common so you can target your next programmes to prospects that have similar characteristics. See exactly which market segments buy. You might think you already know your best segments, but through analysis you can uncover market segments that have purchased significant amounts, but you did not realise it. This process can enable the firm to improve its market segmentation by refocusing and redefining existing segments or may highlight totally unexpected new segments.
- Ascertain whether different market segments buy different products. This information allows you to spend marketing and sales resources more effectively by marketing each product to the best potential industries, firms or people. Learn which market segments bring highest average revenues. This is what differentiated marketing is all about, that is, dividing the total market into segments and then having a slightly different marketing strategy for each segment.
- Find out types of industries, firms or individuals that respond to different types of marketing communications so you can decide where to better spend advertising and marketing resources. Find out which market segments not only respond to programmes, but also actually buy and buy repeatedly.

Again, these might be different demographic profiles or different in some other way that might be commercially exploitable, and you might modify your targeting tactics and only market to the segments that buy repeatedly or at least frequently.

- Calculate the average lifetime value of customers. This can be done using discounted cash flow procedures. You can use this information to find out which customers are not living up to their potential and devise marketing and sales programmes to encourage them to buy more. Identify new customers and create programmes that encourage them to buy again. Reward your most frequent buyers and buyers that bring the highest revenue. The concept of 'lifetime' value is central to the idea of customer retention and long-term relationship marketing, a subject that was covered in detail in Chapter 13.

18.3.3 Data mining

Database marketing is a process that enables marketers to develop, test, implement, measure and modify marketing programmes and strategies more accurately and efficiently than non-database methods. By applying data mining techniques, marketers can fully harvest data about customers' buying patterns and behaviour and gain a greater understanding of customer motivations. Data mining and CRM software allows users to analyse large databases to solve business decision problems. Data mining, as the name suggests, involves 'interrogating' a database to discover interesting and commercially exploitable associations, patterns or relationships in the data. Modern data analysis software such as SPSS allows users to manipulate, group and correlate data variables and sets.

In order to implement successful database marketing solutions, management needs to know how to carry out certain basic tasks. The list given below is not intended to be prescriptive or exhaustive. However, it serves to illustrate some of the basic principles:

- identify and gather relevant data about customers and prospects to construct the database in the first place;
- use data warehousing techniques, which are systems of data storage and organising, to transform raw data into powerful, accessible marketing information (this adds value to the data collected by putting it in a format so that it can be retrieved and analysed effectively);
- apply statistical techniques to customer and prospect databases to analyse behaviour and attempt to establish patterns, associations or relationships in the data that may be commercially exploitable;
- establish meaningful market segments that are measurable, reachable, viable and commercially valuable;
- score individuals in terms of probability of their response. This will involve prioritising prospects in terms of the probability of purchase and long-term commercial value.

Data mining is in some ways an extension of statistical analysis. Like statistics, data mining is not a business solution; it is just a technology. CRM, on the other hand, involves turning information in a database into business decisions, for example, consider a catalogue retailer who needs to decide who to send a new catalogue to. The information incorporated into the CRM process is the historical database of previous mailings and features associated with the (potential) customers such as age, post-code, response in the past, etc. Software would use this data to build a model of customer behaviour that could be used to predict which customers would be likely to respond to the new catalogue. This is rather like building a 'virtual customer'. By using this information marketing can target customers who are likely to respond. It provides much greater accuracy and saves time and money.

18.3.4 Data fusion

Data fusion is similar to data mining. As the name implies, data is obtained from a range of different sources and put together like a jigsaw puzzle to form a complete profile of an individual, for example, you may fill in a loyalty card at a supermarket which means a lot of personal information is now on a company database. You may apply for bank account or credit facilities with the same or related company, for example, supermarkets like Sainsbury's' offer bank and credit facilities to customers, and fill in another form that gives further personal details. This data may be merged and integrated with data held about you on other personal databases, for example, those run by Equifax Ltd. or Experien Ltd., which supplies personal data to firms including financial data such as credit history.

Data from all these sources can be 'fused' together, cleaned using a 'filtering system' and will then basically form a complete picture of you as a person and a consumer. Sometimes data will be fused together from fragments held on different databases on different people. These people may share similar characteristics and form part of the same market segment. There may be associations between key variables that link a particular consumer to a particular segment. If you have the right value on one or two of these variables you are then treated as if you have the characteristics of the 'virtual consumer' built up from the fused data fragments. Using these techniques, firms can attribute a probability to you that you will behave in a certain way as modelled by their virtual consumer profile. Data fusion is a formal framework in which are expressed means and tools for the alliance of data originating from different sources. It aims at obtaining information of greater quality; the exact definition of 'greater quality' will depend upon the application.

It has been suggested to use the terms merging, integration, and combination in a much broader sense than fusion, with combination being even broader than merging (Wald, 1998). These terms define any process that implies a mathematical operation performed on at least two sets of information. These loose definitions intentionally offer space for various interpretations. Another domain pertains to data fusion: data assimilation or optimal control.

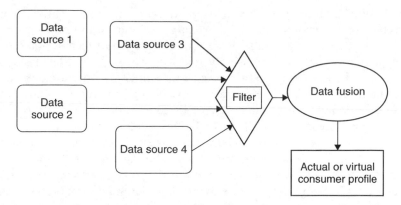

Figure 18.2 Schematic flow chart representing the data fusion process. *Source*: Lancaster and
Reynolds (2002, p. 389)

Data assimilation deals with the inclusion of measured data into numerical
models for the forecasting or analysis of the behaviour of a system.

18.3.5 Filtering

There are many examples in engineering where filtering is desirable. Radio
communications signals are often corrupted with noise. A good filtering
algorithm can remove noise from electromagnetic signals while still retaining
useful information. Another example is voltages. Many countries require in-
home filtering of line voltages to power personal computers and peripherals.
Without filtering, power fluctuations would shorten the useful life span of such
devices. Kalman filtering is a relatively recent (1960) development in filtering,
although it has its roots as far back as Gauss (1795) (see Agostinelli, 1978;
Benham, 1974; Bos, 1976/77). Kalman filtering has been applied in areas as
diverse as aerospace, marine navigation, nuclear power plant instrumentation,
demographic modelling, manufacturing, and many others including data
fusion (see Sorenson, 1985; Anderson and Moore, 1979). Figure 18.2 explains
this process.

18.4 The internet

The internet is a major technological development that will continually evolve. It
heralds the beginning of the next business revolution that will affect the way we
live, work and play for the rest of our lives. The technology involved in setting
up the internet has demonstrated to management that it will significantly change
the way people interact with each other, particularly so in the sphere of business.
The internet crosses boundaries of geography, politics, race, sex, religion, time
zones and culture. Technology helps to make possible and improve the way

we work. Without it many of the things we do, often take for granted, would be impossible, for example, much of advertising relies on communications technology; effective distribution and logistics relies on transport technologies; marketing research and analysis increasingly relies upon computing technology. This reliance on and use of technology in marketing is not new, but the extent to which it is used and the way it is used today is new. Think how different life would be without the calculator, or e-mail or even television. What would our lives be like without the technology to telephone a relative or deliver electricity and power to our homes and offices? Less noticeably, but no less significantly, technology also affects and helps aid marketing and the marketing process. Some marketing techniques are almost totally underpinned by technology and its application, an obvious example being the use of e-marketing. Some new marketing activities like database marketing, data fusion, electronic data 'warehousing' and data analysis, simply could not be done without the new technology.

E-Business, based on internet technology and the variations that have been developed from the original internet concept such as the intranet and the extranet, connects and links employees, customers, suppliers and partners. The internet has reduced the planet to a 'global village', accelerated the pace of technology, opened up tremendous possibilities for marketers and altered the way they think about doing business. It has started the new e-commerce revolution in marketing that is arguably the most important revolution since the development of commercial advertising. Some experts say the new revolution will rebuild the existing economy and change the way business is conducted. There is still a long way to go. Some people are confused by the new technology and many are concerned about Internet fraud and other security issues. These will have to be overcome if the Internet is to be as acceptable as any other form of commerce (see Fletcher, 2001, pp. 128–141).

18.5 World Wide Web

The WWW market will reach £1 trillion by the end of 2003. The WWW has unique features, which differentiates it from other forms of business communications. Because the web is so different from more traditional media such as television and radio its use is revolutionising the manner in which some marketing activities are carried out. In fact they could not be carried out without the use of web based technology.

In the USA more than two thirds of firms are setting up computer-based systems such as intranet and/or extranet facilities. As in many other technological innovations, the USA acts as a driving force for the diffusion of the new technology and new marketing methods that go with it across the world. These are tools that have the potential to increase profits by cutting costs, improving productivity, efficiency and communications and reducing paper work. E-commerce helps improve all areas of business from bringing in new customers, improving service levels, creating growth potential, tracking customers, data mining of databases, better targeting of marketing communications, reducing distribution costs and speeding up growth.

The E-commerce revolution, of which the WWW is at the epicentre, has been hailed as one of the most important developments ever to occur in the world of business. These developments will affect all areas of business operations, especially marketing. These new developments in marketing represent a 'paradigm shift', meaning that the new technology is not simply resulting in marketing firms doing basically the same thing, but with more up to date technology. It means we have to change the whole way we think about doing marketing and need a new model or 'paradigm'.

18.6 The World Wide Web: new model for electronic marketing

The WWW is a form of 'hypermedia computer mediated environment' (HCME) that is networked on a global scale. Basically an HCME is a networked system that allows the users of the system to interact in some way with the system. Both the sender and the receiver of the message can supply information to and interact with both each other, other people such as other users and with the system itself. This makes the WWW very different in form to other systems used in marketing and in particular in marketing communications at the present time. The telephone and other media allow for certain amount of interaction, for example, people can 'telephone in' to the local radio channel, and be heard by listeners participating in the programme. However, the interactivity provided by the WWW goes much further than this. As mentioned earlier, users not only interact with the sender of the commercial message, but with other users of the system and contribute material to the system itself. It is this 'person interaction' and this 'machine interaction' that differentiates the web from other commercial media and has led to its widespread use and adoption as a marketing media (Hoffman and Novak, 1994).

Let us consider for a moment the standard 'one way' simple model of marketing communication that we see in Figures 18.3 and 18.4. These have already been discussed in depth in Chapter 10. However discuss them here in a slightly different context. The conventional 'simple model' of marketing communications has been developed and discussed by a number of writers including Katz and Lazarfield (1995) and Laswell (1948). The model is one where the sender, in this case the marketing firm encodes and transmits a message to multiple receivers, that is, the target audience. In these models no interaction takes place between the sender and receiver although there is a 'feedback' loop whereby the sender can evaluate the effectiveness of the communication using research.

Models of the communications process may be verbal, non-verbal or mathematical. Regardless of form, they share three basic elements: sender, message and receiver. The message may be sent to one receiver or, as is more common in

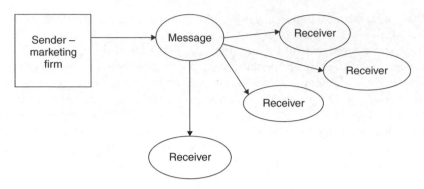

Figure 18.3 A simple communications model

marketing communications, the message is sent to multiple receivers simultaneously. The communications process can be modelled as shown in Figure 18.3.

This model incorporates multiple receivers. The sender (source) is a person or group having a thought to share with some other person or group (the receiver or destination). In marketing, receivers are current and prospective consumers of the company's product. The message is a symbolic expression of the sender's thoughts. The message may take the form of the printed or the spoken word, a magazine advertisement or television commercial being examples. Figure 18.3 shows a simplified model that underlies many such models of mass communications such as those of Lasswell (1948) and Katz and Lazarsfield (1955). The main feature of this model is the 'one too many' communication where the firm transmits a message to consumers. The communication may be 'static' such as a poster, or 'dynamic' like a video recording. A dynamic element can be added to the basic model (Bornman and van Solms, 1993). No interaction between consumers and companies is present in this model. This is typical of contemporary models of mass media effects that are all variations on this particular theme.

Figure 18.4 shows a slightly more complex model. This introduces encoding, decoding, channel and feedback elements. Encoding is the process of putting thought into symbolic form that is controlled by the sender. The encoding process might use music, visual art or a psychological message containing sadness, guilt, etc. Similarly, decoding is the process of transforming message symbols back into thought that is controlled by the receiver. Both encoding and decoding are mental processes. The message itself is the manifestation of the encoding process and is the instrument used in sharing thought with a receiver. The channel is the path through which the message moves from the sender to the receiver. The feedback element recognises the two-way nature of the communications process; in reality, individuals are both senders and receivers and interact with each other continually. Feedback allows the sender of the original message to monitor how accurately the message is being received. Thus, the feedback mechanism gives the sender some measure of control in the communication process. In marketing, it is sometimes acknowledged that customers as originally intended do not receive an advertising message. Based on market feedback, the message can be re-examined and perhaps corrected. This model was discussed in detail in Chapter 10 and reference should be made back to that section for a more detailed explanation.

The key feature of conventional simple models of mass media communications is that no interaction takes place between the sender and the receivers of the message. Hoffman and Novak (1995) construct a new model of communication that is more suitable for a HCME such as the WWW. In this model customers/ receivers actually interact with the medium and both marketing firms and receivers of the message can provide actual content to the medium. In this mediated model, Hoffman and Novak show that the primary relationships are not between the sender and receiver, so much as with the HCME itself with which they interact. Hence in this new model, information or 'content' is not simply transmitted from sender to receiver, but 'mediated' environments are created by all parties using the system and then experienced by them. The model shown in Figure 18.5 is adapted from the model of Hoffman and Novak (1995).

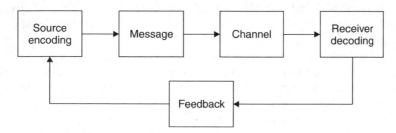

Figure 18.4 A more detailed model of the communication process

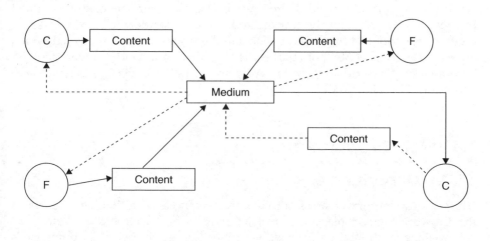

C = Customer
F = Firm

Figure 18.5 A communications model for a HCME such as the WWW (adapted from the work of Hoffman and Novak, 1995)

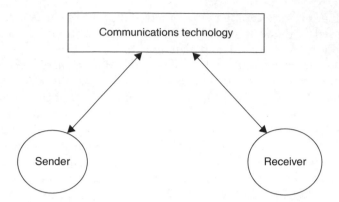

Figure 18.6 A mediated communications model (based on the work of Steuer, 1992)

Figure 18.5 is also based on traditional models of mass communication although the model incorporates a feedback view of interactivity between the firm and customers and customers and customers. Interactivity is the feature that really differentiates Figure 18.5 from the two earlier figures. Figure 18.5 represents a 'many to many' communications model for HCME's such as the WWW. Interactivity can be with the medium, that is, machine interactivity and through the medium, that is, person interactivity. Figure 18.6 is based upon an earlier mediated model proposed by Steuer (1992).

The mediated model shown in Figure 18.6 illustrates that the main form of communication is not between the sender and receiver, but rather with the 'mediated environment' with which both interact. Because of the interaction, the sender is also a receiver and the receiver is also a sender. Hence in this model information is not simply transmitted from a sender to receiver as in Figures 18.3 and 18.4, but instead 'mediated environments' are created which are then 'experienced' by both parties. That is, the sender and receivers actually become part of a simulated, virtual world and actually participate, contribute to and interact in this world.

18.7 E-commerce

18.7.1 Opportunities

Of the most important areas affected by advances in technology has been the growth of electronic commerce, referred to as 'electronic marketing' or 'e-marketing' or more generically as 'e-business' or 'e-commerce'. E-commerce is a collective term to describe a variety of commercial transactions that make use of the technologies of electronic processing and data transmission. The majority of these are based on the internet and its hybrids such as the extranet and intranet.

Electronic commerce is defined as the use of electronic technologies and systems so as to facilitate and enhance transactions between different parts of the value chain. All types of companies and all sizes of companies can make affective use of e-commerce. Smaller firms particularly seem to be particularly adept at using the new technology successfully (see Thelwall, 2000, pp. 149–159).

This definition focuses on the fact that all electronic commerce is designed to improve the business transaction processes. E-commerce would not have grown to the extent it has and will continue to do, had it not provided potential improvements to the marketing process. Often these potential improvements, as already stated, will be in the form of cost reductions for the marketer, but much more important, are those improvements that can be passed on to the customer. Put another way, the growth of e-commerce would not have been possible without the growth of the 'e-customer'. For example it will be some time before e-commerce becomes a major 'mass' force in carrying out business transactions in developing countries such as India. That is because the majority of the rural population in India does not even have electricity, gas or the telephone yet. Even if such people can make use of 'cyber café' or other internet facilities, most would not have a credit card to facilitate such commercial transactions.

The marketing concept states that marketing is about identifying and satis-fying customer needs and wants more efficiently and effectively than the competition. If customers did not want to become e-commerce customers the technology would have never have been adopted by so many people. The definition points to the fact that e-commerce and the technologies that under-pin it can, and do, relate to the total value chain including not only customers, but also intermediaries, suppliers and other external agencies such as advertis-ing and market research companies. In fact the ability to link and co-ordinate all members of the 'value chain' is one of the primary reasons for the growth of e-commerce. E-commerce is extension of internet technology to online market-ing or online shopping, 24 hours a day, 7 days a week with the world as a market place. A theatre or restaurant can use e-commerce applications to book tickets online for a film, drama or concert or to book a table. A school, college or University can use e-commerce applications for marketing and on-line admission to courses.

E-commerce can facilitate small businesses to market their goods globally with minimum cost without travelling overseas; this is allowing small and medium sized enterprises to market their products and services internationally without being disadvantaged by their size. E-commerce can save enormous expense, time and effort on marketing, accounting, financing and billing. There is no need for printing catalogues or price lists. Leading publishers of newspa-pers, magazines and books are doing lucrative business on internet. Electronic commerce is serious business and attracting money, out of total on-line busi-ness, retailing accounts only for approximately 10 to 15% of business, the rest is made from business to business commerce.

18.7.2 Challenges

The main challenge to prospects of e-commerce is infrastructure and security. There is the threat of unauthorised access to confidential information stored on the intranet and extranet (see Zugelder *et al.*, 2000, pp. 253–271, for a discussion on security and legal aspects, see also Fletcher, 2001, pp. 128–141). Many potential e-commerce customers are held back from ordering over the internet, not because they cannot use the technology or do not like what they see on the web page, but because they have fears about security. This worry is usually particularly acute when asked to give their credit card details. Unless the problem of security can be solved it is likely to inhibit the growth of e-marketing amongst a significant segment of the security conscious segment market. The company's database system has to be protected, at the same time allowing legitimate users access to the data they require. Most data requires some kind of conversion for it to be read from another system. Incompatible data formats can be a problem. Business wants to provide easy access to information, but needs secure corporate networks. Hackers can surmount barriers. There has to be adequate security against potential hazards of opening business information to the world. Industrial espionage and the inappropriate use of private commercial data is a problem. Computer fraud and computer crime is big business. We can see from the limited list of applications discussed that the range of industries and markets now affected by e-commerce is diverse and the list is growing all the time. From its original business-to-business market usage, the effect of e-commerce and the technologies that underpin it are becoming more and more widespread. Clearly, e-commerce and new technology is having significant effects on marketing and markets.

18.7.3 Intranet

An intranet is an electronic system of internal communication throughout an organisation. Similar to the internet but operating within an organisational system, the intranet connects functions and activities within an organisation thereby facilitating rapid and effective internal systems of communication. The intranet is similar to an internal management information system, which is open to all approved users within the firm. The use of the intranet is good for achieving 'internal marketing' within an organisation. People feel they are 'included' and this helps create the right internal culture and makes them feel they are valued and are part of a team. Intranets allow, for example, employees to access information from other parts of the company though some of this may be restricted. This allows greater management of communication and can be used to advantage for relaying for example information on important developments from outside an organisation like competitor actions. The intranet may also be used to advantage for internal promotional material such as company newsletters.

The intranet is a secure internal network that uses technologies developed for the internet, WWW and browsers to share information and knowledge among employees of a single company. It connects different departments within an organisation. It interconnects all departments across all branches within the country and around the world. Companies start publishing information on their homepage or websites that can be accessed by employees around the world. The same information can be circulated all around the organisation irrespective of location, distance, time or hierarchy. It increases transparency within an organisation and confidence and morale among employees. It can empower employees, cut down managerial hierarchies and change fundamental business processes. Any employee can talk and communicate with any other employee irrespective of hierarchies. It cuts down time and cost of accessing information. It is no longer necessary to print and circulate copies to employees. It also reduces cost and facilitates training. Employees can learn on the job what and when they need to learn without leaving work. The intranet not only reduces cost and effort, but also stimulates co-ordination between various departments and branches of the organisation. Such communication results in more efficiency, more profits and faster growth.

18.7.4 E-mail

Direct e-mailing can be an effective tool for marketing a firm's products, services and website. Firms have to persuade recipients to read messages, and then follow these up by contacting the receiver again. Promotional e-mails should be interesting, and it is a good point to offer the receiver something like a special offer or discount to make the message valuable to them. You may then write to them to thank them for doing business with you or for visiting your site. A list of customers and potential customers who have e-mail address are starting points. E-mail can be an effective tool to transmit the firm's marketing message as well as handling routine communications with clients. Many larger firms give selected clients access to the firm's e-mail system to speed up the flow of communication and to foster contact and utilise electronic invoicing. Communications with clients can also be made through organisations such as CompuServe, Lexis Counsel Connect and America On Line. On-line services are also a good source of business information on prospective and existing clients. Where communications are confidential, documents can be encrypted to ensure that the wrong party does not read them.

18.7.5 Extranet

Many firms want to be able to communicate confidentially with a selected group of other firms and individuals to help them achieve their business objectives and in a sense help them to run their business. As a group, these other organisations are referred to in marketing as the 'task environment' and technology developed for the internet has been developed further to form what has become known as the extranet. The internet has been used as a model to form variations on the basic application of the technology. This has taken the form of intranets and extranets resulting in significant opportunities for increased efficiencies and profits within the value chain. The potential of the extranet is limited only by business strategies and methods used by companies to make use of it. Extranets are a natural evolution, taking advantage of the basic internet infrastructure and previous internet investments to focus communications to exchange information and share applications with business partners, suppliers, and customers. The extranet is similar to the internet except it links downstream and upstream business 'partners' such as agents, distributors and suppliers, that is, other organisations in the 'task environment'.

There follows examples of extranet applications indicative of the kind of issues this technology can be used for:

- a way of using high volumes of data using Electronic Data Interchange (EDI);
- sharing product catalogues and inventory levels exclusively with partners;
- collaborating with other companies on joint development efforts;
- share news of common interest exclusively with partner companies;
- making 'partner' organisations part of the team, that is, relationship marketing;
- project management tools for companies and collaborating third parties;
- everyone involved in the project can be kept informed as to what everyone else is doing;
- sharing ideas and information with select a select group such as suppliers, agents and other intermediaries;
- online training for resellers like agents or dealers.

The extranet has helped facilitate the application of the concepts of relationship marketing and internal marketing within organisations. The marketing firm may be depending on other firms to help them achieve their own business success. These other independent organisations may be suppliers, logistics specialists, product components suppliers, sub-contractors and others. The marketing firm wants all these other 'business partners' to feel they are valued and are an intrinsic part of the business 'team'. These relationships are mutually beneficial ones where participants are engaged in a 'win–win' situation where every member of the team is benefiting in some way by being part of the network. Not only does the extranet bring various business collaborators and 'partners' together by allowing them to share information, but often the sharing of such information is vital to the functioning of the business relationship. In project management situations, for example, it is paramount that each team member of the project is aware of what is going on elsewhere and what other teams are doing. The fact that staff members from each of the organisations are able to share information and participate and contribute across ordinary organisational boundaries makes them feel more important, valued and part of the 'team'. Hence the extranet contributes towards the achievement of 'internal team spirit' and belongingness to the network of organisations in the value chain, that is, it facilitates and internal marketing outcome.

18.8 Principles of internet marketing

The growth of the internet as a commercial medium is good for business as it provides enormous commercial opportunities for companies and customers to communicate with each other via a mass medium on a new mediated environment. At the same time the new medium challenges business, because the web and its relationship marketing business model may conflict with more established marketing methods. Using a HCME which is at the very core of the internet and the WWW, is very different from conventional marketing tactics (see Pickton and Broderick, 2005, p. 127).

Firms need to redefine their businesses in terms of organisational structure, production, marketing, communications, sales, after sales services and overall strategic planning processes. Successful web strategies can only be achieved by embracing the medium proactively from a comprehensive organisational viewpoint supported and formulated by top management. Internet marketing strategies should be integrated throughout the organisation and not simply viewed as an additional marketing and advertising channel. It has opened opportunities for business people to link into global sourcing. It is projected that there will be over 250 million internet users by 2005 and one billion users by 2010. It is not difficult to sell products and services over the internet, but what is important for e-marketing success is that firms take into account a number of points when considering using the internet to market their goods or services (see Tjan, 2001, pp. 78–85):

- What is your site and what is in it? Are the contents correct for the type of business you are running? Is the amount and type of information on your site correct and suitable for the type of potential customer you hope to attract?
- How big is the internet budget and is the organisation fit for web traffic? Is your firm taking the internet venture seriously and does it have all the necessary facilities in place to handle both the volume and type of internet traffic expected? Do you have support lines and product return strategies worked out? Are there people who can answer enquiries on-line or off-line?
- What purpose does the website serve and how do you justify the website? Is the firm clear as to what the objectives for the website are? Is it to provide information and educate? Is it merely a backup for other more 'mainline' marketing communications tools such as conventional media advertising?
- What value does the website add to your customers? Is it informative, interesting or valuable from an operational point of view? For example, can industrial customers re-order industrial consumables from your website?
- What do your website customers know about the internet? How often they use the internet? What do you they want to know from your site and what internet connection do they have?
- What goal and objective do you get for your website and who/how are you going to measure, control and act on these metrics? How are you going to track enquiries? What kind of analysis are you going to employ in the evaluation process?

It is important not only to attract visitors once to the site, but to make them come back often. That is why it is necessary to keep web content updated and changed regularly and 'refreshed' with information and articles. Visitors should be given reasons to come back with regular articles, newsletters and stories. Web content and web promotion is not a one off affair, but an on-going process to market and build relationships. The website should be a place of community atmosphere. Internet web content should have definite project goals, and not just be launched due to internal excitement.

18.9 Website construction and operation

18.9.1 General principles

A website is analogous to television. It has to have some of the same qualities of creativity and interest and be intriguing, exciting, stimulating, etc. Web 'surfers' have similar characteristics to television channel 'zappers', the difference being that there are hundreds of millions of channels on the internet, so an individual website has to stand out to be noticed. There are no definitive rules for website design, but to be more successful, a website should take into account the following basic elements:

- Ensure visitors come back and visit again.
- Promote word-of-mouth communication.
- Does the website communicate with potential customers?
- Whether to use traditional marketing methods on the internet?
- How to use internet based technologies to increase sales?
- Provide means of attracting website visitors otherwise there is little point having one.
- A commercial website should retain interest long enough to market a product or service.

A commercial website has a prime objective which is to stimulate visitors to take some form of desired action such as placing an order. This key motive is behind every element of a commercial website design and content. Companies should start with the idea that they have one chance to reach customers. They may never return to a site unless the company makes it worthwhile, and they will not buy unless they are encouraged to do so.

18.9.2 Improving web sales

A business website may receive a lot of visits or 'hits', but are these visitors buying? Attracting visitors to a site is half the battle, but the majority of visitors will buy nothing. Many will simply be 'looking around' or 'surfing' the web. Attracting attention in today's crowded business culture is difficult. A business needs to turn web surfers into dedicated web buyers for the site to be commercially viable (see Venkatraman, 2000, pp. 15–18).

An important website consideration is whether one can quickly see where it involves humans, or could it just as easily be a front-end for a database or search engine? Many e-commerce sites are unwelcoming and need to do substantially more to make visitors 'feel at home' and welcome them to the site. This is no surprise, as their focus is on the sale and not the customer. The key point to remember is that the web is a communication tool directed at humans. Marketing firms have to give customers what they want and this means a user friendly and attractive website which reassures them and allows them to contact people from the marketing firm if necessary. The key is to create opportunities for visitors to interact with actual humans or at least get the sense that there is someone behind the site. A free telephone number that lets customers talk to a person is invaluable. An internet marketing company would rather have a customer's telephone number than have them leave a website with nothing. Listing the address of your physical location will reassure customers. Consider offering live, instant customer service through the internet, using a chat-like interface. Several companies offer this service at small cost, or even free. It adds a valuable human dimension to a medium that can appear cold and unfriendly to some customers.

Many potential website customers are concerned about carrying out transactions on the internet for security and other reasons. Newspapers stories regularly appear about unethical companies operating on the web and 'fleecing' customers. People need reassurance. Customers want to know that a site is legitimate, and they can trust the people behind it. They want to know who they can contact if something goes wrong. Some internet firms include a 'Comments from Our Customers' page to show newcomers that others like to buy from your site. Some sites have customer 'chat' facilities where they can discuss products and related issues. Others, like Amazon.com and Napster.com, allow visitors to post their own product reviews. If a site feels comfortable, visitors will be more likely to purchase and tell others about the site and their experience. Website providers should consider joining a trade association, a professional organisation or an industry group as such an official affiliation provides comfort, for example, franchisees can display the logo of the British Franchise Association or the Direct Marketing Association which tells users of the site that the company is ethical and abides by a recognised code of practice.

E-marketing firms should create and prominently display a return policy. If customers buy a product from a conventional retail store they can normally take the product back and have it replaced if it turns out to be faulty. Many potential internet customers are worried that they may not be able to do this if they purchase from a website. A clear returns policy will give customers information to make informed purchasing decisions. Customers often leave sites because they are too slow or difficult to navigate, so a site should make the shopping experience convenient for users.

Site providers should provide e-mail links for users to ask questions and provide answers effectively and efficiently. A facility should be included for a 'frequently asked questions' (FAQ) list. Most sites offer credit card facilities, but more inclusive ones also offer a facility for on-line cheques, money orders and cash on delivery (COD) as companies like Gateway Computers do.

Providers should try to identify reasons why customers abandon transactions on their sites. Reasons might be relatively simple, for example, a firm may be receiving a lot of e-mail about returns policy or some other aspect of the business they are not happy with. A company should carry out tracking and analysis of customer exit behaviour.

18.9.3 Improving profits with existing customers

Existing customers are the most valuable and important assets of a company. In a sense they are the business, for without them there is no business. Many entrepreneurs feel they should be attracting new customers all the time. They sometimes do this at the expense of existing customers who they neglect. This process is analogous to trying to fill a tub with water whilst the plug is out. As soon as you put the new water in the old water is forced out of the plughole.

Existing customers are more profitable and cost less to retain than new customers cost to attract. Generally, when firms think about building bigger profits, they think of acquiring more customers, not realising that it is easier to market more to existing customers (see Reichheld and Schefter, 2000, pp. 105–113 for a discussion of the importance of customer loyalty on Internet marketing programs).

Before a purchase can be made from a website there are typically four stages to conclude:

1 Obtain their attention (the hardest stage of all, as we are bombarded with a multitude of marketing messages every day and people are selective in what they choose to look at).
2 Get the prospect to think about your offer that has to be interesting to the prospect and give value. There has to be some USP that is intriguing to the prospect and makes them consider the possibility of placing an order.
3 Have the prospect decide to buy from you, which is a key stage. The material on the website must be sufficiently enticing to make the prospect decide to buy. Security and other commercial safety issues will come in to play in the prospect's decision-making process. These must be addressed for the purchase to go ahead.
4 The prospect must take action to buy. This is the most important stage for if the prospect does not place an order then everything is wasted. Even in e-marketing, ways must be found to actually 'close' the sale with a prospect; the fundamentals are no different from traditional personal selling.

After someone buys they may not come back to buy again. Studies show that many people cannot accurately remember where they bought items several weeks after purchase. Current and past customers are the easiest ones to sell to again, and this leads to a need to stay in touch with present customers. Much internet business is based on repeat business and customer retention, for example, once someone has purchased a book on-line from Amazon.com that same person usually purchases a book again in the future. The internet marketing company should not only include these customers in a database, but should also include 'hot' prospects that have shown an interest in the business in the past. These are the best audiences that can be found for targeted marketing offerings. A well-constructed database will allow the marketing firm to analyse data and prioritise customers in terms of their probability to purchase and allow effective segmentation of the customer base. There are many database programs to keep lists organised and most include a basic database feature, or more specialised programs like Microsoft Access can be used.

The main reason for working on an in-house list of customers and 'hot' prospects is to keep business in people's minds. People have many options to spend their money on even when buying specialised products and services. There are numerous firms on the internet that can take customer credit card orders and quickly deliver products. If a provider does not work to stay in the minds of customers, others will. How can a list be worked upon without incurring too much expense? Many e-marketing firms have found their best low-cost marketing tools for working an in-house list are postcards and e-mail. Postcards are cheap to send and do not require a customer to open an envelope. Many people throw away enveloped direct mail material as 'junk mail' without even opening them. Some firms put a colour photograph or graphic on one side of their postcard, this adds interest and brings the communication to the prospect's attention. The other side should have the main offer in a bold headline again so it can be noticed and have impact plus a clear indication of the website for more information. There should be a deadline for an offer, as busy people often put off buying, with the intention of returning, and then forget about the communication. A postcard offer is never more powerful than it is at the moment the customer has it in his or her hands. Make sure that information on the card briefly tells people how to buy and make the process as simple as possible. List the company's website, phone number, store location if appropriate and e-mail address. Unlike a postcard, e-mail messages can contain as much information as you want. Forms can be put on a website to gather e-mail addresses from prospects wanting to be sent information.

There are a number of principles for increasing the number of quality visitors to a website:

1 Track the number of visits received to each page of the website at least once a month, including repeat visits. This is a way of tracking the effectiveness of advertising campaigns to establish what works best. If a firm has an e-commerce site, then track money generated by that site at least once monthly. Find out what works (in terms of site marketing) in a particular industry. If something does not work, then this is valuable information.
2 Market very specifically to the target audience to get high quality visits to the site. These customers are most interested in the product or service and are most likely to buy. Segmentation and targeting are of paramount importance. Prioritise and concentrate on marketing to those prospects that represent the highest probability of success.

3 Find out where (on the web and otherwise) people who want your products like to go to, and actively communicate in that medium using internet and non-internet communications like conventional direct mail, posters and advertising.

4 Register the site with many search engines and link exchange services. Re-register monthly to ensure you are on them. You can list your site with over 2,000 search engines monthly. Specialist management companies can provide this service.

5 Exchange links with sites you can find that have the same target audience as you. This can be a great source of high quality and profitable visits, for example, if you are targeting academics, have hotlinks to your site on other sites which may also be of interest to academics.

6 Know the purpose for the site. What do you want it to do? Sell your product? Have people place orders? Gather data about your site's visitors? Sell advertisers' products so you can sell more ads on your site? Get people to call you for more information? Make sure your web designer understands what your business is about, and make sure the web page design effectively communicates what you are as a business.

7 It is important that prospects know whom you are and where to find you. Put your URL (site address) on every communication that leaves your company. Add clear labels with the URL printed on it to outgoing packages, as this is a cost effective way of getting internet details in front of prospects without wasting resources.

8 Ensure the site is a quality one, as a poorly constructed site will produce annoyance that could be worse than not having a site. A site should be easy to use, attractive, and informative.

9 People should have as many opportunities as possible to see the website address on posters, newspaper advertising, direct mail shots, van livery, etc.

10 Ensure that graphics communicate who you are as a business including the type of business you are and what you have to offer. Theme graphics including overall colour themes and page layout structures. Be clear about the brand image(s) being portrayed.

18.10 Website management

Web design is more than just coding web pages. It consists of navigation that allows users to find what they need, the file structure that supports organised maintenance and the planning that allows the site to successfully fulfil its objectives. It has an ergonomic aspect in that users have to feel comfortable when using the website and must feel they are competent to navigate around the site. There are millions of web pages on the internet, but many are unimaginative and boring. Some do not work properly, or do they supply the user with the type of information they say they are going to hence wasting people's time.

Out of all the sites on the web, only a small fraction account for the majority of web visits and even less account for the majority of web sales. People are bombarded with commercial information in all aspects of their daily lives. To be able to cope with this enormous amount of information, people have to be selective. This is true when people are on the internet visiting websites. For a site to be successful, it has to have certain qualities (see Gulati and Garino, 2000, pp. 107–114).

It has to work for a start, and has to deliver the type of information the user is expecting in a way that makes navigating the site easy and enjoyable. The main stages of the process for establishing a commercial website should be:

1 The initial consultation. Here the general needs of the client are determined, the purpose of the site sketched out, and the pricing and payment terms are set.
2 The server is prepared, and any necessary domain registrations are performed.
3 The site's design proposal is prepared, and presented to the client. This document outlines the file and directory structure, and provides an organised overview of the various components that will make up the site.
4 All necessary materials and data are gathered. Images are scanned, text assembled and copied, and the client's background information collected. This is a critical phase, as site design is on hold until it is completed.
5 The site design is initiated. Lead-time is usually set at approximately two weeks, although this can vary.
6 The finished site is posted for final inspection. Necessary alterations are performed.
7 The site goes public and marketing takes over.

An important consideration in the analysis of the WWW as a marketing media is that it possesses unique qualities that other marketing environments do not have. The WWW is a virtual hypermedia environment that incorporates interactivity with people and computers. The web does not really try to simulate a real world shopping experience, although some of the characteristics one would expect to see in a normal shopping expedition are built into the web experience to make users feel familiar with the environment and comfortable when using the technology. What the web provides is a virtual experience and the experience of being in a mediated environment rather than a true 'real world' environment. Within this virtual environment, both experiential behaviour, such as 'surfing the web', and goal directed behaviours, such as 'on-line shopping', compete for the user's attention (Hoffman and Novak, 1996). The user of this virtual marketing environment must develop certain competencies and capabilities. Users are challenged through using the web, and the concept of competency and 'flow' as the user goes from site to site or action to action on a single site is important and needs to be factored into all web design and operational considerations.

18.11 Summary

The world of sales and marketing is constantly changing. The internet, e-commerce, the continuing rise of direct marketing and the increasing marketing emphasis on customer retention over customer acquisition are only a few of the salient factors affecting the way firms carry out business in the modern world. Firms have to move fast, keep up with the latest developments and trends and invest in the most relevant software and systems to stay ahead of competition. Business in general, and marketing in particular, have become more and more affected by, and dependent upon, technology. Technological progress itself is changing and accelerating at an exponential rate. Not since the Industrial Revolution has the marketing firm been affected so much by changes in the technological environment. Firms that are not fully aware of technological advances and developments will fall behind in the commercial race as this huge 'step' change in the way marketing firms do business. Marketing is all about staying ahead of the competition. This in turn means that the marketer must also have skills to use the new technologies of today and tomorrow to assist the marketing process. Similarly, those organisations whose management and marketers are unaware of, or unable to, use advances in technology will become increasingly uncompetitive. The marketing manager of the future will need an understanding of the use of technology within the discipline and be able to appreciate how they can factor in the use of new technology into all aspects of their marketing plans and operations. Some argue that a totally new model of marketing is required for a web based society. In the USA, more than two thirds of firms are setting up computer-based systems like intranet and/or extranet facilities.

The e-commerce revolution, of which the WWW is at the epicentre, has been hailed as one of the most important developments ever to occur in the world of business. These developments will affect every area of company business operations, particularly marketing. These new developments in marketing represent a 'paradigm shift', meaning that the new technology is not simply resulting in marketing firms doing basically the same things, but with more up to date technology. It means we have to change the whole way we think about doing marketing.

References

Agostinelli, C. (1978), 'Some aspects of the life and work of Carl Friedrich Gauss and that of other illustrious members of the Academy', *Atti Accad. Sci. Torino Cl. Sci. Fis. Mat. Natur.* 112 (suppl.), 69–88 (Italian).

Anderson, B. and Moore, J. (1979), *Optimal Filtering*, London: Prentice-Hall.

Benham, W. (1974), 'The Gauss anagram: an alternative solution', *Annals of Science* 31, 449–455.

Bornman, H. and von Solms, S.H. (1993) 'Hypermedia, Multimedia and Hypertext – Definitions and Overview', *Electronic Library*, 11(4–5), 259–268.

Bos, H.J.M. and Gauss, C.F. (1976/77), 'A biographical note' *Nieuw Tijdschr. Wisk.* 64(4), 234–240 (Dutch).

Curry, A. (2001), 'What's next for interactive television', *Interactive Marketing*, 3(2), October/December, 114–128.

Fletcher, K. (2001), 'Privicy: the Achilles heel of the new marketing', *Interactive Marketing*, 3(2), October/December pp. 128–141.

Gulati, R and Garino, J. (2000), 'Getting the right mix of bricks and clicks for your company', *Harvard Business Review*, May–June, 107–114.

Hoffman, D.L. and Novak, T.P. (1994), 'Commercialising the information superhighway: Are we in for a smooth ride?', *The Owen Manager*, 15(2), 2–7.

Hoffman, D.L. and Novak, T.P. (1995), 'Marketing in Hypermedia Computer Mediated Environments: Conceptual Foundations', Project 2000 Working Paper No. 1. Owen Graduate School of Management, Vanderbilt University.

Katz, E. and Lazarsfeld, P. F. (1955), *Personal Influence*, Glencoe: Free Press.

Lancaster, G.A. and Reynolds, P.L. (2002), *Marketing a one Semester Introduction*, Oxford: Butterworth Heinemann, p. 389.

Lasswell, H.D. (1948) 'The structure and function of communication in society', in Bryson (ed.), *The Communication of Ideas*, New York: Harper and Brothers.

Pickton, D. and Broderick, A. (2005), *Integrated Marketing Communications*, 2nd edition, Financial Times, London: Prentice-Hall, p. 127.

Reichheld, F. and Schefter, P. (2000),'E-loyalty, your secret weapon', *Harvard Business Review*, July–August, 105–113.

Sorenson, H. (1985), *Kalman Filtering: Theory and Application*, IEEE Press.

Steuer, J. (1992), 'Defining virtual reality: dimensions determining telepresence', *Journal of Communication*, 42(4), 73–93.

Thelwall, M. (2000), 'Effective websites for small and medium sized enterprises', *Journal of Small Business and Enterprise Development*, 7(2), 149–159.

Tjan, A. (2001), 'Finally, a way to put your Internet portfolio in order', *Harvard Business Review*, February, 78–85.

Venkatraman, N. (2000),'Five steps to a dot-com strategy: how to find your footing on the web', *Sloan Management Review*, Spring, pp. 15–18.

Wald, L. (1998), 'A European proposal for terms of reference in data fusion', *International Archives of Photogrammetry and Remote Sensing*, XXXII (7), 651–654.

Zugelder, M., Flaherty, T. and Johnson, J. (2000),'Legal issues associated with international Internet marketing', *International Marketing Review*, 17(3), 253–271.

Further reading

Bocij, P., Chaffey, D., Greasley, A. and Hickie, S. (2003), *Business Information Systems. Technology, Development and management in E-Business*, 2nd edition, Financial Times Harlow: Prentice-Hall.

Chaffey, D., Mayer, R., Johnson, K. and Ellis-Chadwich, F. (2003), *Internet Marketing, Strategy, Implementation and Practice*, Financial Times Harlow: Prentice-Hall.

Chaston, I. (2000), *E-Marketing Strategy*, Maidenhead: McGraw-Hill.

Dussart, C. (2000), 'Internet: the one plus eight "re-volutions"', *European Management Journal*, 18(4), 386–397.

Hafner, K. and Lyon, M. (1996), *When Wizards Stay Up Late: The Origins of the Internet*, Simon & Schuster.

Hardaker, G. and Graham, G. (2001), *Wired Marketing: Energising Business for e-Commerce*, New York: John Wiley and Sons.

Kalakota, R. and Robinson, M. (2000), *E-Business. Roadmap for Success*, Reading, MA: Addison-Wesley.

Slevin, J. (2000), *The Internet and Society*, Cambridge: Polity Press.

Smith, P.R. and Chaffey, D. (2001),*EMarketing Excellence – At the Heart of EBusiness*, Oxford: Butterworth Heinemann.

▎ Questions

Question 18.1

Using specific examples to illustrate the points being made, distinguish between the 'intranet' and the 'extranet' and explain the use of these two systems within a marketing context.

Question 18.2

Explain what is meant by the term 'hypermedia computer mediated environment' and discuss how this environment differs from more conventional marketing communications media.

Question 18.3

When evaluating the benefits of a web site, which factors must forms take into account?

Question 18.4

How can e-marketing companies reduce the perceived risk inherent in a website transaction for a new potential customer?

Question 18.5

Explain the basic principles of database marketing and data fusion techniques.

Question 18.6

Give reasons explaining why a website may have to integrate with the rest of the firms marketing mix.

Question 18.7

Explain how the Internet can help smaller firms enter and serve customers in international markets.

Question 18.8

Which factors would a company take into consideration when evaluating the suitability of its product for Internet marketing?

19

Marketing Strategy, Planning and Control

19.1 Introduction

The contemporary view of customer orientation has been adopted by most companies. However, many tend to neglect a systematic approach to planning, analysis and control. Not only does attention to the latter facilitate customer satisfaction, it helps to guarantee survival by ensuring profitability.

Some businesses are directed by leaders who have a 'feel' for the market and whose intuitive decisions lead to success. Intuition is an important ingredient of successful management, but few can say that it is so frequently correct that we can use it as the basis for managing a company. Markets change rapidly and the intuitive leader runs risks that are unacceptable to shareholders and employees.

Some companies merely respond to current demand. Providing the order book is full, they see no need for planning. When sales slow down pressure is put on the sales force to sell more.

Planning systems that have not evolved from the origins of marketing planning are often based on the company's financial budgeting process. Available resources are allocated to functional managers in an indiscriminate manner and there is no facility available to evaluate expenditure in terms of what it has achieved. So long as a department has not overrun its budget allocation, everyone is satisfied.

19.2 Formalised planning procedures

19.2.1 Central to marketing

A formalised planning procedure that takes account of the firm's environment, its internal resources and its longer-term objectives is required. Planning is complicated in practice, but its concept is relatively straightforward as illustrated in Figure 19.1.

An organisation wide commitment to planning has been assumed throughout this text, and chapters relating to marketing mix elements, for example, have referred to the design and implementation of strategy. In practice, strategies are the result of careful preparation and hard work. Contained within Figure 19.1 are the combined efforts of senior management in the various functional areas that make up the company. The planning process is continuous. Throughout the year, information should be collected and analysed and performance should be constantly reviewed. At given intervals, problems are assessed and decisions made as to the most appropriate course of action (see Dobni, 2003, pp. 43–46).

Planning is at the heart of marketing and is not an abstract or separate function within business. This chapter brings together the elements of marketing

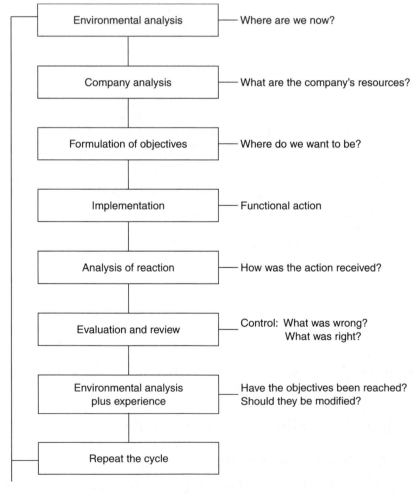

Figure 19.1 A simple planning system

and shows how they are practised concurrently and in conjunction with each other. Figure 19.1 outlines the contents of planning, strategy formulation and control. Each of these basic themes is important to the company. Strategy formulation is an exciting activity for marketing practitioners because of its creative content. Control provides the means to discover whether or not the strategy has been appropriate and provides the information that allows corrective action to be taken if necessary.

Another simple view of planning is incorporated in the acronym 'MOST' that stands for:

Mission	The business we are in
Objectives	What we need to accomplish
Strategies	In general terms how are we going to do it?
Tactics	In specific terms how are we going to do it?

19.2.2 Terms in common use

The area of planning contains a wide range of words and titles in its description. Confusion arises over the meaning of the word 'strategy' and its use in the terms 'corporate strategy' and 'functional strategy'. It is useful to clarify these terms:

- 'Planning' is the process of decision-making that relates to the future. The term can be used at all levels of company decision-making.
- 'Corporate planning' refers specifically to decision-making at the highest levels of management. Decisions made here refer to the future of the total business. Corporate planning is sometimes referred to as 'strategic planning' and some older texts refer to it as 'long-range planning'. Corporate or strategic planning is not concerned with forecasting sales, devising marketing mix strategies or organising production and raw material supply to accommodate this forecast. Corporate planning involves asking: What business are we really in? Is this the right business? What are our basic objectives? Are our markets growing or declining? Are new technologies threatening our products? After analysis, strategic plans can be drawn up based on the answers to such questions.
- 'Operational' or 'functional planning' is the process that develops the corporate or strategic plan. One strategic corporate objective may be to enter a new market and achieve x per cent market share with y per cent return on investment within 2 years. Operational planning will indicate how this should be best achieved (for instance, by adopting a particular marketing mix strategy and financial allocation).
- The word 'strategy' can be used at an operational level (product, price or advertising strategy) because it describes medium- to long-term actions.
- 'Tactics' are actions that bring about temporary modifications to operational plans, for example, a price change or an increase in advertising intensity

necessitated by unexpected competitive action. These are essentially short-term in nature.

- 'Objectives' should be 'SMART' which stands for:
  - ○ Specific
  - ○ Measurable
  - ○ Achievable
  - ○ Realistic
  - ○ Time related.

A logical planning hierarchy is:

1 corporate planning,
2 functional (e.g. marketing) planning,
3 sub-functional (e.g. sales) planning.

The above can be expanded as follows:

1 *Strategic corporate planning:*
  - ○ define organizational mission,
  - ○ establish strategic business units (SBU's) which is defined later,
  - ○ anticipate change.

2 *Marketing planning for SBU's:*
  - ○ set marketing objectives,
  - ○ develop marketing strategy,
  - ○ make formal marketing plans.

3 *Operational marketing plans.*

19.3 Strategic planning at the corporate level

The term 'corporate planning' has evolved in line with the increasing size of companies and numbers of multi-product, multi-market companies. Takeovers, mergers and multi-national activity have created a complex and wide-ranging business environment so larger companies are indirectly responsible for the direction of several firms who are involved in various, often unrelated, markets. The task is to define a 'corporate mission' or 'corporate goal' and develop plans that enable this to be accomplished. The mission should be stated in marketing terms so as to encourage as wide a view of opportunities as realistic within resource constraints.

Objectives are defined and communicated to individual parts of the company whose managers develop their own plans for achieving these objectives. Such a process facilitates a marketing mission rather than a product orientation.

To illustrate marketing evolution, a company whose principal activity is the manufacture of fountain pens should perhaps consider itself to be in the 'gift market', or perhaps the 'graphics market'. In addition to adopting a marketing orientation, businesses can include a social dimension in their corporate mission statement (e.g. the achievement of goals by means of a commitment to reduce pollution). Whatever the mission, it should serve to generate a common theme throughout the company and motivate staff towards a common goal (see Dobni *et al.*, 2001, pp. 400–408, for a discussion on marketing strategy implementation).

19.4 Strategic business units

In order to realise corporate objectives, management must break down areas of responsibilities into identifiable and manageable units. This facilitates analysis, planning and control. A method of identifying such business areas is to divide the total business into 'strategic business units' (SBUs) or operational entities to which corporate strategy is delegated. A major criterion of SBU management is that SBUs should be easily identifiable. They should represent the key business areas of the company. Although it is not always possible to delineate business areas exactly, ideally SBUs should be single businesses that can be planned independently of the company's other businesses. This suggests that they have an identifiable management, with responsibility for managing and controlling resource allocation and direct competitors can be identified. For multi-market or multi-industry organizations, SBUs may be whole companies in themselves. Single industry or 'product-line dominant' companies may be able to identify SBU's based on specific market areas.

19.5 Audit and SWOT

Having defined corporate objectives and identified SBUs, the company proceeds to the stages of planning outlined in Figure 19.1. The first stage is 'environmental analysis' (sometimes called the external audit) and it is known through the acronym 'PEST' analysis (short for political, economic, socio-cultural and technological analysis). Some authors cite the acronym as 'STEP' as there is no chronological sequence in the way each factor should be considered. Each of these four categories should be investigated in turn. These separate 'PEST' factors have later been broadened to include legal aspects that made the acronym 'SLEPT'. Later, Environmental factors were considered as a separate category and the acronym became 'PESTLE'. The latest factor to be included is ecological factors and the acronym has now become 'STEEPLE'. However, it is felt that the introduction of so many extra factors unnecessarily complicates what is a sound tool of analysis, and for most situations, 'PEST' analysis works well.

As well as this external audit, the company also performs an internal company analysis. In this stage the company analyses its own internal strengths and weaknesses and its external opportunities and threats (called 'SWOT' analysis). Bullet pointed strengths and weaknesses are listed from an internal company perspective along with opportunities and threats from an external macro-environmental point of view. This latter part of the analysis uses information that has already been identified from the 'PEST' analysis. With this information to hand, planners can consider the strengths and opportunities of their SBUs, situate them in their respective environments, and then formulate plans designed to realise corporate objectives.

19.6 Portfolio analysis

19.6.1 Boston Consulting Group (BCG) Matrix

A popular approach to planning called 'portfolio analysis' was pioneered in the USA by the Boston Consulting Group (BCG) and it is also referred to as the 'Boston Box'. This method identifies the company's SBUs and places these on a matrix that considers 'market growth' and 'relative market share' as can be seen in Figure 19.2.

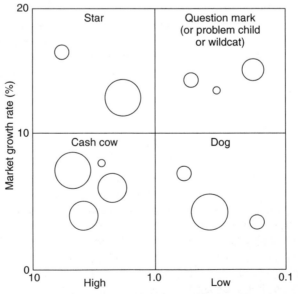

Figure 19.2 The BCG portfolio analysis matrix

Four business types can be distinguished:

1 'Stars' are SBUs that have a promising future. Significant investments of cash are necessary to develop their full potential. If managed correctly, they will develop into a valuable source of revenue as the market evolves.
2 'Cash cows' have achieved a high market share in a mature market. They deserve detailed attention because the cash they generate can be invested in newer market areas with high growth potential.
3 'Question marks' (or 'problem children' or 'wildcats') pose a problem for management. Whilst market growth prospects are good, question mark SBUs have a low relative market share. If they are to be moved to the left (i.e. increase relative market share) substantial investment may be required. Based on available information, management must decide whether such investment could be better employed in supporting other SBUs.
4 'Dogs' show no growth potential and their relative market share is low. Although they may not necessarily be a 'drain' on company resources, they are unable to make a positive contribution to profits.

The BCG model was originally designed for multi-industry companies and SBUs, as depicted in Figure 19.2, represented competing companies. BCG analysis is now more frequently used by individual companies where SBUs relate to individual product lines. The size of each circle represents the relative value of sales between different SBUs.

A major object of business is to optimise performance so corporate objectives can be realised. Not much can be done by a single company to change the market growth rate that defines its position on the vertical axis. The options are, therefore, to eliminate SBUs from the 'portfolio', or to move them from the right to the left along the horizontal axis (i.e. increase their market share). Of course increased sales will increase the size of the SBUs themselves.

Suppose that the SBUs in Figure 19.2 are the 12 individual companies that make up a large organisation. These represent the 'corporate portfolio' (it would be called the 'product portfolio' for a smaller company). The upper-left quadrant reveals one small star and one large star, although three large cash cows with a high relative market share are in evidence below this complemented by a small cash cow. The company should protect its cash cows and attempt to improve the star situation so that a new generation of cash cows can be developed. The company might have problems when attempting to move the most promising question marks from the right-hand to the left-hand quadrant. As far as the dogs are concerned, they should be examined individually, to decide whether they should be kept and improved (perhaps in the interests of ensuring a more comprehensive portfolio) or sold off or abandoned.

The accuracy of any model is only as good as the information on which it is based. A BCG matrix-type model requires a great deal of accurate market and company information before the model can be used as a meaningful management tool. In addition to presenting strategic alternatives, a well-prepared BCG matrix is valuable because it compels objective consideration of the elements of the portfolio in relation to each other. However, the most significant criticism is that it too simplistic, because variables used do not take into account the circumstances of growth or market share. For example, Pringle knitwear only has a small share of the overall knitwear market, but it is a leader in the luxury knitwear market. Similarly, market growth may be high, but such growth may attract competitors who might adversely affect profit margins.

19.6.2 The General Electric (GE) matrix

General Electric of America's matrix overcomes some of the criticisms of the BCG matrix by using industry attractiveness and competitive position as its parameters. It was developed with management consultants McKinsey and is sometimes referred to as the GE/McKinsey business screen. This matrix contains nine boxes and offers a wider strategic choice than the BCG matrix by using broader market and company factors. It uses 'business strength' on the horizontal axis and 'industry attractiveness' on the vertical axis. It is graphically represented in Figure 19.3.

Each of the boxes suggests a strategy that is appropriate for the SBUs that it contains.

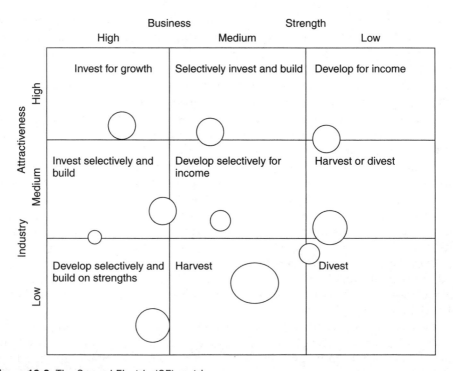

Figure 19.3 The General Electric (GE) matrix

19.6.3 The Shell directional policy matrix

This was developed by Shell Chemicals and was designed to cope with a dynamic market place. The requirement was that each strategy should be evaluated against potential contingencies. Figure 19.4 shows how the vertical axis looks at measures of the company's competitive capability, for example, market growth, the industry situation and environmental issues. The horizontal axis examines prospects for sector profitability from an industry point of view.

Each of the SBUs is given between one to five stars along each axis. This is then quantified, and the result places each SBU at an appropriate point in the matrix.

19.6.4 Ansoff's matrix

Ansoff's matrix was described in Chapter 3 and illustrated in Figure 3.3. It is a useful starting point for a strategic review of a company's position and a precursor to marketing action. Whether the matrix is used at a corporate or

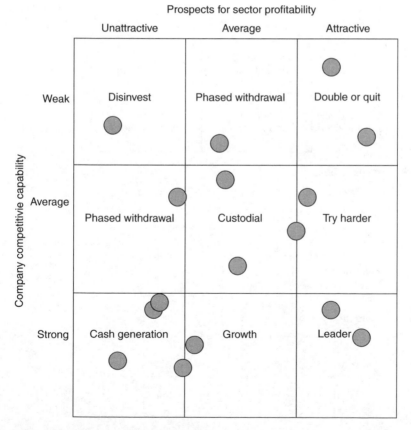

Figure 19.4 The Shell directional policy matrix

operational level, the act of examining each of the quadrants shown in Figure 19.5 focuses attention on where the company is and where is could, or should, be.

19.6.5 Hofer's product/market evolution approach

Marketing strategies for each stage of the product life cycle were outlined in Chapter 6. The PLC concept can also be used for corporate planning as shown in Figure 19.6. Products or companies can be arranged in terms of their competitive position in the relevant stage of the product or market life cycle.

19.6.6 Industry/market evolution

Porter proposed that the strategies for success are not necessarily financial coupled with high market share as shown in Figure 19.7.

	New markets	Existing markets
New products	Conglomerate diversification	Product diversification
Existing products	Market diversification	Market intensification

Figure 19.5 Strategic alternatives

	Competitive position		
	Strong	Average	Weak
Introduction			
Growth			
Maturity			
Decline			

Figure 19.6 An adaptation of Hofer's product/market evolution portfolio matrix

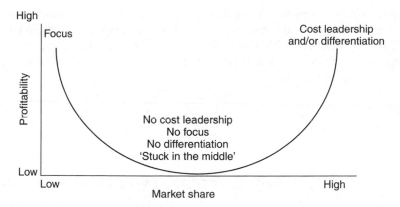

Figure 19.7 Porter's generic strategies

		Growth (emerging industry)	Maturity (and transition to maturity)	Decline
Strategic position	Leader	Keep ahead of the field	Cost leadership; raise barriers to entry; deter competitors	Redefine scope; divest peripheral activities; encourage departures
	Follower	Imitation at lower cost; joint ventures	Differentiation; focus	Differentiation; look for new opportunities

Figure 19.8 Strategic position in industry life cycle

- 'focus' means the company consolidates its efforts on a small range of products in a market niche;
- 'differentiation' means to establish a USP or other feature that the competition cannot match;
- 'cost leadership' means the lowest price in the market;
- 'stuck in the middle' describes companies at the bottom of the curve.

In 1985 Porter further developed his ideas based on evolutionary stages and whether the company was a leader or follower as shown in Figure 19.8.

Depending upon whether the company is a 'leader' or a 'follower' depends on which strategy should be adopted. Individual evolutionary stages are explained:

- 'Growth' or emerging industry is characterized by conservatism amongst buyers over the attributes of new products and the fact that they might become dated in either function or style.

- 'Maturity' and transition to maturity can mean reduced profit margins as competitors come in and sales begin to slow. Buyers become more confident as they are familiar with the product and manufacturing emphasis is on features and intangible factors like image. Attempts should be made to serve specialist market segments.
- 'Decline' indicates that the market has become saturated. Alternative products might appear that supplant traditional products and this is when companies should look for alternative products.

19.6.7 Industry maturity/competitive position matrix

Management consultants Arthur D Little developed a matrix that looked at life cycle stages for the industry under review and considered where individual companies fitted into each stage under criteria ranging from 'dominant' to 'weak'. This idea is illustrated in Figure 19.9.

19.6.8 Product (or market) life cycle matrix

Barksdale and Harris (1982) developed a model that combined the BCG matrix with the product life cycle concept in an attempt to overcome the problem in the BCG matrix that ignores the position of the industry in relation to its stage of development. The resultant matrix is described in Figure 19.10.

- 'Infants' are in a situation where R&D costs are being recovered with high promotional expenditure in term of educating the market.
- 'Stars' have high promotional costs, but good future potential once the product/service has been accepted by the market.
- 'Problem children' (or wildcats or question marks) are in a high growth situation, but low market share. They are costly to maintain and market

	Embryonic	Growth	Maturity	Ageing
Dominant				
Strong				
Favourable				
Tentative				
Weak				

Figure 19.9 Industry maturity/competitive position matrix

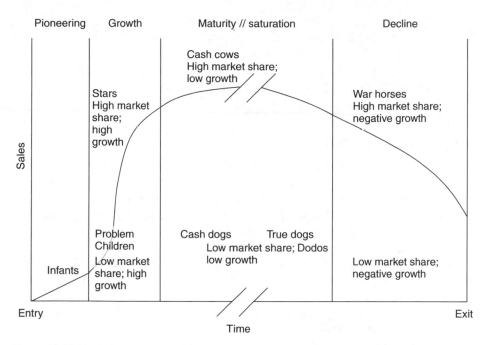

Figure 19.10 Barksdale & Harris BCG/PLC combined portfolio

action should be taken to move them to 'star' and ultimately 'cash cow' positions.

- 'Cash cows' earn money in a high market share/low growth situation. Promotional costs are lower as the market is familiar with the product/service.
- 'Cash dogs' with a low market share are to the maturity side of the box in a saturated market and have a flat cash flow. 'True dogs' have a low market share towards the saturation side of the box with a negative cash flow.
- 'War horses' are in a declining market, but still have a relatively high market share, probably as a result of competitors exiting from the market. This contributes to a positive cash flow.
- 'Dodos' are in a declining market with a low market share and negative cash flow. They should be deleted, but might still exist because management hopes they will stage a revival.

In concluding this insight into corporate planning through the medium of portfolio analysis, we should refer to the planning stages illustrated in Figure 19.1. All planning begins with an analysis of the company's widest environment and proceeds to analyse the company's marketing environment through the marketing information system. The information gathered and resultant analyses are the base on which strategic corporate objectives can be formulated. These indicate the basic direction that the company wishes to follow. Corporate objectives are then communicated to operational management for implementation.

Later planning stages are similar at both corporate and operational levels and are now considered in more detail in terms of marketing planning.

19.7 Marketing planning at an operational level

19.7.1 TOWS matrix

The success of marketing planning at this level depends on a prudent deployment of the marketing mix. Before a mix strategy can be developed, operational management must consider the company's position in the market with reference to 'SWOT' analysis. A practical tool is 'TOWS' analysis that facilitates the formulation of strategies. A number of stages are considered:

1 evaluate the influence of environmental factors (PEST or STEEPLE issues) on the company;
2 formulate a diagnosis about the future;
3 assess company strengths and weaknesses in relation to operations management, finance and marketing;
4 develop strategic options.

An application of 'TOWS' is illustrated through a simple example of refrigerators. Suggested strategies are contained below and to the right of SWOT factors, and these use the SWOT factors that are indicated:

Product: refrigerators

	Strengths 1. Brand name 2. UK sales force 3. Good after sales 4. Competitive price	Weaknesses 1. International markets 2. UK specified products 3. Logistics
Opportunities 1. EU market 2. Disposable income 3. Second homes 4. Cheaper transport	Use existing brand name and after sales support to market to EU countries (S1, S3, W1, O1)	Establish manufacturing plant in potential EU entrant country to market new low capacity range (W1, W2, W3, O1, O3, O4, T4)
Threats 1. Far East imports 2. Currency variations 3. New low-cost countries entering EU	Establish depots in EU and recruit sales force using UK trainers (S2, S3, S4, W1, W3, O1)	Source components in Far East for new ultra-low cost range of additional home freezers (S1, S3, S4, O3, T1, T3)

19.7.2 Procedure for marketing planning

Figure 19.11 outlines a basic marketing planning routine and this encapsulates the whole activity that comprises marketing in a strategic framework.

1.   Mission
2.   Corporate objectives
                                   Goal setting

3.   Marketing analysis – External audit (PEST) and Internal audit
4.   SWOT analysis
5.   Assumptions
                                   Situation review

6.   Marketing objectives and strategies (SMART) ◄ – – – – – – – – – – – – – – –
                                                      Feedback

7.   Estimate expected results from sales forecast
8.   Identify alternative marketing mixes and plans
                                   Strategy formulation

9.   Budget
10.   Year 1 implementation of plan (time scales)
                                   Resource allocation/monitoring

11.   Measurement and control –

Figure 19.11 A model of marketing planning

The strategic planning process should have now taken place and an individual plan is required for each SBU or product line.

According to Abell (1979) in essence, the marketing plan should include the following:

1 analysis,
2 setting objectives,
3 forecasting,
4 budgeting,
5 organization,
6 selecting targets,
7 developing the mix,
8 control.

These are now discussed separately in the context of marketing planning at an operational level:

19.7.3 Analysis

Marketing research can provide a detailed picture of the market and profiles of potential consumers. Information is needed about competitive activity, patterns of distribution, prices, products and trends. Analysis of pricing data, particularly price elasticity and the price sensitivity of various market segments is of particular importance. However price is an area where marketing planning seems to have less influence than in other marketing mix areas, which is a bit odd considering the importance of pricing decisions (see Murphy, 2002, pp. 22–24). We must ask potential consumers where they buy, how they buy and what they consider to be problems with current supplies/suppliers. The evaluation of customer satisfaction is a key issues now in many firms.

Relatively simple marketing research methods can be used to collect data on customer satisfaction and customer service appreciation (see London and Hill, 2002, p. 12). In particular, we need to know the market size and likely repeat purchase. If the company is operating a long term relationship marketing strategy then management will be concerned with the long term or 'life time' value of customers (see Garau, 2002, pp. 203–219).Within a company, costs should be analysed and production and distribution capabilities assessed.

19.7.4 Setting objectives

Based on marketing research/analysis and knowledge of its internal capabilities, the company must decide on its objectives, that is, the market position the company will seek. The objectives of a marketing plan must be realistic, attainable and specific so that they can be easily communicated throughout the company. 'To increase sales' or 'to increase brand awareness' are meaningless. More specific (SMART) objectives provide a focus for marketing effort and permit subsequent evaluations of such effort, for example, a useful objective would be 'to increase sales by x per cent in market y during period z'.

19.7.5 Forecasting

This activity is distinguished from marketing research and marketing control as it is based on analyses of past events. The precise location of forecasting as a stage in the marketing plan varies according to the type of product (new or existing) and the objectives that have been set (purely marketing based – for example, increasing brand awareness, or financially based – for example, reducing costs or increasing sales). An existing product can be adapted to a different market, so it is likely (because of lack of knowledge of the market) that forecasting will precede the objective-setting stage in this case. If we are dealing with an existing product and a known market, analysis should have provided sufficient information to permit the setting of objectives. Specific estimation of buyer intentions (i.e. sales forecasting) can then follow.

The total market potential is estimated, and then information is refined into a specific company sales forecast. Whatever forecasting techniques are used, the net result is the company's best estimate of its expected participation in a given market during a given period (usually one year). The sales forecast (combined with marketing objectives) thus becomes the basis for company-wide corporate planning.

Production, human resource and financial decisions, as well as appropriate marketing mix strategies can only be based on anticipated sales. However, forecasts are estimates rather than predictions. Accurate sales forecasting can be expensive and fraught with difficulties as discussed in Chapter 15.

19.7.6 Budgeting

When the company has forecast future sales, it can allocate resources on the basis of anticipated revenue. Marketing objectives can influence resource allocation. Procter & Gamble is known as a company that achieves high market share through assertive promotion. This requires high advertising expenditures during the product's introduction and growth stages, which could not really be justified on purely financial grounds. The option to inject funds into the marketing budget is also important when, for example, in BCG terms, the company wishes to transform a 'question mark' SBU into a 'star'. In general, when considering costs of production, distribution and marketing, expenditure should not exceed expected revenue. Sometimes finance does not allocate a set amount of money as a budget for marketing, but will require a certain level of forecasted profit. The amount of money that is available for marketing will then be the amount of profit forecast in excess of company requirements (see Weber, 2002, pp. 705–717, for a more detailed discussion of marketing budgeting).

How money is then apportioned to individual elements of the marketing mix is the responsibility of marketing. One technique for arriving at the optimum profit level is to forecast the effect of different levels of expenditure on different marketing mix elements. For example, operating a high service level will incur high costs, but these may be more than offset by increased sales. There will be a point at which further investment in the level of service is superfluous and other mix elements assume greater importance. The relationship between marketing and sales is called the 'sales response function' (see Donaldson and Wright, 2001, pp. 276–284 for a discussion on the use of sales data and sales information systems in marketing planning).

With unlimited funding, there is little that a marketing manager could not achieve. Budgeting emphasises the 'realistic' nature of marketing. Financial resources are always limited and in demand elsewhere in the company. There is pressure on the marketing manager to transform financial resources into profitable results.

19.7.7 Organisation

This is a vital element of the marketing plan. Too often, extra responsibilities are given to employees without due consideration of how this will affect their overall performance. Similarly, personnel are sometimes 'misplaced' in terms of experience and expertise. As well as numbers and types of personnel, the company must consider the relationships between departments that might be overstaffed, whilst others might be under pressure coping with their workload.

19.7.8 Target selection

This involves defining market segments to be approached (see Chapter 5). It might be that a demographically based segmentation strategy is appropriate, or perhaps behavioural variables such as benefits sought or usage rate might be better.

19.7.9 The marketing mix

When the first five planning stages described in Figure 19.11 have been carefully executed, specific marketing strategies can be developed. Each market segment should have its own marketing mix. The marketing mix strategy is the means for achieving company objectives in a specific marketing situation. It is developed within the framework of available financial and company resources.

19.7.10 Control

The effectiveness of a marketing mix strategy should be monitored and after a predetermined period of time, it must be evaluated and reviewed. This is the 'control' process.

Before considering control in more detail, the following observations can be made:

- goals and objectives only assume value when they are translated into action;
- we should be aware planning is not an end in itself, only a means to an end; the 'end' being the provision of customer satisfaction by a means that provides the company with a profit;
- only if it makes profits, can a company's customers be best served and employment sustained.

19.8 Marketing control

Figure 19.1 portrayed a simple planning system that can be applied at strategic and operational levels. Whilst we make a distinction between these planning levels, the process itself is essentially the same for each. Implicit in successful planning is the need to look back with the light of experience so that performance can be evaluated and improved (see Bourne et al., 2000, pp. 754–771 for a discussion of control measures). We know from everyday experiences that plans do not always work out. Control systems enable us to find out what has gone wrong and why practice has deviated from the plan (see Bowman, 2002, pp. 32–40, for a discussion on the use of knowledge systems in planning and control).

People can be given independence when plans are being implemented, but responsibility must be borne by all levels of management and operational personnel. It acts as a powerful stimulus, because success can contribute to their personal future. In contrast, control tends to have a negative connotation. People are less inclined to respond positively to requests for information and analysis of their performance for control purposes.

Whilst it is clear that control procedures are vital to the success of marketing plans, we should not lose sight of the fact that plans are implemented by people. From an organisational point of view, control (if it is to be effective) should be approached with thought and sensitivity. Senior management is ultimately responsible for the success of marketing plans. Logically, managers are also responsible for organising control procedures. These should be set up with the human factor as the starting point. They should be aware of the 'law of diminishing returns' as it applies to the usefulness and efficiency of gathering information. Managers should try to establish a priority of information needs and ascertain the minimum rather than the maximum requirement.

This will mean greater, not less efficiency. At the functional level, marketing personnel tend to see their vital role as 'doing' rather than accounting for their activities.

The aims of control are often misunderstood. Often, the word is seen as being synonymous with coercion and allocation of blame. These are not the objectives. The analogy of a rocket launch and a space programme is often used to illustrate marketing control. A rocket is launched with a clear objective or mission. During its flight, for a variety of reasons, numerous modifications may be made to ensure that the craft stays on course. The analogous function of marketing control is to identify changes in the marketing situation before they become serious problems, and to initiate corrective action. This is referred to as 'driving control'. Management must also ensure that targets are reached satisfactorily. This is done when a particular activity has been completed and only then can evaluation and recommendations be made. This is 'results control'. Marketing is essentially concerned with results, so it is very important. Unfortunately, what marketing management considers to be driving control may appear to be results control by marketing staff and it takes on a punitive connotation, for example, salespeople might be blamed. This behavioural observation highlights the sensitive nature of marketing control management.

Having taken these critical human or organisational factors into account, there are a series of elements that must be included in any control system (see Figure 19.12). In addition to these essential elements, the system should be designed to maximise communication and minimise noise – the distortion that can occur when messages are passed through a system via a series of 'human filters' as in the game 'Chinese Whispers'.

Marketing control is essential because it:

1 Enables running or 'driving' corrections and modifications to be made in response to problems which, if not detected at an early stage, could have serious consequences for the marketing plan.
2 Provides information that can be used to review at regular intervals (e.g. bi-annually) on how effectively objectives have been implemented. Deviations caused by internal or external forces can be identified and corrected.
3 Provokes analysis that, in turn, can cause opportunities to be identified.
4 Acts as a motivating force at all levels of operational activity.

Put succinctly, control serves to minimise misdirected marketing effort.

19.9 Execution of control systems

We now examine the execution of control in more detail. Figure 19.12 outlines the basic steps in the control process. Just as planning must have objectives in

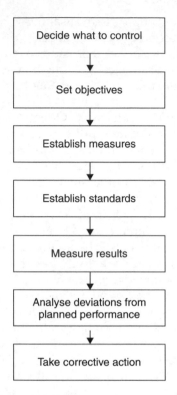

Figure 19.12 Steps in the control process

order to be meaningful, control systems must also set objectives and establish how these are to be achieved.

'What to control' (the parameters) is the foundation of the control process. Typically, sales, costs and profits are the major preoccupations of management. These are central indicators of the firm's efficiency. Marketing activity extends beyond these basic criteria and each marketing function has individual objectives that must be subject to control (see Pickton and Broderick, 2005, p. 513, for a discussion on the monitoring and control of the communications element of the mix).

When parameters of control have been established, 'control objectives' can be defined. Usually, they are defined in terms of financial, as well as functional performance. If planning objectives have been well defined, the control process can also use them. The sales manager's target must be achieved within a given budget and there are sub-objectives that must be controlled and included in the 'sales plan', for example, an optimum call-frequency-to-sales ratio. Other functional objectives can be identified in a similar manner.

Measures of success should be incorporated into the control process. Sales objectives may be to achieve a certain level of sales force efficiency (e.g. the quality of their contribution to marketing information or their ability to obtain new accounts). Success can be measured in terms of cross-references to other sources of information or the contribution to annual sales turnover.

Objectives are rarely achieved in absolute terms. Standards must be established which refer to the 'real life' environment in which objectives are implemented. A 'standard' may refer to upper and lower limits for a particular budget, or to a required level of brand awareness.

Once the preceding steps have established a framework for control, measurement of results can begin. Management must decide how often and at what level this should be undertaken and considerations of cost and time allocation are crucial in such decisions. Measurement procedures should be such that their costs do not exceed the value of their contribution to the company. Management should take steps to ensure that activities associated with data collection for 'measurement' reasons do not detract from the efficiency of operational activities: on the other hand, measurement should be conducted often enough to detect 'early warning signals' of deviations from the plan.

In analysing results, there is a danger that wrong conclusions may be drawn. Analysis may reveal shortcomings in performance, but care should be taken to ensure that the original objectives were realistic. In addition to simply comparing results with what was planned, emphasis should be placed on the identification of changes, either internal or external and new information that genuinely affects the ability of those concerned to meet objectives. Analysis should be sufficiently detailed to uncover individual factors that affect the performance of a basically sound plan. Sometimes a single product can be the cause of poor profitability of an otherwise sound product line. Necessary action in such a case could be to remove this product rather than alter the whole product line. The ability of a company to take appropriate corrective action depends on the efficiency of the analysis process.

The marketing audit provides systematic appraisal of the company's activities at the corporate level. The purpose of the marketing audit is to consider the company in its entirety and its objectives are:

1 To consider the marketing environment in both macro and micro terms to identify changes and tendencies which might affect the firm's future activities.
2 To re-examine corporate strategy in the light of the above. What new or revised objectives should be communicated to operational marketing management?
3 To consider the efficiency of marketing at an operational level it should be appreciated that the marketing audit is not concerned with measuring results. Rather, it is concerned with examining objectives and how well the company is equipped to fulfil them. The marketing audit at this level encompasses all marketing functions as well as marketing's organisational structure. It is particularly important that organisation is not overlooked, because the efficiency of any plan relies on the skill, proper deployment and relationships between people who carry out the plan.

Companies that carry out a full-scale marketing audit display a high level of commitment to marketing orientation. They recognise that in order to provide customer satisfaction, the company must endeavour to optimise efficiency at all levels. Control systems are the means by which efficiency can be assessed.

19.10 Summary

Strategy, planning and control embrace all marketing activities. At the corporate level, marketing information systems (Chapter 14) and the marketing environment (Chapter 2) link with this topic. At an operational level, functional marketing mix areas (Chapters 6–11) are involved. Financial analysis is referred to at various points in the text, but is elsewhere more concerned with using these techniques in the execution rather than the formulation and control of marketing tactics and plans.

The control process is concerned with all marketing activity. As well as being a continuous process that permits 'fine tuning' of plans whilst they are being implemented, it involves a review of activity after it has taken place. Usually this is an annual event that allows a company to look objectively at the total value of its efforts. Such a review should occur at both corporate and operational levels.

At the operational level, the company is concerned with the marketing plan. When considering 'what to control', sales, costs and profits are of particular significance. Again, we must address the reality that marketing costs must not exceed the profits that sales provide. It is logical to suppose that if each functional activity efficiently achieves its objectives, then the net result for the firm would be overall success. However, this is not necessarily true. Often objectives are achieved at cost levels that are disproportionate to the value of the achievement. Annual control of the marketing plan allows the company to consider whether or not its financial resources are being optimised across the marketing mix. In a competitive environment, cost control is usually the key to profitability. Some management systems consider each functional area as a separate profit (or loss) centre with its own accounting procedures. This ensures functional managers are close to financial reality.

References

Abell, D. (1979), *Strategic Market Planning: Problems and Analytical Perspectives*, Englewood Cliffs, NJ: Prentice-Hall, Chapter 4 and 5.

Ansoff, I. (1957), 'Strategies for diversification', *Harvard Business Review*, September, 38.

Barksdale, H.C. and Harris, C.E. (Jr), (1982), 'Portfolio analysis and the product life cycle', *Journal of Long Range Planning*, 15(6).

Bourne, M., Mills, J., Willcox, M, Neely, A. and Platts, K. (2000), 'Designing, implementing and updating performance measurement systems', *International Journal of Operations and production Management*, 20(7), 754–771.

Bowman, B.J. (2002), 'Building knowledge management systems', *Information Systems Management*, Summer, 32–40.

Dobni, B. (2003), 'Creating a strategy implementation environment', *Business Horizons*, March–April, 43–46.

Dobni, B., Dobni, D. and Luffman, G. (2001), 'Behavioural approaches to marketing strategy implementation', *Marketing Intelligence and Planning*, 19(6), 400–408.

Donaldson, B. and Wright, G. (2001), 'Sales information systems: are they being used for more than simple mail shots?', *Journal of Database Marketing*, 9(3), 276–284.

Garau, C. (2002), 'How to calculate the value of a customer', *Journal of Targeting, Measurement and Analysis for marketing*, 10(3), 203–219.

Kotler, P. (1988), *Marketing Management, Analysis, Planning, Implementation and Central*, 6th edition, Englewood Cliffs, NJ: Prentice-Hall, p. 65.

London, S. and Hill, A. (2002), 'A Recovery Strategy Worth Copying', *Financial Times*, 16th October, p. 12.

Murphy, D. (2002), 'Cause and effect', *Marketing Business*, October, pp. 22–24.

Patel, P. and Younger, M. (1978), 'A frame of reference for strategy development', *Long Range Planning*, April, 6–12.

Pickton, D. and Broderick, A. (2005), 'Integrated marketing communications', 2nd edition, Financial Times, Englewood Cliffs, NJ: Prentice-Hall, p. 513.

Porter, M. (1980 and 1985), *Competitive Advantage*, New York: The Free Press.

Robinson, S.J. (1978), 'The directional policy matrix – tools for strategic planning', *Long Range Planning*, June, 8–15.

Weber, J.A. (2002), 'Managing the marketing budget in a cost-constrained environment', *Industrial Marketing Management*, 31(8), 705–717.

Further reading

Aaker, A. (2001), *Strategic Marketing Management*, Chichester: Wiley.

Davidson, H. (2002), *'The committed enterprise'*, Oxford: Butterworth Heinemann.

Dwyer, F.R. (2002), *Business Marketing: Connecting strategy, Relationships and Learning*, 2nd edition, New York: McGraw-Hill.

Jobber, D. (2004), *'Principles and Practice of Marketing'*, 4th edition, New York: McGraw-Hill, pp. 35–64.

Lambin, J.J. (2000), *'Market Driven Management: Strategic and Operational Marketing'*, London: Macmillan.

Lynch, R. (2000), *Corporate Strategy*, 2nd edition, Harlow: Pearson.

Piercy, N. (2002), *'Market led strategic change: transforming the process of going to market'*, Oxford: Butterworth Heinemann.

Questions

Question 19.1

A significant proportion of marketing effort is devoted to satisfying the demands of control systems. How would you justify such a claim on a company's financial and human resources?

Question 19.2

Differentiate between *corporate goals* and *operational, or functional, marketing objectives*. How are these planning activities related?

Question 19.3

What is the relationship between strategic marketing planning and overall corporate planning?

Question 19.4

How does clearly defining the firm's 'mission' help marketing planners?

Question 19.5

Outline the contents of a marketing plan and discuss the marketing activities carried out at each of the stages.

Question 19.6

'Plans are nothing but planning is everything'. Discuss this statement.

Question 19.7

Explain how short, medium and long term sales forecasts contribute to the marketing plan.

Question 19.8

Why is a monitoring and control procedure needed as part of an integrated marketing plan?

Question 19.9

What is the relationship between the marketing plan and the sales budget?

Question 19.10

Critically evaluate the product life cycle concept as a marketing planning tool.

Question 19.11

Compare and contrast the usefulness to marketing planners of the General Electric Matrix and the Shell Directional Policy Matrix.

Index